*The A-1 Skyraider in Vietnam*

# The A-1 Skyraider in Vietnam

## The Spad's Last War

Wayne Mutza

**Schiffer Military History**
Atglen, PA

Book Design by Ian Robertson.


Library of Congress Catalog Number: 2003100015



Printed in China.
ISBN: 0-7643-1791-1

We are interested in hearing from authors with book ideas on related topics.

Published by Schiffer Publishing Ltd.
4880 Lower Valley Road
Atglen, PA 19310
Phone: (610) 593-1777
FAX: (610) 593-2002
E-mail: Info@schifferbooks.com.
Visit our web site at: www.schifferbooks.com
Please write for a free catalog.
This book may be purchased from the publisher.
Please include $3.95 postage.
Try your bookstore first.

In Europe, Schiffer books are distributed by:
Bushwood Books
6 Marksbury Avenue
Kew Gardens
Surrey TW9 4JF
England
Phone: 44 (0) 20 8392-8585
FAX: 44 (0) 20 8392-9876
E-mail: Bushwd@aol.com.
Free postage in the UK. Europe: air mail at cost.
Try your bookstore first.

# Contents

# Acknowledgments

A book of this magnitude is not possible without the support of numerous individuals. Many of those listed here participated in the events that forged the Skyraider's proud history in Southeast Asia. This is their history. I am most fortunate – and honored – to have been entrusted with their memories and their mementos. My heartfelt thanks to Heinie Aderholt, Richard W. Albright, Steven P. Albright, William L. "Bags" Bagwell, O'Dean "Stretch" Ballmes, Edd G. Barnes, Ed Barthelmes, Robert "Black Bart" Bartunek, Barrett Thomas Beard, Manny Benero, Michael Bennett, Steve Birdsall, Robert E. Blood, Paul Boyer, Ralph Brannan, Billy C. Butler, Robert Christiansen, Ernest L. Connors, Robert DeGroat, Win DePoorter, Donald C. Dineen, Thomas E. Doll, Richard S. Drury, Melvin C. Elliott, Mark Eyestone, Ed Fancher, Walt Fink, Bernard F. Fisher, Fred Freeman, Jack M. Friell, Richard A. Gaebler, Tom Garcia, David J. Gardner, James G. George, Linden Gill, Forrest H. "Frosty" Goodman, Hill Goodspeed, Gary L. Gottschalk, Albert Grandolini, Edwin A. Greathouse, Frederick M. Guenzel, John Gulow, Dan Hagedorn, Richard M. Hall, David A. Hansen, Robert Heisler, Richard R. Higgins, Joseph Hoang, Douglas Hudgens, Byron E. "Hook" Hukee, Marty Isham, Edward R. "Randy" Jayne, Marty Jester, Richard Kaufman, Paul Kimminau, Vic Kindurys, Leo Kohn, Jeffrey L. Kolln, John Konek, John L. Larrison, Kenneth T. Lengfield, Terry Love, Elof Lundh, Winfred G."Glenn" Mackey, Mike Marron, Gene McCormack, Dwayne Meyer, Herbert C. Meyr, Richard E. Michaud, Eric Micheletti, Robert C. Mikesh, Stephen Miller, Frank J. Mirande, Stephanie Mitchell, Terry Moore, Ted A. Morris, Frank Musick, Dale Mutza, Lawrence New, Qui Nguyen, Robert L. Nicholson, Tom Novak, Merle Olmsted, David Ostrowski, Robert Patterson, Lionel Paul, Ron Picciani, Ron Pickett, Donald H. Plagge, Ralph Poore, Joe Reynes, Paul Rhodes, Tom Risch, William H. "Speed" Ritzman, Jr., John W. Rochester III, Scott Roe, Seabie "Gunner" Rucker, Robert L. Russell, James Salter, John Santana, Tom Schornak, Robert M. Senko, Kenneth R. Shatzer, Ashby Shoop, Michael Smith, Ronald E. Smith, Thomas K. Stump, Gerrald R.Tabrum, Norm Taylor, Kirsten Stephens, Dr. Istvan Toperczer, Ngoc Van Tran, Harold M. Troxell, Francisco Vazquez, Joe Vincent, Will Ward, Tommy G. Wardlow, John C.Waresh, "Bud" Watson, Lawrence D. Webster, David Wendt, Darrel Whitcomb, Richard White, Scotty Wilkes, Nick Williams, Leon Wohlert, James F. Yealy, Ralph B. Young and Roger L. Youngblood.

No historical treatment of the Skyraider would be complete without the superb photos taken by Tom Hansen during his days as an Air Force flight mech. His air-to-air views, taken from the open hatch of his *Albatross* rescue aircraft, are unequaled. Tom's knowledge and admiration of the A-1 is evident in his descriptive portion of the introduction. Special mention goes to the late Harry Gann, whose expertise in the field of Douglas aircraft was unrivaled. Special thanks are due Greg and Ralph Davis, and Byron "Hook" Hukee, who manage the Able Dog and Skyraider Association web sites, respectively. I'm indebted to friend and fellow writer/historian Lennart Lundh for his astute analysis of my work, to Ron Thurlow for his perseverance in providing the details so necessary to this history, and to my wife, Debra, for understanding why those remodeling projects were on hold.

And I am indebted to the following organizations: A-1 Skyraider Association, American Aviation Historical Society, Air Commando Association, Pima Air & Space Museum, U.S. Air Force Museum, Naval Air Systems Command, and the National Museum of Naval Aviation.

I have made every effort to credit the photographers of the images that appear in this book.

# Preface

Most are graying, balding, paunchy, and wear glasses. Some are slightly stoop-shouldered. But mention the word "Spad" and a gleam comes to their eye. They straighten a bit and set their jaw. The gleam turns to fire as their memory becomes energized with images of decades past. The grin speaks volumes and makes me wish I too could see the glowing orange sunset against the silver sea from a lofty perch, feel the wind through the open cockpit, smell the leather and oil, and feel the awesome power and rapture of controlling the thundering beast.

The next best thing, it seemed, was to research their involvement with the Spad, to tap their rich memories and present fresh insight to their achievements, in their airplane, during their war. They were warriors once. They did not do their job for political ambition or for the treachery of power. They fought for their beliefs, even when some stopped believing they were fighting for freedom. They fought for each other and for their own survival. And they did it superbly.

They flew an airplane military leaders mistakenly assumed had seen its heyday in Korea. Often they were viewed as the bastard children of aviation, for no other reason but that their airplanes had propellers on the front of them. Theirs was a bond of survival and honor that knew no boundaries. Still heard among their ranks are the words from an old song carried over from World War II: "Throw a nickel on the grass, to save a fighter pilot's ass." The phrase was used through the years as a salute to fallen comrades—to say, "You are honored and remembered."

You see, they did not preach the brotherhood of man – they lived it. To them this book is dedicated.

# Introduction

Lightning flashes on the horizon, piercing the darkness. Thunder rumbles in the distance. The damp air is heavy, the heat oppressive. Flashlight beams dart through the gloom as someone moves around a dark shape, inspecting. Faint sounds, off-key singing to a rock hit, a truck passing nearby, tools against metal, a curse. A light cart casts an eerie glow and a power unit hums incessantly. The pungent aroma of damp vegetation, cooking fires, sweat, 50-weight oil and 115/145 avgas—the purple stuff.

A guy encumbered with gear and carrying a helmet gets off a truck. Words are exchanged and he walks around the dark shape—looking, thumping, grabbing, wiggling. Satisfied, he tightens straps and clambers up on a wing. Grasping handholds and stepping in kicksteps, he hoists a leg over the cockpit sill, awkwardly climbs in and squirms down into a hard, uncomfortable seat. The chief is at his side, handing him harness straps, his helmet, and pulling pins. Leads are plugged in, and a mask is held in place for a quick oxygen check.

Toggle switches click in the darkness. Dim lights begin to brighten—a hum from some deep corner. The chief jumps down and moves out in front and to the left side of the shape. Another man appears with a wheeled fire bottle, at the ready. The warrior looks over at the chief and nods. The chief, hand upraised, smartly twirls a light wand in a circle. A metallic whine—the huge blades begin to turn. The warrior counts the blades, then fingers a toggle switch with gloved finger. He watches the chief, light wand held straight up, who in turn watches a little drain tube underneath. A primer solenoid actuates, sending impulses of the cold purple stuff to its destination. A cough, an explosive, ragged rhythmic sound accompanied by a huge, swirling cloud of dense, white-gray oil smoke curling back past the tail.

Primer on steady—oil pressure comes up within 30 seconds. The ragged, barking thunder evens out. Mixture lever to auto rich—primer switch off. Fuel flow steady, temps starting to rise. A radio call, the warrior looks to the chief, who goes through a series of hand signals. The warrior responds by moving various controls. Temps now in the green, the thunder calms down, noticeably. One can hear individual beats. A sudden second or two of quiet, then the thunder resumes. Warrior looks at chief, who jabs thumbs outward to each side.

Chocks are pulled and the chief motions the shape forward. As it begins to lumber forward, the chief steps back and snaps a crisp salute, which the warrior returns. Amid the rumbling racket, twin light beams stab ahead, pointing the way, lighting a worn yellow centerline, puddles, black tire marks, and oil stains.

The shape motors down to the end of the field between two rows of dim blue lights, swings around into the wind, brakes set, burbling waves of sound increase to a steady, powerful roar, then stabilize.

Pressures, temps, supercharger, cycle the prop through a few times, mag check. The noise slacks off—a radio call. Warrior holds hands up in the air and men run out from the shadows, darting here and there with practiced movements, pulling off red streamers and holding them up. Warrior nods—the canopy slides forward and locks. Brakes off, the machine rolls, turns, and lumbers onto the end of the long, wet ribbon of pavement.

A pause on the centerline, tailwheel locked, rudder trim cranked in, a quick wiggle of elevators, ailerons, and rudder. Then the smoking, rumbling hulk announces an ear-splitting crescendo, its flashing blades becoming invisible. Orange flames from the big stacks on both sides flash in the darkness. Brakes off, rolling, then faster, every bump transmitted up through the entire structure—faster now. The tail comes up as thousand-foot markers flash past. The machine is bellowing and getting lighter on the oleos.

At an exact instant, the pounding vibration suddenly stops. Tires spin madly but don't touch anything. The thick airfoil takes over the load and the forces of lift, thrust, weight, and drag assume their finely-balanced states. The warrior slams a lever up and the spinning tires soon tuck into their recesses with a satisfying thump. A specific combination of events has transformed the charging beast into a creature entering the element for which it was carefully designed.

Similar scenes were played out aboard American aircraft carriers in the South China Sea. On their decks, Skyraiders of Navy attack squadrons huddled, wings folded, awaiting launch as plane captains, ordnancemen, and other hands scurried among the poised machines. In ready rooms below deck, mission details were finalized and pilot banter masked the anxiety of facing enemy guns. On deck these "Blue-water" warriors would scrutinize their beasts during the familiar preflight before climbing up on the wing, the brown-shirted plane captains faithfully at their sides.

Signaling the start of events was a voice that boomed across the flight deck: "Check chocks, tie-downs, and fire bottles—check for all loose gear about the deck—check props, intakes, and exhausts—prepare to start all engines—start all engines!"

The launch itself transformed the deck into a kinetic montage of gray aircraft and nimble handlers wearing colored shirts. Deck crew braced against the warm wind during the fast-paced but well-orchestrated drama. The carrier deck during launch and recovery operations was, and remains, one of the most dangerous workplaces.

The smell of avgas and exhaust hung heavy in the humid salt air. Steam rose from catapults, and huge props blurred into deadly discs just inches from rudders and wing tips as Spads jockeyed toward catapults. Wings were spread and locked, followed by an exchange of signals between warrior and deckhand. The airplane's launch weight was confirmed between warrior and flight deck officer, and the growling Spad was bridled into the catapult holdback. Warrior released the brakes, throttled to full power, and scanned his engine instruments. With the mighty Wright roaring, and vortices spiraling back from the huge prop, the warrior and cat officer exchanged salutes.

The Spad hurtled down the deck and, for a brief moment, seemed suspended over the water. Warrior relished the moment, knowing the day ahead and recovery aboard the "boat" would be much more difficult.

Whether slipping away from a carrier in the Gulf of Tonkin, an air base in Thailand, or a remote airfield in South Vietnam, machine and warrior became one. This was the Spad on its way to work. This was "Sandy," "Arab," "Zorro," "Viceroy," and "Phoenix," to name a few. It came from El Segundo and passed through places named Litchfield Park, Quonset Point, Alameda, Eglin, Pleiku, and NKP. This was the culmination of a concept born during the first world war, never to be repeated in any future conflict—the single-seat, single-engine, piston-powered, propeller-driven, tailwheel fighter-type ground attack aircraft—dented, patched, oil-streaked, cannon-stained, exhaust-burned, and heavily laden.

For the pilots who flew the Skyraider, there was romance—no dishonor, no delusion in saying they loved what they did. The Spad, for them, evokes memories of a huge, round, thundering engine, tail hook, folding wings, long on-station time, massive ordnance loads, and lots of right rudder. The romance dimmed to a flicker in Southeast Asia, where theirs was a serious, grim job. For some, flying the Spad to take the war to the enemy, and protecting their comrades on the ground, reflected their attitude toward life in general.

Like their fellow combatants, Spad pilots did not have the overwhelming support of Americans back home when they unleashed their lethal firepower in a war whose political dimension was pervasive. Colonel William A. Jones, while recovering from injuries

**The unofficial slogan of the Skyraider pilot says it all—"Jets Are For Kids." This Spad driver's helmet, complete with tuft, and reminiscent of World War I aviators, is perched upon an A-1H on alert in Southeast Asia. (Tom Hansen)**

sustained during the mission for which he received the Medal of Honor, in 1969 wrote:

> "This is a time perhaps unprecedented in history, when pacifism and passive resistance have become the *in* thing. The *good guys*—those who believe in fighting for what they believe is right and just—have become the *bad guys* in our society...those men at arms believe that certain ideals, such as love of homeland, liberty and human dignity are worth defending—even to the death."

Even less recognized were South Vietnam's Skyraider pilots, who were no less fond of the airplane. Since their homeland was the battleground, some Vietnamese pilots not only acquired the flying skills of their American counterparts, they amassed thousands of combat hours. The vast cultural gap and insufficient time necessary to build a competent air force proved detrimental to the Vietnamese Skyraider program. Since the Vietnamese had been involved with war since childhood, and expected that to continue, their perspectives contrasted sharply with those of the Americans.

The Spad's endurance, ordnance load, and the skill of its pilots earned it the respect of the "grunts." It became the preferred fixed-wing support aircraft of beleaguered ground units, special operations teams, and downed aircrew in Southeast Asia. Special Forces teams, who manned remote camps, swear that were it not for Skyraider support, they would have been overrun. They clearly remember Spads roaring out of smokescreens, extremely low, accurately laying down massive amounts of ordnance. Many "SFers" profess that were it not for A-1s, they would not be here. For Spad drivers, there is no greater debt of gratitude.

Navy old-timers, who nurtured the Skyraider, refer to it as the "Able Dog." It was also called the "Pedigreed Pulverizer," "Big Oily Monster," "Flying Dump Truck," and, my favorite, "The box the T-28 came in." It became best known as the Spad. Its pilots were a special breed of warrior. When they strapped into their Skyraiders, it was with the intent of carrying out their mission with the skill, courage, and dedication expected of them. This book is testimony to how often they exceeded those expectations.

Gone are the open cockpits and heady smells of hot oil and leather. The passing of time may have dimmed images of anti-aircraft fire and the echoes of anxious radio calls, but some recollections of Spad pilots remain clear. Therefore, throughout this book, I have passed the pen to them so they could write their own history.

We are naturally curious about the past, and when it comes to aviation history, the Skyraider has universal appeal. Although not as sexy as jet-powered aircraft, the battle-hardened Spad is a classic. As such, the more time that passes, the more pronounced its heritage. It has withstood the tests of time and battle, having outlived and outfought many of its jet contemporaries. It epitomized versatility, having served the Navy in countless roles. And it was the most successful attack bomber of the Korean and Southeast Asian wars. The Skyraider is also a link to times many say are best forgotten, but we should never forget. These pages, therefore, speak of a time when, despite national discord, the Spads of Southeast Asia not only performed in stellar fashion, they fortified the American spirit under the most adverse conditions. It is my hope that this book preserves that heritage.

# 1

# The Airplane

Although much has been published about the Skyraider, an overview of its development is helpful in understanding its involvement with the war in Southeast Asia.

The Skyraider was the brainchild of Edward Henry Heinemann, who was involved with aircraft design and development throughout most of his life. His career track began in 1926 with his position as a draftsman at the Douglas Aircraft Company. Not only was he responsible for the design and development of 19 aircraft, he and his staff developed a number of aircraft components, including ejection seats, bomb racks, autopilots, and flight computers. Heinemann's designs maintained Douglas' prominence in the aviation industry, first established with the DC-3. Especially noteworthy among his long, remarkable list of achievements is the famed Skyraider.

During early 1944, the El Segundo design team led by Heinemann was busy designing a replacement for the SBD *Dauntless* dive bomber. Their goal was to meet World War II Navy requirements for a carrier-based, single-engine, long-range, high-performance dive bomber. Initial designs fell short of specifications, so in June 1944, Douglas, eager for inclusion in the Navy's competition, came up with plans, literally overnight, for a fresh design. The Navy approved the concept and awarded Douglas a contract for 15 evaluation aircraft, which were given the designation XBT2D-1 and named "Dauntless II."

Douglas wasted little time producing their new airplane, since four other manufacturers (Boeing, Curtis, Kaiser Fleetwings, and Martin) had begun work on competing designs. The Dauntless II made its first flight on 18 March 1945, and shortly thereafter went to the Naval Air Test Center, where it received high marks in flight characteristics and ease of maintenance. Navy test pilots took an immediate liking to the airplane, citing its superior balance and responsiveness to control input at all speeds, which meant excellent carrier wave-off ability.

The BT2D-1 was a large, sturdy airplane with a length of 39 feet and a 50-foot wing span. Its empty weight was 10,740 pounds. Its wings folded hydraulically overhead, reducing the wing span to 24 feet. Unique to the Dauntless II were dive brakes built into the sides and bottom of its fuselage, thereby simplifying the wing structure. The huge panels kept 500 mph dives in the safer region of 300 mph. In compliance with Heinemann's insistence on weight reduction, Douglas did away with the usual bomb bay, which saved 200 pounds. Although external stores would induce drag, designers felt the speed of an airplane with no bomb bay and empty racks was more important when leaving the target area. External attachment points also allowed more flexibility in the types of stores that could be carried. It's doubtful the design team envisioned the positive impact that decision would have on the airplane's role in future wars.

**The Skyraider's designer, Ed Heinemann (center), and his design team in 1952. (Douglas)**

**This A-1J (AD-7 BuNo. 142079) was one of only 72 built of an initial Navy order for 240 of the type. The "J" featured stronger landing gear, wing spars and attachment points, plus the new Wright R-3350-26WB engine. It was also the first Skyraider model ordered with a centerline "buddy store" tanker configuration. (Douglas)**

Although the Dauntless II's experimental predecessors featured tricycle landing gear, Douglas designers, in the interest of saving weight, used a simpler, lighter tail wheel configuration. Its main landing gear retracted rearward and rotated 90 degrees for flush storage in the wings. Armor plating protected the cockpit area, and a 20mm cannon was installed in each wing. The Dauntless II had three bomb racks: one on the fuselage centerline and one on each wing.

Power was supplied by a Wright R-3350-24 radial engine delivering 2,500 horsepower at 2,900 rpm for takeoff. A huge 13-foot, 6-inch diameter Aeroproducts variable-pitch, constant-speed hollow steel propeller permitted a rapid rate of climb at steep angles.

The aircraft was clean, simple, and functional, reflecting the talent of Douglas engineers. In keeping with Heinemann's weight-saving doctrine, it was 5,000 pounds lighter than the nearest competitor. Unfortunately, much of its structure later proved inadequate and a great deal of strengthening was necessary, which added much of the weight saved in the initial design.

One month after its maiden flight, the Navy placed an order for 548 BT2D-1s, which was reduced to 277 after the war with Japan ended. After service trials at NAS Alameda, California, 20 XBT2D-1s underwent landing gear strengthening and were assigned to VA-19A in the Pacific. In February 1946 the Dauntless II was renamed the *Skyraider.* When the Navy revised its aircraft designation system in April, the BT2D became simply "AD" (Attack, Douglas) which, in the phonetic alphabet of that period, translated appropriately to "Able Dog." Production ADs were delivered to VA-3B and VA-4B, which put the Skyraider through carrier qualification aboard the *USS Sicily* during mid-1947. By October AD-1s were aboard the *USS Midway* for cruises in the Atlantic and Mediterranean.

The U.S. Navy was quick to recognize the potential of its Skyraider and capitalized on its wide range of abilities. The result was an interesting variety of configurations, especially in models AD-1 through AD-5, each of which was given its own designation.

Versatility became a buzzword in the Able Dog community, as Skyraiders proved adept at torpedo attack, night attack, reconnaissance, target-towing, drone control, electronic countermeasures, sub hunting, and nuclear weapons delivery.

Success with the AD-1 through AD-3 series led to the AD-4, of which 1,051 were built, more than any other series; it also spawned the most sub-variants. Among the improvements introduced in the AD-4 were an autopilot, multi-seating, and additional 20mm cannons.

Prior to the Korean war, a widespread belief in the aviation industry was that the all-purpose airplane had no future, compared to aircraft designed for specific tasks. Ed Heinemann agreed, in principle, but maintained that an all-purpose airplane could be a

**The AD-5W, which became the A-1G under the 1962 revised designation system for U.S. military aircraft. Douglas Aircraft billed its AD-5 line of wide-bodied Skyraiders the "Multiplex Bomber." (Douglas)**

valuable asset, especially in war. Backing its chief engineer, Douglas began work on the AD-5, the first of which flew on 17 August 1951. The AD-5 embodied revolutionary advances in design and the experience gained from its wide range of Able Dog predecessors. The unique concept was billed as the "Multiplex Bomber," since its *universal chassis* allowed conversion to more than a dozen configurations without altering the structure. This was accomplished through packaged kits supplied with each aircraft. Although Heinemann was unsure about the concept, Douglas's claims for the -5's quick and easy transition to various attack modes or submarine hunter-killer combinations appealed to defense budget planners. Navy acceptance of the AD-5 kept the Skyraider line open longer than originally expected, which paved the way for additional models.

The AD-5 featured a massive, boxy fuselage, which was lengthened by 23 inches and widened to seat two crewmembers side-by-side. A cavernous aft cabin could accommodate ten passengers, four litters, cargo, auxiliary fuel tanks, or a wide variety of mission gear. The vertical fin area was enlarged by nearly 50 percent, and the side fuselage dive brakes were deleted. The uprated R-3350-26WA powerplant was moved forward eight inches to compensate for the change in center-of-gravity. All AD-5 versions weighed just over 12,000 pounds empty, had a design gross weight of 17,000 pounds, and an overloaded weight of 25,000 pounds.

The number of stores provisions was increased, and two M3 20mm cannons in each wing became standard. A single 380-U.S. gallon fuel cell was located in the lower center fuselage, and a 38.5-gallon oil tank was mounted forward of the firewall; both were standard through all models. Production versions were the AD-5, AD-5N night attack, and AD-5W airborne early warning (AEW). An AD-5Q electronic countermeasures (ECM) variant was derived by modifying AD-5Ns. A total of 668 AD-5s were built, with the last one rolling off the production line in April 1956.

Produced concurrently with the AD-5, the AD-6 reverted to the single-seat design for the day attack mission. The "Six" combined features of the AD-4B and AD-5, plus refinements that broadened its mission. Like the AD-4B, it was capable of nuclear attack, although former pilots are convinced the delivery technique ruled out the return trip. The AD-6 was equipped for low-level bombing and it had the stores provisions developed for the AD-5; they were a centerline station and a stub pylon on each wing, just inboard of the fold-joint (for fuel tanks and heavy ordnance), and six racks on each outer wing. The Six also had a strengthened center section and armor plate on the sides and bottom of the cockpit. Other improvements included simplified electronics and all-weather instruments.

The AD-6 was powered by Wright's R-3350-26WA, which produced 2,700 hp for a top speed of 343 mph. Its service ceiling was 28,500 feet and it had a combat range of 1,143 nautical miles. A total of 713 were produced.

Since low-level operations imposed severe strain on the airframe, the last 72 Skyraiders built received strengthened wing spars and fittings. The landing gear and engine mounts were also made stronger. Upgrades were substantial enough to warrant a new model designation, which was AD-7. A more powerful R-3350-26WB engine was installed, matching the heavier -7's maximum speed with that of the AD-6. Its service ceiling was 25,400 feet, and it had a combat range of 1,128 nautical miles.

The Skyraider was no exception to the rule that aircraft design involves compromise. Accordingly, Skyraiders became heftier throughout development as improvements were added, which had an adverse effect on performance. To overcome that effect and minimize the level of compromise, Douglas prudently used the Wright engine to power every Skyraider built.

The R-3350 was a stalwart in the industry. It was an 18-cylinder, two-row, air-cooled powerplant. Compared to other reciprocating engines, such as those built by Pratt & Whitney, the Wright's

**A Vietnamese Air Force A-1H undergoing overhaul at Tan Son Nhut Air Base in 1968. Clearly visible are the details of the powerful Wright R-3350 engine. The wing gun access panels are open, and the cockpit armor has been removed, revealing the original light gray paint. (Roger D. Fetters)**

dry sump type lubrication system used external oil lines to lubricate almost all engine components, versus internal lubricating paths. Consequently, Wright engines had a reputation for leaking oil; so much, in fact, that leaking oil became a Skyraider trademark. Pilots joked that the leaking oil was part of a designed-in corrosion control system. So common was the condition that some pilots and ground crew said an absence of oil made them suspicious. For ferry flights from the Philippines to Southeast Asia, U.S. Air Force A-1Es sometimes carried spare oil tanks in the aft cabin since the aircraft would run out of oil before it consumed its allowable fuel load.

To help counter the left turning tendency of the airplane caused by the engine's tremendous torque, the vertical stabilizer was offset three degrees to the left. Despite the design feature, it was said that Skyraider pilots were easily identified by their overdeveloped right leg, which resulted from applying so much right rudder. The offset stabilizer had an opposite effect at top speed, which required left rudder to fly straight.

As testimony to the Wright's power, the Skyraider proved itself a champion at carrying tactical loads. On 21 May 1953 an AD-4 took off from NAS Dallas with a bomb load of 10,500 pounds, with a total useful load (ordnance, ammo, fuel, and pilot) of 14,491 pounds, which was 3,143 pounds more than the aircraft's weight. Its total weight at takeoff was a staggering 25,839 pounds.

The last of 3,180 Skyraiders rolled off the assembly line on 18 February 1957. A total of 28 sub-variants grew from the 7 basic models. Under the 1962 Department of Defense redesignation system the AD-5, AD-5N, AD-5W, and AD-5Q became the A-1E, A-1G, EA-1E, and EA-1F, respectively, while the AD-6 became the A-1H, and the AD-7 became the A-1J. The AD-5, -6, and -7 variants went to war in Southeast Asia. Their pilots, crewmembers, and mechanics dubbed them "Spads." The nickname's origin is dubious, however, and a number of possibilities have been offered. Some believe it makes reference to the Skyraider's antiquity, a kinship with the Spads of World War I and the dashing bravado of their pilots. The most logical explanation comes from Navy pilots who flew the AD during the 1950s. William "Speed" Ritzman remembers being called a "Spad driver" in 1960 when he checked in to Training Squadron 30. Walt Fink, who also flew Navy ADs during the Fifties, claims the term originated with the introduction of the multi-place AD-5. To differentiate between single-place and multi-place models, carrier deck spotters shortened "Single-Place AD" to SPAD to identify the single-seat version. The term not only stuck, but was exploited by Navy jet pilots aboard attack carriers, who scorned the oil-dripping, pattern-clogging throwbacks to World War I. Much of the Skyraider's reputation is based on remarkable feats, one of which is unbelievable, yet documented in Navy records. Not only has the Skyraider flown with its wings folded, it has done it four times: on three occasions accidentally and once intentionally. The first bizarre incident occurred during October 1949 at NAAS Charlestown, Rhode Island. A 21-year old pilot of Attack Squadron 34, with 32 hours in the type, neglected to lower the wings of an AD-2 following a folded-wing taxi, took off, and reached an altitude of about 200 feet before crashing. The Spad was destroyed but the pilot survived.

It happened again when a Composite Squadron 35 pilot on 11 May 1951 took off in an AD-4N from Kangnung air strip, South Korea. It too crashed, but not before reaching an altitude of 200 feet. The third incident occurred during fall 1954 when an AD-4Q of Composite Squadron 12 took to the air with wings folded from Lawrence Airport, Massachusetts. Personnel at the Naval Air Test Center found the first folded-wing Skyraider takeoff so incredible, they decided to duplicate the event in the interest of the Fleet and to determine the AD's extreme limits. During March 1951, NATC test pilot Edward L. Feightner taxied the test center's AD-5 (BuNo 133860) with the wings folded and locked.

The plan was to reach flying speed and lift off from the runway. To everyone's surprise the AD did not require a longer than

**One of more than 100 AD-4s delivered to France beginning in 1960. Under the French flag, Skyraiders saw combat in Algeria and Chad. (Jack M. Friell)**

normal takeoff run. Three times Feightner took off and flew a few feet above the runway—wings folded. NATC personnel concluded that a *channel wing* was formed, which provided lift on both surfaces of the wings. Feightner noted that when airborne the folded wings spread apart to near vertical and the airplane was fairly stable.

Despite the Skyraider's popularity and renowned versatility, few were exported to foreign air arms. Although some countries expressed an interest in obtaining Skyraiders, Douglas' production schedules left little room for foreign orders, and the U.S. Navy—the largest operator of Skyraiders—was not ready to relinquish one of its front-line aircraft.

Under the Mutual Defense Aid Program (MDAP), the first exported Skyraiders went to Great Britain beginning in 1951 to fulfill the Royal Navy's need for early warning aircraft. A total of 50 AD-4Ws were acquired, which the Royal Navy designated AEW.1s and operated until 1960. Thirteen AEW.1s were passed to Sweden, where they were converted to target tugs and operated by Swedair under contract to the Swedish Air Force. During February 1960 the first of 113 AD-4 variants were delivered to the French Armee de l' Air, which flew them in support of French forces in Algeria. In 1976 France sent six AD-4s to Chad, where they were flown by French mercenaries until 1984. Four went to Gabon in 1976 to serve with the Presidential Guard.

In a move to which the U.S. strongly objected, France in 1965 delivered the first of 15 AD-4NA Skyraiders to Cambodia. They equipped a squadron of the 1st Intervention Group, which also operated one squadron each of T-6Gs, T-28Ds, and MiG-17Fs.

Supplementing Cambodia's Skyraider fleet were two VNAF A-1Hs whose pilots had defected. The first crash-landed at Phnom Penh after being heavily damaged during an attempted coup against South Vietnam's President Diem in 1960; his wing man was shot down and crashed into the Saigon River. The defector Skyraider became the first placed in service by the Cambodians. The Khmer forces acquired their last Skyraider when a VNAF pilot defected in 1966.

When the war in Vietnam spilled over into Cambodia in 1970, most of the Cambodian Skyraiders were grounded, pending overhaul in France. However, when the French military advisory mission ended in March 1970, the aircraft were placed in storage. A request by the Cambodian government for U.S. aid, unsurprisingly, went unanswered. Attacks by North Vietnamese forces during early 1971 all but obliterated the Khmer Air Force, and the fate of Cambodia's Skyraiders seems doomed to conjecture. Some reports indicate that Cambodia may have received from France as many as 40 Skyraiders during late 1970, most of which were supposedly destroyed in hangars at Phnom Penh by North Vietnamese attackers. In addition, several U.S. officials reported having observed a great deal of Skyraider wreckage at Phnom Penh during the early 1970s.

As testimony to their satisfaction with the Skyraider, the U.S. Navy in 1962 sought to reactivate its production. Management at Douglas obliged to the extent they began work on jigs and dies, but they could not generate enough political support from the Air Force. Although the idea thrived in some Air Force circles—especially since the Skyraider was considered perfect for the counterinsurgency (COIN) role—it did not fit into the master plan for an all-jet air force. Nor did it help that Douglas was at odds with Secretary of Defense McNamara over cancellation of the nuclear-tipped *Skybolt* air-launched ballistic missile. Harry Gann of Douglas offered his view:

> "There were plans to place the AD back into production. Since the tooling had been destroyed, the plan was to ship two Navy AD-7s back to Douglas for new tooling. A similar arrangement was to be made with Curtis for the engines. In the end McNamara decided it was not cost-effective for the small number of aircraft they wanted. The idea of a turboprop version never went beyond the rumor stage."

While no production Skyraiders were modified with turboprop powerplants, Douglas built the turboprop-powered A2D-1 *Skyshark* as a proposed successor. Although a vast improvement over the Skyraider, the Skyshark program suffered major design setbacks and ended in September 1954. Helping to seal the Skyshark's fate was the advent of Douglas' jet-powered A-4 *Skyhawk*, which prom-

**The first exported Skyraiders were AD-4Ws, which went to Great Britain's Royal Navy as early warning platforms. The Royal Navy redesignated them AEW.1s. (Jack M. Friell)**

ised superior performance. Older Navy Skyraiders were placed in storage as they were replaced by Skyhawks, however, production of both types continued, and they shared space on carier decks well into the war in Southeast Asia.

Like the Skyraider, the Skyhawk was popularized as a Heinemann classic and proved to be one of the world's best attack aircraft. Intended as a replacement for the Skyraider, it was later joined by Grumman's *Intruder* and Vought's *Corsair II.*

Although Navy leaders shared the Air Force vision of an all-jet air arm, the Department of the Navy in early 1965 asked Douglas to prepare a study to reactivate A-1J production. The proposal submitted by Douglas on 23 April 1965 quoted complete figures for quantities up to 500 A-1Js, building up to a production rate of 25 aircraft per month. Included were commitments from Wright Aeronautical for new engines and the Allison Division of General Motors for new propellers.

During communications during June 1964 concerning new production, Navy Attack Squadron Program and Assignment Officer, Commander Billy Spell, stated, "There is serious consideration being given to provide Vietnam's air force with the new aircraft under MAP (Military Assistance Program), with the COIN mission secondary." The deletion of catapult and arresting gear listed among configuration changes in the report clearly indicated the new Skyraider would not be flown from carriers. A proprietary memo from Douglas' marketing department dated 16 June 1965 stated:

> "As you know, the final decision on whether additional A-1Js will be purchased rests with McNamara's staff. McNamara has made statements which are conflicting. At the outset, he stated that no propeller aircraft would be purchased for the present inventory, and particularly since it would have to remain in the inventory for ten years. Recently, however, he made the statement that the A-1s are doing a fine job, and that if his staff gave it an up he would buy it.
>
> The Navy still would like to have 200 A-1Js, but not if it means compromising future A-7 or A-4E buys for their five-year force structure plan. Both the Navy and DoD (Department of Defense) feel the only real advantage for buying A-1Js now is time. There is less enthusiasm for buying A-1Js this week than there was earlier. The decision still rests with McNamara's staff. It is estimated that this decision will be in two to three weeks."

The decision was indeed made, ending the possibility of reopening the Skyraider line.

Air Force leaders faced a similar dilemma, having been caught up in the concept of limited warfare. Indicative within its command level of opposing views concerning an all-jet air force was a search for a successor to the A-1, publicized during March 1967. The Air Force announced it had invited 21 aerospace firms to bid on design studies for what it called the *A-X*. The plea to builders to come up with an inexpensive aircraft with capabilities equal to or better than the A-1 was based on a fruitless search by the Air Force to find and restore additional Skyraiders. Fairchild Republic won the competition with its jet-powered A-10 *Thunderbolt II*, the only modern Air Force aircraft considered somewhat on a par with the Skyraider. As late as the 1990s, some "Old heads" in A-10 squadrons lamented, "Wish we still had the Skyraiders."

**During the early 1960s, Great Britain passed 13 AEW.1s to Sweden, where they were used as target tugs. (Tom Doll)**

# 2

# Overview of a Long Air War

What became largely known as the "Vietnam War" overshadowed what was, in actuality, a Southeast Asian war that extended far beyond Vietnam's borders into Laos, Cambodia, and Thailand. Decades of conflict and intervention in all four countries by Western, Asian, and European governments led to the 1954 Geneva Accords. The agreement resulted in a communist North and Western-backed South Vietnam, while both Laos and Cambodia were declared neutral. In observance of that neutrality, the accords forbid the U.S. and its Southeast Asia Treaty Organization (SEATO) allies from stationing forces in those countries. Political infighting in Laos, however, prompted a marked U.S. response, which included the establishment of a civilian office in the Laotian capitol, effectively sidestepping the Geneva directives. In addition, Washington found it increasingly difficult to address guerilla warfare within South Vietnam's borders without conducting operations in neutral regions. Another term of the agreement held that jet aircraft not be introduced into the signatory nations—the United States and South Vietnam attended the accords, but did not sign the treaty.

The commitment of U.S. Army Special Forces training teams to Laos in mid-1959 set the stage for more than a decade of combat actions in neutral countries that became difficult to hide from a watching world. When President Kennedy took office in 1961 he faced the daunting task of maintaining peace in Laos. Resolve was beyond reach, and years later President Nixon would admit the U.S. was waging war outside Vietnam's borders to check communist use of Laos and Cambodia for bases and supply lines into South Vietnam.

The first U.S. presence in the region, though meager, dates back to 1950, soon after the onset of the Korean war. A Military Assistance Advisory Group had been sent to French Indochina, along with USAF personnel, to support French air operations. After South Vietnam's President Diem ignored the Geneva requirement for a free election in 1956, for fear communist leader Ho Chi Minh would win, Ho's forces began a campaign of terrorism in South Vietnam. The South Vietnamese government's response included cross-border forays beginning in 1958. The first installment of American fixed-wing air support, in the form of AD-6 Skyraiders transferred from the U.S. Navy, coincided with U.S. Navy training in the U.S. of a handful of Vietnamese Air Force (VNAF) pilots beginning in 1959.

Two weeks before President Kennedy took office, Russian leader Nikita Khrushchev proclaimed his nation's support of wars of liberation, specifically in Vietnam and Algeria.

Kennedy responded to the Kremlin's announcement—and the likelihood of communist insurgency in developing countries—by instituting a program of counterinsurgency (COIN). The fight was on, which, for America, was a plunge into quicksand. After Special Forces teams entered Laos, the CIA in 1961 received permission to assist the South Vietnamese in conducting covert operations in North Vietnam and Laos—the South Vietnamese government added Cambodia to the arrangement for good measure. Also that year, the U.S. Air Force established several bases in northern Thailand in conjunction with SEATO exercises designed to display a show of force in the region. By early October 1961 a Tactical Control Group was operational at Vietnam's Tan Son Nhut Air Base, signaling the U.S. Air Force's active involvement in the war.

In response to President Kennedy's call to establish COIN forces, the USAF's air commandos, who had gained fame as jungle fighters in Burma during World War II, were revived at Hurlburt Field, Florida, in April 1961 when the Tactical Air Command (TAC) activated the 4400th Combat Crew Training Squadron (CCTS), code-named "Jungle Jim." True to the air commando legacy, just four months after activation the squadron's Detachment One was deployed to Mali, West Africa, followed in early November by Detachment Two, code-named "Farmgate," which shipped to South Vietnam. The 4400th was staffed with aircrews and maintenance personnel, who operated a mix of vintage propeller-driven C-47 transports, B-26 bombers, and T-28 fighter/trainers. Aircraft flown by American advisors wore the insignia of the Vietnamese Air Force.

As air commando forces grew, so did resentment towards them over everything from wearing of the bush hat to budget appropriations. Many senior Air Force commanders viewed the use of funds on outmoded aircraft as an infringement upon their blueprint for modernizing the Air Force. The level of disdain slowed the development of COIN aircraft to the extent the air commandos resigned themselves to acquiring and modifying existing aircraft. The U.S. government's half-hearted attempt to honor the Geneva directive that prohibited the use of jet aircraft in Southeast Asia actually lent validity to the air commando's plan. The Navy's consent to turn over enough A-1E/G Skyraiders to equip two air commando squadrons formed in 1963 could not have been better timed, since weary Air Force B-26s and T-28s were experiencing wing losses.

From the onset, air commandos in Southeast Asia were subjected to the many operational restrictions that identified the protracted conflict. The aggressiveness of air commandos turned to frustration as they, along with the Vietnamese they were sent to train, became embroiled in bureaucracy. The Farm Gate detachment was prohibited from engaging in combat unless a Vietnamese was aboard, or if the VNAF proved ineffective in a combat situation. This doctrine paved the way for acquisition of the two-seat A-1E. When a Viet Cong mortar attack on 10 September 1963 prevented Soc Trang's T-28s from defending two villages in the area under attack, four USAF air commando pilots got two T-28s airborne and attacked the mortar positions. Along with their commendations for repelling the attack, the pilots received reprimands for engaging in combat without the requisite VNAF personnel on board. It would be a long war.

The situation in Laos was similarly bleak. By 1960 its unstable political front led to growing U.S. support. When the Soviets provided air support of the communist Pathet Lao, U.S. military leaders prepared for possible intervention in Laos, fearing that its loss would not only give rise to the domino theory, but that it would demonstrate lack of American resolve. As a U.S. task force steamed north from Subic Bay in January 1961, President Eisenhower, bent on finding ways to avoid direct U.S. involvement in Laos, favored a CIA scheme of training Hmong military forces and supporting them with Air America, the CIA's air arm. A network of remote airstrips, called Lima Sites, were carved out of mountainous terrain in northern Laos to interconnect Hmong outposts.

As North Vietnam expanded its areas of control in Laos, President Kennedy in 1963 authorized the CIA to expand its operations. In February 1964 the U.S. Military Assistance Command-Vietnam (MACV) established its Studies and Observations Group (better known as Special Operations Group, or SOG) to handle the broad mission of clandestine operations in the denied regions of Laos and, eventually, Cambodia. After full-scale fighting broke out in Laos in March 1964 President Johnson approved SOG missions, thereby setting the stage for what would become known as "The Secret War."

Support of indigenous ground troops and SOG missions in Laos was provided by Air America and U.S. military aircraft. It quickly became clear, however, that the intensifying war in Laos overwhelmed Air America search and rescue capabilities. Compounding the situation was the flow of equipment and personnel from the north to support the enemy's guerilla campaign in South Vietnam. The seemingly endless supply line moved along the vexation known as the Ho Chi Minh Trail, most of which wound its way through *neutral* Laos, beneath triple canopy jungle.

To keep pace with the intensifying war, U.S. Air Force unconventional capabilities were expanded in April 1962 by upgrading the 4400th CCTS to the Special Air Warfare Center (SAWC) at Eglin AFB. As the organization enlarged, its 1st Air Commando Group became the 1st Air Commando Wing in May 1963, which, in March 1964, deployed Detachment Six (code-named "Water Pump") to Udorn, Thailand. The detachment trained indigenous soldiers to fly the T-28 in combat.

During early August, in the much publicized *Tonkin Gulf Incident*, North Vietnamese patrol boats attacked U.S. destroyers in retaliation for raids on naval bases, giving President Johnson all the reason he needed to escalate the war. The Skyraider had joined the ranks of the USAF's prop-driven air commandos and, like their carrier-based brothers, joined the fray in Southeast Asia. The U.S. initiated the *Barrel Roll* air campaign in December 1964 to support Laotian ground forces.

The face of the war in both Laos and Vietnam changed abruptly during 1965. Although U.S. airmen were continually forced to fight with one hand tied behind their backs, the commitment of regular ground combat units to Vietnam eased the constraints against the use of jet aircraft. Moreover, air commandos no longer were required to fly with Vietnamese nationals aboard, or with VNAF insignia on their aircraft. March 1965 signaled the beginning of *Rolling Thunder*, a sustained air campaign against the North that was waged simultaneously with other major air operations. Those included interdiction strikes against the Ho Chi Minh Trail, attacks against the Viet Cong in South Vietnam, and attacks against targets in North Vietnam. Despite the ever changing tactical environment of air combat in Southeast Asia, limiting *rules of engagement* not only prevailed, but often bordered on the ridiculous. For example: initially, North Vietnamese MiG bases were not targeted for fear that Chinese or Russian advisors might be killed, with subsequent reprisals. Nor did surface-to-air (SAM) missile sites—the first of which was spotted in April 1965—appear on target lists, as long as they were not used against aircraft. Often, permission to strike targets spotted by pilots had to come from high-level offices as far away as Washington. In other instances, pilots could not attack obvious targets unless they were being fired upon. Spad pilot Tom Dwelle remembers:

> "We had a directive in 1965-'66 never to hit a Buddhist *Cao Dai* sect temple. They were absolutely off limits so as not to alienate this particular religious group. The Cong knew this, and one morning I got directed onto the biggest temple I had ever seen—up in II Corps, as I recall. The FAC directed me to take out the temple. I refused, and he said the place was completely full of ammunition and added, 'What do *you* think you ought to do?' The FAC had people on the ground and convinced me he knew what

he was talking about so, against my better judgment, I put two 750-pound napalm bombs in the front door and was rewarded with a ride on a tidal wave. It was by far the biggest *secondary* of my tour. *Wingey* said, 'Well, we know where they store their explosives, I wonder where they go to church.'"

Other restrictions included a ban on bombing dikes that dammed rice paddies in North Vietnam, which only helped the enemy select the most favorable sites for anti-aircraft batteries. The list goes on.

Following close on the heels of Rolling Thunder was *Steel Tiger*, a limited air campaign aimed at severing the Ho Chi Minh Trail in Laos. Augmenting Steel Tiger was *Tiger Hound*, a major campaign that pitted every available type of weapon and aircraft of all services against the Trail. The quarry most hunted on the Trail was a ragged, battered, but capable truck able to haul a few tons of war material and soldiers from supply points in North Vietnam to South Vietnam. Bombing halts during the Johnson administration, implemented as gestures of good faith to bring Hanoi to the peace table, were ignored and simply provided the enemy with ample opportunity to bolster his air defenses, much to the dread of aircrews. Those airmen, in jet, prop, and rotary-wing aircraft alike, would face the fiercest air defenses in the history of aerial warfare. The Trail's 2,000-mile labyrinth alone was guarded by 10,000 anti-aircraft weapons, comprising mainly a lethal trio of 37mm, dual-barreled 23mm, and 12.7mm guns. By the late 1960s the war was in full swing. On pilots' maps, North Vietnam was divided into six operational areas called *Route Packages*. Air strikes launched from bases in Thailand, South Vietnam, and Guam, and from carriers off the coast. As armadas of jets rained bombs on targets, the air war *on the deck* belonged to helicopters and a few fixed-wing aircraft, especially the Skyraider. The Navy retired their Spads in early 1968, while the USAF and VNAF flew them to the bitter end, mainly in support of ground and SAR forces. Rolling Thunder ended in 1968 as part of the on-again, off-again peace negotiations in Paris which, throughout President Nixon's term, would prove to be nothing more than political follies. When President Nixon took the helm in 1969 he stressed the importance of turning the war over to the Vietnamese. In a move that ultimately contributed to his downfall, he sanctioned strikes in neutral Cambodia.

The *other* war in Laos, which was no longer a secret to anyone, did not fare well, as North Vietnamese Army (NVA) divisions continued their relentless assaults. Air America and U.S. air units suffered heavy losses, and by the end of 1971 the North Vietnamese were largely in control. In response to the North Vietnamese invasion across the demilitarized zone (DMZ) into South Vietnam, which began in March 1972, *Linebacker* kicked off in May. The goal of Linebacker was to break the back of the North Vietnamese supply system by hitting major complexes in the Hanoi and Haiphong areas. The North's offensive stalled and the flow of supplies was reduced, however, the results were short-lived. The North feigned moves toward the peace table, which relieved the bombing, but it had actually used the lull to restore its war machine. Their deception resulted in *Linebacker II*, which started in December 1972 and brought around-the-clock strikes to the heart of North Vietnam's industry and supply points.

Linebacker II, which many agree would have met with greater success years earlier, drove North Vietnam, once again, to the peace table. On 23 January a cease-fire was signed, with one of its most noteworthy terms calling for the return of American POWs. Shortly after the Vietnam truce went into effect a cease-fire agreement was signed in Laos, leading to the establishment of a coalition government. American forces gradually vacated Thai air bases, and the last Air America aircraft crossed from Laos into Thailand on 3 June 1974.

It is estimated that nearly seven million tons of ordnance rained upon Vietnam, Laos, and Cambodia during the conflict—another impressive, but dry statistic during a war in which success was measured by body count, and by the number of bridges, trucks, structures, and encampments destroyed. What *is* more important historically is the fortitude of the soldiers sent to fight it. They knew that had they been used as intended, the war would have taken a dramatically different course. And *they* knew that when you fight a war, you fight to win.

# 3

## Things Under Wings

Skyraider enthusiasts have long wondered about the wide variety of objects suspended from the airplane, and Spad drivers themselves admit there were too many stores designations to remember. Since carrying external stores seemed to be the Skyraider's natural state, it's time to take a closer look at those things under wings. Wars, in their own sinister way, nurture the development of weaponry, and the conflict in Southeast Asia was no exception. If anything, it was the most remarkable weapons proving ground in the history of American warfare, and the Skyraider was a major participant. The range of external stores carried by Skyraiders throughout that war was incredibly vast. Due to their massive payloads and accuracy in placing ordnance, Skyraiders were unquestionably the best aircraft for taking the war to the enemy. This capability was vital to ground forces, who needed close air support—lots of it—and for longer periods of time than other aircraft could provide.

When the Skyraider first became operational during the early 1950s it was armed with ordnance developed prior to and during World War II. After proving itself a most capable weapons platform during the Korean war, the Skyraider joined the ranks of naval aircraft assigned to the Naval Air Special Weapons Facility (NASWF) for tests of special weapons and nuclear warheads. The Naval Ordnance Test Station (NOTS) at China Lake, California, teamed with Cal Tech and became largely responsible for the development of all other munitions. Eventually, anything associated with naval weaponry passed through China Lake before going to the Fleet.

At the beginning of the 1960s, President Kennedy recognized the likelihood of America's involvement in limited warfare, prompting a shift to the development of conventional weapons and deviating from the nuclear weapon mindset of the 1950s Cold War. It was the limited warfare concept that influenced weapons research and development to the extent that more than 75 percent of weapons and supporting systems in Southeast Asia came from the NOTS-Cal Tech team. By 1967, when China Lake NOTS and the Naval Ordnance Laboratory at Corona, California, merged to become the Naval Weapons Center, many of their products had proven successful in Southeast Asia. Those mated with Spads included pod-launched rockets, the "Eye" series of freefall weapons, and fuel-air explosives.

Meanwhile, the U.S. Air Force was well involved with its own weapons development program, most of which was conducted at Eglin's Air Proving Ground (APG). Part of the Air Force's realignment prompted by the emphasis on conventional weaponry included changing the APG to the Armament Development and Test Center (ADTC). Its vast ranges, which included the Gulf of Mexico Test Range, provided ample space for evaluating the wide range of weaponry used by Skyraiders. It did not take long for the ADTC to be-

**In the South Vietnamese Air Force, the Skyraider replaced the Grumman F8F Bearcat, seen here in 1960 with an ordnance mix carried over to the Spad. (Albert Grandolini)**

**Skyraiders assigned to the NOTS at China Lake were instrumental in the development of a wide range of ordnance. Here, A-1G BuNo. 132510 is loaded with 12 practice bombs, a Mk 88 practice bomb on the centerline rack, and a pair of Mk 79 Model 1,000-pound fire bombs. (Ron Picciani)**

come immersed in developing systems to keep pace with the expanding, yet limited, war and a cunning, elusive enemy.

In the field of ordnance, the device, and each of its components, including aircraft racks, fuses, igniters, fins, arming wires, suspension lugs, fillers, and sub-munitions, were given letter/number designations, creating an encyclopedic identification chart. Compared to today's system of joint services, years ago each service developed and labeled much of its own weapons and related systems, with very little crossover. However, the series of external racks, along with bombs and fuel tanks of various sizes, originally labeled under the *Aero* brand name, retains the Douglas trademark, having been designed by Ed Heinemann and his staff.

Before examining the Spad's hardware, it's helpful to look at the airplane in terms of carrying and delivering stores. Skyraider pilots learned in training the importance of *drag indexes* and how they relate to gross weight and flight performance. The drag index of a "clean" A-1E/G—without external stores—was 80, figuring in wing guns, 15 stores racks, cowl flaps closed, and landing gear and flaps up; the basic drag index of the A-1H/J was 0. Each external store was assigned a drag index number, which depended upon the size and shape of the item and its location on the airplane. The more drag it induced the higher its number. The total of these numbers, when added to the clean airplane drag number, gave the drag index for that particular mission configuration. The index then de-

**The first Spads deployed to Udorn RTAFB in 1965 for search and rescue coverage for F-105s carried this stores configuration. U.S. Air Force A-1s rarely carried two external 300-gallon fuel tanks, which was the maximum that could be carried due to fuel/oil ratio limitations. Assigned to the 602nd ACS, this Spad was shot down and its pilot killed on 12 September 1966. (Bernard Fisher)**

**An A-1J of VA-196 during a pre-Vietnam cruise, as indicated by single wing guns. Ordnance consists of 260-pound fragmentation bombs and 5-inch High Velocity Aerial Rockets (HVAR) with high explosive warheads. The single mount lugs on the bombs were for use on British aircraft. (Paul Rhodes)**

**This musclebound VA-196 Spad carries 1,000-pound fire bombs, and 250-pound "fat boy" bombs on its outer wing racks in 1965. (Paul Rhodes)**

**A VA-196 A-1H makes an emergency landing aboard *Bon Homme Richard* due to loss of hydraulic pressure. The pilot dumped external stores, but both inboard Aero 7D rocket launchers hung up. Prior to aircraft in trouble trapping aboard carriers, the ship announced, "Heads up on the flight deck, hung ordnance in the groove." The bag hanging from the starboard Mk 51 rack holds 80 pounds of tie-down chain. (Paul Rhodes)**

termined the performance of the airplane in that configuration. The total drag index and the airplane's gross weight—plus other mission factors, such as distances—was used for determining the fuel load. As stores were dropped or emptied during the mission the external configuration changed, and thus the drag index. External stores that induced the most drag and, therefore, had the highest drag numbers were flat-faced "funny bombs" and empty rocket launchers. A number of operating restrictions, such as speed, altitude, and G forces, applied when external stores were carried and released.

External ordnance was controlled through an armament panel located below the instrument panel. Special stores were controlled through additional panels installed on the consoles. All stores could be released electrically by the pilot, and some could be jettisoned manually. As a safety feature, the master armament switch, which energized all armament circuits, had an open circuit when the landing gear was extended. The pilot's control stick incorporated a trigger switch for firing guns, a release switch identified by a B for releasing stores on the center wing racks, and a release switch identified by an R to release stores on the outer wing stations. A Mark 20 gun sight, which could be used for guns, rockets, bombs, or torpedoes, was mounted atop the instrument panel. In the A-1E/G it was mounted on the left side.

All ordnance and stores were carried externally on racks mounted to the wings or fuselage. Each outboard wing section had six stations, each with an Aero 14D, E, or G (14-inch distance between suspension lugs), which were numbered 1 through 12, starting at the left outboard wing. One Mk51 rack (14 and 30-inch suspension) was mounted beneath each inboard wing station, and one Aero 3A (14 and 30-inch suspension) ejector rack was mounted to the fuselage centerline station. The latter incorporated an electrically fired 10-gauge shotgun cartridge that propelled a two-plate ejector foot to "kick" clear an empty fuel tank, which otherwise would strike the fuselage when released, or to ensure that large ordnance cleared the propeller arc during a diving attack (perfecting this feature proved troublesome after a 2,000-pound inert bomb went through the prop when released in a vertical dive during an early test flight, forcing test pilot Bob Rahn to bail out). The centerline rack could carry 3,600 pounds on 30-inch suspension. The Mk51 rack could carry 2,300 pounds on 14-inch suspension and 3,000 pounds using 30-inch suspension. The maximum outboard wing load was 2,500 pounds. Only a two-inch clearance between stores was required. Large stores could not be carried on Aero 14 racks at stations 5 and 8 since they would interfere with shell and link ejection from the outboard wing guns.

The Mk51 and Aero 3A racks featured screw jack pad sway arms that were tightened down against the store to hold it firmly during flight maneuvers. In place of a Mk51, a Mk61 (with 20-inch suspension) was also used, although the former was more com-

**Visible on this Navy A-1H are cannon flash suppressors, and arming wires running to bomb fuses. Also visible is a bi-fold access panel for the outboard cannon, and a similar panel for the inboard cannon abutting the wing fold seam. (Gary L. Gottschalk)**

**View looking into the wing upper surface access panel of the outboard 20mm cannon feed mechanism. Linked cartridges are visible at upper left in the opening. (Ted A. Morris)**

**Ordnancemen ("Ordies") aboard *Oriskany* in 1965 load 20mm cartridges in an A-1 of VA-152. (Bud Watson)**

mon. External stores could be fitted with suspension lugs at different intervals to adapt to various racks. The 500-pound capacity Aero 14 racks were equipped either with the threaded jack arms or retractable spring-loaded sway arms. The Aero 14 also had provisions for firing stores electrically, with power supplied through "pigtail" wires plugged into wing receptacles just aft of each rack.

Ordnance arming wires were secured in the racks by a solenoid actuator. The wires ran to fuses in the front and back ends of ordnance where they were held with two *Fahnstock* clips. When the ordnance fell away the clips were stripped away, allowing the fuse vanes to turn and mechanically arm the device. The arming wires remained with the aircraft and were easily discarded for reloading.

The U.S. Air Force made use of a MAU-63/A Multiple Bomb Rack (MBR), which was designed for counterinsurgency (COIN) aircraft to carry six 250-pound stores on a single station, providing they did not exceed 64 inches in length or 10.8 inches in diameter. Each of the MBR's six racks had all the features of the Aero 14 rack. The MBR released stores in single sequence only. The Navy equivalent was designated A/A37 B-3 PMBR.

An important component of the Spad's arsenal was its wing guns (also called cannon) intended for air-to-air combat and strafing. Four forward-firing M3 20mm guns were mounted in the wings, one on each side of the wing-fold joint. The guns were charged hydraulically in pairs and could be fired simultaneously or in pairs. The M3 was an automatic combination gas-recoil operated, link-belt fed, air-cooled weapon. It differed from other 20mm guns in that it fired percussion-primed ammunition. Each gun weighed 100 pounds and was 6 feet, 6 inches long. Its rate of fire was 650 to 800 rounds per minute, and it had a muzzle velocity of 2,730 feet per second. The guns were supplied by a total of 796 rounds of ammunition. Each outboard gun had three ammo boxes that held 66 rounds each, and were accessed through hinged upper wing panels. Each inboard gun had two ammo boxes that held 100 rounds each, and

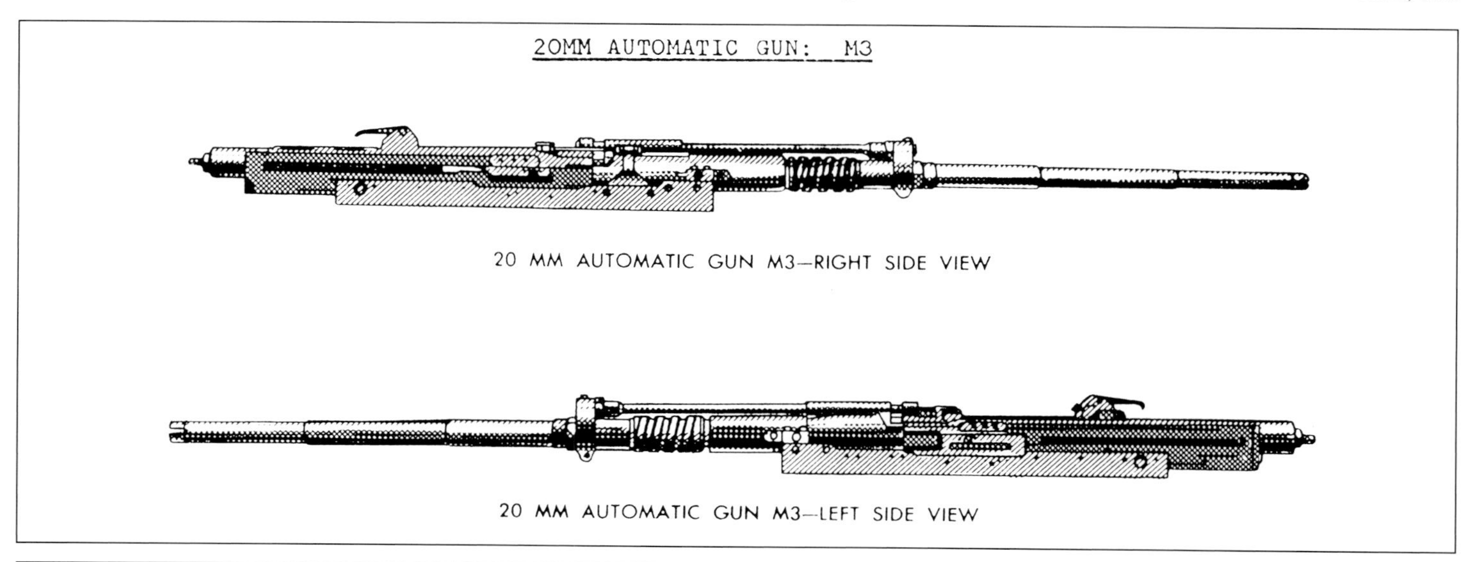

**Although the Mk 8 fuel tank was not to be jettisoned from A-1s since it had no fins and would bump the underside of the aircraft on release, it was sometimes done anyway. The tank featured a lengthwise pressed steel flange. This example, attached to a USAF Spad in 1967, still wears its Navy Glossy Sea Blue paint. (Tom Hansen)**

**The Skyraider's 300-gallon Aero 1A fuel tank carried on the centerline rack was not complete without a liberal coating of engine oil. (Tom Hansen)**

were accessed through the wheel wells. The 20mm cartridges were high explosive (HE), high explosive incendiary (HEI), armor piercing (AP), tracer, and practice. The type and combination of ammo used was usually determined by the target and unit policy. Flash suppressors normally attached to the gun barrels were seldom used in combat. Failure of the Spad's wing guns is believed to have caused aircraft losses, although the Air Force never officially confirmed an A-1 loss as a result of gun failure. The Navy and South Vietnamese Air Force did not report wing gun failure incidents. Worn components and percussion ammunition were the factors contributing to gun failure, usually with disastrous results. If gun breeches were worn or shell extractors cracked, a round would project too far into the chamber and misfire. The extractor could not remove the shell, and the next one entering the chamber detonated the first. Typically the explosion resulted in an A-1 being downed by its own guns during strafing runs. A program was begun to procure replacement gun parts, and to replace several million rounds of dated 20mm ammunition with bore-safe ammo. Unfortunately, the Department of Defense directed that the use of outmoded ammo be continued. Although other factors, such as gun maintenance, ammo loading, care of ammo, and duration of firing bursts were investigated, non-bore-safe ammo was found to be directly responsible for gun failure.

Especially helpful in pinpointing the cause of gun failure was the examination of a Spad flown to Da Nang AB following a wing explosion. On 10 January 1969 "Stretch" Ballmes had just begun a strafing run with an A-1G when an explosion occurred in one of his wings. Since he prudently had gained sufficient speed and altitude, and was near Da Nang, he decided to stay with the airplane. Although his wing was on fire and his Spad had no hydraulic pressure

**Aviation ordnancemen of VA-165 use "hernia bars" to load a 250-pound Mk 81 "Snakeye" bomb. Two additional Snakeyes are cradled into a 14B skid used to transport ordnance to the aircraft. A smoke marker/drift signal is attached to the outboard rack. (U.S. Navy)**

**One hundred-pound bombs are loaded aboard an A-1G's multiple launcher at McConnell AFB, Kansas in September 1967. The T-28 in the background was also used for ordnance training. (Merle Olmsted)**

**An ordie arms a parachute flare of a VA-152 Spad. Ejection and ignition fuse setting dials were in the flare's fuse cavity. An arming lanyard is visible on the flare's casing. (Bud Watson)**

**Twenty-pound AN-M41 frag bombs and 100-pound white phosphorous bombs stored at Pleiku during late 1965. (Raymond A. Young III)**

for flaps and speed brakes, the landing gear locked down and he was able to touch down at 200 knots. Ballmes said, "There wasn't much skin left on that wing."

Built into the leading edge of the right center wing panel was an AN/N6 or AN/N9 gun camera installation. The camera operated automatically when the guns or rockets were fired. Some Spads were modified with an electrically operated KB-18A 70mm strike camera, which was mounted in the underside of the left wing, inboard of the wheel well. The camera operated automatically when stores were released, providing panoramic images for battle damage assessment. This was accomplished by a rotating prism that scanned 180 degrees fore and aft and 40 degrees laterally during each photograph. Strike cameras were seldom used, and some pilots agree that they were effective only if they flew straight off the target. That was considered foolhardy, since pilots jinked to avoid ground fire, often giving intelligence people shots of trees and the horizon.

The only cameras used by the 1st ACS were wing-mounted versions for photographing other aircraft on strike missions, a task that was not popular with Spad pilots. It has been said that President Johnson had a voracious appetite for combat footage. Tom Dwelle, who flew Spads with the 1st and 602nd ACS, recalls that during mid-1965 he flew 15 missions with a 500-pound napalm can modified with cameras. Built into the canister were a 35mm rapid-sequence, still camera with color film, and a forward and backward-looking 16mm movie camera. Both cameras were activated by releasing external stores or by the pilot's rocket-firing button. The images were widely distributed throughout the press during 1966.

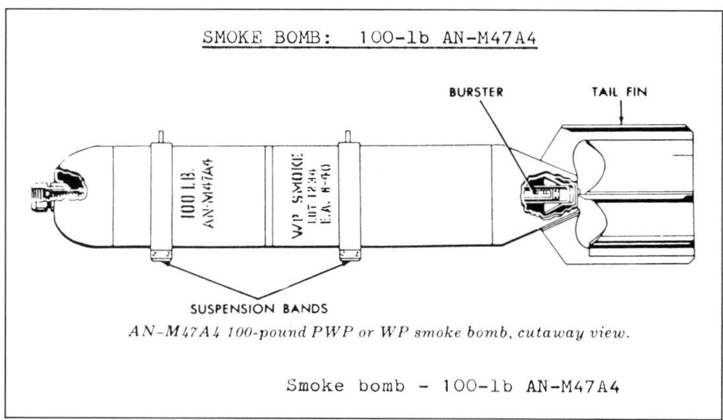

**The display placard near this A-1E's left wing states the typical ordnance load is 250, 500, or 750-pound general purpose bombs, few of which are on this aircraft. Instead it carries alternating 7- and 19-tube rocket launchers, for a total of 156 rockets, plus six 250-pound bombs on an MER on the left inboard rack, and what is believed to be depth bombs on the right inboard rack. A 150-gallon fuel tank occupies the centerline rack. (USAF)**

**Parachute flares next to the 19-tube rocket launchers indicate a night mission for this VA-25 A-1H in 1966. A 300-gallon centerline fuel tank was standard for Navy Spads. (Tom Hansen)**

Fuel tanks were common external stores on Skyraiders, augmenting their 380-U.S. gallon capacity main fuel cell; aircraft modified with a self-sealing fuel cell had a 368-gallon capacity. External tanks were either of Douglas' Aero design or standard Mk 8 types. The 300-gallon Mk 8 saw little use compared to the high-speed Aero design. Its bulbous shape and lack of fins ruled out a clean separation when jettisoned, thereby increasing the likelihood that it would strike the aircraft. Although the trademark streamlined shape was seen throughout the Aero series, their sizes and tail sections varied.

The Aero 1A(1), 1B, and 1D were 300-gallon tanks. Those with a short tail cone without fins were limited to mounting on the centerline station, while those with a long tail cone and horizontal

**The inboard rack of this A-1E at Bien Hoa AB in 1965 mounts an early style MAU-63 rack with six 100-pound bombs. The lightning bolt on the centerline fuel tank was a personal marking of the crew chief. (SMSGT Paul Lake, Ret.)**

**Napalm and white phosphorous bomb strikes in South Vietnam's Delta in 1965, seen by the rear-facing strike camera of an A-1E of the 1st Air Commando Squadron. (USAF)**

**A white phosphorous bomb strike by an A-1E on an enemy stronghold in South Vietnam's Delta. White phosphorous was nicknamed "Willie Pete." (USAF)**

**The symmetrical outer wing loads of this 602nd SOS Spad in 1970 comprise SUU-14/A CBUs, Lau-3/A rocket launchers, and WP/PWP bombs. The left stub has a SUU-11/A minigun, while the stub opposite has a 150-gallon fuel tank. A 300-gallon tank is on the centerline. (Richard Michaud)**

fins were carried on inboard stations. Aero 1A and 1C tanks were 150-gallon capacity and had horizontal fins. They could be carried on either centerline or inboard stations. Like the Mk 8, the 300-gallon Aero tank without fins could be jettisoned in emergencies, however, minor flap damage was certain, the extent of which increased with speed. Since the Spad's high rate of oil consumption dictated the fuel-oil ratio, no more than two 300-gallon external fuel tanks could be carried at one time.

The effectiveness of rockets was proven by the Skyraider during the Korean war and by its predecessors during World War II. Rockets fired by Spads in Southeast Asia were of the 5-inch and 2.75-inch variety. Paul Rhodes was a Navy Aviation Ordnanceman (AO) with VA-196 aboard the *USS Bon Homme Richard* during its 1964 and 1965 Vietnam cruises. He explains:

> "The 14E racks also accommodated 5-inch High Velocity Aerial Rockets (HVAR) that were fired electrically. They attached to the rack fore and aft on the HVAR slots made for that purpose. The rockets were plugged into the plane's electrical system just before launch, and we always did a stray voltage check just before the plane saddled up on the catapult gear. We never had any stray voltage, so we just plugged 'em in. When the planes returned, the plugs that had ripped out of the rocket when it was fired were still plugged into the wing. These were removed at rearming. Sometimes the rockets were duds, and they tended to come off when the returning plane trapped back aboard. The rocket could not be manually jettisoned the way stores hung on hooks could. I saw this happen more than once. When they came off they came bouncing down the deck. No one was hurt by these when I was aboard. We just picked them up after they stopped and heaved them over the side. They weighed about 130 pounds."

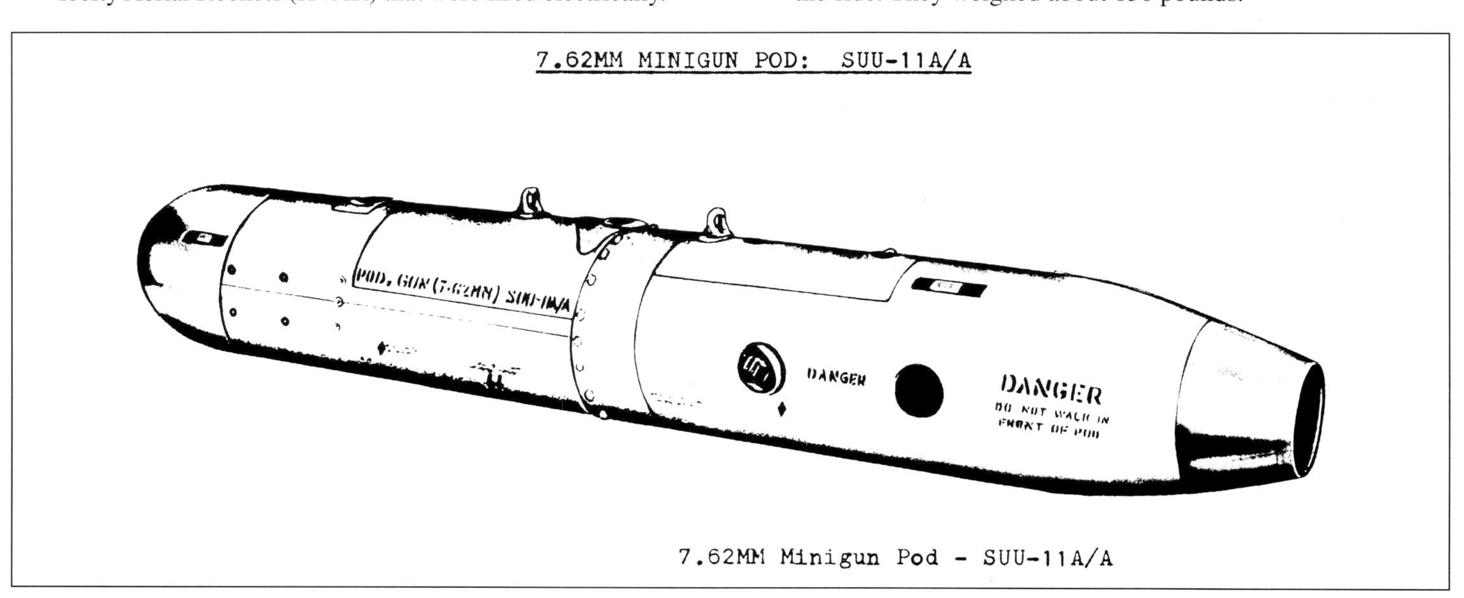


7.62MM Minigun Pod - SUU-11A/A

The A-1E no. 135141 of the 1st SOS carries a typical "Sandy" load for the 1966-1967 period. The opposite inboard stub has a minigun, while the outer wing load mirrors this view. (Tom Hansen)

Major Tommy Wardlow of the 602nd SOS poses with a squadron Spad loaded with red-painted fire bombs on Christmas Eve 1968. The wording stenciled on the Mk 116 reads, "Dear Charlie, may these gifts add warmth to your Christmas." (Wardlow collection)

The *Zuni* was an improved supersonic 5-inch rocket that went into service in 1960. Its high velocity contributed to greater accuracy and shock effect over other rockets. It was 15 feet long, carried a 48-pound high explosive warhead, and was fired from the LAU-10/A four-tube launcher. The launcher was primarily of aluminum construction and had a breakaway nose fairing. Zunis could be fired singly or in ripple mode. Zunis with delay fuses for penetration of the target before detonation were known as "Bunker Busters."

The 2.75-inch Folding Fin Aerial Rocket (FFAR), also known as the "Mighty Mouse," saw its heyday in Southeast Asia, where it became the most-fired non-bullet ordnance in combat. Also a successful China Lake product, the tube-launched, electrically fired FFAR consisted of a motor, warhead, and fuse. The rockets varied in length, weight, and warheads. Weights ranged from 17.9 to 22.2 pounds, and lengths from 47.9 to 52.9 inches. Warheads were Mk 1 high explosive (HE), Mk 5 high explosive anti-tank (HEAT), Mk 151 fragmentation (PMI – Pearlite Malleable Iron), WDU-4A/A flechette (2,200 steel darts), M156 white phosphorous smoke (WP), and practice. Early rocket motor bodies were blue-gray, while later versions were white.

The family of 2.75-inch rocket launchers has changed little since their introduction during the early 1960s. Their nomenclature varied somewhat between the services, and Spad units commonly used what was available. Since the differences between models of rocket launchers were slight, they were more easily identified as 7 or 19-tube types. The original 7-tube launchers were designated LAU-32A/A and –32B/A, which were replaced by the improved LAU-59/A and LAU-68A/A. A non-reusable version, which had paper tubes, was LAU-49/A. The standard USAF 19-tube launcher was the LAU-3A/A. It, along with the –60/A and –69/A, had paper tubes and saw use on Navy aircraft. The LAU-61/A and –71/A had metal tubes and were reusable. In Navy parlance, the 7-tube launcher was known as the Aero 6A, and the 19-tube the Aero 7D. The 2.75-

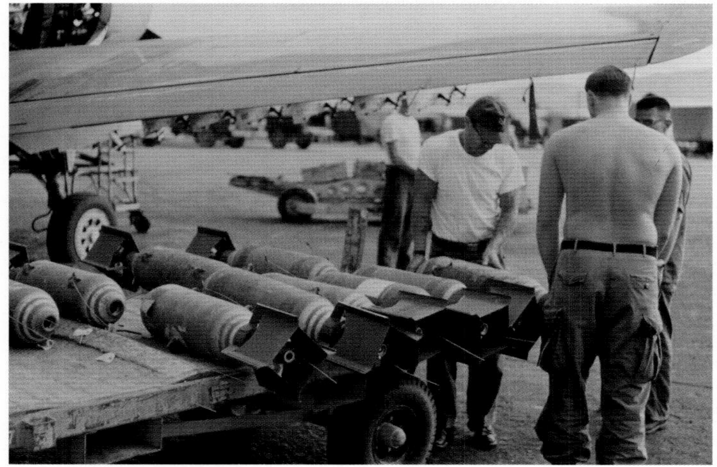

Air Force armorers load old series 100-pound GP bombs on an A-1E at Pleiku in December 1965. Arming wires protruding through the box fin assembly will be attached to rear fuses. (Raymond A. Young III)

Banded clusters of fragmentation bombs fill the MERs of this 1st ACS Spad at Bien Hoa AB in 1965. Fifty-six rockets complete the antipersonnel arsenal. (USAF)

## FRAGMENTATION BOMB CLUSTER: 100-lb AN-M1A2, AN-M1A3, & AN-M1A4

ARMING WIRE
SUSPENSION LUG
SUSPENSION LUG
CLUSTER ADAPTER
VANE LOCK SPRINGS
FRAG BOMBS
8.9"
10.3"
TOGGLE STRAP CLAMP
VANE LOCK SPRINGS
NOSE VIEW
TAIL VIEW

Frag bomb cluster - 100-lb AN-M1A2, AN-M1A3, & AN-M1A4

## MISSILE CLUSTER ADAPTER: 500-lb MK44

Lazy Dog missile, slightly oversize.

Missile cluster adapter - 500-lb MK44

**The A-1E no. 132445 of the 1st SOS at Pleiku armed with wall-to-wall CBU-14s and two BLU-1B fire bombs. (Ted A. Morris)**

**Fused and armed Mk 81 GP bombs on racks numbered one through six. (Ted A. Morris)**

inch rocket launchers were carried on outboard wing racks. On the rear face of 2.75-inch rocket launchers was an intervalometer dial for presetting ripple or single firing mode.

To significantly reduce the launcher's drag index, a molded fiber fairing, which shattered from rocket impact, could be attached to its front. The LAU-3A/A and –60/A also had breakaway tail fairings, while the LAU-61/A and –69/A had aluminum open-ended fairings to direct debris away from the aircraft. The use of breakaway fairings on Spads in Southeast Asia depended upon their availability and unit policy. Early production launchers and fairings were white, with the switch made to olive drab during the mid-1960s. The tip of the fairing was red or black.

Another means by which Spads could clear jungle or stop large numbers of enemy troops was the SUU-11A/A pod, which contained a 7.62mm GAU-2B/A minigun. This unit provided highly accurate concentrated firepower in a self-contained unit. The GAU-2B/A was a lightweight derivative of the proven 20mm M61 Gatling gun. Besides the minigun, the pod contained a linkless feed system, control system, battery, and 1,500 rounds, which lasted for 15 seconds of firing at the maximum rate of 6,000 rounds per minute. The gun was operated by an electric drive motor and gearing that rotated six barrels and the feeder mechanism. The pod was seven feet long, one foot in diameter, and loaded weighed 325 pounds. The SUU-11A/A was most often carried on the left Mk51 rack, and sometimes occupied both Mk51s. Favored as a close-in weapon, the minigun became a standard element of a USAF "Sandy" SAR load, but was seldom, if ever, used by Navy or VNAF Spads.

Napalm, despite having gained notoriety during the war in Southeast Asia, actually dates back to World War I when both Germany and the Allies exploited gasoline's volatile properties for use in flame throwers. It was not until 1942 that Harvard scientists and the U.S. Army found a way to slow the burn rate of gasoline. The answer was mixing aluminum soap powder—*na*pthenic and *palm*etic acids, hence *napalm*—with gasoline to produce a sticky

**One hundred-pound GP bombs fill the wings of A-1E no. 132665 at Bien Hoa in 1965. One hundred-pound WP smoke bombs are attached to the Mk 51 racks. (USAF)**

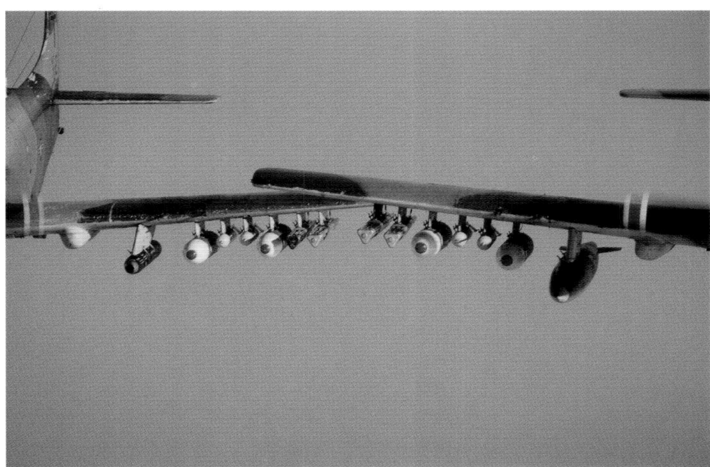

**This interesting view, taken from the rear of an HH-3 helicopter, of Sandys One and Two of the 1st SOS in April 1970, shows the complete SAR loads. From outboard on the outer wings are CBU-14, LAU-3/A, AN-47A and LAU-3/A. The left inboard stub has a SUU-11/A, while on the right is a 150-gallon fuel tank. (Richard Michaud)**

Six M41A1 20-pound, spiral-wrapped HE fragmentation bombs are braced with pieces of wood to help fit clusters tight to the rack. Clearly shown are the two types of rack mounting devices: screw jack pad sway arms and retractable spring-loaded sway braces. (Ted A. Morris)

This VA-25 A-1H, BuNo. 137517, carries Zuni rocket launchers and two variations of the 7-tube rocket launchers. (Tom Hansen)

gel that burned more slowly and adhered to targets. After the fire rained upon Japan during late Word War II and the success of napalm bombs against enemy troops in Korea, the substance had become a mainstay in the U.S. arsenal. Type M2 thickener was the standard agent mixed with aviation gasoline (avgas) or jet fuel, however, other mixers were developed for use in varying climates. A safer form of napalm that burned longer and hotter (called "Napalm B") resulted from its refinement.

Containers filled with napalm were called "Fire Bombs," which were thin-skinned aluminum tanks, usually dropped during low level attacks. The container ruptured upon impact and spread flaming, sticky fuel, which was ignited by one or more fuses and igniters. Like other ordnance, fire bombs came in a variety of shapes and sizes, had 14-inch suspension lugs, and used arming wires to arm fuses when the device was released.

Fire bombs came in four sizes: 250, 500, 750, and 1,000-pound. The 250-pound (BLU-10 series) was generally used by aircraft smaller than the Spad, such as the T-28 and A-37. Navy Spads used three types of fire bombs: the Mk77 Mods 0, 2, and 4; the Mk78; and the Mk79 Mod 1. The Mk77 was filled with 75 gallons of fire bomb mix and weighed approximately 500 pounds. Combinations of fuses and igniters were attached to each end to ensure detonation. The Mod 4 differed from the Mod 2 in that its two filler holes were relocated, and it permitted the use of alternate fuses and igniters. The Mod 0 was slightly longer. All models of the Mk77 were nonstabilized, meaning they had no tail fins and tumbled toward the target. Finned fire bombs, on the other hand, offered a greater degree of accuracy through a predictable trajectory path. The Mk78 Mod 2 held 110 gallons of napalm and weighed 750 pounds.

The 1,000-pound Mk79 Mod 1 was a four-finned streamlined design of steel and aluminum, which telescoped together for shipment and storage. Painted dull red, this fire bomb was a staple Skyraider ordnance aboard carriers during Vietnam cruises. Paul Rhodes describes their use:

In preparing to load a 1,000-pound bomb to a Mk 51 rack, VA-165 ordnancemen use the rack's access door to reach safety and sway brace controls. (USN)

Air Force munitions specialists load 100-pound bombs on an A1E, no. 132410, at Pleiku in December 1965. (Raymond A. Young III)

**Fire bomb casings at Pleiku in December 1965. The "cans" were filled with napalm mix after they were attached to the aircraft. (Raymond A. Young III)**

**This 1st SOS Spad in 1969 is armed with frag clusters, Mk 82 bombs, rockets, and finned 750-pound fire bombs. (Richard S. Drury)**

"These were brought up the bomb elevators empty, in the collapsed storage condition. On the flight deck we wheeled them back to our AO (area of operations) on the fantail. There ordnancemen extended the units by pulling out the front and back. They pulled out easily and snapped into the assembled position. Then the tanks were hung on the Mk51 racks and the sway braces deployed snugly against them. The fill cap was removed from the inboard side and a four-pound box of inert napalm powder was poured in. The fuels division then pumped them full of 115-145 fuel and immediately sealed the opening with a concave cap. This was then fitted with a cylindrical explosive charge that was secured with a steel snap ring. In the top of that was a threaded hole for the four-vane spinner arming fuse. We then installed the arming wires from the solenoid in the Mk51 rack to the fuse vanes. The reaction

**Very unusual on this VNAF A-1H are LAU-3/A rocket launchers, totaling 114 2.75-inch rockets. (Author's collection)**

**This A-1E carries a total of 156 rockets. Rocket launchers were later painted olive drab. Fire bombs are carried on the inboard stubs. (USAF)**

**Five A-1Es of the 4407th CCTS fly formation with a Navy NP-2E Neptune enroute to Panama in early 1967 to conduct tests of ADSID sensor drops. (Herbert C. Meyr, Jr.)**

of the napalm powder with the gasoline happened rapidly. It sometimes oozed from the fuse cavity. They were ready for use when the planes left the ship. These were one-shot loadouts only! They were NEVER brought back to the ship."

More familiar to USAF and VNAF Spads was the "BLU" family of fire bombs, also called "Napes." Those used by A-1s were of the 500 and 750-pound variety. The aluminum fire bombs were armed through electrical cables that connected front and back fuses and white phosphorous igniters with an initiator between the suspension lugs. When the bomb was released, a lanyard connected to the initiator and the rack armed the device. End caps streamlined the bomb and protected the fuses and igniters. The 500-pound fire bombs were designated BLU-23/B and -32/B, while the 750-pound category comprised the BLU-1/B, -1B/B, -1C/B, and –27/B. Very similar to the BLU-27/B, but shaped slightly different was the M-116A. Both finned and unfinned versions of the BLU series fire bombs were used. The BLU-32/B and –27/B had welded cases and were factory-filled with the relatively stable Napalm B. Fire bombs initially were of bare aluminum finish with red instruction placards, but were later painted olive drab with red bands denoting incendiary munitions.

Despite the effectiveness of fire bombs, they were not without problems. Since napalm mixture continually gelled in the container, it was important not to prepare the mix too early before use. Of primary concern was the seemingly inherent failure of fuses and igniters. Air Force units addressed the problem by dropping fire bombs and white phosphorous bombs together to ensure napalm

**An Air Force armorer attaches a 36-inch fuse extender, called a "daisy cutter," to a 500-pound Mk 82 GP bomb on A-1E no. 132448 of the 1st SOS in 1970. Fire bombs occupy the Mk 51 racks. (Richard S. Drury)**

**"Bad News" of the 6th SOS at Pleiku in October 1969 fully loaded with daisy cutter Mk 81 GP bombs and CBU/SUU-30s on the inboard stubs. (S. Pargeter)**

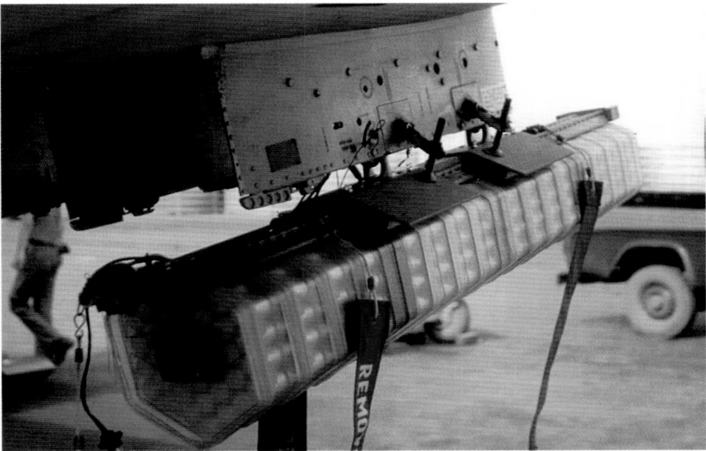

**The CBU-19 was developed by combining two Navy XM 15 CS (tear gas) units for a total of 528 CS canisters. The unit was 5 feet long and weighed 100 pounds. (Ted A. Morris)**

**Left: This 1st ACS A-1E in 1966 carries eight CBUs, two fire bombs, and a 300-gallon centerline tank. Unusual are the miniguns carried on the outboard racks. (Robert E. Blood)**

ignition. Having a wing man strafe napalm that did not ignite also worked. A solution tried by VA-165 and –176 aboard the *USS Intrepid* in 1966 involved two flights of A-1s, one armed with general purpose (GP) bombs, and the other with fire bombs. The bombs were dropped first, followed by napalm, which was then strafed if it still had not ignited.

The largest category of ordnance carried by Spads was labeled "General Purpose," or GP bombs. These were also called "hard bombs," "iron bombs" and, with the advent of "Smart" weapons, "dumb bombs." The range of GP bombs is so vast and many are so similar in appearance that one would have to read the data stenciled on the bomb's casing to identify a specific device. Skyraiders, like other prop-driven *slow movers* committed to the war in Southeast Asia, made do with a large supply of World War II bombs.

Bombs hung on Spads ranged in sizes from 20 to 2,000 pounds, the most common of which was the low drag, general purpose (LDGP) type. Nearly half of the bomb's weight was explosives—either composition B (least stable), TNT, Amatol, Tritonal, or H6. Bombs with contents other than high explosive (HE) are explained separately. General purpose bombs are divided into two basic interservice classifications: older AN series bombs and Mk 80 series, the latter of which are still in use. All are commonly referred to in terms of weight.

The *old series* of GP bombs were called "Fat Bombs," or "Fat Boys." Although they were designed primarily for internal carriage and low-altitude attack, they were easily adapted to the Spad's external racks. They used both nose and tail fuses, with the latter serving as backup. Box fins were original equipment, but were replaced in favor of conical fins, which proved more accurate and stable when dropped from high altitudes and high speeds. Suspension lugs were spaced 14 inches apart on bombs weighing 1,000 pounds or less, and 30 inches apart on 2,000 pound bombs.

Under the old system, fat bombs had yellow bands around the nose and tail of their olive drab casings to identify the explosive filler: one band was TNT, two for composition B, and three denoted Tritonal. The new system used a single three-inch wide yellow band around the bomb's nose, and stenciled markings were changed from black to yellow.

Old series bombs were the 100-pound AN-M30A1, 250-pound AN-M65A1, 500-pound AN-M64A1, 1,000-pound AN-M65A1, and 2,000-pound AN-M66A2. As with other munitions, suffix designations identified slight differences in basic types. A number of old series bombs were modified with conical fins, which extended their length and significantly changed their shape.

The *new series* general purpose bombs, which are recognizable by their slender shape, include the 250-pound Mk81, 500-pound Mk82, 1,000-pound Mk83, 2,000-pound Mk84, and 750-pound

**The yellow band around the nose cap of this SUU-14A/A indicates the tubes are loaded with CBU-14 or CB-25 category BLUs, or bomblets. (Ted A. Morris)**

M117. Tritonal was the standard explosive filler, however, a compound labeled H6 was also used. These bombs were designed for both mechanical and electrical fuses. The latter was possible with conduit, through which ran fuse wiring that connected nose and tail fuses with a receptacle installed between the suspension lugs. The Mk81 and Mk82 could accept the Mk15 "Snakeye" retarder fin assembly. This opened into four dive-brake like flaps to slow the bomb and allow the aircraft to clear the target before bomb impact. A similar MAU-91 fin assembly was later adapted for use with Mk83 and M-117 bombs. Bombs could be dropped with retarder fins in the open or closed position.

Fragmentation bombs—commonly called "Frag Bombs"—were grouped with general purpose bombs, but differed in that their casings had square bar stock spirally wound around them, which became shrapnel. Frags came in four sizes: 20-pound AN-M41, 100-pound AN-M30A1, 220-pound AN-M88, and 260-pound AN-M81. The difference between the AN-M81 and AN-M88 was the size of their windings, and subsequent weight disparity. The AN-M81 had one-inch square windings, while those of the AN-M88 were 3/16-inch smaller, resulting in a larger explosives capacity. Both featured a single lug welded opposite their double lugs for use with British aircraft. The 220 and 260-pound frag bombs used box or conical fins. To achieve maximum effect, frags were fused for airburst or instantaneous impact. An exception in the 100-pound class was the AN-M28A2 fragmentation bomb cluster. Basically an earlier type of CBU, its casing split into halves, releasing 24 four-pound M83 frag bombs.

Six 20-pound frag bombs were used to form an AN-M1A2, -M1A3, or –M1A4 cluster. All were secured by a metal strap to a quick-opening frame in two clusters of three each. Their nose fuse vanes were tension locked with springs until the cluster was released, which pulled their arming wires free from strap clamps and released the lock springs. General purpose bombs up to the 250-pound size in similar groups of six were also attached to multiple ejector racks (MERs).

Fuse extenders on bombs, often thought to have been a product of the Vietnam war, made an appearance in Korea. According to veteran Navy Aviation Ordnanceman Seabie Rucker:

> "We made daisy cutters in Korea for fragmentation bombs by welding a bomb nose cavity plug on a worn out .50 caliber machine gun barrel, and welded a flat plate on the other end. We installed an instantaneous fuse so the bomb would explode above ground."

Old habits die hard, as evidenced by Mel Elliott's memory of walking out to his 1st ACS Spad in 1965 to find 12 bombs similarly fitted with worn out 20mm gun barrels. Welded to the front of each makeshift daisy cutter were 12-inch squares of PSP runway material. "Store bought" fuse extenders used on bombs in Southeast Asia were either 18 or 36-inch long steel tubes filled with tetryl, a booster explosive. One end was threaded to mate with the bomb nose fuse cavity, and the other end was threaded to accept the M904E1/E2 nose fuse. Daisy cutters were by no means limited to the two standard lengths. Don Dineen, who flew 6th SOS Spads, recalls carrying a 2,000-pound bomb on the centerline rack. It had a long fuse extender which, he says, "Wasn't very far behind the prop." The bomb was dropped during the late 1960s in the middle of a large village and did significant damage.

A special bomb that was regularly seen suspended from the wings of Spads was the 100-pound AN-M47A4 smoke bomb. It could be used as an incendiary device or to create a smoke screen. The smoke bomb was 52 inches long, 8 inches in diameter, and had a box fin tail. Two suspension bands with lugs were clamped around its body. Early versions were filled with approximately 74 pounds of white phosphorous, which was commonly referred to as WP, or "Willy Pete." This gave way to plasticized white phosphorous (PWP), which burned longer and had an increased antipersonnel effect. Running the full length of the bomb was a well for an AN-M18 or -M20 burster. A fuse ignited the burster, which shattered the bomb and dispersed the WP. White phosphorous was ignited by atmospheric oxygen and produced dense white smoke. Smoke

**The A-1E-5 no. 135201 of the 6th SOS in 1968 being loaded with XM 3 dispensers filled with "gravel" mines. (USAF)**

**The A-1E no. 132653 of the 4407th CCTS heads for one of Eglin's ranges with more than two tons of napalm in August 1972. Six 500-pound fire bombs fill the outer wings, while 750-pounders are hung from the inboard stubs. (USAF)**

bombs were light gray with yellow stenciling and yellow bands identifying the filling—one for WP and three for PWP. Later versions were painted light green with red stencils and one yellow band.

Unique among the Spad's arsenal were incendiary bomb clusters, best known as "Funny Bombs." How this specialty ordnance got its name is anyone's guess, but there was nothing funny about its devastating effects to anyone unlucky enough to be on its receiving end. Funny bombs were used against Japan during World War II, during which they were called "Tokyo Fire Bombs." A large supply remained and found its way to U.S. air bases in Southeast Asia. Among the large family of incendiary munitions, those used in Southeast Asia were designated M31, 32, 35, and 36, and ranged in weight from about 500 to 900 pounds. So effective were funny bombs that their production resumed, although in limited quantities, until 1967. An improved version—the M36E1—was placed in production in early 1969 when CBU-53/54 ordnance proved inadequate.

The funny bomb's basic design comprised a finned hollow casing containing incendiary bombs. The M31 held 38 M74 10-pound incendiary bombs and weighed 562 pounds. Also in the 500-pound class was the M32, which held 108 AN-M50A3 4-pound incendiary bombs and weighed 617 pounds. The M31 and M32 were approximately five feet long and 15 inches in diameter. Although their weight varied considerably, the M35 and M36 funny bombs were grouped in the 750-pound category. The M35 contained 57 M74A1 incendiary bombs and weighed 690 pounds, while the M36 weighed in at a hefty 900 pounds when filled with 182 4-pound M126 incendiary bombs. The M35 and M36 were nearly eight feet long and 16 inches in diameter.

The funny bomb's awkward barrel-shaped, blunt-nosed design—which may have contributed to its nickname—had a high drag index, which was more than compensated by its destructive capability. Throughout its development, slight variations in the casing and sub-munitions resulted in numerous designations. The M31 and M32 had standard fins, while the M35 and M36 featured circular shrouded fins. All versions were gray with a purple band and markings.

**A ground crewman paints a heartfelt message on a 1,000-pound bomb attached to the inboard pylon of a 602$^{nd}$ ACS A-1E in 1965. (Win DePoorter)**

**An A-1E of the 1$^{st}$/6$^{th}$ SOS composite unit carries SUU-30C/B dispensers in 1968. The Spad was shot down on 25 March 1969 after it had been transferred to the 22$^{nd}$ SOS. (Author's collection)**

When M31s and M32s were released, mechanical time fuses detonated a burster in the firing mechanism, which ejected a framework to which the individual bombs were attached. The framework broke apart, allowing the bombs to fall and spread. The M35 and M36 used a split casing held together by a hinge tube running its length. After release a fuse ignited, detonating cord threaded through the hinge tube. The casing then blew apart, freeing the incendiary bombs.

Incendiary bombs used as their filler either PT1 thickened gasoline-magnesium mix or TH3 "Thermite" (also called "Thermate"), which burned hot enough to melt steel and provided long periods of burn time. If directed by an able forward air controller (FAC) and delivered properly, a funny bomb could cover an area three to four times larger than napalm. Its widespread blanket of intensely burning thermite proved deadly for trucks and area targets. The FAC gave the Spad pilot the target elevation, and it was then up to him to calculate his dive angle, airspeed, and the bomb's opening altitude for an effective delivery.

Few Spad pilots recall the funny bomb's nomenclature, but they vividly remember its spectacular effect at night. Charlie Holder, a Spad pilot with the 22$^{nd}$ SOS, remembers:

> "Funny bombs didn't have the signature 'ring effect' of the normal CBU, but dispersed in a large filled-in circular pattern. It burned with an intense, bright white light, which we hoped would adversely affect the gunner's night vision if we missed. However, when we hit something, it became 'toast.' That stuff would melt through the barrel of any AAA gun unlucky enough to be within the lethal circle! In *Barrel Roll* I caught a fuel truck with one on one dark and stormy night. It lit up the sky for miles around! The ground forward air guide was ecstatic."

In describing their use on truck parks in jungle, 1$^{st}$ SOS Spad pilot Michael Smith said:

> "On one mission my wing man and I dropped four of them and got lucky. We stopped counting secondary explosions around 30-plus in less than half an hour and went home. Some of the secondaries were pretty big."

Air Commandos strongly favored funny bombs over other ordnance, especially if they were targeting trucks. A single bomb carried within the cluster could destroy a truck, or at least create a sizeable fire to aid bombing corrections. Funny bombs were carried not only on Skyraiders, but externally on A-26s and internally on B-57s. They were, without a doubt, the best truck-killing ordnance in the Air Force inventory.

Adding to the Spad's muscle were cluster bomb units (CBUs), which encompassed a vast array of sub-munitions. CBUs were the result of mating an SUU dispenser with BLU bomblets, and came in two basic forms. The first involved the line of SUU-30 dispensers, which were cylindrical, finned casings divided in half lengthwise. A locking cap at the nose and plate assembly at the tail locked the halves together. The nose fuse fired detonating cord in the casing seam, separating the halves and dispensing the BLU load. A more streamlined SUU-30 had a fuse booster that blew off a locking nose cap, separating the halves. Minor differences in the fins of SUU-30s resulted in individual designations, as did the nose shape, which depended on whether mechanical time or lanyard fuses were used. Numerous combinations of dispensers and bomblets resulted in a wide range of CBUs, which armed many aircraft types. Those common to the Skyraider included the CBU-24 and –29 class and the CBU-52 and –58 class; the latter was introduced in 1970. All averaged 800 pounds in weight and had 14-inch suspension lugs. They averaged 7 to 8 feet in length and were 16 inches in diameter.

The BLUs, or bomblets, contained within the SUU casing were of aluminum alloy and were from tennis to softball size. Most were imbedded with 1/2-inch diameter steel balls, which decimated most targets. Factory installed internal fuses became armed after spinning during freefall. They could detonate on impact, when disturbed, or be preset for timed delay detonation. Also available, but seldom used due to their sensitivity, were anti-withdrawal fuses, which ensured detonation if a dud bomb was disturbed. Most CBUs using the SUU-30 series dispenser contained approximately 650 BLUs, except the CBU-52B/B, which held 217 BLU-61A/B bomblets. Bomblets dropped from the SUU-30 family of dispensers formed a doughnut shaped pattern on impact. Dispensers were olive drab with a 3-inch wide yellow band around the nose.

The second primary type of CBU employed the SUU-14A/A dispenser, which was a triangular shaped device formed by six aluminum tubes held together by a "Strong-back," which incorporated the suspension lugs. A blunt nose fairing not only helped to hold the tubes together, but housed the electrical firing system, a single or ripple firing selector switch, and six gas ejection cartridges and pistons. The unit loaded weighed from 250 to 300 pounds—depending on its BLU content—and stretched 7 feet in length. The SUU-14A/A was unpainted, however, since its outward appearance did not reveal its contents—color bands on the nose indicated the types of BLU in the tubes. The variety of bomblets ejected from CBUs included fragmentation, smoke, incendiary, mine, and tear gas types. Other types of CBUs employed an SUU-13/A dispenser for spreading bombs or mines.

Rectangular in shape with a rounded top surface, the SUU-13/A contained 40 tubes to accommodate various bomblets or mines. The unit was nearly 8 feet long and weighed between 385 and 850 pounds, depending on its BLU load. Among the many innovative munitions dropped from Spads was a group of mines known as "Gravel." Gravel resulted from the massive effort to interdict the flow of personnel and vehicles along the famed Ho Chi Minh Trail. Developed at the U.S. Army's Picatinny Arsenal, New Jersey, the mines were of two basic types: those for use against personnel and vehicles (gravel); and those designed as movement detector alarms ("Micro-Gravel" and "Sandwich Button Bombs") to trigger air-dropped seismic and acoustic detectors.

**A technician prepares to load 500-pound bombs on A-1E no. 132649. (USAF)**

**This VNAF A-1E, no. 132628, has a strike camera pod attached to the left stub, a most unusual store for a VNAF A-1. (Richard Oliver)**

The standard dispenser for carrying gravel was the XM3 loaded with four XM canisters containing the mines. The 7-inch diameter canisters were double-walled, with the outer chamber pressurized with nitrogen for ejecting the mines. The inner chamber was packed with mines in liquid freon. The mines themselves were small camouflaged cloth bags filled with a pressure sensitive explosive compound. Freon rendered the mines safe; however, when the mines were ejected and the freon evaporated, the mine became armed. When stepped on or driven over, gravel not only activated nearby camouflaged sensors, it could cause injuries, puncture truck tires, and inhibit enemy movement and discourage searching for sensors. Like the sensors, gravel had a limited life and had to be replenished. Mines and canisters were produced with slight differences, which resulted in separate designations.

The XM3 dispenser was nearly 8 feet long and 18 1/2 inches in diameter. It weighed between 525 and 565 pounds, depending on its sub-munitions load. An aerodynamic nose fairing was placed on its aft end during storage so pressure gauges on the forward end of each canister could be monitored. The four canisters could be ripple-fired or fired in sequence.

Gravel was first used by Army UH-1 "Huey" helicopters flying from Long Binh, South Vietnam, during January 1967. Shortly thereafter, A-1Es of the 1st ACS at Pleiku began carrying them. However, after a short period of use gravel was found to be too unstable, so it went back to the drawing board at Picatinny. By December gravel was again shipped to the squadron, which had relocated to NKP.

Gravel quickly found its place on search and rescue missions, where it was used to discourage the enemy from closing in on downed flyers. Pioneering gravel's development was a large group of scientists and technical experts gathered by Defense Secretary McNamara and called the Defense Communication Planning Group (DCPG), more popularly known as "Disneyland West" (at NKP) and "Disneyland East" (in South Vietnam). The DCPG originally called for a flight of A-1s, led by a Navy special LORAN equipped P-2 Neptune, to fly straight and level, low and slow over the target to drop gravel. A follow-on analysis by the folks at Disneyland predicted that any unit that did so would lose so many aircraft that it would become non-operational in 30 days. The results of the report preceded gravel's arrival in Southeast Asia, producing the expected cold reception by Spad pilots. Pilots of the 1st ACS proposed instead that they approach the target from 10,000 feet, nose over, and cross the target low level at maximum speed, then quickly pull up, thereby increasing their survivability. Disneyland wisely agreed.

A similar endeavor is described by Spad pilot Herb Meyr:

> "In the spring of 1967 I participated in a flight test of 'McNamara's Electronic Fence.' We took six A-1Es from Hurlburt and flew in formation with a Navy P-2 to Panama via NAS Guantanamo Bay. The idea was to have the P-2 at low level drop sensors that would pick up troop movement, with the A-1s flying 1,000 feet in trail, stacked high and in-line abreast formation dropping CBU mines. This became an exciting mission at night low level, especially when the P-2 flew into the clouds and it became 'every man for himself.' I thought the whole thing was ridiculous, and that many aircraft would be lost in Southeast Asia trying to do this."

The Navy Neptune unit tasked with dropping sensors (VO-67) did, in fact, suffer such high losses that it was pulled out of action.

Due to gravel's nitrogen and freon components it was difficult to maintain. Dick Gaebler explains one example of Gravel's instability:

> "A real attention grabber occurred when the Eglin weapons test engineers had us drop the then new CBU 'briquettes' at night. Jim Johnston got a low-pressure warning light one day and radioed the range safety officer for advice. *Mister Safety* said to pickle the whole tank into Choctawhatchee Bay, so Jim did. The only trouble was, who knew the deadly little briquettes would float! Swimming and boating in the bay was canceled for the next couple of days until many hundreds of floating bomblets

**A Mk 81 "Snakeye" bomb with its high-drag fins deployed. The small circular area between the two lugs is a handling well, while the larger one is an electrical well. (USAF)**

were corralled. If there is anything to be said for a war, I do find a 'Make your own rules' environment refreshing."

One night the gravel ordnance on a Spad taking off from Pleiku malfunctioned, spreading hundreds of armed mines over the runway. No procedures had been developed to render them safe. Luckily a base Explosives Ordnance Disposal (EOD) expert came up with a solution. He poured oil on the bags and then very carefully injected oil into the mines using a jury-rigged hand pump. Thanks to his quick thinking and dangerous work, the runway was useable in several hours. Gravel's use was discontinued, and Spad pilot William Neal explained the last gravel mission:

"In May 1969, 7th Air Force decided to dispose of the remaining stock by having a C-123 haul the stuff, canisters and all, over the Trail and just dump it. A *one-star* [general] came up to oversee the operation and requested an A-1 to escort the '123. He wanted pictures of the drop and the impact, and instructed me as his pilot what he wanted me to do.

When we reached the drop area we were in trail with the '123, as instructed. As the stuff was pushed out the back of the '123 on pallets, he snapped a picture and said to follow it down. I had been led to believe the pallets would remain intact as they fell. Just after I rolled in behind it everything came apart. Pallets, canisters, 4 by 8 sheets of plywood, etc. were all over the sky, with us right in the middle. I dodged and jinked till we were off to one side while still following the flying debris in its erratic descent.

I pulled out at a thousand feet as the stuff crashed through the trees. My passenger looked a little pale and shaken and had little to say as we returned to NKP. Upon arrival he thanked me and departed. Prior to the mission, he had promised to send me some pictures. I never received them and highly suspect he only took one."

One of the most controversial weapons used by Skyraiders in Southeast Asia was tear gas (CS), which was delivered either as a CBU package or in powder form in the shells of BLU-1C and BLU-52 series napalm tanks. The BLU-52A/B used a concoction of tear gas mixed with napalm. Officially called the "Riot Control Canister Cluster," the CBU-19/A was custom made for Air Force Skyraiders by joining two Navy XM15 CS units. The result was a 63-inch long unit incorporating 16 plastic modules, each of which contained 33 BLU-39/B23 tear gas canisters, totaling 528. It was triggered by an electrically fired explosive bolt, which sheared a rod holding spring-loaded end clamps. The package then split in two with the halves forced downward by strong-back leaf springs, releasing all the modules and igniting the canisters. Beginning in 1970 the CBU-30, which consisted of the SUU-13 downward ejection dispenser and 1,280 BLU-39/B23 CS sub-munitions, became the favored tear gas ordnance.

One of the most unusual munitions taken into combat by both Navy and Air Force Spads since the war's onset was called "Lazy Dogs." Technically this consisted of a 500-pound Mk44 missile cluster adapter, which resembled an old-series 500-pound general purpose bomb, and a large quantity of small darts, called Lazy Dog missiles. The darts were packed into the hollow canister in 40 ten-pound bags. When the pilot dropped the store a mechanical time fuse separated the halves, allowing the missiles to free-fall. The finned, solid steel darts were 1 1/2 inches long, .41 caliber in size and had a pointed nose. When released above 2,000 feet the darts were said to have enough kinetic energy to pass through an engine block. Their kill probability within an oval 50 by 100-yard impact pattern was 80 percent. As an area weapon Lazy Dogs were not accurate, so they could not be used for close air support. They were, however, very effective against dug-in troops, and for clearing ambush sites adjacent to convoy routes. Spad pilot Jim Harding noted:

"Lazy Dogs were great for dropping on enemy runways. They would stick in the runway, and the little fins on the back of the 'bullet' flattened the tires of aircraft trying to take off or land. They had to dig each one of them out before they could use the runway."

Due to their penetrative abilities and wide area coverage, the use of Lazy Dogs required clearance from the *Country Team*. Lazy

**An early USAF A-1E at Hurlburt Field in 1965 during tests of the M4A, which could hold 100 to 500 pounds of supplies for ground troops. The Navy version was the CTU-1/A, which featured an improved parachute mechanism. (USAF)**

Dogs were also called "Elda," which was a phonetic take on the official abbreviation LDA, for *Lazy Dogs, Antipersonnel.*

Somewhat similar to the Lazy Dog was the original version of the Mk20 "Rockeye," which was used by Skyraiders only during the Son Tay Prison raid. The Rockeye contained 247 dart shaped Mk118 anti-armor sub-munitions that could penetrate 7 1/2 inches of conventional armor.

Among the special munitions carried by Spads were fuel-air explosives (FAEs), which were as politically sensitive as tear gas. The NOTS worked in conjunction with private research agencies during the early 1960s to develop the family of FAEs, which ranged from small devices to bombs that weighed in excess of 2,000 pounds. Developers of fuel-air explosives undoubtedly took their cue from liquefied petroleum gas (LPG) disasters that plagued refineries and the transportation industry. Basically LPG, when released from a pressurized container where it is stored as a liquid, expands rapidly, giving the appearance of a white cloud. Being heavier than air, it easily filled tunnels and caves. When ignited, the overpressure from the explosion—far more powerful than that of conventional bombs—crushed everything in its path and spread destruction far beyond the blast zone. Their detonation also consumed the oxygen within a given radius, thereby causing suffocation. Pilots who dropped FAEs agree they looked like small atomic bombs.

Initially, FAEs were so unwieldy they were test-dropped from cargo aircraft. Eventually their design was refined to the point they could be dropped from smaller aircraft, specifically the A-1 and F-4 Phantom, which carried the BLU-72 (Pave Pat I) and BLU-76 (Pave Pat II), respectively. Both types weighed approximately 2,500 pounds, and were 14 feet long and 30 inches in diameter. Externally, they were differentiated by the BLU-76's additional fins and more conical nose. Although there are various forms of LPG, Spad pilots commonly referred to them as "Propane Bombs." The prototype is said to have been fabricated from a commercial propane tank.

One or two BLU-72s were carried on the Spad's Mk51 racks. If one was carried, it was counterbalanced by a 300-gallon fuel tank on the opposite Mk51. When dropped, a parachute slowed its descent so the container would simply split open on impact, allowing the LPG to rapidly escape. To achieve maximum effect it was important that the LPG vaporize and fill the target area prior to ignition. After 20 to 30 seconds, fuses ignited thermal devices that detonated the lethal cloud. Stateside testing of the BLU-72 was conducted on the ranges of Nellis and Eglin Air Force Bases. In remote regions, other tests, which would have had animal rights activists reeling, resulted in herds of decimated sheep, testifying to the weapon's complete devastation. It then went to the 1st SOS during fall 1968, with the first drop made in South Vietnam's Delta region. Combat evaluation of the BLU-72 showed problems with the igniters. With modified igniters, the FAE was used against tunnel complexes in South Vietnam, and it also proved useful in clearing jungle to create helicopter landing zones. Approximately 50 BLU-72s were produced, which were used by A-1s until 1972.

Equally controversial, yet effective, was the follow-on CBU-55, explained here by Spad pilot Randy Jayne:

> "The CBU-55 fuel-air explosive consisted of a 600-pound canister with rounded nose and a flat back plate. Packed inside, with a compressed air ejection device, were three individual FAE canisters. When preflighting, the pilot set the time delay on the unit fuse and the selected number of seconds after release (and extraction of the arming wire). The air ejection device fired, the back plate separated, and the three canisters were shoved out the back of the falling CBU cylinder. Each canister, in turn, deployed a small parachute from its top and extended a four-foot fuse from the bottom. Upon impact, the fuse tripped a small charge that split the can and spread the fuel at the right mix with the air. A fraction of a second later, the fuse ignited it.
>
> A team from Eglin arrived at NKP in early December 1971, and I was designated the combat test evaluation pilot. Between 2 and 8 December we flew four sorties, each with an A-1H and an A-1E as a two-ship, with the young Eglin program manager engineer in the right seat as an observer. We learned the hard way, without drag tables, that the max load was six canisters on an H and four on an E/G. The wind drift with the chutes was significant, so

**Under Project Pave Pat, the original BLU-72 FAE bomb is reported to have been fashioned from a commercial propane tank. This 4407th CCTS A-1H uses a 300-gallon Mk 48 fuel tank to counterbalance the awkward, but lethal, device. (USAF)**

accuracy corresponded to very low altitude release. The stuff was impressive to watch when it went off, and the visual was like a tiny nuclear blast, with a very strong shock wave emanating outward on the ground. With essentially no fragmentation from the thin aluminum canister, the predominant weapon effects were blast and severe local overpressure.

The 5 December mission, with Dave Blevins as my wing man, was clearly the most significant. Supporting a 'Raven' (FAC) in Steel Tiger, south of the 'Catcher's Mitt,' we used CBU-55 in support of a 'mild' TIC (troops in contact). Because the enemy force was apparently small, and the area not wildly hostile, the friendlies on the ground were able to quickly overrun the NVA/Pathet Lao position after our eight CBU-55 passes. Most were right on target due to lack of heavy ground fire and thus releases below 2,000 feet. The BDA (bomb damage assessment) was impressive—both KIA and numerous incapacitated POWs who in general could not hear and were found lying dazed in various positions around their lines. Subsequently, the CBU-55 team visited the A-37 squadron at Bien Hoa, and they conducted a similar test. We all concluded that, while the FAE was an impressive way to go after a cave or bunker, the recently introduced Paveway Mk-82/84 seemed to have a much safer delivery method. As for TIC and troops in hiding, our traditional CBU/rocket/20mm combo was far better in terms of accuracy, cost, drag, loadout, etc."

Depth bombs, which were designed for attacking submarines and were widely used during World War II, were hung from the wings of some of the first Navy Skyraiders deployed to Southeast Asia. Armed for a preset depth, the depth bomb created a pressure wave against underwater targets great enough to crush their hull plates. To prevent impact damage to its thin casing, the depth bomb was dropped from low altitude, and its flat nose prevented ricocheting on the water. A tail fuse was used for an attack on a submarine, however, a nose impact fuse could be armed by the pilot for surface targets. In Southeast Asia, Navy ordnancemen exploited that feature by adding fuse extensions to the depth bomb's nose. Although depth bombs ranged from 325 to 700 pounds, the only type carried over into the 1960s was the AN-Mk54 Mod 1, which weighed approximately 350 pounds.

**This Stateside A-1E carries a pair of BLU-72 propane bombs, which barely clear the ground. (USAF)**

Like the depth bomb, the flat-faced 750-pound BLU-31 demolition bomb was an anti-ricochet munition also designed for low-level delivery. Its strong casing, however, made it suitable for use against hardened structures. The demolition bomb was approximately 8 feet long and had four conical fins. The BLU-31 was also designated the MLU-10 penetration bomb/land mine, as well as the BLU-14 skip bomb. Korean war era Air Force jet aircraft first qualified with the BLU-31, and it was last used with Southeast Asia-based A-1s and F-4s.

Last, but certainly no less important in the bomb category, were practice bombs, which were of 5, 25, 250, and 1,000-pound varieties. The 5-pound Mk106 practice bomb was a cylindrical, flat-nosed casing with modified box fins. The 25-pound BDU-33 had a slender streamlined body with a modified box fin assembly. The 1,000-pound Mk88 practice bomb was similar in appearance to the Mk83 series LDGP bomb. It usually contained only enough smoke filler compound to place in the 500-pound class. Practice bombs, upon impact, discharged white smoke rearward through a central tube. Although blue was designated as the standard color for inert munitions, they also appeared in orange and black.

Although various aircraft types were tasked with "Psywar" (psychological warfare) operations, Skyraiders periodically made leaflet drops. This was accomplished with the M-129 leaflet bomb, which resembled the M-117 GP bomb. Constructed of fiberglass-reinforced plastic, the body of the M-129 was split lengthwise in two sections, which were held together by four latches. After release a time delay fuse in the nose ignited a detonation cord, which separated the halves and released the leaflets. Another non-ordnance store was the M4A delivery container for dropping between 100 to 500 pounds of supplies to ground troops. Although originally intended for use by the F-100 jet, the Air Force-developed M4A proved ideal for delivery by the A-1, since it was best released at an altitude of 300 feet. The Spad's use of the container meshed with its role in supporting ground special operations teams. The M4A used a parachute to slow its descent, and it was often camouflaged to aid in concealing its bulk in enemy territory. The aluminum canister was 104 inches long, 21 inches in diameter, and had four 12-inch fins. The M4A had 10.5 cubic feet of cargo space, and when empty weighed 215 pounds. A Navy modification of the M4A was the 230-pound CTU-1/A, which featured a more reliable parachute deployment mechanism. It entered service during mid-1967 for use by the A-1, A-4, A-6, and both Navy and Air Force F-4s.

A refined version of the M4A was tailor-made for downed flyers. Named after one of its developers—Captain James Madden of the 56$^{th}$ SOW—the "Madden Kit" was essentially a gutted flare container to which lugs were attached for mounting to the A-1. Filled with combat survival gear, the kit was designed for pinpoint delivery from an altitude of 100 feet and with the survivor in sight. Tests were conducted at NKP during early 1971, and it proved highly successful on SAR missions.

Flares were a common item among the wide variety of stores carried by Spads, especially in view of their involvement with search and rescue and close air support. The standard flare was the Mk24 series parachute flare, which was 3 feet long, weighed approximately 25 pounds, and burned at 2 million candlepower. Its aluminum outer casing incorporated a fuse cavity with dials for setting ejection and ignition fuses. Modifications of the Mk24 were the LUU-1/B and LUU-2 target markers, which had cross-shaped parachutes to snag them in the top of heavy foliage. The target marker burned on its top (parachute) end with a brilliant red flame that was visible from great distances.

Representing a new concept in flare technology was the MLU-32/B99 "Briteye" flare, which used a hot air balloon and heat generator that allowed the 5 million candlepower flare to hover as it burned. Although it was earmarked for use by the A-1 and nearly a dozen other aircraft, it is not known if the Briteye was used by Spads operationally.

To counter the SA-7 missile threat following Spad shootdowns during 1972, the LAU-10 Zuni rocket launcher was modified to carry and eject eight Mk24 flares to divert SA-7s. The flares were set to ignite immediately after ejection. Designated the SUU-25, the launcher could also carry Mk45 flares and target markers. The SUU-40 was similar, but weighed only 325 pounds compared to the 500-pound SUU-25.

Often seen on the outer wing racks of Navy Spads during the war were gray Mk6 Mod 2 smoke marker launchers. These were 16-pound rectangular wooden boxes rigged to eject four floating AN/Mk5 night drift signals and pyrotechnic candles that were water activated and burned for nearly an hour. Besides target marking, the Mk6s were ideal as floating practice targets since they produced a great deal of smoke. When released, an arming wire lit an igniter and a metal nose piece made it float nose down. Air Force squadrons, like their Navy counterparts, used the markers, called "logs," for practice or to train student pilots. The markers played a large part in what was, for some USAF Spad pilots, their most daunting mission.

Those missions were played out over Eglin's Gulf Test Range beginning in 1964. At the behest of the Air Force, the Navy sent a few A-1 people to Hurlburt to train Spad pilots in laying mines. This involved low-level formation flying over water at night. Mel Elliott, who was in training during that time, recalls:

> "I never saw what the real mine laying mission would have been like for a Spad, and was thankful we never had to do it for real, if it was anything like the training mission at Hurlburt. That night mission at Hurlburt was the hairiest thing I ever did in an airplane. The instructors hated the mission so badly that there were only one or two IPs (Instructor Pilots), out of 12 or 16 airplanes on our mission."

Another of the *fortunate few* to have undergone the training was John Larrison. He explains:

> "I have not heard of any Air Force types dropping sea mines from the A-1, however, I was in class Express 8 at Hurlburt in fall 1964, and we were trained to do it. The way Hurlburt set up the training, it was one hairy mission. I can almost believe the real thing would have been better.
>
> A Navy type came over from Pensacola to give us some ground school on the subject of low-level piloting over water. All I remember from it was that he kept telling us over and over again that 'waves don't move—they just go up and down.' Must have been a Navy thing. He gave us a handout with some drawings to help estimate the wind speed by looking at the condition of the waves. We then flew two or three low-level DR nav missions out over the Gulf to see how close we could hit a given landfall after about an hour over water at about 100 feet altitude. This was day VFR and was fun. Then we flew low level up the beach back to Hurlburt.
>
> Then the big show. We did the VFR once during the day and then again at night. As I recall we had about 12 aircraft in the formation, led by a pathfinder. In actuality, the mission would have been a night launch to hit the target at sunrise, and it was to be done at 100 feet to stay under any radar. Once at the target, the pathfinder would split off and the large formation would split into four-ship elements. We performed *procedure turn* maneuvers to provide some spacing between the four-ship formations. We all then ended up heading toward the target area on a heading to lay our mines. The pathfinder laid a string of floating smoke flares as aiming points. As each four-ship came in on the reference markers, we spread out and picked our marker according to our position, from right to left. Once over your marker, you took up a control heading and started to drop your mines in a random release pattern. Our heading gave us separation from the wing man, and we had laid down a large rectangular mine field. So far, so good with day VFR. We dropped floating smoke markers as simulated mines, so when completed we could pull up and take a look at it. I can't believe any ships would have gotten through it.
>
> We used one of the 'Texas Towers' oil rigs as an Initial Point (IP) for the minefield. Being excellent fishing locations, there were many small boats around the rigs when we arrived. After we dropped—although clear of the fishermen—all we could see were a lot of wakes as the boats departed the area at full throttle.

**Barely visible behind the starter cart of this BLU-72 equipped A-1H of the 4407th CCTS is an orange-painted camera pod. (USAF)**

Now the hairy part. The next training mission was at night. Since the instructors did not want to get up and take off in the middle of the night to hit the IP at sunrise, we took off late in the afternoon to hit it at sunset. I guess they believed that would simulate sunrise. We got to the IP just after sunset and started the mine-laying maneuver. As we all spread out to come in on the reference marker flares, no one could get a visual on them. After a few radio calls, we figured out the problem. The pathfinder forgot to arm his flare launcher, so he didn't drop any. Now there were 12 aircraft spread out over the water, low level, and by now it was very black.

The call went out to join back into the original formation and make another run—again at 100 feet, at night, and over water. This was the hairy part. I don't remember how many times the lead had to circle to get all the aircraft back in formation. Towards the end of this rejoin, one of the aircraft tried to play submarine when he dropped very low. Someone saw his lights and called out to pull up. We all made it back together and completed the maneuver on the next setup. The minefield looked good, but at that point I don't think anyone cared.

Our grade books were filled in, and we pressed on and tried to forget the event. When, in early 1965 there was talk of a blockade of Hanoi and mining its harbor, none of us told anyone we had received this training, and we hoped it was not on our records. It looked like a great Navy mission to me."

On several occasions during 1965, Navy squadrons loaded six 500-pound mines on their Spads for three-plane strikes into Haiphong, however, they were ordered removed each time politicians reached an impasse about their use. Later in the war the Navy did, in fact, mine North Vietnamese channels. They used A-6s. Until the development of mines suitable for use by attack jets, the Spad was the only carrier aircraft without a bomb bay that could carry mines having high drag indexes.

The first Skyraiders flown in Southeast Asian combat were those handed over to the South Vietnamese Air Force (VNAF), which used a mix of available ordnance. Ordnance stocks consisted mainly of napalm, rockets, and older-series GP bombs originally intended for F8F Bearcats.

The magazines of carriers that steamed into the South China Sea at the war's onset were filled with a variety of ordnance for their Spad squadrons. Typical of Navy A-1 attack squadrons at that time was VA-196 aboard the *USS Bon Homme Richard*. The carrier was near completion of a WestPac cruise when the Gulf of Tonkin incident occurred. After being diverted to Vietnam, VA-196 began flying Rescue Combat Air Patrol (ResCAP) missions, followed by air strikes. Aviation Ordnanceman Paul Rhodes remembers:

"There was no time for anything except work—ass-busting work—sometimes for 16 to 18 hours a day, 7 days a week. The longest we were at sea was 52 straight days, and we flew combat strikes on every one of them. Maintenance was done between three hops a day and after *flight quarters*, which was late at night after the last plane had been recovered and we turned out of the wind. The ship's company ordnance worked around the clock, breaking 'ord' out of storage and readying it on 14B skids to be delivered topside to the flight deck.

We loaded ordnance, including 1,000-pound bombs, by hand—and by back. We used 'hernia bars,' which were pieces of steel pipe welded to a screw-in plug that fit into the bomb's fuse cavity. We screwed hernia bars into both ends of the bombs, with two to three guys on each end applying the back power to lift them into place. 'Heave ho, ya swabs' took on a whole new meaning."

Attack Squadron 196's ordnance loadouts usually consisted of 250 to 2,000-pound old-series GP bombs and new-series bombs (often with "daisy cutters"), rockets (both 5 and 2.75-inch), 1,000-pound fire bombs, 260-pound frag bombs, and flares. A 300-gallon centerline tank was standard for loadout. Loads were similar for night strikes, but with 4 to 6 flares carried on outboard racks to illuminate targets on "road recce" flights. Navy Spads seldom, if ever, loaded all racks. They were not to bring ordnance back to the ship unless it was hung up.

**A BLU-72 equipped A-1E, no. 132455, at NKP during September 1968. (USAF)**

The hazards of having large amounts of ordnance aboard carriers was underscored by three disastrous carrier fires during the 1960s, two of which occurred in the war zone. On 26 October 1966 a flare lit accidentally aboard the *USS Oriskany* caused a catastrophic fire, and on 29 July 1967 leaking fuel ignited and fired rockets aboard the *USS Forrestal*. The following January, disaster struck the *USS Enterprise* enroute to the war zone when a jet's exhaust on the cramped flight deck ignited a Zuni rocket, which hit other aircraft. After the Forrestal fire, old-series ordnance was banned from carriers.

Air Force A-1s seemed to carry everything ever invented. During the early period of the war, Spad loads consisted mainly of old-series GP bombs, frags, anti-personnel ordnance, and all rockets or all napalm. Drop tanks were seldom used unless missions, such as those flown into A Shau, required them. During 1966, when USAF A-1s began flying into North Vietnam, a relatively standard load consisted of a 300-gallon centerline tank, a 150-gallon tank on the right stub (Mk51 rack), an SUU-11/A minigun on the left stub, and a mixed bag on the dozen wing racks. Search and rescue missions usually used this arrangement, along with smoke bombs and 2.75-inch rockets with WP warheads. By 1970, "Sandy" missions included a pair of miniguns, plus a mix of four CBUs, four "napes," and two 19-tube rocket launchers. These were the norm, of which there were many minor variations.

Loads obviously depended mainly on missions requirements and, in some cases, unit policy. It was not unusual to see USAF Spads carrying stores not USAF-approved. Often these were acquired at Navy, Marine, and Army facilities where traditional USAF stores were unavailable. Throughout periods of bomb shortages, aircraft were ordered flown with partial loads, versus using less aircraft with full loads, to give the impression—only to those interested in favorable statistics—the same number of sorties were being flown.

Mark Eyestone, who served as an aircraft mechanic at NKP in 1971, describes his experience with Air Force Spad ordnance:

> "During the dry season, the war was on 12 hours a day, 7 days a week. There was a special area on the north end of the runway overrun called the 'North Hammerhead.' That was where the Munitions Maintenance workers, called 'BB Stackers,' had a little shack painted orange and white, per military regs. They were there during launches and recoveries to arm and disarm the external munitions. When the truck supervisor thought you had enough experience, he would send you up to the North Hammerhead to marshal A-1s. You had no problem hearing the warbirds coming up the taxiway. There were lines on the ramp so you could figure out where you needed to be to give the pilot maneuvering instructions to get him where the BB stackers wanted him. When he got there, he set the parking brakes, shut off his engine, and raised his hands to show them to the munitions workers. He then rested them on the windshield's edge so the workers knew he wasn't fooling around with the master switches, firing buttons, etc. They went under the wings and pulled all the "Remove Before Flight"safety pins on the ordnance. Then the weapons were all *hot*. Then I would signal the plane's restart, watch the fuel prime lines, and have my fire bottle ready. Imagining a stack fire on a fully loaded warbird, I was all that was standing between keeping the fire from taking out the airplane and pilot.
>
> If the pilots had hot targets, they would come back in to rearm. If they came back unexpectedly they were probably empty, but the munitions workers had to safety the minigun and all four cannon. Sometimes the planes would not restart and they had to be towed back to the Hobo revetments. If they had a good target or there was a battle going on, the planes would be back in 45 minutes and you would go through the whole procedure again. Some of the pilots would be hopped up on adrenalin and not remember all the little details of safety procedures. They still had the enemy in sight and wanted to get back as soon as possible. Some of the pilots really liked this old fashioned combat."

Many specific types of ordnance had their own peculiarities and consequences surrounding their use. For example: funny bombs, it's told, when used on the Trail at night, were most effective against a line of trucks after napalm had been dropped in front of the convoy to bring it to a halt. Successive funny bombs were usually dropped "on instruments" since the first one ruined the pilot's night vision. At the beginning of the 1970s, when thermite bombs were dropped north of the Plain of Jars in Laos, the 7th and 13th Air Forces pulled them out of the theatre, explaining that thermite was too terrible a way to die—as though napalm was more pleasant!

During the late 1960s, some USAF Spads carried napalm on all SAR missions. It was also a special request ordnance for SAR support. Likewise, WP/PWP smoke bombs were standard on SAR loads until the end of USAF Spad missions. They were used mainly for marking targets or holding areas for rescue helicopters. Occasionally a flight of four A-1s, carrying 12 smoke bombs each, was

**Some of the ordnance load carried by this 1st SOS A-1H, no. 139803, in July 1972 is unusual in that Zuni rocket pods more commonly appeared on Navy Spads. Even more unusual, on the inboard stub, is a SUU-25 flare dispenser, which was a LAU-10/A Zuni rocket launcher modified to carry and eject eight Mk 24 Mod 4 parachute flares. (Byron Hukee)**

**The familiar Aero shape of this AD-5Q houses the ALT-2 noise jammer carried by "Electric Spads." (Douglas)**

special-ordered to lay smoke screens to cover a rescue. Such flights equipped for a specific mission were given their own call signs, such as "Smoke," "Strike," and "Gas." Some not so obvious included "Chop" and "Twiggy," which identified Spads equipped with area denial ordnance. Rather than to confuse the enemy, the purpose of ordnance related call signs was to help the Rescue Coordination Center (call sign "Joker"), FACs and mission leaders keep track of the resources on scene.

The introduction of some stores, such as the SUU-25 flare launcher, resulted in a change in tactics. Modified from a Zuni rocket launcher, the SUU-25 was designed to counter the SA-7 missile threat in 1972. In addition to carrying the launcher, it was decided the wing man fly above 7,500 feet to watch for missile launches, while the lead flew a normal low altitude attack/search pattern. Flying fully loaded at higher, safer altitude was ruled out since evasive maneuvering became difficult, and the SAM's effective range was 13,000 feet.

Tear gas, which was used judiciously by Spad units mainly to support rescue operations, was the most controversial ordnance. As the enemy bolstered its defenses to thwart rescue efforts, tear gas (which often went by the code name "Vodka"), was introduced as a viable option to counter those defenses. Although tear gas had been authorized for use in Southeast Asia since November 1965, it wasn't until February 1968 that it was officially approved for use on SAR operations in Laos. The on-scene rescue commander had the authority to use tear gas, however, he had to notify 7th Air Force and 3rd ARRG in Saigon of its use. Besides rescues, "Gas birds" were used to deny the enemy use of hidden spaces (such as caves and tunnels), in offensive and defensive combat operations, and to clear areas prior to defoliation. The authority to drop tear gas from A-1s in support of special operations in Laos was held by the US Ambassador to Laos. In specific rescue missions, the downed flyer was gassed if he was surrounded, had been captured, or was injured and faced imminent capture. Wearing gas masks, a helicopter crew could then attempt the rescue.

Spads of the VNAF rarely utilized all ordnance racks. Specific policies were in place governing VNAF A-1 loads, however, they were not observed at all times. VNAF A-1s are not known to have used CBUs, smoke bombs, flares, Zuni rockets or special purpose ordnance. Nor did they use drop tanks, fly at night or commonly fly multi-plane strikes.

Seldom included in mention of the Skyraider's external stores is the equipment carried by Navy EA-1F "Electric Spads," which flew electronic countermeasures (ECM) support missions for Task Force 77 until late 1968. In conjunction with its onboard electronic suite, this variant carried a relatively standard array of stores that included a 300-gallon centerline tank and AN/APS-31C search radar in a bulbous housing beneath the right wing. The left stub mount and a single rack on each outer wing were occupied by AN/ALT-2 noise jammers, and either AN/ALE-2 or MX-900A chaff dispensers. Their specific arrangement was based on unit policy and mission.

# 4

# Blue Water Warriors

Throughout its history, Naval Aviation has measured its success by its ability to take up positions anywhere in the world to protect American interests. Such awesome mobility is derived from a fleet of aircraft carriers which, in 1964, numbered 24 operational carriers, 15 of which were designated attack types (CVAs), with the remainder used for antisubmarine warfare (ASW) support (CVSs). The *USS America* and *USS John F. Kennedy* were under construction. With the exception of the *Kennedy*, all of the attack carriers, along with five ASW carriers, made at least one Vietnam cruise during the course of the war. For Naval Aviation, that time frame officially spanned from 2 August 1964 to 15 August 1973. Carriers from both the Atlantic and Pacific Fleets rotated to the war zone. Until mid-1966 the attack carriers served on *Dixie Station* off South Vietnam, before deploying north to *Yankee Station*, where Task Force 77 (TF 77) was the operational command; TF 77 came to be known as "The Tonkin Gulf Yacht Club." Dixie Station was discontinued in mid-1966 when it was decided to maintain three to four carriers on Yankee Station.

The Navy had maintained a presence in the Western Pacific (WestPac) and Southeast Asia since World War II. For nearly two decades Task Force 77 monitored communist activities in the region and served as a deterrent to communist aggression. The Navy's indirect involvement with Indochina centered around support of French forces that operated Navy-supplied aircraft. Up until the Vietnam war began in earnest in Southeast Asia, Task Force 77 had served as the Navy's representative in supporting the Southeast Asia Treaty Organization (SEATO) by participating in several joint ASW exercises in the region. When war broke out in Laos between the

**Framed by an Air Force Grumman Albatross headed for Da Nang, an A-1H of VA-152 pulls alongside following the successful rescue of an RF-101 pilot on 1 November 1965. (David Wendt)**

**The Cat Officer aboard *Oriskany* in 1966 gives the go signal to a Spad of VA-152. The A-1 carries a typical load for gunfire spotting. (Bud Watson)**

**Lt. j.g. Kinsley of VAW-11 (in orange flight suit) kicks the tires of his EA-1E during preflight aboard *Bennington* in April 1964. The Navy changed from khaki to orange fight suits during the early 1960s. Shortly after Navy planes began combat operations in Vietnam, an emergency supply of camouflaged flight suits was ordered in mid-1964. (Richard W. Albright)**

government and communist forces, aid to the Laotian government, along with U.S. assistance being provided through South Vietnam, increased the American naval presence in the South China Sea.

The relationship between the Navy and the Skyraider was reciprocal. The Skyraider, having its roots in the Navy, helped the Navy achieve its goals, while the Navy, having nurtured the Skyraider, formed the foundation for its success. At the time of the Tonkin Gulf Incident, the Navy's carrier aircraft inventory (both Atlantic and Pacific Fleets) included 200 A-1H/J Skyraiders and 30 each EA-1F and EA-1E variants. Approximately two-thirds were aboard Pacific Fleet carriers. A typical complement of aircraft aboard each carrier comprised 90 fixed-wing and rotary-wing types. Half of that number embarked on four carriers that were not configured for operations with the 1960s generations of jet fighters. These carriers were the *USS Hornet*, *Yorktown*, *Kearsarge*, and *Bennington*—which were used exclusively for ASW operations. *Kearsarge* was the first on station during mid-1964, followed by *Yorktown* beginning in February 1965. *Bennington* arrived in July, and the *Hornet* in October. Air elements aboard these ASW carriers, which comprised two S-2 squadrons, an SH-3 squadron, and a detachment of EA-1Es or E-1Bs, formed Carrier ASW Air Groups (CVSGs). The *Bennington* also had an additional detachment of four A-4 Skyhawks for Combat Air Patrol missions. These four carriers combined made 13 Vietnam cruises. The *USS Intrepid* and *USS Shangri-La* also served in the war zone as attack carriers, but were limited to attack and close support missions. Aircraft aboard the more capable and modernized attack carriers were organized into squadrons, usually having 12 aircraft each, while detachments comprised the balance of Skyraiders embarked. Squadrons were organized into Carrier Air Wings (CVWs). The *Intrepid* deployed with newly formed Air Wing 10, which consisted of four attack squadrons. These were two A-1 squadrons (VA-165 and VA-176), plus two A-4 squadrons.

**A Skyraider propeller advertised VA-122's Spad School at NAS Lemoore during the 1960s. (Tom Doll)**

The first Skyraiders to arrive in Southeast Asia were AD-6s passed in September 1960 to the Vietnamese Air Force to replace Grumman *Bearcats* of the VNAF 1st Fighter Squadron. In conjunction with the transfer, a group of Navy petty officers and chief petty officers, led by Spad pilot Lt. Kendall E. Moranville, was sent to Bien Hoa, South Vietnam, to train VNAF Skyraider pilots and ground crew. Navy Spad pilots again would assist the VNAF when a portion of VA-152, called "Det Zulu," trained VNAF A-1 pilots at Bien Hoa from April to November 1964. The first American Skyraiders to participate in the conflict were AD-5Qs (later EA-1Fs) of Carrier Airborne Early Warning Squadron 13 (VAW-13) Detachment Lima. In September 1962 they replaced Tan Son Nhut-based USAF F-102 interceptors, which were to intercept North Vietnamese or Russian transport aircraft flying low-level supply missions at night over South Vietnam's Central Highlands and Laos. In November 1961 Lt. Forrest Goodman, who was known for his te-

**VAW-13's many detachments that provided ECM support during air strikes into North Vietnam operated from land bases and carriers. Here EA-1F BuNo. 133770 stands by at Da Nang AB during late 1966. (Tom Hansen)**

**An EA-1F at Da Nang during 1966. (Tom Hansen)**

nacity and fairness, was selected to head VAW-13's all-volunteer Detachment *Lima*. He describes the interesting assignment:

"In early January 1961 the air group deployed to the Far East for a ten-day readiness exercise. Det. Lima received the highest grade for performance of the entire air group. I was most proud of my detachment. We did it again in Hawaii.

In March, after departing Hong Kong, one of the admiral's staff asked if we could plot radar sites. I told him that was one of our capabilities, so I was launched as the ship departed Hong Kong. I took a position about 50 miles off the *Chicom* coast and headed north. An hour or so into the flight, the ship asked if I had high-speed jets in sight that were heading in our direction. I didn't, but my radar operator picked them up on his scope and noted that their closing speed was around 500 knots. When the MiGs obviously got us on radar and started to circle and look for us, the ship radioed the deck was clear. After securing all equipment I went down to 50 feet off the water and headed home. Things were a bit tense, but we did plot several radar sites."

In April, Detachment Lima was ordered by the Joint Chiefs of Staff to leave the air group and fly to NAS Cubi Point. Following SEATO exercises in May, the detachment received another message from the JCS detailing the mission to intercept enemy resupply aircraft in Southeast Asia. Two Spads were stripped of ECM gear and outfitted with 20mm cannons. Goodman continues:

"I flew the first test hops and test-fired the guns. What a thrill. It was the first time I'd fired since advanced training. When I got back I told the others to get acquainted with strafing as an attack Spad once again.

Intelligence sources discovered the Russians were flying on moonlit nights. They would come over the mountaintops in low, slow aircraft, drop into the valleys and drop their supplies. We were to fly the valleys, and with our APS-33 radar with up-tilt ability, spot them as they came over the mountaintops. We would then arm our rockets—six or more on each wing—pour the coal to the 3350 and make the intercept.

**An EA-1F of VAW-13 leaves the *Constellation* off the coast of South Vietnam in August 1966. (USN)**

An EA-1E, BuNo. 135207, of VAW-11 Det. T snags the wire aboard *Yorktown* during its 1965 Vietnam cruise. (USN)

This VA-152 Spad was involved in the second day of a SAR mission during early November 1965 when the Air Force suffered the first HH-3 rescue helicopter loss of the war. Lt. Gordon Wileen was flying in a two-ship section in search of the helo's crew when he took hits at low altitude, which knocked out his hydraulics and forced a belly landing at Da Nang. (USN)

> We flew out of Cubi Point because the mountains in the northern Philippines were similar to those in Vietnam. We coordinated training flights with full moonlit nights that occurred about three times every two weeks. We flew in the valleys with our lights out to avoid being spotted by ground forces. The flights were hairy, so we worked hard on timing should we fly in the shadow of a mountain."

It was not until he was out of the Navy and received in May 1963 a commendation for his work that Goodman discovered how he was selected to lead the special mission. His commander, in a meeting with the Joint Chiefs of Staff—which was attended by President Kennedy—was asked by Air Force General Curtis LeMay which detachment of four then in the Pacific he would recommend for the mission. Commander John Peterson replied, "Detachment Lima on the *Hancock*." When asked by President Kennedy why he picked the junior officer-in-charge among the four, Peterson answered, "He's the only one I could trust to properly do the mission." Goodman was stunned. He adds:

> "Having flown the AD-5s, as well as working to set up the special mission with one of the finest groups of men in the Navy, was one of the most fascinating highlights of my entire life."

Goodman's logbooks record pilot time in 119 of the Navy's AD-5 variants.

Since the AD-5Qs, like the F-102s, did not locate or intercept enemy aircraft, Detachment Lima's rotational deployment ended in December 1963.

Navy reconnaissance flights began on 19 May 1964, marking the first time carrier pilots came under fire in the war in Southeast Asia. In retaliation for attacks by the North Vietnamese in the Gulf

Armed with Zuni rockets and FFAR rockets, the pilot of A-1J, BuNo. 142070 of VA-25, with his plane captain close at hand, prepares for launch. (USN)

The Zuni-armed A-1H, BuNo. 137576 of VA-152 is marshaled forward for a cat launch aboard *Oriskany* in 1965. (Gary L. Gottschalk)

**A VA-152 A-1H grabs the wire aboard *Oriskany* in 1965. (Gary L. Gottschalk)**

**An A-1H takes the short trip down *Oriskany's* catapult. (Gary L. Gottschalk)**

of Tonkin on U.S. destroyers on 2 and 4 August 1964, President Johnson ordered strikes against North Vietnamese naval bases and petroleum storage depots. On 5 August the first U.S. strikes against North Vietnam were launched from the carriers *USS Constellation* and *Ticonderoga.* Besides F-8 Crusaders and A-4 Skyhawks, Skyraiders of Attack Squadron 52 (VA-52) aboard the "Tico," and VA-145 aboard the "Connie," did their part in amassing 64 sorties, which severely damaged or destroyed 25 patrol boats and 9 petroleum storage tanks. Unfortunately, President Johnson's announcement of retaliatory strikes gave the North Vietnamese ample time to set up heavy gun positions, which downed VA-52's Lt. j.g. Richard C. Sather, the first U.S. Navy pilot to be killed in the war. A VA-145 Spad flown by Lt. James S. Hardie was hit in the fuel tank and hydraulics, but he managed to land safely aboard *Constellation.* Before day's end Lt. Everett Alvarez's Skyhawk would be shot down, giving him the unenviable distinction of being the first U.S. Navy prisoner of war in Southeast Asia.

The first major search and rescue effort of the war foreshadowed the Skyraider's role as the ideal support aircraft for such missions. On 18 November 1964 one of two F-100s escorting a naval reconnaissance flight was shot down in central Laos. An HU-16B airborne controller requested Navy A-1s to aid in the search for the F-100 pilot and to provide firepower, if needed. Shortly after their arrival on scene the Spads were hit by antiaircraft fire, but turned the attack on the enemy guns, receiving only minor damage. Six Navy A-1s took part in the mission, which ended with the deceased pilot being located the following day.

Early in the war, until USAF air rescue aircraft became widely available, Navy Spads occasionally supported Air America helicopters on rescue missions. Former Spad driver Walt Darran describes one such mission:

> "On 15 July 1965 two VA-165 Skyraider divisions (four Spads each) were sent to cover the pickup of the crew of the first A-6 *Intruder* shot down in the war. 'Mustang' (*Coral Sea)* was on Yankee Station. The crash site was in Laos, so we made an 0400 launch and flew direct over Vinh; our friends on the ground celebrated our overflight with a delightful fireworks display to greet the new day.
>
> We split at the Laotian border. Division 2, led by the squadron executive officer, Harry Parode, went to Udorn to top off and stand by. Division 1, led by the skipper, Ken Knoizen, rendezvoused with the Air America H-34 choppers and started searching. We soon picked up a PRC-49 (survival radio) signal. The lead Air America chopper sighted a man on the ground, but after several low passes, had to retire due to a fuel leak caused by Pathet Lao playing with automatic weapons. There was considerable confusion, partly caused by the fact that the downed pilot's transmitter was working, but not his receiver; vice-versa for the BN (bomber/navigator). We did not figure it out at the time, and they were a mile apart, so the communications sounded like me and my ex-wife. After we contributed some thunder and lightning to the festivities, another H-34 picked up both crewmembers. Then we destroyed the A-6 and adjourned to the infamous Air America bar at Udorn for a debrief.

**A VA-152 Spad gets expert care in the hands of maintenance technicians below decks in 1965. (Gary L. Gottschalk)**

**A pair of VA-152 A-1Hs during the squadron's second Vietnam cruise in 1966. Both are armed with four Zuni rocket launchers. The five purple hearts painted on the cowl of BuNo. 139770 say much about its combat experience. (Tom Hansen)**

**Navy Spad pilot Gary L. Gottschalk dressed for work in early 1966. He wears overalls, a leather jacket, steel-toe flight/hiking boots, leather gloves and a G suit, which was worn on flights involving dive bombing and high G pullouts. In the pockets of the Mae West flotation survival vest, normally worn on long overwater flights, were sea survival items, such as shark repellent, a flashlight, strobe light, and whistle. (Gottschalk collection)**

Assuming we were staying for the evening, we happily accepted celebratory drinks offered by our new friends. A couple hours later we were brought up short by a message from 'Mustang' telling us to get our young asses back home ASAP. It was a colorful recovery at 2040."

Often the downing of one aircraft resulted in successive events that included the loss of additional aircraft. Such was the case in 1965 when a USAF A-1E (BuNo 132439, flown by Capt. McKnight) was shot down during a SAR for a downed F-105. That prompted a massive SAR effort that included USAF helicopters and both Navy and USAF Spads. One of the helicopters, a CH-3E "Jolly Green," was downed, becoming the first loss of its type in the war. Spad pilot Gary Gottschalk picks up the story:

"Aboard the *USS Oriskany* on 6 November, orders came to my attack squadron, 152, to man a two-plane section for a search mission. Four rescue helicopter crewmembers were down about 40 miles southwest of Hanoi. The skipper chose Commander Gordon Smith, our squadron executive officer, to lead the flight, and I volunteered to fly wing with him.

Our two Spads were strapped to the catapults and launched at 1730 hours into a lowering sun, followed by a two-hour flight heading northwest. En route and *feet dry* we started receiving a weak emergency signal from a pilot's survival radio. Responding to the signal with onboard homing equipment, we diverted toward the signal since it could be a credible one. It could also be a false one, since some emergency radios had fallen into enemy hands. Our flight of two was soon circling an area of rough terrain where the signal was coming from. Shortly after we were bracketed by intense AAA and automatic weapons fire, some of which put holes in both aircraft, but with no major or disabling damage. It was a 'flak trap,' and we got out of the area.

Continuing on to the area of the downed helo crew we arrived after sundown, but with visual conditions and

**Their bomb racks empty, a pair of *Wild Aces* Spads head for the carrier. The unit's tail fin chevrons were reduced in size for the squadron's second Vietnam cruise. (Gary L. Gottschalk)**

**A pair of VA-115 Spads await their turn for *Kittyhawk's* catapult in 1965. (Author's collection)**

a rising half moon. We started to search with the hope of establishing communication with any of the downed airmen. As we circled an area approximately three miles in radius we encountered AAA and automatic weapons, which we avoided. We searched for perhaps an hour with some help from moonlight as we flew low over the precipitous mountainous terrain, with dense jungle canopy in the valleys between. Then we received a weak signal from nearby, terrain having blocked the line of sight signal earlier. We homed on the signal and were able to establish radio contact with one of the airmen. Gordon then had me climb to about 2,000 feet above the area and plot the position as closely as possible, while he tried to pinpoint the survivor's location from low altitude.

We made many low passes close to the airman's position as Gordon communicated with him. We hadn't yet pinpointed a location that would enable the rescue helo to make the pickup. On one of the low passes Gordon clipped some of the jungle canopy, which we later found on his aircraft. Fuel was now becoming a concern. Then an idea occurred to Commander Smith that probably saved the airman's life. Gordon asked him if he had a flashlight in his survival equipment. He didn't. Smith asked, 'Do you have a cigarette lighter?' He did. Gordon told him to flash on the lighter whenever he heard the airplane fly directly overhead. Gordon located the position precisely after a few more passes by spotting the small flame in the darkness through the jungle canopy. On a subsequent pass he flashed his navigation lights momentarily from over the position and I was able to accurately plot it on my charts. We got what we came for, but now fuel was more of a concern since we were about two hours from the *Oriskany*, and with about two hours fuel remaining.

We remained on station for about another 15 minutes waiting for another flight to relieve us. A flight of four USAF F-4s arrived and we departed. Now it was a game

**Early in the war, ordnance shortages resulted in an equal number of sorties, but with less punch. This A-1H of VA-25 in 1966 carries two each Mk 81 and Mk 82 bombs, plus two Zuni rocket launchers. (Tom Hansen)**

**Rocket launchers occupy only four of the 14 ordnance racks available on this A-1H waiting to be spotted on *Ticonderoga's* catapult in 1966. The "double nuts" of its side number "300" indicate the squadron commander's aircraft. (Author's collection)**

A Spad looks for trouble over Vinh, North Vietnam, in 1965. This activity would prove even riskier a few years later, when the North beefed up its antiaircraft defenses. (Gary L. Gottschalk)

Carrying 42 rockets, a VA-52 Spad, named "The Whip," comes in close while escorting an HU-16B Albatross rescue amphibian. (David Wendt)

of 'do we have enough fuel to make it to the *Oriskany* and, if not, where to land.' We flew at a power setting and speed for maximum range. The closest land base was Da Nang in the northern part of South Vietnam, a farther distance than the *Oriskany.* We took up a heading for the carrier, while having the option to ditch in the ocean alongside the rescue destroyer on station in the gulf, about half the distance to the carrier. From over the gulf, Smith radioed the destroyer with a request to be relayed to the captain of the *Oriskany*: 'If conditions allow, would the *Oriskany* steam in our direction during the one-hour flight to the ship?' This would give our flight about 30 less nautical miles to fly and possibly preclude ditching. Being one hour's flight from the carrier, our options were: land in enemy territory; ditch alongside the rescue destroyer; attempt flying to the carrier before fuel starvation; or ditch short of the carrier and hope for a night, or next day, rescue. Captain Bartholomew Connolly III magnanimously turned the carrier in our direction and steamed flank speed for a successful trap aboard. Gordon told me to land first. I did and made certain the approach for the arrested landing would be successful on the first try. It was a good arrested landing and, as the tail wheel touched the deck in a nose-up attitude, the engine quit. Gordon had a good trap landing shortly after." It wasn't until 1990 at an air wing reunion that the Spad pilots heard, from an officer who

Navy Spads that accompanied Air Rescue HU-16Bs frequently obliged picture-taking crewmen aboard the Albatross by lowering their gear and tail hooks. (David Wendt)

They had a reason to smile. The Air Force A-1 pilots who helped rescue Dieter Dengler after his five-month ordeal, seen here at Da Nang AB in August 1966. They are, from left, Capt. Robert E. Blood, Lt. Col. Gene Deatrick (1st ACS commander) and Maj. Gail Anderson. Not shown is Capt. Frank Urbanic. (Robert Blood collection)

**The A-1J named "Puff The Magic Dragon" of VA-165 at Da Nang AB on 10 September 1966. Lcdr "Speed" Ritzmann diverted to Da Nang after missing the scheduled recovery time on *Intrepid*, having flown a 4 to 6-hour ResCAP. He went aboard the carrier during the next recovery cycle. (Tom Hansen)**

**This A-1H of VA-52 wears graffiti after having landed aboard a carrier other than that to which it was assigned. (Tom Hansen)**

was with Captain Connolly that night, how he ran the *Oriskany* into dangerously shallow water to bring the pair aboard. "The skipper of VA-152, Cdr Knutson, was upset with Smith's nearly 7-hour vigil, which was supposed to be only a 'look-see.' I sympathize with Knutson's concerns, but I also take my hat off to Smith, who went above and beyond to find those airmen.

At first light the next morning the rescue helo hoisted the survivor that we located from the jungle. Commander Smith was involved in the search for the other airmen, but without success. It was later discovered they had been captured. Another A-1 was lost during the attempt, and Smith led that SAR also. Gordon Wileen was his wingman, who took hits from low altitude that knocked out his hydraulics and forced a belly landing at Da Nang. Smith also escorted one of the rescue helos to a safe haven after it was shot full of holes and leaking fuel profusely. Smith located a clear zone on a mountaintop, where the helo put down safely and its crew was rescued."

As the war intensified, so too did the Spad's role. Shortly after *Barrel Roll* missions over Laos were approved, four VA-95 A-1s escorted by eight F-4 *Phantoms* launched from *Ranger* for armed reconnaissance missions over major Laotian roads. When the Viet Cong attacked U.S. barracks at Pleiku, South Vietnam, on 7 February 1965, the Navy retaliated with *Operation Flaming Dart.* The strike against enemy facilities in North Vietnam was carried out by 83 Navy aircraft launched from the *USS Coral Sea*, *Ranger*, and *Hancock.* Skyraider squadrons aboard these carriers were VA-165, VA-95, and VA-215, respectively. Just three days later a Viet Cong bomb killed and wounded a large number of Americans at Quin Nhon, South Vietnam. Retribution was swift, as 99 aircraft from the three carriers launched *Flaming Dart II* against North Vietnam.

When *Operation Rolling Thunder* got under way on 15 March 1965, VA-95's Lt. j.g. Charles Clydesdale failed to make it back to the *Ranger*, becoming the Navy's second loss of a Spad pilot. When 40 aircraft from the *Hancock* and *Coral Sea* attacked North Vietnam's Ha Tinh radar sites on 26 March a VA-215 Spad was hit, but the pilot, Lt. j.g. Gudmunson, survived after crash-landing at Da Nang AB. During the early phases of Rolling Thunder, small groups of A-1s and A-4s flew 'round-the-clock strikes. The tempo increased and, by April, up to 100 aircraft were launched almost daily from carriers in the Gulf of Tonkin. The sustained *Rolling Thunder* campaign fostered *Alpha Strikes,* which were preplanned strikes against targets pre-approved by the Joint Chiefs of Staff and assigned to TF 77 and 7th Air Force.

When it became painfully apparent in mid-1965 that surface-to-air missiles (SAMs) posed a threat to U.S. air operations, military leaders reevaluated electronic reconnaissance and countermeasure (ECM) capabilities. Aircraft in the Navy inventory designed for such tasks were the Douglas EA-3B and EA-1F. In Navy jargon they were known as the "Queer Whale" and "Queer Spad," respectively, since their pre-1962 designations included the mission suffix "Q" (A3D-2Q and AD-5Q). After redesignation, the EA-1F be-

**"Baby" was an A-1J BuNo. 142033 assigned to VA-145 seen here at Da Nang in August 1967. The squadron was called "The Swordsmen" and used the call sign "Electron." (Tom Hansen)**

**Escorting Navy Spads provided great photo opportunities for Albatross crewmen. Here A-1H BuNo. 139680 of VA-25 closes the distance with an Air Force HU-16B during a rescue orbit on 16 September 1966. (Tom Hansen)**

**An A-1J displaying VA-176's colorful markings nears an Albatross in 1966 as the Spad pilot holds a note. Writing above the Spad's side number on the cowl reads, "Cdr Ray Ashworth." (Tom Hansen)**

came known as the "Electric Spad." Although the Navy normally did not assign ECM aircraft to its standard compliment of carrier air wings, detachments of both types, which were usually shore-based, were assigned to carriers deployed to the Western Pacific. Detachments were in demand and often *cross-decked* to carriers as they took up positions on the line. The EA-3Bs flew electronic intelligence gathering missions and warned of SAM and MiG launches, while EA-1Fs jammed North Vietnamese radar during air strikes. Detachments of Airborne Early Warning (AEW) EA-1Es served as airborne radar eyes for the Fleet to guard against Soviet and Chinese submarines.

Although the EA-3Bs that operated from carriers and Da Nang AB did a credible job, EA-1E and EA-1F "Electric Spads" bore the brunt of AEW and ECM work beginning in 1965. Typically, each WestPac Carrier Air Wing (CVW) had a two or three-aircraft detachment of EA-1Fs assigned to one of its carriers. VAW-13's "Zappers," which called NAS Alameda home, set up shop at NAS Cubi Point, Philippine Islands, to provide TF 77 with detachments of Electric Spads. VAW-33, whose Spads played a significant role in tracking and intercepting Soviet ships during the Cuban Missile Crisis, also supplied the Pacific Fleet with EA-1Fs; VAW-33 was redesignated VAQ-33 on 1 February 1968. VAW-11, which was home-based at NAS North Island, embarked aboard ASW carriers. On one combat cruise aboard *Kearsarge*, VAW-11's Detachment R set a record by having EA-1Es in the air for 501 mission hours.

Equipped with noise jammers, chaff dispensers, and radar, EA-1Fs usually operated in pairs, launching well ahead of strike aircraft to arrive first in the mission area. Flying at 5,000 feet, just three to four miles off North Vietnam's shore, they monitored enemy radar activity. When a radar source was identified, the Electric Spads flew slowly toward the source, jamming the signal and dispensing chaff. Although their perilous path brought them within range of enemy guns, only one EA-1F was lost in combat.

**This A-1H of VA-115 was experimentally camouflaged in 1966. The Spad taxis with a partial load of general purpose bombs. (NMNA)**

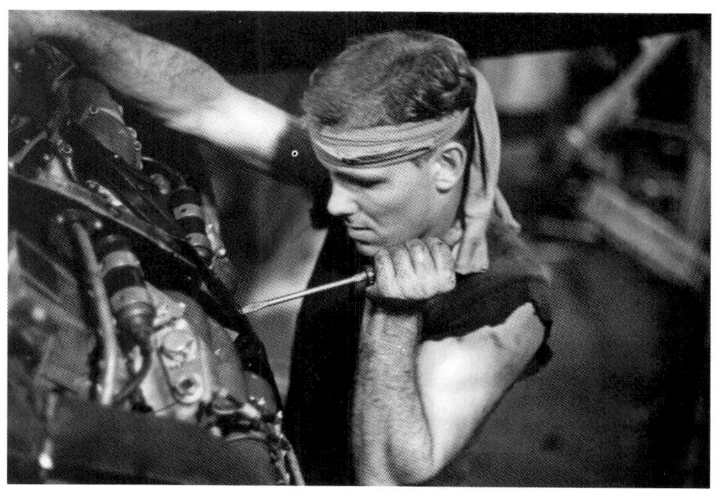

**U.S. Navy mechanics aboard carriers worked long hours in sweltering conditions to maintain Skyraider availability rates. (Bud Watson)**

VA-152 pilots in *Oriskany's* ready room in 1965. (Bud Watson)

A VA-52 Spad makes a rocket run against an antiaircraft site near Cape Bang, North Vietnam in 1965. (Bud Watson)

The Navy channeled pilots to the A-1 community through its pipeline, known as the Advanced Training Syllabus for Attack. Until 1960 training was conducted in units segregated by aircraft type within the Air Training Command. Skyraiders comprised Advanced Training Unit (ATU) 301 which, on 1 July 1960, became a squadron designated VT-30—in Navy jargon "V" stands for heavier-than-air, and "T" stands for training. During the early 1960s VT-30, which was based at NAS Corpus Christi, Texas, trained both U.S. and Vietnamese Air Force pilots in the single-seat A-1, an arrangement that severely reduced the number of Navy A-1 pilots. When VT-30 was disestablished in 1965, not only pilots, but Spads were becoming scarce, as additional A-1s were relinquished to the Air Force. Navy officials, however, viewed the loss of Skyraiders as a large step toward modernization with jets.

Although Spads and jets shared deck space on carriers, rivalry among their pilots was common. Because of the variation in roles, Spad pilots during the early 1960s found the effort to transition to jets frustrating. Fanning the embers of rivalry was the Navy's contention that pilots in the attack community were not fighter pilots. That, of course, made the transition from one community, or mission specialty, to another difficult. As the war in Southeast Asia intensified, the transition became easier. And when the Navy retired its Spads, most pilots with remaining service were assigned to jets. Although the argument about A-1 pilots logging fighter time was lost to a definition of terms, in the end it seems the A-1 pilots preferred being known as "Spad drivers" or "Attack pilots."

Attack squadron 122 (VA-122) at NAS Lemoore, California, took over training Spad pilots when VT-30 closed its doors. When VA-42—the east coast training squadron—transitioned to the A-6 in 1963, VT-30, and subsequently, VA-122, became responsible for training all replacement Spad pilots. As the new A-1 replacement air group (RAG), VA-122 established a training program similar to that used by VT-30, but added nuclear weapons delivery, low-level navigation, and night operations. Prospective Spad pilots, called "Nuggets," arrived monthly, first attending survival school, a T-28 instrument course, and ground school before climbing into a Spad cockpit.

Scott Smith, who checked into VA-122 as a Lieutenant Commander and instructor in June 1964, recalls:

> "Our main training problems at Lemoore consisted of the winter fog and the summer heat. Otherwise, problems revolved around the usual military exercise of trying

A *Wild Aces* Spad at work over North Vietnam in 1965. (Bud Watson)

> to do more with less. At one point, the Navy supply people dumped the A-1 spare parts onto the surplus market prematurely and we had to buy them back.
>
> Pilots soon learned to preflight the aircraft while wearing gloves in the summer. Some parts of the aircraft could get hot enough to burn the skin. It was pointless to wash a flight suit because it was soaked with sweat before getting into the plane, let alone flying without air conditioning in the Spad or T-28. Everyone knew they earned their pay after flying on a hot day."

Since thick fog in the San Joaquin Valley hampered Spad training during California's winter months, classes went on special detachment to NAS Fallon, Nevada, where the air was cold but clear. Smith continues:

> "I went to Fallon with over 20 T-28s and A-1s and 30 pilots, including instructors and replacement pilots. Normally we only went to Fallon for weapons training. This time we scheduled familiarization, instruments, and formation flying outside the target areas."

When the Navy training command realized early in the war in Southeast Asia that its weapons training program was inadequate, a full week of weapons training was added to the training syllabus. No time was wasted on nuclear weapons delivery, although that mission existed in Fleet squadrons throughout the war. RAG instructors dolefully noted that successful combat tactics used during World War II and Korea had quickly been forgotten.

After weapons training, Fleet replacement pilots began field carrier landing practice (FCLP), which consisted of one week each of day and night operations. The few weeks following a carrier's return from a WestPac deployment were spent with carrier qualifications (car-quals). These were conducted every other month, usually off San Diego. Spad pilots had to make 10 day landings and 8 night landings to qualify. The carrier then started training with the air wing, by which time the next carrier sailed into port to repeat the process.

As Spads became more scarce, instructors flew chase flights in T-28s. At one time VA-122 had more T-28s than Spads, which proved detrimental to instructors trying to stay proficient in the type before rotating back to Fleet A-1 squadrons.

Since prospective Spad pilots were culled from the jet pipeline, or were volunteers from the S-2 *Tracker* community, none had flown a tail-wheel equipped aircraft. Therefore taxi flights were used, which had students taxiing into a takeoff with an instructor in a T-28 following closely behind. Getting the Spad's tail wheel off the runway constituted a sufficient flight mode. Fledgling Spad pilots learned quickly that the Spad, like any tail-dragger, had its center-of-gravity aft of the main landing gear, making conditions ripe for a ground-loop. Pilots also learned to counter the tail-over-nose tendency by making quick corrections with rudder and brakes to keep the heavy Spad pointed straight down the runway. Jet-trained students were found to have difficulty managing the Spad's engine and rudder control. When it became apparent that students from the S-2 pipeline were more motivated and more adept at handling recip-powered aircraft than jet-trained pilots, it was decided to draw only from their ranks to create Spad pilots. That decision would be affirmed by the involvement of three former S-2 pilots in two incidents in which MiGs were downed by Spads.

A few months after a jet pilot ground-looped and destroyed a Spad, VA-122 evaluated an A-1E borrowed from the Air Force, hopeful the side-by-side pilot arrangement would prevent the loss of more Spads. However, the S-2 pilots' progress and use of the T-28 ruled out the need for A-1Es.

By the time students had completed training, they lacked only operational experience to qualify for the hard-earned title of Spad pilot. It did not take long for them to realize that not only was landing a Spad on a carrier a major challenge, they would endure the pressure of 20-second landing intervals…and reputations were at stake.

As the Spad crossed the carrier's *round-down*, the landing signal officer (LSO) flashed a light and gave a voice "Cut" signal for a reduction to idle speed. At that moment the pilot settled the airplane into the landing area and, hopefully, his tail hook snatched the number-two wire. After picking up the wire, the Spad did a full run-out and it rolled back slightly. Simultaneously, the pilot's hand left the throttle to raise the hook handle, raise the flaps, and unlock and fold the wings. At the same time, he tapped the brakes so the nose swung around to the right and the shortest distance clear of the landing area. Throughout the process, the pilot held the stick

**The VA-152 pilot of A-1H BuNo. 139770 leaves *Oriskany's* deck in 1966. (Bud Watson)**

U.S. Navy deck crewmen work dangerously near a Spad's prop to ensure the aircraft is ready for launch. (Bud Watson)

Added to the unit markings of this A-1J of VA-145 was the Tonkin Gulf Yacht Club emblem on the fuselage. (Tom Hansen)

back—usually with his right wrist—while on the deck, and a deckhand slammed the loose arresting wire with a bat to ensure the tail hook released it. The pilot's left hand swept from the hook handle to the flaps, to the wing fold, and back to the throttle to apply power to quickly leave the landing area. Experience came quick, and by the end of deployments Spad pilots were clear of landing areas in less than 15 seconds. No pilot wanted to be responsible for having caused a wave-off behind him. Done correctly, a flight of four Spads could be recovered in 45 seconds and clear the landing area. It was vital during carrier landings that the tail wheel be unlocked.

As carriers steamed to stations in the South China Sea practice hops were flown, with gunnery runs made against the "spar," a target towed 400 meters behind the ship. Spads typically used four Mk-76 practice bombs and fired 20mm just aft of the spar. Other preparations for combat included changes to the aircraft, such as the addition of nearly 700 pounds of armor around the cockpit, the addition of outboard wing guns (Navy Spads used only two guns outside the combat zone), and the removal of most decorative markings.

Spad squadrons were usually positioned farthest aft on a carrier's deck, making them the last to launch and the last to recover. If the carrier's bow faced into the wind Spads could launch without the catapult, a feat matched only by the S-2 if there was sufficient room on the deck. Air operations aboard carriers ceased during underway replenishment (UNREP); a supply ship alongside meant slow going for the carrier.

The Navy assigned call signs to all aviation units, which seldom changed them, and then only with approval from the Navy *brass*. Detachments, including those of VAWs, used the squadron's call sign. In true military fashion call signs went beyond air squadrons, having also been assigned to targets, which became "Skunks." Trawlers were called "Hookers," and even carriers got in on the act. For example: *USS Bennington* was "Big Boy," and *Yorktown* was "Cactus."

After arriving on station in the combat zone, Spad squadrons operated on hectic schedules preparing for and launching on a variety of missions. At the war's outset Spads flew strikes against heavily defended major targets, however, in less than one year concentrated

This A-1H of VA-115 *Arabs* was the subject of an elaborate "zap" consisting of footprints applied from wing tip to wing tip. The prints are suspiciously similar to those associated with Air Force pararescue crewmen of "Jolly Green Giant" rescue helicopters. (Tom Hansen)

antiaircraft fire necessitated changes in Spad roles. Coastal and land armed reconnaissance missions—which targeted dams, bridges, buildings, sampans, trucks, caves, and roads—became the norm. Close air support and convoy cover were added, along with Barrier Combat Air Patrols (BarCAPS) and Force Combat Air Patrols (ForCAPS) to protect the battle group.

Foremost among the roles undertaken by Navy Spads was search and rescue, called Rescue Combat Air Patrol (ResCAP). Spad pilots considered ResCAPs their most important mission, during which they searched for downed aircrew, prevented their capture, suppressed ground fire, and escorted rescue helicopters. Carriers on Yankee Station carried only two helicopters, none of which were equipped for firefights with ground forces. Therefore, the express purpose of ResCAPs was to protect downed aircrew until other resources arrived. ResCAP also involved flights of two or four Spads escorting Air Force HU-16B *Albatrosses* that flew tracks off the coast of North Vietnam. When the amphibians made water landings to pick up downed aircrew the Spads provided close-in cover, usually keeping enemy boats at bay and silencing shore gun batteries. Such missions involved long on-station time and were usually boring and not particularly dangerous...until Albatrosses went in for a pickup. The mission then became anything but dull and routine.

For example: on 14 March 1966 an F-4C Phantom—call sign "Pluto 2"—was badly damaged by antiaircraft fire during a strike in North Vietnam. Knowing the chance of rescue was greater if he reached the Gulf, the pilot nursed his crippled jet to the coast. The VA-115 Spad pilots escorting the Albatross—Lcdr Jerry Tabrum ("Arab 506," flying BuNo.139778) and Lcdr Manny Benero ("Arab 510," flying BuNo. 139789)—collaborated to provide their account of the incident:

> "We had been on station for about two hours flying a racetrack pattern (10-mile legs) over the Tonkin Gulf when we heard the Mayday call on the guard channel. An Air Force F-4C Phantom had been hit by AAA, and the two-man crew ejected over water between the North Vietnam coast and Hon Me Island. The HU-16 took up a direct heading for the site and began a gradual descent. I remember seeing 220 knots on the airspeed indicator during the descent, which surprised me, as I had about 350 hours in the HU-16 and had never been above 195 knots. We arrived at the site in about 12 minutes. After spotting the survivors, the HU-16 made a nice water landing and taxied toward them. We scanned the general area for water traffic, but there was only one vessel, a junk, approximately one mile north that was heading away from the site at best speed.
>
> As the HU-16 began the task of picking up the Phantom crewmembers, I noticed a splash in the water approximately 200 yards west of the site. I asked Lcdr Benero if he had released something from his aircraft, and he replied, 'Negative.' We both then saw a second splash about 75 yards east of the HU-16. Approximately ten seconds later the right wing of the HU-16 exploded in orange flame and dense black smoke. I looked toward the mainland beach to the west and saw numerous muzzle flashes. We made several rocket runs on the beach using 5-inch rockets. After expending the HVARs we made strafing runs using 20mm cannons, which seemed to halt the mortar fire for the time being. LCDR Benero assumed the duties of SAR on-scene commander, and he made an immediate request for rescue helicopters for the eight men now in the water.
>
> The NVA attempted to capture the survivors by sending three small boats to the scene. I made one rocket run firing two 19-shot pods of 2.75-inch FFARs in salvo on the boats and they disappeared. We continued remaining in sight of the burning amphibian, eventually vectoring in two 'Fetch' SH-3 helos from *Yorktown* who, despite taking enemy fire, rescued five crewmen and were forced out of the area. By this time a very low overcast had come in from seaward, forcing us to remain at a very low altitude in order to remain in visual contact with the amphibian. The final crewman was rescued by a UH-2 helo vectored in from the guided missile cruiser *USS England*, terminating a two and a half hour ordeal. Two HU-16 crewmembers had been killed by the direct hit on their aircraft."

**Spad pilot Jack Smith of VA-152 rolls in on a target in 1965. (Gary L. Gottschalk)**

Albatrosses ceased flying ResCAP missions during September 1967 since the more maneuverable HH-3E *Jolly Green* rescue helicopter could air-refuel and land on water. Navy Spad pilots who escorted helicopters during ResCAPs often found such missions high risk, and that not all had favorable outcomes. Scotty Wilkes, a VA-215 Spad driver, tells of working a ResCAP with a helicopter:

> "Not all ResCAPS went well. A flight of four of us were coming back from up north and had just reached *feet wet* when we received a *Mayday* from a Marine flight just below the DMZ. We still had *juice*, so we checked with the *boat* and responded, along with a chopper who was also in the neighborhood. The chopper was first on scene and spotted the Marine A-4 that had pancaked on the top of a mesa just ten miles north of his destination, Chu Lai. Just as we got on scene the weather set in, and the very low clouds prevented even the chopper from getting close,

but he was taking ground fire. Since we knew the exact location, we arranged with the chopper to meet the next day and see if there were signs of life, though we found none initially.

It was as if someone had ordered good weather, so there we were working with the same chopper driver. In we went, and all of a sudden the chopper pilot radioed, 'Back off!' We asked the obvious, and he came back with, 'The body is in plain sight, very conveniently sitting upright, clear of the wreckage.' The chopper pilot knew that wasn't what he saw yesterday. He had put two and two together and, as the on-scene commander, made the right decision. But he got too close to the bait and got the hell shot out of him. He also noticed a lot of bad guys in the area, so he called us in and in we went. The next day they got some good guys in there, and we got credit for 110 KBA (killed by air), and the chopper driver got the Distinguished Flying Cross.

It was later determined that the A-4 pilot had indeed died either prior to, or during, the ditch, for no sane jet jock would try to ditch if he had a choice. His mother received a body that was slightly worse for wear, but should have been awarded the Navy Cross for service as a forward air controller. Rest his soul."

Wilkes explains how he became the subject of a SAR mission:

"Frank Morrow and I were in Laos on 27 April 1965 running the Trail, looking for targets of opportunity—foolishly, in daylight. All hell broke loose, and we were both hit pretty bad. I was hit in my inboard gun ammo storage, and 200 rounds of my 20mm started to blow off my left wing. Discretion being the better part, I went out on the right as the airplane went left. Despite being shot up Frank had the Mayday out, I landed, a chopper landed about 100 yards away, and off we went to NKP. I was greeted by the base skipper; they force fed me a six-pack of San Miguel, along with a turkey dinner, put me on a plane to Da Nang, and then back to the *Hancock.*

We made two cruises for a total of 18 months out of two years. During those cruises we lost six good men out of eighteen. One of our four commanders, CDR Robert Hessom, 'bought it' on his 265th mission. I ended up with 151 missions, was shot up 26 times, got shot down once, and had a forced landing."

Despite the punishment from antiaircraft fire the Spad could endure, Doug Clarke, who amassed 2,400 hours in Navy Spads, offers this interesting contrast from one of his memorable ResCAP missions with VA-152:

"The mission was on 13 November 1965, when I was called off a strike mission to hunt for CDR Harry Jenkins, who was shot down just north of Dong Hoi flying an A-4. I was given the coordinates and went to look for Harry. It was several miles inland, clear of the main highway and a fairly rural area, so I was down around 300 feet with my wingman on a high perch. I must have orbited the general area for 20 to 30 minutes, and the only person I saw was a farmer crouching behind a bush. Then on one pass I noticed the son-of-a-gun had a rifle pointed at me, and the next thing was the thud of the bullet hitting my plane. As luck would have it, he got my hydraulic tank. I called out that I had been hit and my wingman replied that I was on fire. But what he thought was smoke was really just the hydraulic fluid vaporizing. Since I wasn't sure I could get both main gear down and locked with no fluid, I elected to make a wheels-up landing at Da Nang. The Air Force foamed the runway and, as I recall, they had a primitive arresting cable, which I caught. The landing was relatively uneventful. The squadron later jacked up the bird (A-1H BuNo 139810), put a new engine on, and put her back in service."

Navy Skyraider operations changed to keep pace with the intensifying war. When sea infiltration by enemy trawlers and junks increased, Task Force 115, code named "Market Time," was established to counter the problem. Skyraiders from carriers on Dixie Station provided cover for Market Time patrol aircraft and vessels that conducted surveillance of suspicious vessels, as well as intercepted enemy craft trying to enter South Vietnam.

By the end of 1965 the Spad proved too vulnerable to concentrated antiaircraft fire and was pulled off of Alpha Strikes. Its role then shifted to armed reconnaissance and naval gunfire spotting in the coastal interdiction effort off North Vietnam, called "Sea Dragon." When a flight of Spads orbited on ResCAPs off major points along the North Vietnamese coast, the enemy, unsure of the Spads' objectives, prepared for incoming Alpha Strikes. Spad squadrons kept up the ruse by scheduling coastal recon sorties 'round-the-clock, using rocket and cannon fire to disguise ResCAPs and inbound flights of strike aircraft.

During its 1965 combat cruise VA-152 recorded the first time SAMs were fired at A-1s. The sobering milestone occurred during a ResCAP on 17 October, during which four Spad pilots searched for two downed Navy pilots near the Chinese border. During its 1966 cruise, on 18 August the squadron experienced one of its more colorful events. While checking out a road near Cape Bang, Lcdr Eric Schade and Lt. Garvey spotted tracks leading into a wooded

**Spotted on *Oriskany's* fantail, a *Wild Aces* A-1H awaits taxi orders for a strike mission. (Gary L. Gottschalk)**

area. Schade, on a hunch, fired several Zuni rockets into the area and was rewarded with secondary explosions. Every rocket and strafe run produced more secondaries. The pair was relieved by two pilots, who met with the same results. The pattern continued even after four more of the squadron's A-1s joined in. Smoke rose to 7,000 feet, and it was estimated that 22 trucks and up to 800 barrels of fuel and oil had been destroyed. The huge burned out area became known as "Eric's Truck Park."

Undoubtedly, the most publicized Navy Spad incident of the war involved the downing and evasion efforts of Lt. j.g. Dieter Dengler of VA-145. Dengler's A-1J was among a flight of four Spads that launched from the *USS Ranger* on the morning of 1 February 1966. Flying in formation at 10,000 feet, the flight began taking fire from radar-controlled guns. When one of the pilots spotted an antiaircraft battery, Dengler rolled his Spad on its back and started to dive. A large shell blasted apart his right wing. Another hit the engine, which sputtered and quit. After calling Mayday, he leveled out and dumped all his ordnance, obliterating the gun that got him.

Dengler crash-landed in a small clearing, but trees sheared off his wings and the Spad's fuselage rolled two or three times. He regained consciousness 100 yards from his mangled, burning Spad. Injured, and with only a meager survival kit and a .38 cal. revolver, Dengler set out on a grueling odyssey that was punctuated by three escapes from torturous capture. More than five months after he was shot down—22 days after his third escape—weighing only 93 pounds and near death, Dengler used a crude SOS to signal an Air Force A-1E, whose pilot summoned rescue forces. Dengler's rescue helicopter flew him to the hospital at Da Nang, and he was later flown back to the U.S.

During *Coral Sea's* 1967-1968 combat cruise, it was decided that overall operations would be more efficient if less aircraft were aboard the carrier. Therefore, each squadron took turns rotating for two days one or two aircraft to NAS Cubi Point in the Philippines. There were also logistic advantages to sending aircraft to Cubi Point on a daily basis. On 12 February it became VA-25's and VAW-13's turn for the rotation. Lt. j.g. Joe Dunn requested the flight so he could telephone home to Massachusetts on his wedding anniversary.

On the 14th Dunn departed Cubi Point in his A-1H, along with an EA-1F from the VAW-13 detachment. The pair apparently set a course that was ten degrees too far north, and that took them straight to the Chinese island of Hainan.

The Chinese scrambled a pair of interceptors that met the errant Spads head-on. The MiG-17s fired when within range, hitting Dunn's Spad with cannon fire on the first pass. The EA-1F pilot dove for a nearby cloud, got under the radar, and headed to Da Nang. Dunn's guns were without ammunition, since it was standard practice to fly the rotational hops unarmed. Loaded guns may not have made a difference, since the Spads were caught by surprise straight and level. One of Dunn's squadron mates, Lcdr "Speed" Ritzmann, recalls:

> "I was on a mission sortie just south of the DMZ that morning when the message was broadcast that an A-1 had been shot down. When I returned to *Coral Sea,* the information was that a VA-25 Skyraider had been shot down about ten miles east of Hainan Island. Somewhere along the line, a report that an emergency beeper had been heard was included in the information passed to us. This, of course, implied that Joe Dunn had made it alive, either in a life jacket or a raft. This report could not be verified at the time, so the decision was made for *Coral Sea* to depart Yankee Station and investigate the area of the incident early on the morning of the 15th.
>
> Our squadron CO had himself scheduled to take the lead of four VA-25 A-1s in the SAR effort. I was scheduled to fly lead of the second section of two for the predawn launch. Our mission was to go and listen for an emergency signal and report a bearing if it was heard. Rescue helicopters would be on a tactical frequency, and were to attempt a rescue if the position indicated by the signal was outside the Hainan twelve-mile limit. We in the search teams were ordered to remain at least 20 miles from the

**The A-1H BuNo. 135300, while assigned to VA-52 during late 1966, flies in the shadow of an Air Force HU-16B Albatross. On 20 February 1968 it would fly the last Navy single-seat Spad mission. (Tom Hansen)**

island of Hainan. This order, in effect, made the rescue attempt appear futile, because it would be unlikely that Joe would hear aircraft ten miles away. No signal was heard, and Joe was presumed lost. Days later, intelligence indicated the original report of the beeper could not be verified and probably did not occur."

Joe Dunn was the last Navy A-1 pilot lost in the war.

Although the Spad had the unmatched ability to remain on station for long periods and its slow speed allowed better target acquisition and ordnance delivery, its days in the Navy were numbered. Navy planners did find, however, that replacing the Spad was not an easy task. A Navy report on replacing its A-1s reveals that ResCAP and Sea Dragon missions would have required from 75 to 100 percent more jet aircraft, depending on the aircraft type and its refueling requirements. Alternatives to the A-1 included staggering, or doubling and tripling, launch cycles of jets, and using the less maneuverable and more vulnerable ASW carrier-based S-2 for gunfire spotting. The following excerpts from the 1967 report say it best:

> "None of the jet aircraft have provisions for carrying any 20mm firepower in quantities comparable with the A-1. This weapon is one of the most useful on the ResCAP mission, and the phasing out of the A-1 heightens the requirement for a satisfactory externally mounted gun pod. Without attempting to exhaust all of the possible alternatives in replacing the A-1, it is evident that the services it is now providing can only be provided by a very much larger (and probably unrealistic) number of jets. Compromises will have to be made in the conduct of present Southeast Asia operations if it is desired to carry out the ResCAP and Sea Dragon spotting missions with a comparable number of jets. Although the A-1 flight schedules shown in this study are typical of current operations in Southeast Asia, they have never been duplicated exactly, nor is it likely they will ever be."

Those sentiments were echoed by Spad pilots, who felt the Navy was placing too much emphasis on speed and sophistication. One commented:

> "The Navy needs planes here in South Vietnam that can fly slow and low, and I'm afraid we may be making a mistake by getting rid of the Spad." Another said, "Only time will tell whether we did the right thing or made a mistake."

When attack squadrons traded in their Spads for A-4s, A-6s, or A-7s, the A-1s were turned over to the USAF or VNAF, first undergoing overhaul and repair at NAS Alameda or NAS Quonset Point. Others took a more direct route back to the combat zone. Scott McIntosh notes:

> "At the end of my 1964-'65 Southeast Asia cruise on the *USS Ranger* in March 1965, we flew all 12 of our VA-95 Skyraiders to NAS Cubi Point for transfer."

At the end of *USS Midway's* 1963-1964 WestPac cruise, VA-25 pilots flew the squadron's 12 A-1s from Cubi Point to Bien Hoa Air Base, where they were turned over to the VNAF. Some retired Spads that had been purchased for scrap by contractors and earmarked for the smelter were purchased back by the Navy and refurbished at NAS Litchfield, Arizona, for transfer to the Air Force.

It seems fitting that the first Navy squadron to take the Skyraider into combat—VA-25 flying from the *USS Boxer* against North Korea in 1950—would launch the Spad on its last Navy attack mission. The squadron took its Spads aboard the *Coral Sea* in August 1967 and, near the end of its combat cruise, flew missions in support of ground troops near the DMZ and at Khe Sanh. "Speed" Ritzmann relates his part in the mission:

> "I was the Operations Officer in VA-25 from September 1967 through February 1968. On February 19th we were assembling the schedule for the 20th, which would be our last day on the line.
>
> Naturally all the squadron pilots present in the ready room at the time wanted to be scheduled for the last Navy Skyraider sortie. Our CO, CDR Cliff Church, decided that he would lead the last flight, and that Lt.j.g. Ted Hill would be on his wing. His rationale was that Hill was the last Naval aviator to complete both flight training in VT-30

**Cdr J.B. Linder, Commander Carrier Air Wing 15, congratulates Lt. J.G. Hill on the final combat mission flown in BuNo. 135300. (USN)**

**VAQ-33's EA-1Fs were the last Spads deployed aboard a carrier. This "Electric Spad," spotted on the *Kennedy's* deck during late 1969, may have flown the last Navy Skyraider mission. (Franco Saya)**

and VA-122's Skyraider syllabus, and obviously this would quiet the volunteer contenders (including myself) in the bidding for the final flight. I passed the CO's desires along to Lcdr "Zip" Rausa, and he wrote the schedule to comply with the skipper's wishes.

Later I was informed of a message from the Chief of Naval Operations that ordered, that upon recovery, the Skyraider that flew the last mission was to be stricken below decks on the *Coral Sea*, and was not authorized to be flown except for a ferry flight or flights to Pensacola. There it was to be stricken from the Navy inventory and delivered to the curator of the Museum of Naval Aviation as a historic artifact."

Bureau Number 135300 was randomly assigned to Ted Hill because it happened to be spotted on the flight deck, fueled, armed, and assigned to the flight. Following a retirement ceremony for the Skyraider at NAS Lemoore in April, Lt. j.g. Hill was selected to fly the Spad to Pensacola. Hill received his Naval Aviators Wings on 21 December 1966, and on 5 February 1967 checked into VA-122 as a student in the last A-1 pilot class before it became an A-7 training squadron. On 9 June 1967 he reported to VA-25, the same day the "Fist of the Fleet" celebrated its 20th anniversary as a Spad squadron. Prior to the final A-1 attack mission Hill had flown 78 combat missions, many in support of ground troops along the DMZ.

The Navy Spad community is quick to point out that Hill's flight signaled the end of the *Attack* Spad. Three-plane detachments of EA-1Fs continued flying ECM missions in the combat zone until December 1968, when the last combat sorties were flown by EA-1Fs of VAQ-33 Detachment 11 aboard the *Intrepid.* The EA-1F earned the distinction of being the first and last Navy Spad type to fly combat in Southeast Asia.

VAW-13 (Det. 63) made its last combat cruise aboard *Kitty Hawk* from November 1967 to June 1968. The EA-1Fs of the "Zappers" flew alongside EKA-3B "Electric Whales," which filled the need for a new EW platform, having joined the squadron during early 1967. The last VAW-13 Spads were phased out in mid-1968. The EA-1E was first replaced by the E-1B "Tracer," until the arrival of the E-2A "Hawkeye." VAQ-33's Detachment 67 boasts the last carrier deployment of Spads, with the final launch of a Spad made 20 December 1969 from the deck of the *John F. Kennedy.*

Navy Spad pilots found that career opportunities were limited, since it was difficult to compete for promotions and commands within their warfare specialty. But the Spad had become legend, and many were content with having been "Spad Drivers." And most felt in their hearts that it could never be replaced.

# 5

# Defiance

"You've been had by a Spad, dad." It was said on the radio by a cocky, grinning Skyraider pilot to an unsuspecting jet jockey, whose "stovepipe" had just been pounced upon by a diving A-1; it was maliciously applied as a "zap" to jet aircraft, whose misfortune was to be loitering within view of Spad types; and it was the epitome of defiance of Spad drivers who refused to believe that any airplane, regardless of how new or how fast, was better than theirs. Navy officials frowned on such tactics, but took them in stride, fully aware that such rivalry was the substance of good pilots. Realistically, a duel between prop and jet aircraft was unthinkable, but it happened on rare occasion during previous wars. Spad pilots in Southeast Asia did not seek air-to-air combat, for the odds favored the nimble, jet-powered MiG-17 in the outcome. But Spad pilots, being a special breed of aviator, would defy those odds—twice.

The first Spad-MiG encounter occurred on 20 June 1965, when four A-1Hs (call sign "Canasta"), flown by Lt. Cmdr. Ed Greathouse, Lt j.g. James Lynne, Lt. Clint Johnson, and Lt. Charles Hartman, were launched from the *USS Midway* on a ResCAP mission over North Vietnam. The objective was an F-105 pilot who had been shot down in the vicinity of Dien Bien Phu. The squadron was beginning to feel the frustration and fatigue of being one month into its third period at sea. Operational tempo was at its peak, and VA-25 had suffered its first loss of the war, Spad pilot Lt j.g. Carl Doughtie, on a strike mission ten days earlier.

Lieutenant Commander Greathouse led the flight "feet dry" at about 10,000 feet, a relatively safe altitude from ground fire at that time, since SAMs had yet to become a major threat. Heading inbound, Greathouse signaled the flight to split into two sections, a half-mile apart, to form a "combat spread," which offered full coverage from attack. Lynne flew on Greathouse's wing, while Johnson and Hartman formed the other section. When the four were about 50 miles northwest of Thanh Hoa, 90 miles south of Hanoi, they received a radio message from the destroyer *USS Strauss* that their radar showed an unidentified target at their one o'clock position, 48 miles away. When it closed to 21 miles at the flight's six o'clock position, the ship lost radar contact. Greathouse describes what happened next:

> "All pilots were looking, and shortly I saw two MiG-17s, in right echelon at my nine o'clock position, slightly above and about two miles away. They were on the same course as our flight and appeared to be cruising at about 300 to 350 knots. They passed us until they got about five miles ahead, and I thought they missed seeing us, so we started a fairly gentle descent on the same heading, as we still had an important mission ahead. With our heavy, and drag inducing, load of fuel and ordnance, I didn't believe we could successfully engage them at that altitude. I didn't want to jettison it, as our primary mission still lay ahead, and I thought the MiGs had not seen us.

**Complete with 19 combat mission symbols and a MiG kill marking below the cockpit, "Papoose 9" awaits its fate at NAS Quonset Point in 1968. (Roger Besecker)**

I am convinced the MiGs were under radar control and had merely overshot us in their turn for a rear attack, and then missed seeing us as they went by, since we were lower and not silhouetted against the sky below a 14,000-foot overcast. I was sure they had radar control when they started a sharp left turn and continued it until they had us on their nose, at about our eleven o'clock position. I was just about to turn toward them when I saw the lead MiG fire two fairly large rockets at us, so I figured my best escape was straight ahead, as that gave us about 30 to 40-degree deflection and almost opposite courses. I then started a rapid descent and watched the rockets until I was sure they would pass to port and astern. The rockets either were pure ballistic or IR types, and did not have enough discrimination to get a lock-on.

As we headed down, with mountain ridges across our path and parallel ridges below, I did a quick 180-degree turn. We dove at about a 50-degree angle and leveled off sharply at about 500 feet in the river valley between two parallel ridge lines. I really hadn't expected the MiGs to follow us down all the way, but as I looked left to my other section, I saw one of the MiGs about 300 feet behind, firing his cannons. I glanced behind and saw the other MiG right behind my section, but not firing yet. We were now headed southeast down the river valley with ridges and mountains between 500 to 1,500 feet to either side of us. We couldn't break left due to the higher ridge on that side, and I wasn't sure we could reverse in the width of the valley. Since the ridge on the right was ending just ahead of us, I called for both sections to break right and got as low as I could, about 200 feet, and turned right around the end of the ridge, holding it as close to its face as I dared.

Just as I turned and started pulling about three Gs, two more rockets passed just below my section and hit the ground ahead of us. I continued the turn for 180 degrees, looked back, and saw that the MiG on our tail had pulled up. It was making a reversal at 1,500 to 2,000 feet and was coming back down on us from our seven-thirty position. Once again I broke hard through a small dip in the karst ridge, holding as tight a turn as I could and as low an altitude. I called the flight to drop their external loads, as our tanks held over 200 gallons of fuel, adding 3,000 pounds to the aircraft. In a steep turn of about two and a half Gs, we really started turning as they released. The MiG went outside the turn, climbed, and did another low altitude reversal. We had completed a 360, and once again had the same ridge on our right. I spotted my other section at about ten o'clock and 1,000 feet above, in a starboard turn toward me.

The MiG was coming down on me again from my seven o'clock position, so I broke right, repeating my ridge-hugging maneuver, holding the turn as steep as possible. This denied the MiG a sufficient firing lead and he started climbing, but by this time my second section was coming down on him and both fired long bursts at extremely short range. He passed right between them in nearly 90 degrees of bank at about 700 feet. The MiG's nose dropped and he continued the turn, hit the side of the hill, and exploded. I don't believe he saw the second section until the last moment, and he was taken completely by surprise as he pulled off my section. When he impacted I had completed my

**Euphoria reigned when *Midway's* crew turned out to greet Lcdr. Greathouse when he deplaned. Next to Greathouse (in cap) is VA-25's commander, Cdr. Harold Ettinger. (USN)**

full turn around the ridge, and looked across the valley to the north and saw the other MiG at my seven o'clock position, climbing out to the northwest and disappearing. I assume he either fired all his ammo or his guns jammed. He did not want to get into the action."

Although Johnson's main radio was knocked out from the cat shot, he knew what was happening when the fight started and followed the flight down. Their best hope was to get very low and try to outturn the MiGs. When Hartman dumped his stores, his Spad leaped upward and at that precise moment, cannon fire from a closing MiG filled the airspace he had just occupied. Greathouse adds:

"Our basic plan was to attempt to separate the opponents, then get into a position where we could get both sections on one of their planes, which worked perfectly in this case. I was surprised at the maneuverability of the MiGs and the pilot's skill in staying behind me at all times by his low altitude reversals, denying me time or latitude to reverse my turn and bring my guns to bear. The value of section integrity is illustrated in this action. Both wingmen did a superb job of holding their positions on their leaders, despite the radical, low-level maneuvering."

The *Strauss* reported that other bogeys were inbound to the Spads' position. They joined up low-level over the Gulf for the flight back to *Midway.* The setting sun meant a night landing aboard the carrier, but the euphoric Spad pilots did not experience the usual anxiety of the tricky recovery. Aboard *Midway*, the Spad's radio report was misunderstood as one of the Spads having been downed. Greathouse finally convinced the carrier that they were fine, but North Vietnam was minus a MiG.

Just three days earlier, F-4B Phantoms of VF-21, also aboard *Midway*, had scored the first two MiG kills of the conflict. The Spad pilots and F-4 crews were presented awards in a full dress ceremony on *Midway's* flight deck on 23 June. Credited with half a MiG kill each, Johnson and Hartman were awarded Silver Stars, while Greathouse and Lynne received Distinguished Flying Crosses. In the true tradition of inter-service rivalry, the commander of the Seventh Fleet reveled in presenting the awards and beating the Air Force. Bolstering that rivalry was the following message sent to the *USS Midway* from the commander of Task Unit 70.2.5:

"For CO ATKRON 25, current color scheme at 5th AF HQ: envious green on USAF faces (after MiG kills by F-4) has been replaced by white (astonishment) and red (impotent rage) at the news of the superb performance by your pilots in destroying another MiG."

The news spread quickly. South Vietnam's Premier Ky, himself an A-1 pilot, when he heard of the shootdown, recognized Greathouse's name as a Skyraider RAG instructor. Ky insisted that the Spad pilots be his guest in Saigon, where they were awarded Air Gallantry Medals, Vietnamese pilot's wings, and honorary commissions in the South Vietnamese Air Force.

After the MiG incident, the four A-1s were inspected and placed in *up* status. BuNo. 137523 (Hartman, "Canasta 73"), just four days later, lost power on approach to the carrier and was ditched. Bureau Numbers 139768 (Johnson, "Canasta 77") and 134609 (Greathouse, "Canasta 79") completed the cruise. BuNo. 135300 (Lynne, "Canasta 71") not only completed the cruise and was with VA-25 for the last Spad cruise, but is now on display in the National Museum of Naval Aviation at NAS Pensacola, Florida.

Seldom emphasized about the second Skyraider-MiG encounter of the war is the probability that three MiGs were destroyed by Spads. By late 1966, North Vietnam's air defenses had intensified to the extent that losses during air strikes were inevitable. On 6 October, three massive strike groups would run the deadly gauntlet into the North, with the predictable outcome. ResCAP coverage included four VA-176 Skyraiders (call sign "Papoose") launched from the *USS Intrepid*, led by Lt. Cmdr. C. Leo Cook, with Lt j.g. James Wiley on his wing; Lt. Peter Russell and Lt j.g. W. Thomas Patton comprised the second section.

Orbiting with a helicopter off the coast southeast of Hanoi, the Spad pilots were keenly aware that if strike aircraft went down, their quickest, most direct route would be over anti-aircraft and SAM sites. Just when it seemed all strike aircraft had survived the mission, a Navy Phantom was reported downed by ground fire, and its two-man crew had ejected 20 miles from Hanoi. Looking at their maps, dotted with enemy gun sites, the ResCAP pilots were faced with the unsettling prospect of running the deadly gauntlet between their position and the downed crew. Cook made the decision to go in, and he and Wiley headed inland. Russell stayed with the helicopter, while Patton covered the rear to deal with ground fire. Almost immediately after going *feet dry* Russell, Patton, and the chopper were met with a barrage of anti-aircraft fire. Hoping to keep the enemy gunners' heads down, Patton made several firing passes, but the flak never slackened. The helo took some hits, but was able to continue.

Suddenly the firing stopped. It was the eerie calm before the storm, for moments later, Cook radioed that four MiGs were in the area. When Russell sent an urgent request for air cover to the radar-monitoring destroyer, the Spad pilots received the unsettling news

**In language understood universally by fighter pilots, Hartman and Greathouse describe their MiG shoot for Radm. Bringle (seated), commander of TF 77, and Cdr. Weiland (flag staff). Johnson and Lynne are at right. (USN)**

that all the covering jets were low on fuel and a tanker aircraft could not be located.

Wiley saw them first—"I've got three MiGs making turns on me!" to which Russell calmly replied, "Right Pud...we're on our way with two Spads and a helo," as though he were confident that would turn the tide of overwhelming odds. It was do or die—the fight was on. In thick clouds over the mountainous region, the MiGs got between Cook and Wiley. One engaged Cook, while the other had Wiley trapped in a deadly wheel pattern. He stayed alive by hugging the ground. Wiley broke left to avoid a mountain peak and a pursuing MiG broke right, then sharply left, giving Wiley a shot. His cannon fire tore off the MiG's wing tip and produced a vapor trail from the crippled jet. Although no one saw the MiG crash, Wiley was credited with a *probable* kill.

Russell and Patton got into the melee, spotted two MiGs, and maneuvered for a head-on attack. Russell fired all four cannons at the belly of one, which was not seen again, earning him a *possible* kill.

Patton, still at 9,000 feet, spotted a MiG headed in his direction, skimming the treetops. When Patton estimated the MiG to be within range, he rolled his Spad into a split-S and dove straight down, exceeding 350 knots, and pulled out of the dive behind and to the right of the MiG. A short cannon burst missed, but got the attention of the MiG pilot, who made the fatal mistake of executing a reverse turn. His airspeed bled off in a climbing attitude, while Patton had plenty of speed, placing him on the MiG's tail. Having the advantage, Patton waited for the MiG to fill his gunsight and, in what he describes as the most exciting moment of his life, poured cannon fire into the MiG's tailpipe. With both aircraft at a 75-degree upward angle, he closed to within 100 feet (close enough to watch the MiG's tail disintegrate) when all four guns quit—two were empty and two, he learned later, had jammed.

Dissatisfied that the MiG had not exploded, Patton fired three of his Zuni rockets, which narrowly missed. As the MiG flipped over and fell toward the clouds, Patton fired his last rocket. Following *his* MiG down, he broke out of the clouds to see the Mig pilot eject. The helicopter crew witnessed the duel and Cook verified the crash site, ensuring Patton a MiG kill.

Patton and Russell escorted the helo to the coast while Cook and Wiley resumed the search for the downed Phantom crew, who were never found. Thankfully, their egress route was cloud-covered. When the exuberant quartet reached the carrier, they performed an echelon formation flyby before landing. For his aerial victory in combat Patton was awarded the Silver Star, while Cook, Wiley, and Russell received Distinguished Flying Crosses. Russell returned for a second combat tour flying OV-10 "Broncos" with VAL-4 "Black Ponies." On 25 May 1969, a single bullet killed Russell as he dove on an enemy position while supporting Navy patrol boats. He had encountered his "Golden BB," the term pilots used for the round with their name on it.

The Skyraiders' victories had various effects on different fronts. Premier Ky told VA-25's pilots that their MiG kill was a tremendous morale booster in the VNAF A-1 squadrons. Conversely, the North Vietnamese significantly minimized MiG flights to increase pilot training. The Spad pilots relished in the belief that they embarrassed the North into withdrawing their MiGs. Although the Skyraider was known for its ability to carry a tremendous load, it was never lost on Spad pilots that it was also designed to defend itself from air attack. That belief is evident in the following anecdote from Navy Spad pilot William "Speed" Ritzmann:

> "In January 1968, just before the Tet Offensive, Lt j.g. Dunn and I were on an afternoon coastal reconnaissance flight. We were assigned to reconnoiter the islands from Haiphong east to the Cam Pha coal mine loading pier near the Chinese border. We had just started our last westbound leg from the Cam Pha area at about 6,500 feet when we heard a warning that two MiGs were *feet wet* southeast of Haiphong and headed southeast toward Yankee Station. This essentially put them between the *Coral Sea* and Joe and I. Further information led us to believe

**The A-1H flown by Lt. Clint Johnson during his MiG kill. His MiG kill silhouette appears immediately aft of the glare shield below the windscreen. (NMNA)**

that the Combat Air Patrol (CAP) over Yankee Station had been vectored to intercept the two MiGs. The MiGs started a wide sweeping left turn in our direction, which put the CAP in a chase position 50 to 60 miles behind the MiGs. Joe and I prepared ourselves for what I expected to be the third encounter. I suspect that the North Vietnamese air controllers saw the pursuit by the CAP and vectored the MiGs back toward Haiphong and, ultimately, their base near Hanoi. We saw the two bogeys high above and south of us as they were heading northwest.

When we arrived back at *Coral Sea*, I sought out Lcdr. Dick Gralow, who was the flight leader of the VF-151 F-4s that were on the CAP. I asked him why he did not take up a vector that would cut the MiGs off from their home field. His reply was, 'We were coming to protect you.' Severely rebuffed by his good natured jibe, I replied, 'Since the box score is Spads four - MiGs nothing, I thought we were capable of taking care of ourselves, and you may have missed out on your own opportunity.'"

In the years following their victories, the Spad pilots, when asked what they were flying when they brought down a MiG, enjoyed saying "Skyraider." The reactions were always the same. Not so fortunate were three Skyraider pilots lost to MiGs during the war. Ironically, the only Navy Spad pilot shot down by a MiG was from VA-25, tempering the squadron's earlier triumph.

The Spad's slow speed, the untenable SAM and flak-filled skies over Southeast Asia, plus the arrival of the A-6 Intruder may have brought the A-1's career as an attack bomber to a close, but not before it added MiG kills to its long list of achievements.

**MiG killer Lt. j.g. Patton poses with one of his squadron's Spads, which wears the kill marking on the cockpit armor plate. (USN)**

# 6

# Perfect Fit

U.S. Air Force interest in the Skyraider dates back to 1949 when Air Force planners were searching for close support aircraft. It wasn't until counterinsurgency became a catchword, and when the South Vietnamese acquired A-1s from the U.S. Navy in 1960, that Air Force officials considered the Spad for the limited warfare role. Having studied the Skyraider and agreed that it might have a place in the Air Force, USAF Headquarters staff on 12 June 1962 ordered evaluation of the A-1E.

To evaluate the A-1E, two Special Air Warfare Center (SAWC) pilots and seven ground crewmen received training at NAS Jacksonville, Florida. Both pilots completed 16 hours of ground school and 10 hours of solo flight in aircraft check-out and acrobatics, as well as instrument, formation, and gunnery training. Ground crewmen received one week of aircraft systems training and two weeks of flight line training. Upon completion in August 1962, two A-1Es—Bureau Numbers 132417 and 132439—were flown to Hurlburt Field, Eglin Air Force Base (AFB), Florida, for further evaluation by the 1st Combat Applications Group of the SAWC.

Until 12 November 1962 the Spads were put through their paces to test operational capabilities and limitations, as well as maintenance and logistical support requirements. Navigation, cargo transport, and combat day and night attack missions up to maximum gross weight were flown, along with gunnery sorties to test dive, glide, and skip bombing, and rocketry and strafing. A pair of Navy AD-5Ns was flown in to enable the pilots to test the capability of the APS-31B radar.

Since part of the evaluation's purpose was to determine changes needed in the A-1E if adopted for Air Force use, the SAWC came up with a number of interesting observations and recommendations. For example: a great deal of attention was given to modification of the A-1E's speed brake well by installing doors through which eight paratroopers could be dropped. One mission profile assumed that, carrying a 300-gallon external fuel tank, an A-1E could carry the paratroopers and 3,000 pounds of ordnance a distance of 250 nautical miles, and then loiter for three hours to provide fire support.

It was also determined the A-1E could carry 2,000 pounds of leaflets or supplies to be released through the speed brake well. Mounting cameras in the well was also considered for day reconnaissance. The modification itself involved lowering the rear half of the cargo compartment, relocating the speed brake actuating cylinder, repositioning radios, strengthening the fuselage, and installing inward-opening doors. Although the mods would be simpler if the speed brake were removed, it was to be retained as a decelerating device. No Skyraiders are known to have undergone the speed brake well modifications.

The Air Force found the APS-31B radar useful for ground mapping for navigation, but it was deemed unsuitable for detecting

**This view of Da Nang Air Base in 1966 evokes an aura of wars past, illustrating the contribution of prop-driven aircraft during the war in Southeast Asia. In the foreground is A-1E no. 132668 sharing the ramp with an HU-16B Albatross, a C-47 and an EC-121. Parked in the distance, and completing takeoff, are C-123 Providers. (Tom Hansen)**

**Still wearing its Navy color scheme, an A-1E is displayed with full ordnance racks at Hurlburt Field shortly after the type entered the Air Force inventory. (USAF)**

aircraft flying at low altitude—concern about communist aircraft slipping over the Laotian mountains at night to supply troops was addressed by Navy EA-1Fs. Air Force evaluators found an abnormally high failure rate for the ARC-27 UHF radio. Similarly, radio problems would plague the A-1 throughout its Air Force career. Also noted was the number of washings required to clean the aircraft of oil and exhaust.

Modifications recommended for Air Force use included replacing the R-3350-26A powerplant with the more reliable –26WD. Personnel at the San Antonio Air Material Area facility informed the SAWC that 600 R-3350-26A engines were surplus to Navy requirements and that they could easily be converted to –26WDs. An additional 129 –26WD engines reportedly were in the Navy inventory, ready for issue to the Fleet.

Other changes proposed included replacing the N-6 gun camera with the improved N-9, installing a parking brake, and replacing the hard rubber tail wheel with a low pressure wheel.

The A-1E's limitations on soft runways due to the small solid tail wheel were discussed in July 1964 between Douglas officials and the Limited War Directorate. Douglas offered that a pneumatic tail wheel was feasible, but it had not been developed and tested. The Air Force was prepared to enlarge the tail wheel opening to accommodate a tail wheel already in use. Although larger and lower pressure main gear tires were also suggested, only the pneumatic tail wheel later appeared, which allowed operations at fields with surfaces substandard to the common pierced steel planking (PSP).

Dual controls in some A-1Es were considered a must for check-out flights. Spads without dual controls acquired by the Air Force early in the program provided anxious moments for the Instructor Pilots (IPs). James Elliot, one of the first four USAF A-1 IPs, reports:

> "I and Quint Evans, John Patter, and Bob Walker were checked out in the A-1 by Iwo Kimes, the A-1 project officer, in the spring of '63. The only thing available to the IP in the right seat was an intercom button on the floor. This made for interesting initial check-outs, especially with studs with little or no tail wheel or torque experience."

Since the Air Force insisted upon landing and taxi lights, a landing/taxi light was added to the A-1E's left landing gear strut fairing, also called the "Knee." Some A-1Gs had a light installed

**Wearing VNAF insignia, a U.S. Air Force Skyraider makes an ordnance drop in South Vietnam. (USAF)**

**A pair of *Hobo* A-1Es takes the war to the enemy in the form of fire bombs. Number 133855 was shot down in May 1967. (USAF)**

**Maj. C.B. Holler of the 1st SOS was rescued after being shot down in South Vietnam flying this A-1E in 1967. (Ed Lemp)**

**Little remains of this Spad that crashed on takeoff during a mortar attack at Bien Hoa AB on 1 November 1964. The Spad caught fire and exploded after the pilot escaped. (Gene Traczyk)**

on both knees. Anti-collision lights were later added to the vertical stabilizers of many USAF A-1E/Gs. The Navy had already installed the light on most A-1H/Js. Additional radios for close support of ground troops were recommended, and slight changes in outboard ordnance racks and armament circuitry were deemed important to increase the types of ordnance that could be carried.

Although A-1s were designed to withstand 7 Gs, several instances of cracks in wing spar caps were discovered after the catastrophic loss of an A-1E (132661) and its two pilots at Hurlburt on 22 October 1968. The aircraft's left wing separated during its fifteenth weapons pass. The tragedy prompted various degrees of limitations, which were based on airframe hours and condition of the wing spar. A review of Spad airframe hours revealed that 179 A-1s in frontline service with the TAC, VNAF, and USAF units in Southeast Asia were in a high-risk category. The commander of the Air Force Logistics Command recommended the A-1 be placed out of service. However, he was overruled by the Air Force Chief of Staff, who approved a repair program. A 3 G restriction was placed on A-1s with more than 3,500 hours. The restriction was lifted after the installation of new spar caps, wing straps, and new wing fold fittings. On 9 April 1969 the Air Force awarded McDonnell Douglas Corporation's Tulsa Division a contract for wing structural improvement of two A-1s from the Sacramento Air Material Area, McClellan AFB, California. A follow-on contract for the modification of 34 aircraft was awarded on 2 October. The procedure was later included during scheduled maintenance at the IRAN facility at Thailand's Don Muang Airport. The modification program continued at China Air Lines, Taipei, Taiwan, until 30 July 1974, when all affected VNAF A-1s had been modified.

One crew chief was considered adequate to perform flight line maintenance, and it was certain that pilot transition could be accomplished in 18 hours. A pilot would be combat ready after an

**An A-1H flies along the Mekong River after having taken off from NKP. Spad pilots knew that once they left the relative safety of Thailand, danger awaited them across the river in Laos. (USAF)**

**Spad pilots agree that you had to watch the airplane carefully to avoid ground looping it. Since the A-1 was directionally unstable, fast but small rudder inputs were necessary to keep it headed straight down the runway. (Martin P. Jester)**

**Female North Vietnamese soldiers retrieve parts of a USAF A-1E, believed to be no. 132408, shot down over North Vietnam in June 1967. (Istvan Toperczer)**

additional 25 to 30 hours of day and night gunnery and ordnance training missions. The A-1E's conventional landing gear and torque were considered the only difficulties that would require additional pilot technique. As one pilot put it:

> "Us young guys in the Air Force never had any prop time except the Cessna T-41 in pilot training. But the transition to the A-1 was really pretty easy. Flying it was a piece of cake—if you could just figure out how to taxi!"

It was concluded that the A-1E was well suited to COIN warfare because of its simplicity of operation, versatility, maintainability, and minimum runway requirements at maximum gross weight. Its ability to not only carry 8,000 pounds of ordnance, but individual stores up to 2,000 pounds in the Air Force arsenal, plus its long loiter time, appealed to tactical planners. The Spad was a *perfect fit* for the Air Force and for the Air Commandos who would take it into battle.

The SAWC's final report, dated April 1963, recommended the A-1E be modified and accepted into the SAWC inventory. The report also indicated that 178 A-1E, AD-5N, and AD-5W aircraft were in storage at Litchfield Park, Arizona, all of which could be converted to the A-1E basic attack mission. When the Air Force decision became official, the Navy submitted to the Sacramento Air Logistics Center (SALC) in December 1963 a list of flyable A-1Es and A-1Gs at Litchfield Park, and at various naval air stations. A selection team inspected and selected the aircraft, along with nearly 100 non-flyable A-1s stored at NAS Memphis, which would serve as a source of spare parts. A combined total of 578 Skyraiders would be transferred from the Navy to the USAF and VNAF from 1960 to 1972. They would undergo modifications extending their careers longer than Ed Heinemann and his design team could ever have imagined.

**Capt. Ed Leonard's A-1H, no. 139678, after he crash-landed 24 miles from Udorn RTAFB with battle damage on 17 March 1968. (USAF)**

**Maj. Kyron Hall of the 20th SOS was flying the CH-3 that recovered Ed Leonard's Spad. Hall said it was a real "grunt" to do the lift. He reduced his fuel load to handle the A-1, but flew only 30 knots to Udorn since the Spad vibrated. (Kyron Hall collection)**

VNAF 518th Squadron advisor Capt. Ron Ohnesorge poses with a Spad flown by one of his charges who lost control during landing at Binh Thuy. (Herbert C. Meyr, Jr.)

An Army CH-54 Skycrane prepares to lift a damaged Spad from an air base periphery. (USAF)

The SALC worked with the Special Air Warfare Center at Hurlburt to ease the Spad's transition into the Air Force inventory. For reporting and standardization, the Air Force assigned the prefix "52-" (the production year of AD-6s) to the Navy bureau numbers. Twenty A-1Es acquired by the Air Force were modified to a near standard A-1E configuration and designated A-1E-5s; these had no control stick for the right seat. Upgrades were completed at Douglas, Litchfield Park, NAS Alameda on the West Coast, and NAS Quonset Point on the East Coast. The Spads were then either transported by Navy ship to the Philippines or were flown to Hurlburt, where they joined other rugged and simple vintage aircraft destined for the burgeoning war in Southeast Asia.

Morgan C. Pummill was among the first batch of USAF pilots to receive Skyraider training. The following are his recollections:

> "I went to Hurlburt to be an A-26 pilot. The date was 1 January 1964. After three flights in the A-26 there was an accident involving a wing failure and the resulting termination of that program.
>
> After one week of ground school, I took my first flight in the A-1E on 18 February '64. The 1st Air Commando Wing really made us bust our backsides to complete the program well trained and on time. We completed our flight training before the 20 April deadline and, after a short stay, we were on our way to Southeast Asia.
>
> Bob Campbell and I were the first to arrive at Clark Air Base, Philippine Islands, in May for further assignment to the 1st ACS, 34th Tac Group, Bien Hoa Air Base, South Vietnam. I went to Subic Bay and processed the first six A-1Es, which were arriving by carrier. The first six aircraft were beautiful. They came direct from the Douglas IRAN facility, Palmdale, California, and they were like new. There were 20 excellent enlisted mechanics at Subic Bay to do the dirty work, plus a tech rep from Douglas with carte blanche priority to get anything we needed in parts, and answers to questions.
>
> I was tasked with flying each aircraft and putting five hours on each before launching them for Vietnam. Needless to say, once the test flight was accomplished and released I went to test the next aircraft. None of the other pilots had arrived yet. Fortunately an old friend of mine, Navy Lcdr Johnson, came to the rescue. As commanding officer of the EA-1F 'Queenie' Detachment, he and his

Spads that belly-landed were commonly placed on barrels pending repair. This A-1E bellied in at Da Nang AB in 1967. (Tom Hansen)

**This plaque was given to USAF Spad pilot Tom Stump after he made a forced landing at Udorn RTAFB on 30 March 1970. Tom explains, "I took off in a driving rain for a night mission and lost my engine right after getting airborne. The plane settled back to the ground, so I dropped the hook since I had no chance to stop. I caught the last barrier. It saved my life I'm sure, since skidding across the ground with napalm and funny bombs would not have worked too well."**

**"Fat face" and "skinny face" Spads of the 602nd SOS being prepared for a mission at NKP. (Neal Schneider)**

men were very helpful in processing the A-1s, and he provided some of his pilots to help in putting time in the aircraft. They almost fought for the chance.

By the time the A-1s were ready to go, all the pilots of class *Express 1* had arrived. That made seven A-1E qualified pilots, plus Ed Blake and a navigator. Lt. Col. John M. Porter led the flight of six—three elements of two. Crossing landfall into Vietnam we made a flyby over Tan Son Nhut, then over Bien Hoa. After landing we were mobbed by photographers, but alas, all the pictures showed us with a 'welcome beer,' and the film was destroyed since they were not appropriate for public relations."

The T-28s the A-1s replaced had operated from Soc Trang, South Vietnam, which had a 3,000-foot runway. The need for more runway to get a fully loaded A-1 airborne prompted the switch to Bien Hoa.

Aircraft and personnel were attached to the 34th Tactical Group, which teamed with the Navy's VA-152 Detachment Zulu to train VNAF pilots. Operations with the original six A-1Es were delayed two days pending replacement of the aircrafts' USAF insignia with that of the VNAF. Since political pressure banned U.S. military advisors in South Vietnam from flying solo missions (which would indicate direct U.S. involvement), the A-1E's side-by-side cockpit conveniently accommodated the requisite VNAF observer or pilot. To complete the deception, U.S. aircraft were also required to wear VNAF insignia. Unsurprisingly, Air Commando pilots were displeased with the restrictive arrangement, and the watching world was not fooled for long.

Meanwhile, back at Hurlburt, the A-1 training syllabus was under way. From 1964 to 1973 the sprawling Air Commando facility would host 110 A-1 classes, with the number of students per class ranging from two to nearly thirty pilots. A total of 934 pilots

**Since the canopy of this fat face Spad was not blown, it may have been destroyed during a fire that occurred on the ground. (USAF)**

**Air Force Skyraiders that arrived in the Philippines by ship were protected from salt water with "spraylat," a process called "cocooning." (USAF)**

**Up close with "Blood, Sweat & Tears" and its young pilot of the 1st SOS. The A-1H, no. 139608, has a replacement cowl ring and cowl flaps. (USAF)**

**A-1E no. 133873 seen with battle damage. It crashed in March 1966 and was recovered and repaired, only to be shot down one year later. (USAF)**

entered the USAF's A-1 training pipeline. Until late 1967 classes were called "Express," with those thereafter designated by year and numbered sequence.

Express classes were filled with pilots culled from various Air Force commands. Contrary to popular belief, not all Air Commando pilots were volunteers, as Ken Beaird explains:

"I and several others were T-37/T-38 IPs in the Air Training Command (ATC) in 1965. Most of us who received orders to RVN (Republic of Vietnam) had not volunteered. In fact, I had no idea what an A-1E was until I got my orders, and looked in *Janes* to find out what I was getting in to. The luck of the draw."

Many of the older students started in T-34s and T-28s, and even in the T-6. Others came from the ATC, where they were jet instructors, while some flew jets in the Air Defense Command (ADC). This accounted for high ranks in the Spad community. It was ADC policy to give pilots at least their second choice of aircraft when they received orders for Southeast Asia. Frank Twait adds:

"All of us old timers had prop time in flight school, but the youngsters came out of T-37/T-38 programs. Every one of them who came to Spads had graduated in the top of his flying training class, and it showed when they got into combat."

According to Charlie Holder;

"In the 1969-1970 time frame, my experience was fairly typical. I was a T-38 First Assignment Instructor Pilot (FAIP) in Air Training Command. In fact, I graduated from pilot training, went to instructor training at Randolph, then returned to the squadron and flight I had graduated from at Moody AFB. All I did was switch sides of the table I had been at as a student pilot. After about three years gaining experience there, I received assignment to A-1s at Hurlburt with a follow-on to NKP. In those days of the 'Momyer Air Force,' I had never even heard of the prop-driven Skyraider. I had to ask my flight commander what the heck it was! As I recall, my Hurlburt training class consisted of about five to six 'Butter Bar' recent pilot training graduates, five to six of us FAIPs, and seven to eight 'Old Heads' who had already had at least one assignment elsewhere in the *real* Air Force. All in all, a good mix."

A few USAF A-1 pilots did not go through training at Hurlburt, but instead were checked out in theater by Navy Spad pilots. Some transitioned from vintage O-1s, T-28s, and A-26s. At Kadena Air Base, Okinawa, the Air Force maintained the Pacific Air Forces Standardization Evaluation Group, which had a flight examiner for each aircraft type in the theater. Spad flight examiners seldom gave flight exams, instead spending more time documenting combat tactics and techniques, as well as augmenting the pilot force in Southeast Asia.

Although stateside Skyraider training could not compare with the drama and stress of combat, it had its noteworthy episodes. Tom Schornak offers this memorable account, which praises Heinie Aderholt, then the wing commander at Hurlburt and a legend among Air Commandos. Tom titles this:

**Tapestry, which hung in "Ye Olde Sandy Box," the enlisted mens' club of the 602nd SOS at NKP, in 1970. (Ernest L. Connors)**

**Wearing the composite tail code of the 6th SOS, this A-1H, no. 134502, stands alert at Pleiku in October 1969. The sign near its prop states, "Alert A/C cocked." Miniguns occupy both inboard pylons, while CBU and napalm the rest. The 6th SOS usually supported special operations ground troops. (S. Pargeter)**

**A fat face Spad rolls off the target after dropping *Willie Pete* bombs. (Douglas)**

How Heinie Aderholt saved my butt from the firing squad.

"By the fall of 1964 I had already flown a T-28 tour in South Vietnam, received jump wings at Fort Benning, was a forward air controller, and had just returned from South America after strapping guns on helicopters in the counterinsurgency effort hunting down some of Castro's protégés. Vietnam was spinning up as I began my check-out in the A-1E, and I, like most Spad pilots, was ready to tangle with most anything...well, almost!

I had only flown my first ride in the A-1E when there was a hurricane evacuation from Hurlburt. To dodge the incoming weather, Mick Jones, my instructor, and I flew one of the several A-1Es to McConnell AFB, Kansas, where I was to continue my checkout.

That particular Sunday morning was great—no wind, sunshine, 12,000 feet of concrete runway, and even Mick said that I was making some really super-hot landings for a new guy checking out in the A-1E. Mick had tuned in the local Wichita country western music station on the low frequency radio and was tapping his finger on the instrument panel to the music. What could go wrong? I felt like Chuck Yeager after he broke the sound barrier. My next landing was the most super-hot landing of my career. I landed that damn A-1E gear up! Even now, almost 40 years later, it is not fun telling this story.

My first indication that this landing was going to be different was in the flare; we seemed low, very low...and getting lower! All at once that giant four-bladed prop began to bite into the concrete, throwing chunks of concrete, sparks, and clouds of dust in every direction. It was scary as hell as the big bird settled in and slid down the runway, slowly, ever so slowly, grinding to a halt. The visibility was reduced to inches in dust and smoke. Inside the cockpit, after we slid to a halt, it was as quiet as standing in the middle of an Ohio cornfield. Mick and I looked at each other in disbelief! He began to turn off switches. I thought this was a good idea, so I helped him. The control tower saw the conflagration of sparks and smoke and asked if we needed assistance. Mick coolly advised that we would not be able to taxi off the active runway. Before exiting the wounded bird, we retuned the low frequency radio from country music back to the outer marker frequency.

The next day we flew back to Hurlburt in someone else's A-1E. There was absolutely no doubt in my mind I would not be considered poster boy for Wing Safety that year. As a matter of fact, I really thought I would be grounded and sent to Thule, Greenland, as snow removal officer. Or perhaps summoned to Wing Headquarters, tied to the flagpole, and then shot by a firing squad. For me, I was truly at the bottom of the birdcage...I was at the end of my string...even my cat ignored me.

**Vortices stream from the wing tips of an A-1E as it pulls out of a napalm drop. (Douglas)**

A 6th SOS A-1H in the revetment area at Pleiku in 1967. The 20mm ammo loading access doors in its wings were outlined in black. (John Christianson)

The ordnance of this A-1G, and others in the flight, were appropriately decorated for an Easter Sunday raid from Bien Hoa in 1964. (Gene Traczyk)

That night I got a call from Wing Commander Aderholt. I hardly knew the guy. His late night phone call confirmed my worst fears—I would be shot by a firing squad the next day. In fact, it was none of that! Heinie asked me to go fishing with him the next morning. That next day, never once did he mention the dreaded subject. As we departed from the dock, his only words were, 'Oh Tom, by the way, you are on the flying schedule tomorrow morning.'

So after all these years it is about time to say 'Thanks a bunch' to General Aderholt for a level of thoughtfulness and caring that went far beyond anything that could be expected during the darkest hour and most embarrassing moment of my career.

The sequel to the belly landing:

*The A-1E*—they put air bags under the wings of the tough old girl, lowered the gear, replaced the engine and prop, then flew it back to Hurlburt, where the sheet metal guys got out their ballpeen hammers and pinking shears and pounded out the aluminum belly and wing tips to fly once again.

*My pet cat*—the following month I saw him fail miserably attempting to make an extremely easy bird kill. We soon became friends after that.

*Mick Jones*—I have always admired him for never, never once losing his cool or good naturedness during the

The A-1H named "Big White Horse" is framed by the gunsight of another 1st SOS Spad during a Sandy orbit of Operation Barrel Roll in 1969. (Richard S. Drury)

The jagged mountainous terrain beneath these 1st SOS Spads over northern Laos was called "karst," and had a humbling effect on pilots. (Richard S. Drury)

**Early in the war the 1st ACS called itself the "Raiders," which was represented by the name in red below a skull and crossbones on the tail. In keeping with the popular James Bond theme, 007 (no. 135007) wears the name "Miss Pussy Galore" in small red letters below the number 4 on the cowl. The fetching character was from the 1964 film "Goldfinger." (Raymond A. Young III)**

whole episode. He is one of the last classic, true stick and rudder guys. Maybe it was not country music he was listening to...it could have been semi-classical Irish folk songs.

*Me*—I went on to become a bonafide A-1 instructor pilot. My very first student was a guy named 'Jump' Meyer. We all know how Bernie Fisher got the Medal of Honor by swooping down and rescuing him from the North Vietnamese-held A Shau Valley airstrip after Jump made his own spectacular belly landing under difficult combat conditions.

*General Heinie Aderholt*—on that fishing trip, he followed the example of another extraordinary person in history, 'He went fishing for men instead of fish.' He won over a devoted friend that would follow him Anywhere-Anytime-Anyplace. No doubt the next day he did the same thing for another Air Commando or his family."

Tom adds:

"I never, never want to hear the sound of an R-3350 chewing up concrete again!"

Some incidents that occurred during Spad training at Hurlburt exemplified the Air Commando spirit, which eventually had to be harnessed...at least temporarily. For example: shortly after it was delivered, one of the first two A-1Es (BuNo. 132417) crash-landed after horseplay with a U-10 *Helio Courier*, whose crew lobbed rolls of toilet paper at the A-1E. The paper fouled the Spad's engine and the pilot brought it down. It was repaired and placed back in service.

Far more serious was an aerial incident on 24 June 1965 that caused the death of four A-1 pilots. It was believed to have resulted from the euphoria in the wake of a MiG kill by an A-1 a few days earlier in Vietnam. Near Seva, Florida, a pair of F-100s jumped two A-1Es, which lost sight of each other in the ensuing dogfight and crashed head-on. The loss of four pilots, three of them instructors, and two Spads worsened the unit's pilot and aircraft shortage. Thereafter, flying activities were severely scrutinized.

A total of 14 pilots perished while in the Tactical Air Command's A-1 Southeast Asia pipeline training program, and 12 A-1Es and 1 A-1H were destroyed.

**A-1E no. 132640 is towed after it ran off Bien Hoa's runway in 1964. The Spad was later shot down. (Martin P. Jester)**

Par for the Air Force was the number of times the A-1 training unit and its parent organization were reorganized and their designations changed. In reviving the Air Commando legacy at Hurlburt Field, in April 1961 the Tactical Air Command (TAC) activated the 4400th Combat Crew Training Squadron (CCTS). Less than a year later it was expanded to Group level, finally becoming the 1st Air Commando Wing (ACW) on 1 June 1963. Due to the large number of aircraft and the training tempo, operations were split into two wings—the 1st ACW went to England AFB, Louisiana, and the 4410th CCTW ran the Hurlburt programs—including the A-1—beginning in January 1966. The 1st ACW was redesignated the 1st Special Operations Wing (SOW) during July 1968 and returned to Hurlburt one year later.

Similar changes took place at the squadron level. The Skyraider training squadron was initially the 603rd ACS until a brief period in 1966 when it was known as the 603rd Fighter Squadron. It then became the 4409th CCTS, which changed to 4407th CCTS in December 1967. In 1972 Skyraiders at Hurlburt fell under both the 4407th CCTS and the 317th Special Operations Squadron (SOS), both of which were inactivated on 30 April 1973.

When the first two USAF A-1Es arrived at Hurlburt, each was assigned two crew chiefs, who were members of the 1st Air Material Squadron (AMS) at Hurlburt's Field No. 9. The 1st AMS became the 850th Organizational Maintenance Squadron (OMS) under the 1st ACW, and later 1st SOW. The 850th performed all A-1 maintenance and was kept busy, as the training squadron worked up to five flights per day.

The Air Force organizational chart for Southeast Asia operations was headed by the 7th and 13th Air Forces (AF), which formed a combined headquarters in Pacific Air Forces (PACAF). The 7th AF had cut its teeth during World War II. It had the distinction of being the first American air force organized outside the continental U.S., and it began the air war against Japan in the Battle of Midway. The 7th AF was reactivated on 1 April 1966 to replace the 2nd Air Division (AD), which had formed an Advanced Echelon (ADVON) in Vietnam during November 1961. The 7th and 13th Air Forces, called "Blue Chip," issued a series of orders, called "Theater Rules," designed as safety measures to prevent "unnecessary aircraft losses." These were not to be confused with "Rules of Engagement," which were political restraints that prevented defeat of the enemy. The term "7/13th minimums" referred to the rule for tactical aircraft to stay, and release all ordnance, above 4,500 feet, unless involved in SAR or "Troops-In-Contact" (TIC) situations. This kept aircraft out of effective range of small arms and *light* anti-aircraft fire (12.7mm and .50 cal.), and minimized exposure to heavier AAA and SA-7 missiles. Evidence of going below the minimums—usually small arms holes or mud on the aircraft—could result in disciplinary action. Spads were overwhelmingly the exception to the rules. Many missions they flew, such as "gravel" missions over the Ho Chi Minh Trail, SOG support, and TIC were so low that enemy guns often could not be depressed enough to shoot at them. Spad pilots quickly learned to identify the types of ground fire headed their way: 37mm appeared as red balls, they were fired in clips of seven, and they were slow; 23mm rounds had a yellow-white color and were much faster. ZPU fire was even faster.

The first batch of Spad pilots at Bien Hoa in 1964 used the cover story of training VNAF pilots to fly combat missions, although training of Vietnamese pilots also occurred. Vietnamese observers, who spoke little or no English, were carried on combat missions to support the cover story in the event the aircraft crashed. The charade became frustrating, especially when missions were canceled due to a shortage of VNAF observers. Occasionally an observer would be taken from a Spad that had landed and hustled to another A-1 preparing to depart. Equally absurd was the demoralizing practice before a mission of changing national insignia to match the nationality of whoever was in the cockpit, or to match the nature of the mission. A fine line existed between compliance with the "training only" directive and solo combat flights by USAF pilots. That line was markedly crossed on 8 March 1964 when USAF Col. Thomas A. Hergert was killed flying a VNAF A-1H off the wing of another on a combat mission. On training missions the VNAF pilot occupied the left seat, and only practice missions—with practice ordnance—were flown.

**Although wearing VNAF insignia, an Air Commando crew was aboard this A-1E when it crash-landed at Bien Hoa in 1965. (Martin P. Jester)**

**A flight of seven Spads from both the 1st and 602nd SOS's, including two commander's aircraft, head for the target on a strike mission. (Jimmy Doolittle III)**

**A pair of *Firefly* A-1Hs ready for takeoff at NKP in October 1969. The Spad at right is named "Peacemaker." (USAF)**

**After it was damaged by antiaircraft fire south of Khe Sanh, 007 crash-lands at Da Nang. (USAF)**

Most of the Vietnamese student pilots had only about 150 flight hours, most of which were in the T-28 during stateside training. They then transitioned to the A-1 at Bien Hoa, and finally were assigned to the 1st ACS for combat indoctrination. The remainder of the VNAF pilots had flown VNAF transport or observation aircraft. In 1965 the entire VNAF training program was moved to Hurlburt, where it remained for the duration of the conflict.

Shortly after the 1st ACS began combat operations on 31 May 1964, the decision was made to equip the 34th Tactical Group with a second squadron of A-1E/Gs. U.S. Air Force officials had hoped to have three A-1 squadrons in operation by 1965, but to avoid increasing U.S. direct involvement, the third squadron was denied and additional A-1s were transferred to the VNAF instead. The 602nd Fighter Squadron (Commando), which had been reactivated during April 1963 at Hurlburt, went into business at Bien Hoa on 14 October 1964. The unit evolved from the 2nd FS (C), which helped form the Air Commando legacy during World War II. Like its sister squadron (1st ACS), the 602nd was tasked mainly with training Vietnamese pilots in the A-1.

By the end of June the 34th Group had one dozen A-1E/Gs, and by the end of 1964 that number had risen to 48, with 92 A-1s in the VNAF inventory. These Spads combined flew about 60 combat sorties daily, plus training missions. Typical Farm Gate missions included air support of the Army of the Republic of Vietnam (ARVN), support of U.S. Special Forces camps, escort of VNAF, U.S. Army, and U.S. Marine Corps helicopters, and escort of C-123 transports flying defoliation and supply missions. As enemy ground fire became more intense and accurate, a four-ship attack formation was used so that two A-1s could cover a pair attacking a target.

Like their Navy counterparts, USAF A-1s had a bomb shortage during 1964 and 1965. To keep the sortie count up, rather than send fewer planes on missions with full loads, more were sent with partial loads. Since success was usually measured by attrition of enemy forces, padding the all-important body count also made good press.

Bien Hoa Air Base soon became a beehive of activity, a fact the enemy could hardly ignore. Consequently, on 1 November 1964 Bien Hoa became the first American air base in Vietnam to come under attack. Four Americans were killed, scores were injured, and six aircraft were destroyed; fifteen, including three A-1Hs, were damaged. As the situation got hotter more troops and aircraft were deployed to the region. Heavy ground fighting in early 1965 boosted the 2nd Air Division commitment for air support. When U.S. Air Force strike aircraft flew their first mission over North Vietnam in support of VNAF A-1s on 1 February 1965, they were joined by USAF A-1s. Strikes by F-100s and B-57s against Viet Cong positions in South Vietnam later that month marked the first use of jets in Vietnam. Escalating conflict and the arrival of single-seat F-100 fighters at Bien Hoa in the summer of 1965 ruled out the need for VNAF observers in Skyraiders and prompted the acquisition of single-seat versions for the Air Force. More than 200,000 troops had been committed to the Vietnam war, and the Skyraiders were becoming much more aggressive.

**The 50-ton cranes of Aero Repair/Crash Recovery units at air bases in Southeast Asia got regular workouts. Here, 007 is recovered after its belly landing. (Tom Hansen)**

**"Little Prince" was the name given to A-1H no. 134526. Three 1st SOS pilots earned Silver Stars flying Little Prince during SAR missions in 1971 and 1972. (Richard S. Drury)**

When word came through in August to stop carrying VNAF observers and change aircraft insignia to that of the U.S. Air Force, morale skyrocketed. Elated with the opportunity to continue their proud tradition, the Air Commandos celebrated. Some transitioning of VNAF student pilots to the A-1 continued, however. The primary mission of 1st ACS and 602nd FS(C) Spads then became support of ground troops and limited air strikes. Some SAR missions were flown. It was not long before the Spad became recognized as an effective weapon. Nor was that notoriety lost on the enemy who, on 23 August 1965, lobbed nearly 100 mortar rounds into Bien Hoa's A-1 flight line, damaging 11 of them.

To provide Spad coverage over the war-torn regions of Southeast Asia additional VNAF A-1 squadrons were formed, and detachments of the 602nd operated from Nha Trang, South Vietnam, and later from bases at Udorn and Nakhon Phanom, Thailand. Added to the routine were alert standbys, scheduled Combat Air Patrol missions, landing zone preps, reconnaissance, and sorties flown from Qui Nhon. Pilots favored the latter, since sorties were short and produced good targets.

Shortly after the bombing campaign against North Vietnam began in early 1965, Air Force commanders at bases in Thailand, from which strike aircraft operated, requested Skyraiders to cover SAR operations. The requests were denied until months later when the 602nd FS(C) was directed to fly a four-ship special mission to Udorn Royal Thai Air Force Base (RTAFB). Each of the A-1Es was loaded with a 150-gallon external fuel tank. The mission's urgent status ruled out the timely process of switching to 300-gallon tanks, which would widen the safety margin over unfamiliar territory. Since the purpose of the Top Secret mission was not disclosed to the pilots, each A-1E was loaded with ten 7-shot rocket pods, which had fairings to reduce drag and conserve fuel. Two spare pilots, two mechanics, tools, and spare parts were included in the mission package.

On 27 July Capt. John Larrison led the flight of four, which had to land at Korat RTAFB when one of the Spads ran low on fuel due to a rough-running engine. After skirting politically sensitive Cambodia, Larrison had wisely decided against landing at Bangkok. The Thai government, which downplayed the U.S. presence at its bases, would have been hard-pressed to explain four heavily armed American A-1Es at its largest commercial airport.

At Korat, F-105 pilots told the Spad pilots they were requested to provide low cover for SAR operations during air strikes on SAM sites around Hanoi. The strikes had begun that day and aircraft had been downed, with the loss of aircrew. During strike missions, two A-1s were to fly a holding pattern just west of Hanoi in case radio contact was made with downed flyers. The other pair of A-1s stood runway alert at Udorn.

The next morning a Navy aircraft was shot down. The pilot ejected and was rescued by an H-43 "Huskie" helicopter, which the Spads escorted back to NKP. Since the Huskie (later called "Pedro") did not have enough fuel to take the rescued pilot to Udorn, where Secretary of Defense McNamara was waiting to meet him, the escorting A-1s landed at NKP to pick him up. Thus marked the first time Skyraiders touched down at NKP.

The four A-1s were ordered back to Bien Hoa, and several weeks later the 602nd began rotating four A-1s to Udorn for two-week periods of SAR coverage. The success of those rotations led

**NKP's crash recovery crew works on "Gomer Getter," no. 134562, of the 602nd SOS after Wayne Warner's takeoff abort on 15 March 1969. It was Warner's second day of checkout as "Sandy 4." Two weeks earlier, the hapless Warner had bailed out of an A-1 when its engine quit ten miles from NKP. (USAF)**

**Lt. Col. Robert Wilke considers his good fortune while looking over his Spad, which received extensive battle damage over the North in 1968. (USAF)**

to the relocation of the entire 602[nd] to Udorn in April 1966, foreshadowing the Spad's role in search and rescue.

The first half of 1966 was bloody for the 602[nd]. More than 30 Spads went with the unit to Udorn; only half were left by June. For several weeks, the squadron suffered the loss of a pilot every two weeks, and an A-1 weekly.

The 1[st] Air Commando Squadron, like the 602[nd], suffered heavy losses flying a variety of missions. One of those A-1Es was flown by Capt. Larry Haight, who details his experience:

> "My involvement with the A-1 started at Hurlburt Field during the summer of 1964. There were nine of us in Express 6, the pipeline for A-1E pilots to the Air Commando squadrons in Vietnam. Having successfully experienced the fearful consequences of excess torque in unskilled hands, we were graduated from the A-1E Combat Ready Gunnery program on 30 September 1964. I arrived at Bien Hoa and was assigned to the 1[st] ACS on 26 October.

My 140[th] mission was on 17 April 1965. This was my second mission of the day. It was fragged for IV Corps, a flight of four: two birds loaded with 250 and 500-pound bombs, and two loaded with napalm. Our tactic with this type of armament was to have the bombers attack from different directions and time-separated so that, as the first bomber was pulling off, the second bomber was rolling in. Each pilot was to make two passes and clean his wings. During the bombing passes, the napalmers were setting up from opposite directions to begin their longer, flatter run-ins. They were to make two passes also. As they approached the release point, the bombers were to climb back up and reposition so they could dive at a high-angle strafing pass at about 90 degrees to the napalmer's flight path, and strafe any area that might be a threat to the exposed napalm bird. Each bomber was to cover with guns for one napalmer, and after the second napalm pass all would rejoin and return to base.

Flying the other Spads were Capt. Doyle Ruff, 1Lt. R.Y. 'Dick' Costain, and a new guy, Capt. Dixon. We were to strike a VC-run village in the Delta. When we arrived in the area contact was made with the FAC, who advised that his Vietnamese observer—who was in contact with the province chief—said they didn't want to strike the village. The mission was changed to take out a nearby herd of water buffalo used by the VC. Dixon, being new, wasn't in position to provide good strafing cover for Costain's nape run, and I reversed flight and tried to provide cover for both Ruff's and Costain's napalm runs. The FAC was indicating there was small arms fire from one of the tree lines around the target. On my third strafing pass I picked up a hit in the engine area. I was pulling off the pass and losing power. I got up to 800 feet and the engine was running rough. The FAC said there was smoke coming off the engine and to head north to get across a river and out of the VC area. Costain cleaned his wings, pulled up, and looked me over. He said that the whole underside and complete right side were thickly coated with oil, and that it

**Observers on the ground were greeted with the incredible sight of this Spad fully afire, with only its nose and canopy visible on final approach to Bien Hoa AB in 1965. Its U.S. pilot and VNAF student were rescued uninjured from the battle damaged A-1E. (Martin P. Jester)**

**Local militia pose with Capt. Haight's crashed A-1E, no. 133886, before it was destroyed with explosives on 18 April 1965. (Larry Haight)**

**The A-1E at left "pickles" four fire bombs during a strike in 1965. (USAF)**

was running the length of the fuselage and drizzling off the end. After just a couple of minutes, the engine was getting rougher and I was losing altitude. At about 600 feet it was apparent I wasn't going to get anything more out of the engine. I considered bailing out, but this was before the Yankee Extraction System, and I didn't like the odds of unstrapping, climbing out on the wing, jumping, and pulling the ripcord at that altitude. The engine was so rough and vibrating, I knew I had to shut it down.

Doyle read me the engine-out landing procedure. Costain had climbed and called 'May Day.' I shut down the engine as it started to freeze. Before the radio went out, I was aware that the Mayday had been heard, and that some Army gunship choppers were in the area and headed our way.

I picked a field and set up for a straight-in belly landing. The cockpit of that sturdy bird still felt comfortable, and it looked like it was going to be a piece of cake. We had practiced engine-out landings all the time over the runway. The difference turned out to be that with a windmilling prop you had a certain level of drag, but with a frozen prop the drag increased significantly. I was approaching the flare point and the bird began to stall. To make matters worse, rocks had been piled up in a mound in the center of the field. The rock pile showed up while I was in the flare and it was dead ahead. I couldn't bank and miss it. I pulled up just enough to go over the rocks. The bird stalled completely a few feet in the air and dropped hard.

The impact momentarily knocked me out. The last I remembered was the impact and the canopy slamming closed from the jolt. My helmet had been ripped off when the windscreen left the fuselage. I came to almost immediately, was slumped forward, and saw blood dripping from my nose. My first thought was 'I'm alive.' Then, 'Fire! Get out!' I could move, so I unstrapped and started to climb out the right side. I saw black pajama-clad figures coming out of the tree line toward the plane. I reached back to get my AR-16 rifle that was between the seats. I got my hand on it, but got tangled in the seat and chute straps and fell out of the cockpit and landed on my head on the wing root, still clutching the AR-16. I got oriented and prepared to fire at the area where I saw the black pajamas, but the clip had dislodged from the weapon upon impact. Fortunately there was a spare clip taped to the butt. I sprayed the tree line and the black pajamas hid. By this time, the flight was providing strafing cover.

My thoughts were racing about what to do next. I had seen a large ditch off to the side. I went to it and slid down its bank to hide. I wasn't there very long before I had a vivid image of William Holden in the Korean war movie 'The Bridges at Toko-Ri,' hiding in a similar ditch after crash-landing, and the North Koreans sneaking up on him and shooting him. I didn't want to die in a ditch! I climbed out and headed for the pile of rocks. At least I could see what was coming. Moving to the rocks, I started falling and seemed to be getting tunnel vision. As it turned out, my neck was severely strained when my helmet was ripped off, I had crushed six vertebrae in my lower back and broken my right wrist, which was holding the stick on impact.

Captain Thaddeus Welch, the FAC, landed his O-1 Bird Dog in a plowed field just on the other side of the ditch. He got out and made his way to me and helped me back to his bird. He wanted me to climb in so they could get airborne, as we were taking small arms fire. My back was hurting like hell. The O-1 barely had room for the pilot and his VNAF observer, let alone me. I couldn't see this thing taking off in a short rough field as anything but a disaster. I also knew a chopper was on the way. We were arguing the merits of this when the chopper showed up. The gunship crew pulled me aboard and we were out of there.

**An A-1G of the 602nd SOS has its tail raised for boresighting its 20mm cannons at NKP in 1970. (Ernest L. Connors)**

**An A-1E's rear-facing strike camera captures napalm and WP strikes by the 1st ACS in South Vietnam's Delta in 1965. (USAF)**

I was very appreciative and certainly respect Captain Welch's heroic attempt to get me out of there. He and his VNAF made it out okay. When he got back to base, he had 27 bullet holes in his O-1. He was awarded the Silver Star for his rescue attempt.

The Army chopper took me to a field hospital at Soc Trang, and after some initial medication I was airlifted to the Navy hospital in Saigon, then on to Clark and the States.

I later learned that a detachment was sent out to see if my Spad's guns and radios could be removed to prevent their use by the VC. They took photos of the A-1 before they blew it up to prevent anything being used by the enemy. Had the A-1 been anything less than the sturdy flying tank that it was, I'm sure I wouldn't have walked away from that landing!"

One year later, Capt. Melvin Elliott of the 1st ACS was at the controls of an A-1E that fell at the hands of enemy gunners in a remote corner of Vietnam, called Plei Me. He describes how he avoided a similar fate:

"On the night of 19 October 1965 I was the flight leader of four A-1Es from the 1st Air Commando Squadron stationed at Bien Hoa. We were scheduled for a combat mission in South Vietnam. Just before takeoff I was told we were being diverted to Plei Me, a Special Forces camp approximately 30 miles south of Pleiku. We arrived just before dawn to find a flight of F-100s in the area working with a C-123 with a FAC on board. When the F-100s had expended their ordnance, we were directed into the area and told the compound was under attack by what was later determined to be North Vietnamese troops, the first confirmed in South Vietnam.

Our A-1 flight was operating on an FM radio frequency that was also used by the flare ship and the American compound commander. During the attack, the commander directed the A-1s to drop their napalm on the camp's perimeter. We noticed that some igniters from the napalm cans were going over the wall into the trenches inside the compound. After all ordnance had been expended the flight returned to Bien Hoa. Upon landing, several small caliber bullet holes were found in three of the four planes.

Two days later I was in the officer's club having a drink with a friend from Hurlburt who was flying the AC-47 gunship. He asked me what medals I had been awarded during our tour, and I replied, 'The only ones left are those that hurt or scare you.' Then the phone in the club rang and it was the command post directing A-1E pilots to go on alert. The pilots on alert had just taken off on their third mission of the day, after which they would have to be replaced. I told the duty officer I would round up four new pilots who would report to the command post ASAP. We went to the command post, were briefed, assigned aircraft, picked up our flight gear, and went to the aircraft to 'cock' them for alert. We had just loaded out gear in the planes when the command post called and ordered two planes to launch. My wingman, Robert Haines, and I were to be the second two to launch, so we went to the alert trailer to try to get some rest.

About midnight we were ordered to fly to Plei Me and rendezvous with a flare ship and an Army Caribou transport. The flight to Plei Me was uneventful, and we

**This view from an A-1E strike camera illustrates the extremely low altitude at which Spads flew to accurately deliver ordnance. (USAF)**

rendezvoused with the flare ship. The weather in the area was about 1,000-foot ceiling with good visibility under the clouds. The flight set up an orbit around Plei Me awaiting the Caribou. The flare ship was keeping the area lit from above the clouds.

After about an hour I advised the flare ship that we would be able to stay longer if we expended our external ordnance—napalm, CBU, and rockets. The compound marked an area with a mortar round, and we expended our ordnance. The flight again set up an orbit awaiting the arrival of the Caribou to resupply the compound. Sometime after 2 AM I requested the status of the Caribou and was told it had been canceled for the night. I informed the flare ship and the compound that we would have to leave the area shortly, but that we could strafe any areas with our 20mm cannon before leaving. The compound again marked an area with a mortar round, and I rolled in on a strafing pass.

As I pulled off the target I noticed that things were quite bright. I looked at my left wing and it was ablaze! I called my wingman and told him I was on fire. He requested that I turn on my lights so he could see me. I thought that if he couldn't see me on fire, he certainly wouldn't see the lights of my aircraft. I planned to maneuver over the compound and bail out—we didn't have the Yankee System. Before getting into position over the compound, the flares went out and it was impossible to see the ground. I continued in the orbit at approximately 800 feet altitude, awaiting the illumination of flares so I could see the ground. Before this happened the aircraft's controls failed, and I notified everyone that I was bailing out.

As I was attempting to bail out I became stuck against the rear part of the canopy. My helmet was blown off immediately when I stuck my head out of the cockpit. A few days before I had cut the chin strap off the helmet, as its snap had become corroded and would not unfasten after a mission. The aircraft was out of control and was rolling due to the fire burning through the left wing. After freeing myself from the aircraft I reached for the D-ring, which was not in the retainer pocket on the parachute harness. However, I found the cable and followed it to the ring and pulled it. The chute opened and, shortly after, flares lit, and I could see that I was going to land in trees. After landing in the trees, approximately 50 feet above the ground, I bounced up and down to ensure that the chute was not going to come loose, and then swung over to the

**Ordnance dropped by a 6th SOS A-1 impacts a truck caught in the open in southern Laos in 1968. (USAF)**

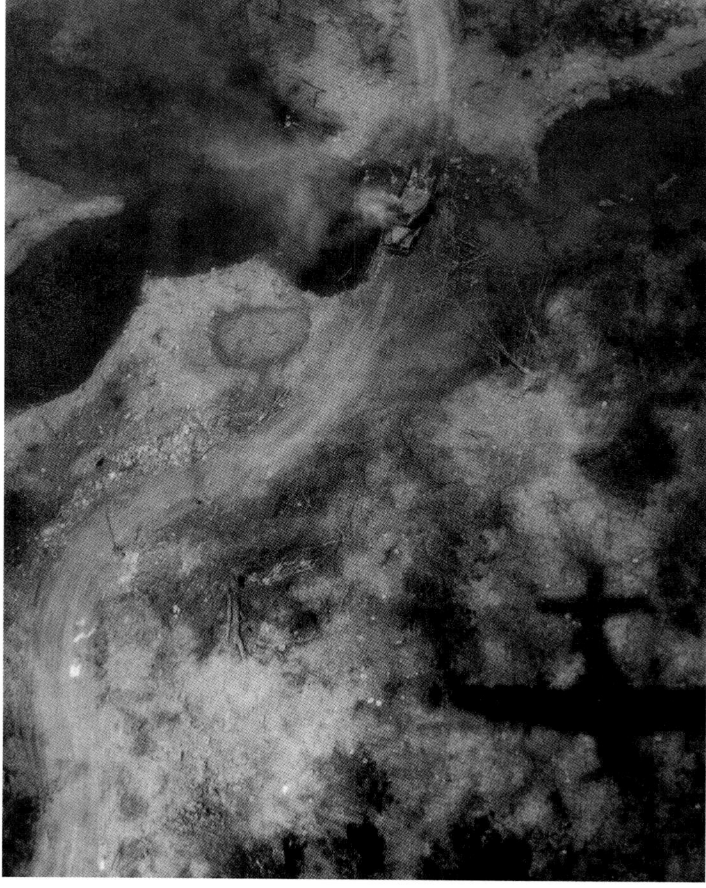

**A second pass reveals the damage to the supply truck. The Spad's shadow is captured in both views. (USAF)**

trunk of the tree and grasped a nearby vine. I had lost my hunting knife during the bailout so I had to abandon the survival kit that was part of the parachute.

After climbing down the vine to the ground I sat down, thought about the situation, and assessed what equipment I had. I had a .38 caliber revolver with five rounds of ammo, a pen-gun flare, a strobe light, a two-way radio (which was a luxury to A-1 pilots), my Mae West, and a brand new 'chit book' from the Bien Hoa officer's club. After regrouping I got out my radio and contacted my wingman, who was orbiting the area. I told him I had him in sight, and that when he was directly overhead, to fly from my position to the compound, and that I intended to make my way there. About 30 minutes later Haines had to leave and go to Pleiku, as he was low on fuel.

I moved toward the compound, and when I felt that I was getting close to its perimeter a severe firefight broke out. I found a likely place to hide out and stayed there the rest of the night. Shortly after dawn I spotted an O-1 aircraft orbiting the area and turned on my radio, calling him several times before getting an answer. I had forgotten my call sign and used my name. By identifying landmarks the Army Bird Dog pinpointed my position. I stayed fast all day, and just after dusk, the same Bird Dog told me that a Huey helicopter was coming to get me out. Shortly afterward radio contact was made, and I was told to get into the best position I could to get picked up.

**Ground crewmen at Pleiku examine battle damage to A-1G, no. 132528. (Bernard Fisher)**

**An A-1J of the 6th SOS unloads four low drag GP bombs on trucks in southern Laos during 1968. The vehicles are barely visible just off the road at lower left. (USAF)**

The Huey arrived, and I moved from my hiding place onto a small trail through the brush. When the Huey came around with lights out, I turned on my strobe. The Huey made two orbits, and on the third circle came in and turned on his floodlight. Suddenly a .50 caliber machine gun opened fire about 50 yards from my position. The Huey turned his lights off and left the area. I put the strobe in my pocket, got off the trail into the brush, and laid as low as possible. About ten minutes later two North Vietnamese soldiers came down the trail with a flashlight. I was about 20 feet off the trail and flat on the ground. They were chatting as if out for a Sunday stroll, and shining their flashlight from one side of the trail to the other. On one of the sweeps the light came to within two feet of me, and the next sweep was beyond me. After the two were satisfied that I was not in the area, I found a new hiding place and settled down for the rest of the night. It was about 8 PM. There was no sleep for me, as aircraft were in the area the entire time. Between them and the mortars it was quite noisy. One thing I learned during my 'tour' at Plei Me was that a bomb must get quite close to a person flat on the ground to cause him any great grief.

About 8 a.m. I contacted a Bird Dog in the area, and through identifying landmarks again pinpointed my approximate position. The USAF FAC said he was going to throw smoke grenades to better locate my position. I didn't really think that was a good idea, but the FAC threw all the smoke he had, never getting any close enough for me to see. He advised he was going for more smoke and left.

Another Bird Dog arrived and advised me that a chopper was coming to pick me up and to get into a suitable area. I moved into an opening clear of brush, but full of six-foot high grass, and rather swampy underneath. Upon reaching the middle of this clearing I contacted the FAC and was told the chopper had been diverted to a 'higher priority' mission. This was really the only time I was completely demoralized. I went back to the place I had hidden out all night and then decided that I was going to move away from the compound to make it easier to get picked up. After moving more than a half-mile I came across a small stream and washed my face and washed out my mouth, which made me feel somewhat better.

I came upon a rise in the terrain, and after the climb came upon a fair sized clearing. I spotted a clump of bamboo and started for it to hide when an object darted out of it. After my heart started again I saw that it was a wild pig. I went into the bamboo thicket and contacted a Bird Dog orbiting overhead. I again pinpointed my position with the pilot, who said he was going for food and water, since they did not know how long it would be before I would be picked up. After he left I realized that the only thing I had to open a can with was my pistol and five rounds of ammo.

A half hour later I again contacted the Bird Dog, and he said to come on the air in 15 minutes. I turned my radio on again and heard several pilots talking on 'Guard,' several of whom I recognized as A-1 pilots. The FAC said that an H-43 chopper was about five minutes out and that the A-1s would be dropping napalm along a tree line about 100 yards from my position. He advised me to move into the middle of the clearing as soon as the A-1s passed over. Doing this, I spotted the H-43 coming in about 20 feet off the ground directly toward me. The pilot got into position and was forced to hover because of the high grass. This created a huge wave of grass that I had to crawl through. Upon getting to the chopper I was dragging many vines that grew in the grass. The PJ (Pararescueman) on the chopper was hanging out the door, and I stepped on to the wheel. As soon as I reached up, the PJ told the pilot he had me and away we went. The wheel rotated, and I was hanging onto the PJ's arm. As he was pulling me into the chopper, I looked up at him and shouted, 'I'm not going down there alone!' This was about noon, after a total of 36 hours on the ground.

**VNAF advisors Capt. Earl Cravens and Capt. Tom Pulham (in black flight suits) sign over VNAF A-1Gs to the 1st ACS at Pleiku in September 1966. Others from left are: Capt. Robert Blood, Capt. Kreiger, Maj. Buzz Blaylock, Col. Bill Bonneaux and an unknown Col. (USAF)**

**Fourteen fat face Spads of the 1st SOS line NKP's flightline in July 1968. (Tommy Wardlow)**

**This 1st ACS A-1E, no. 132666, was recovered at Bien Hoa in 1965 after its VNAF pilot missed the landing approach and rammed the throttle to the firewall in an attempt to go around. However, tremendous torque slow-rolled the Spad 50 feet over the runway and it went in at full power, inverted, at which time the pilot tried to jump out of the open canopy. He was half out of the aircraft when it impacted. Neither Maj. George F. Vlisides or his VNAF student survived. (Martin P. Jester)**

The zap, which reads, "You been had by Sandy Spad, Luv," applied to an F-105F of the 44th TFS at Korat RTAFB, echoes the saying heard throughout the Spad community. (David A. Hansen)

Left: Bomb away somewhere over North Vietnam in July 1966. (USAF)

I was taken to Pleiku, where there was some scrounging around trying to find a way to get me back to Bien Hoa. Ultimately, an A-1 driven by Gail Kirkpatrick was diverted to Pleiku to pick me up. An intelligence sergeant from Saigon was at Bien Hoa to debrief me, and his most redundant question was, 'Captain Elliot, were you scared at any time?' There is no way to say thanks to all the people involved in a successful rescue mission, and there is no way to tell someone who has not been through such an ordeal what it is really like."

In 1966 the 1st ACS moved to Pleiku Air Base, which was located in South Vietnam's Central Highlands. The unit was attached to the 3rd Tactical fighter Wing (TFW), which had both A-1s and F-100s. The 1st ACS had previously been assigned to the 6251st TFW. During March 1966 the squadron came under the 14th ACW, and finally, the 56th ACW during December 1967. From October to December 1967 about half of the 1st ACS was deployed to NKP, with the remainder arriving during late December.

The 56th ACW was activated in March 1967 and became the 56th Special Operations Wing (SOW) on 1 August 1968. On that date Air Commando squadrons were redesignated Special Operations Squadrons (SOS).

As clandestine operations expanded during 1967, Special Forces teams that went into Laos, and probed Viet Cong bases in South Vietnam, relied heavily on Spads for tactical support. When SOG commander John Singlaub became aware the Air Force planned to replace the A-1 he argued for its unmatched close support capabilities. To keep pace with increased operations, the 6th ACS was formed at England AFB during November 1967. The squadron was destined for Pleiku to replace the 1st ACS, which left behind seven pilots to familiarize the 6th ACS with the current combat situation. Although some 6th ACS pilots had served a tour in Southeast Asia, they would find that the war had changed dramatically. Beginning in August, before the unit was officially organized, its first two pilots spent several months ferrying A-1Hs and A-1Js from the storage facility in Arizona to the Naval Rework Facility at

The ordnance under the wings of this 1st ACS A-1E belies the placid scenery below. (Robert E. Blood)

NAS Quonset Point, Rhode Island, and then to McClellan AFB, California, for shipment to Vietnam by carrier. In February 1968 the first group of 6th ACS pilots attended survival school at Clark Air Base in the Philippines and continued on to Pleiku. A total of 20 single-seat Spads earmarked for the 6th were offloaded at Cam Ranh Bay during March. The 6th used the call sign "Spad," as well as "Super Spad," and it's A-1s wore the tail code "ET." The squadron came under the 633rd SOW (which was activated on 9 July 1968) and became the 6th SOS on 1 August.

The Super Spad's primary mission was to provide close air support to South Vietnamese and U.S. ground units in the II Corps area, especially the U.S. Army's 4th Infantry Division operating along the western border of the Central Highlands. The 6th also flew attack missions in Vietnam and Laos, with special attention given to the infamous Ho Chi Minh Trail. Having proved its usefulness, the reputable A-1 was sought by theater commanders. To broaden their coverage, Spads of the 6th SOS, like those of other units, were dispersed to various locations. On 31 March the 6th sent a detachment of two A-1s, four pilots, and eleven support people to Da Nang for assignment to the 56th ACW's Operating Location Alpha Alpha (OLAA). The temporary duty lasted until 9 April, and a second detachment, comprising five pilots and aircraft, was sent during late April. Normally two A-1s were placed on alert and their crews housed with HH-3 "Jolly Green" crews. Five of the squadron's A-1s and pilots were also sent to NKP to stand alert for missions in support of SOG teams. It then became necessary to augment the 6th's Pleiku contingent with ten A-1s.

**The largest antiaircraft gun usually encountered in Laos was the 37mm, often positioned in groups of three to cover air approaches to targets. This Russian made example was captured by the 1st Cavalry Division. (Ray H. James)**

**With much of his right wing shot away by a 37mm gun over North Vietnam on 1 September 1966, Capt Lee Minnick displayed superior airmanship to keep his Spad airborne. He flew it at 2,800 rpm and 56 inches MAP for more than an hour to get back over Thailand. He used the safety pin/flag from his minigun to tie off the control stick before he bailed out near NKP. An escorting Jolly Green helicopter picked up Minnick when he bailed out over a lake. (Norm Legget)**

The insertion, support, and extraction of a SOG team into enemy territory was a carefully planned and well orchestrated event that usually involved about 20 aircraft, including Skyraiders. Because such forays into the lion's den extended far beyond the range of artillery, and U.S. ground troops were prohibited from crossing into Laos and Cambodia, SOG commandos depended completely on air support. When teams got into trouble, their preferred close air support aircraft was the A-1. The distinctive roar of a Spad's engine raised the hope for survival of a team trying to "get out of Dodge." They knew a Spad pilot would fly low and slow, be able to stay in the area much longer than gas-guzzling jets, and place its huge amounts of ordnance in close proximity. SOG team members were often singed by napalm or hit by shrapnel from Skyraider ordnance placed "danger-close," but they remained grateful for the pilots' skill. Such extreme action spoke of profound trust and created a bond between Spad pilot and SOG commando.

Although the 6th SOS was not designated a "Sandy" search and rescue unit, its A-1s flew SAR missions whenever necessary. Shortly after the squadron went into business at Pleiku, two of its pilots, Capt. Robert Smedley and Maj. Paul Johns, flew the squadron's first SAR mission. Returning from a strike mission, they responded to a Mayday call in the A Shau Valley, worked their way down below a 500-foot cloud ceiling, made contact with the pilot, and guided a rescue helicopter to him while providing suppressive fire.

During the first three months of operations the 6th SOS lost eight pilots and twelve aircraft. One of the first fatalities was Lt. Col. Wallace A. "Jack" Ford, who commanded the squadron while at England AFB and later at Pleiku. After eight months of operations the 6th had flown over 3,000 sorties. Although all four USAF Spad squadrons flew support for SOG units, along with two VNAF squadrons later in the war, the 6th SOS flew almost exclusively for SOG.

**Complete with leather helmet, goggles, and scarf, 1Lt. Jim Seith of the 1st SOS enjoyed taxiing his rare shark mouthed Spad past the F-4 Phantom pilots at Da Nang, so they could see a "real warbird." The Spad was A-1J no. 142053. (USAF)**

Their role in providing support for Special Forces teams guaranteed 6th SOS pilots plenty of action. Lt. Col. Sidney McNeil was awarded a Silver Star for covering an SF team that happened upon an NVA base camp on 11 January 1969. The team was surrounded and under attack when McNeil and Maj. Donald Dineen began a sustained period of covering fire. After 40 minutes the pair had destroyed 20 structures and several ammunition caches. The Green Beret leader estimated that 20 nearby enemy soldiers had been killed before the team was rescued by helicopter. During late August 1968 the 6th SOS helped end the siege at Duc Lap, an outpost amid a major enemy infiltration area. Spads of the 6th SOS joined other attack aircraft in halting waves of enemy attacks, which began on 23 August. Countless times the Spad would prove that decisive airpower was a key factor in turning the tide of battle.

After setting up shop at NKP in October 1968 the 22nd SOS became adept at night missions. Under the call sign "Zorro," the 22nd's primary mission became night interdiction during Steel Tiger and Barrel Roll operations. The Zorros flew A-1s whose undersides were painted black to fit the mission.

As the number of Spads in the war zone increased, the types of missions they flew were limited only by the users' imagination. That imagination, it seems, turned to folly in the minds of some, whose hands held the fate of the warriors who flew the missions. Jim Yealy, who served as the operations officer of the 1st ACS, explains:

> "In 1967 an electronic detection system, championed by Robert McNamara, was deployed to NKP under the code name 'Igloo White,' a highly top secret project. It consisted of employing acubuoy sensors dropped by Navy Neptune aircraft along main roads and trails, primarily in Laos, with seeding of 'gravel' ordnance by 1st ACS Skyraiders. The gravel was supposed to activate the sensors when tread upon or run over by vehicles. The sensors would record the activity and simultaneously transmit the information to airborne C-121s. Airborne attack aircraft would then be vectored to the area for interdiction.
>
> A number of factors revealed that the system was flawed. The Neptunes and Skyraiders were to fly as a unit on one pass, and on the deck. Our practice runs quickly showed that this was extremely dangerous, as we presented

**This 1st SOS A-1E, no. 132472, made it safely back to base after taking punishing 37mm fire in Laos in 1969. (USAF)**

**Left: The assortment of antique airplanes at Nakhon Phanom RTAFB was the basis for this cartoon given to the 1st SOS by a jet squadron.**

Maj. Lou Gang of the 1st ACS crash-lands gear-up on a full 150-gallon centerline fuel tank at Qui Nhon, South Vietnam, on 29 July 1965. The A-1E (no. 132670) was destroyed, but Gang escaped uninjured. (John Larrison)

John Flynn stands in the gaping hole of 472's wing, where the 37mm shell tore through. Flynn was shot down and killed at Muong Soi in July 1969. (Richard S. Drury)

slow targets in the highest threat areas. For survivability, it was decided the Neptunes would perform a single-ship mission, with the sensors' position plotted for follow-up delivery of the gravel by two A-1s.

It didn't take the North Vietnamese long to figure out we would make our runs over the road, straight and level, on the deck and slow. It was a nightmare for us and a bonanza for enemy gunners. Within a few weeks the enemy had increased their number of anti-aircraft guns, knowing full well we would return. Their patience paid off.

Prior to being given the mission, these targets were off limits due to their high threat. But there we were low and slow, and straight and level at 165 knots dispensing gravel. The Navy Neptunes fared worse than us, losing three aircraft and crew in quick succession. The Navy found the losses unacceptable and pulled out of the program. Fast movers (F-4s) took over the sensor delivery, but the A-1s still had the unenviable task of seeding roads.

Our aircraft had been modified with six large canisters on the wings, further negating our delivery speed and survivability. When the FAC marked the target with a 'Willie Pete' rocket, the North Vietnamese knew we were coming. After acknowledging our target, we called in from 8 to 9,000 feet in a steep dive, full throttle, with the birds groaning and shaking. Leveling off at or below 50 feet, we started seeding. These choke points on the trail had been hit numerous times and there wasn't a blade of grass or a tree within miles.

The 'pucker factor' became paramount, sitting out there naked with no trees to block the gunners. We began our slow ascent jinking and kicking rudder to present a poorer target. We were subjected to every type of weapon the North Vietnamese could bring to bear. Those climbouts

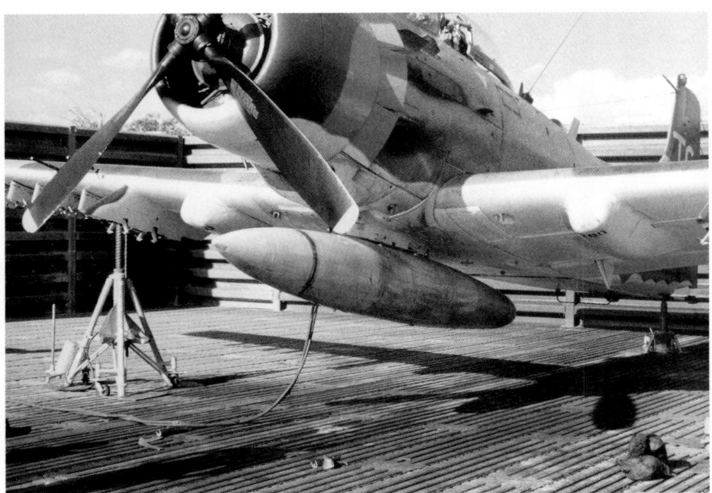

**The A-1H no. 139780 of the 1[st] SOS on jacks for maintenance of its hydraulically controlled landing gear. (Mark Eyestone)**

**During the Spad's start procedure, the crew chief carefully watched the gang drain, signaling the pilot when he could stop priming the sometimes temperamental Wright 3350 engine. (Mark Eyestone)**

were the longest moments of my life. For others less fortunate, it was an eternity.

We lost some great, courageous people trying to prove that McNamara's folly was all it was forecasted to be. Many of us old heads had serious misgivings about the future of this system. After I left NKP in 1968 I was informed the system was found ineffective and abandoned. The program's cost was phenomenal, even under today's expenditures for military hardware.

The system's failure was not due to the pilots. We tried to make it work and paid dearly. It was just another chapter in a war that was unsupported, and had so many restrictions that it was impossible to win. No one was held accountable for the conduct of the conflict in Southeast Asia."

In addition to heavy losses and the lack of U.S. political will, which severely restricted the war effort, Spad pilots had to contend with dissention within the Air Force toward them and their airplanes. The 7[th] Air Force commander, Gen. William Momyer, took a dim view of the Spad community and made known his advocacy for an all-jet Air Force. When asked about the A-1s during a visit to Pleiku in early 1966, Momyer stated, "This is a jet-powered Air Force and I'm not gonna let those damn antiques makes us look bad." Thankfully, the U.S. ambassador to Laos, William H. Sullivan, opposed Momyer's views. The Sullivan-Momyer debate over prop versus jet continued through much of the war.

Increasing the resentment between Spad pilots and those in rear echelon offices was a 1967 headquarters directive stating unit call signs would be changed weekly in the interest of security. A list would be forthcoming. When the list appeared, combat pilots were outraged. The first week of the new system the "Hoboes" of the 1[st] ACS became "Wild Roses." Other units were assigned indignant call signs, such as "Pussy Willow" and "Sunflower." After two months, it seemed everyone except the enemy was confused, and the original call signs were reinstated.

The 602[nd] used the call sign "Firefly," and its Udorn detachment used "Dragonfly." Dragonflies flew missions into northern Laos, while Fireflies covered eastern Laos, including the Ho Chi Minh Trail. Both flew armed reconnaissance and FAC missions, and went into North Vietnam as needed. The 602[nd] detachment that went from Bien Hoa to NKP in 1965 began using the call sign "Sandy." Relief detachments continued using the call sign, which was used throughout the war by A-1s on SAR missions. The 602[nd] detachment sent to Qui Nhon in 1966 used the call sign "Surf." The 6[th] SOS performed all missions, including SAR, under its "Spad" call sign. Unusual call signs were sometimes used to identify A-1s with special ordnance loads.

**Lt. James George of the 602[nd] SOS flew A-1H no. 139779 on a successful SAR mission on 16 November 1969. Despite damage from 37mm rounds, one of which passed between the prop blades, George was able to fly the Spad. With three cylinders knocked out and oil streaming back, George dropped his stores and had his hand on the bailout handle, when he realized the aircraft was holding together. The engine quit on final to NKP so he made a successful "deadstick" landing. The Spad's nickname may have referred to pilots who criticized USAF leaders insistent on a strategic nuclear mindset, who Spad pilots commonly called "SAC types." (Richard S. Drury)**

Missions flown by USAF Spad pilots were based upon specific tactical requirements and the constant tactical changes that occurred during the long war. Whatever the mission, Spad squadrons maintained impressive availability rates. Spads often were placed on alert status, sitting "hot-cocked" in their revetments. A hot-cocked Spad was fueled and loaded with ordnance, its preflight check was complete, and its radios were set. The aircraft was mission ready, down to the last detail, which included the pilot's harness hanging on the inboard cannon, and his helmet perched on the windscreen with its communication cord plugged in. When a pilot "scrambled" his crew chief was faithfully at his side, usually with a frozen canteen.

When looking back, Spad pilots find some missions more memorable than others. Often these were not large-scale operations, but missions that hold special significance. Ed Leonard recalls an effort led by Tom Burden to recover from North Vietnam the body of a pilot who was downed after flying 200 missions:

> "The downed pilot, Karl Richter, was up against a karst (steep, jagged mountain), and a large group of villagers was moving across rice paddies toward the site. Tom told us to cover him, and he dropped down and flew 'naked' in front of the villagers as a warning we would attack them as they neared Richter.
>
> They stopped, turned around, and returned to the village. The Jolly Green helicopter came in, sent down a PJ, made the pickup, and we all left. It was completely unopposed. Tom risked his life, in effect, to save the lives of the villagers. I still feel it was the bravest act I've ever heard of in Southeast Asia. Since no shots were fired, no recognition occurred. I will never forget the bravest man I've had the privilege to know."

Randy Jane tells of high drama in a Skyraider—while on the ground, parked:

> "After a long, hot mission in '72, I sat in the de-arm area at NKP and, as some of us frequently did, safety pinned the Yankee extraction system, opened the canopy, and unstrapped from the very constraining harness and lap-belt. I wasn't surprised when the de-arm crew gave me the 'shut-down-the-engine' sign, pointing at a jammed 20mm gun on the left side. I was very surprised, however, when, seconds after turning the mag switch to off, the entire front end of the Skyraider erupted in flames!
>
> Having unstrapped, the rocket-assisted 'Option A' was no longer available as a cockpit exit strategy, and the flames were lapping at both sides of the open cockpit. In exercising 'Option B,' I put my oxygen mask back on, lowered my helmet visor, pulled down my sleeves (like a good aviator, I had my fire retardant nomex gloves on), and promptly stood up. I 'stepped' through the flames on the left side, ran across the wing, and jumped down to the ramp. Behind me, the crew chiefs and armers were aiming all available fire bottles at the flames. My wing man, in an exercise of good judgment, literally jumped his chocks and taxied away from the scene.
>
> As the fire was extinguished I did a quick post-flight on myself. My nylon survival vest had melted slightly in a couple places, and I was 'sunburned' on the back and front of my neck (the only exposed skin). My hot, sticky, uncomfortable nomex 'green bag' had otherwise done its job exactly as advertised. It was then I realized that my heels and ankles felt like they were on fire; that asphalt was really hard, especially carrying all my normal 200 pounds, plus harness, helmet, vest, pistol, etc.
>
> The airplane postmortem was quite simple. The main fuel line between the fuel pump and the supercharger had a hairline crack. Under pressure, the leaking spray of Avgas was somehow being blown clear of the exhaust stacks while the engine was running. As I shut down the big fan, however, that fuel sprayed onto the hot manifold, with the obvious results. Thanks to the very quick and brave maintenance guys, the flames did only moderate damage. After some wiring and engine components were repaired and replaced, the bird flew again only two weeks later."

The skill and tenacity of Spad pilots, who were the lifeline for ground teams, is evident in a mission flown by 602nd SOS pilots Tom Stump and Ed Gullion on 10 August 1970. An Army long range reconnaissance team, which had been inserted deep within an enemy-infested area, ran into trouble, and helicopters trying to attempt its rescue were driven off by heavy ground fire. Earlier that day a helicopter had been shot down. The recon team leader advised the FAC that enemy troops had moved to within 20 meters of his position.

Stump and Gullion were on station, but very low on fuel. Nevertheless, the FAC directed them to place ordnance on all sides of the surrounded team, to within 20 meters, at the leader's request. This brought temporary relief to the desperate team, but five minutes later, after the Spads had departed, the team leader once again

**With his crew chief assisting, a 6th SOS pilot mans his A-1H. External stores visible are a Mk 8 centerline fuel tank and 750-pound fire bombs on the inboard racks. The squadron's first commanding officer, Lt. Col. Wallace A. Ford, was killed in this aircraft on 24 May 1968. (USAF)**

radioed that the enemy was on the verge of overrunning them. Having heard the radio message, and aware that no other air support was available, Stump and Gullion returned. Although dangerously low on fuel and under heavy ground fire, the pair flew multiple strafing passes within five meters of the recon team. The Spad's accurate fire forced the enemy to break contact. Had it not been for Stump and Gullion's selfless actions the team faced certain death or capture.

Jim George tells of another Spad pilot's mettle, which personalizes one of the many A-1 losses:

"The A-1J number 142030, of the 602nd SOS, was my airplane. It ran off the runway and was consumed by fire and destroyed on 2 October 1970. The pilot, Donald R. 'Bob' Moore, like many of us, was a great, young kid. Bob and I were classmates at the Air Force Academy, class of 1967. I hadn't known him well until we got to NKP, but he was instantly likeable, very competent, and conscientious.

That day, Bob was launching just before sunup on a 'first light' SAR effort. He aborted the takeoff with a rough running engine and, knowing that much of the SAR team would be delayed if he engaged the departure end arresting gear cable with his tail hook, he opted not to do so, thinking he could safely abort without it. But his brakes on the heavily loaded Spad failed, and he lost directional control as the aircraft slowed and the rudder became ineffective. He and '030' departed the runway to the side and, as per the procedure for departing paved surface, Bob dutifully raised the landing gear. This put his hot, and probably burning, brakes in contact with the contents of his now rupturing six cans of napalm, creating a massive fire. For whatever reason—maybe the cumbersome 'Koch' fittings that held the ejection seat harness—Bob wasn't able to exit the aircraft and escape the fire. He died that day—another tragic 'combat loss.'

I lost two good friends that day: 1Lt. Bob Moore, my buddy, and A-1J 030, the first airplane I was ever able to say was 'mine.'"

Many pilots recall the loss of their Spads, and even more vividly how they survived. John Rumph offers this account of a mid-air collision while flying an A-1G on 16 June 1965:

"I was leading a flight of four A-1s, and we were striking a V.C. unit near a Special Forces camp about 30 miles south of Pleiku. We were operating out of Qui Nhon, where we had a detachment of the 1st ACS from our home base at Bien Hoa. We had all made one dive pass, and with number four coming off the target I was preparing to roll in when number two must have lost sight of me and hit my right wing, removing it from the inboard gun out. Unfortunately he went in and was KIA. The aircraft was not controllable, so I departed over the left side, hit the horizontal stabilizer with the side of my head, and lost my helmet. I went out at around 1,500 feet, so I made a couple of swings and landed butt first on the side of a hill. I did a lot of running in hopes I could get to the Special Forces camp. I was on the ground for 30 to 40 minutes when an Army Huey showed up and hauled me into the camp. The Special Forces guys patched up the side of my face, and about an hour later the Huey took me to Pleiku for the night. The next day it was back to Qui Nhon and on to Bien Hoa.

My initial thought was that one of my bombs had armed somehow and had gone off on the pylon. It wasn't until after I was picked up that I found out what actually happened."

**With Spad crew chief Terry Moore positioned off its left wing, no. 134472 of the 1st SOS goes through a run-up at NKP in 1971. The cable from a power cart is draped over the oil stained fuel tank. The container behind Moore was filled with a chemical mix to extinguish white phosphorous bombs that accidentally ignited. (USAF)**

In 1968 Ed Leonard joined the fraternity of pilots who lost multiple Spads, having two airplanes severely damaged in combat less than three months apart. After he was downed the second time Leonard became a Prisoner Of War. He picks up the story:

"I was on a Firefly sortie—a bomb strike—against bridge construction just south of Dien Bien Phu on the Laotian border. We 'make one pass 'n' haul ass.' On climb-out my engine started running rough and finally quit. After spitting and sputtering, and losing several thousand feet, it smoothed out and I resumed climb-out. This went on and on. I called Mayday after about half an hour. I called Mayday again about 45 minutes later. It turned out my situation wasn't serious.

I made it back across the Mekong River into Thailand while slowly losing altitude. About 22 miles short of the Udorn runway I quit trying to save it. I saw what looked like a smooth field and put it into a rice paddy. Fortunately, I thought, the dikes were only about a foot high."

Referring to his shoot-down in an A-1H on 31 May 1968, after which he was captured, Leonard continues:

"Later I learned (walking to the 'Hilton') that typical rice paddy dikes are much higher than a foot. Belly landing into paddies is not smart. I also discovered parachuting into a regular NVA division retreating from getting its collective ass kicked in I Corps wasn't very smart either. But it was either that or rotate home and fly B-52s at Loring (AFB), which would really have not been very smart."

In language clearly understood by his colleagues, Rich Hall offers his view of a day's combat flying in a Spad:

"Charlie Kuhlman augered in about the middle of September 1968. Don Dunnaway was his wingman, and they had a Sandy orbit going near the 'Dragon's Mouth,' east of Ban Ban.

Maj. Tom O'Connor was flight lead for us, and this was my first left-seat ride in actual combat, with Maj. Tom Campbell in my right seat for the obligatory one ride with an IP. We were heavily involved with our 'fast movers' in a strike at Khang Khai, and the air was literally filled with 37mm bursts. I remember looking back over my right shoulder, and every window in every direction had at least two 37 bursts framed, if not more! Flight lead ran out of 'Willie Pete' rockets, and I smartly bombed mine off on the next pass (FNG – 'F...ing New Guy' trick). At that time we heard a Sandy was down, and we headed east to help.

As we cleared the scattered deck of 37mm bursts over 'KK,' another Sandy said he could not see any movement from the downed bird, and no chute. I heard later that Charlie tried a split-S from a little low and didn't quite make it. At his own request Maj. O'Connor landed last, as his Spad had been slightly damaged earlier in the day and he didn't know if the gear would hold. It did.

Over a cool one—or several—that night, I remember thinking, 'You're gonna die boy.' There seemed to be no way to survive that kind of stuff. Surprisingly, many of us did."

The Skyraider lived up to its billing of being versatile, although its designers likely did not foresee their creation in the hands of Air Force pilots over Southeast Asia. Missions flown by USAF Spads varied as much as the stores carried beneath their wings. Skyraiders had many unconventional applications in Southeast Asia, among which was its use as what one pilot called, "A damn big match."

In early 1965 Air Force planners considered a way to use air elements instead of ground troops to deny the Viet Cong the Boi Loi Woods, a tropical forest in South Vietnam known to A-1 pilots as "Sherwood Forest." A plan that would have modern day environmentalists reeling called for *Ranch Hand* C-123 "Providers" to spray chemical defoliants on 19,000 acres and then burn the area with a fuel-fed fire. Ranch Hand operations were preceded in late January by three days of heavy bombing by USAF and VNAF A-1s. After nearly 400 tons of bombs were dropped, the C-123s began spraying on 22 January. As the Providers worked, A-1s bombed and strafed Viet Cong positions.

By March, when all the foliage in Sherwood Forest had turned brown, it was decided that 36 A-1s from the 1st and 602nd squadrons would join up to form a fingertip spread and stacked formation. After C-123s dropped 1,200 gallons of diesel fuel, all the A-1s would drop their full napalm loads on the lead's cue.

**An A-1E of the 1st ACS drops a white phosphorous bomb. The Spad was shot down over Laos on 14 February 1966. (USAF)**

It was stressed to Spad pilots during briefing that prior to releasing napalm loads their aircraft be running on internal fuel tanks. Should their engine be fed from the external centerline fuel tank it could jettison if armament switches were not closely monitored. Kirk Kirkpatrick commented:

> "Takeoff was normal, but joining up was a little slow. Who the hell practices 36 finger join-ups? Not even Canadian honkers heading south! Lead managed to find Sherwood Forest, and after getting everyone on the same radio frequency, his countdown began. Everyone dropped their load on his command, and the fun started because a few dropped a bigger load than they intended. At least five belly tanks departed with the napalm cans. Plus, a few seconds after the drop, lead slowed down and no one could stay behind him. Did he extend his speed brakes? No. His engine shut down when his fuel tank released. Nice move. Aircraft broke in every direction, and why there wasn't a number of mid-airs no one knows. A-1s returned to Bien Hoa in single ships or flights of two. We don't remember a debriefing—could it have been too embarrassing?"

Despite the massive effort, which included eight B-57 sorties dropping incendiary "funny bombs" to spread the fire, two thunderstorms swept through and doused the conflagration.

Several days later at the bar a Spad pilot boasted that the Sherwood Forest mission was a success. When asked why he thought so, he answered, "Even though the fire went out, a fuel tank hit Robin Hood on the head and killed him." The lead pilot who had killed his engine found little humor in the quip.

Although the operation was not repeated on a grand scale, repeated attempts were made to burn the enemy out of strongholds, usually with only moderate success. Ranch Hand C-123s were commonly escorted by A-1s, which often prepped their spray route, and then accompanied them for quick reaction against ground fire. Spads also escorted AC-119 "Shadow" and "Stinger" gunships, as well as C-130 "Blindbat" flare ships.

Spad pilots unanimously agree that were it not for the skill and dedication of their crew chiefs and maintenance personnel their work would have been much more difficult and dangerous. Capable military leaders recognized that the crew chiefs, mechanics, and munitions handlers, who could be fiercely independent, were the heart and soul of flying squadrons. Simple acts, such as listening to their advice, providing for them, and praising their performance paid dividends in gaining their respect and loyalty. They worked under difficult conditions. The airfield they called home was occasionally hit by rockets and mortars, or came under sniper attack. Often, the tempo of activity was unrelenting and the working conditions dismal. They did their best in torrid weather, and often without adequate tools and parts, to keep their aircraft in the air. Unlike the pilots whose daily flirtation with danger and excitement helped them keep their perspective, ground crewmen found less reward and motivation.

**1Lt. R. Bertrand of the 22nd SOS ran this A-1E, named "Midnight Special," into the mud when he aborted a takeoff run at NKP in 1969. (USAF)**

Crew chiefs tended to their planes and pilots, often making a personal connection that was borne by personal names given the aircraft. Pilots and crew chiefs alike felt that some Spads had their own personality upon which names were based. If the prop stopped in the vertical/horizontal position, the crew chief owed the pilot a beer—the reverse if the pilot failed to back off the throttle after the crew chief left it in the forward position. During 1965 PACAF decreed that only 7-level non-commissioned officers (NCOs) could be crew chiefs. Consequently, in some flights with few 7-levels, a crew chief could be responsible for multiple aircraft.

Those who were based at Bien Hoa AB in 1965 recall about 45 "fat face" A-1s lined up on a long PSP ramp. Losses of A-1s and pilots during this period, prior to installation of the Yankee extraction system, were high. Crew chiefs took it hard when they were told their airplane and pilot were not coming back. "Turnarounds," during which the Spad was refueled, re-oiled, and its ordnance and gun bays reloaded, were often completed in 15 minutes. If the Spad was being turned around, minor battle damage was repaired with a special tape, called "supersonic tape," until sheet metal "scab patches" could be applied. A small diesel powered freezer on the ramp froze the water in canteens. Crew chiefs became adept at replacing the tires of A-1s, which often blew under the Spads' heavy loads.

And there was the oil—always the oil. Dwayne Meyer, who was an airborne electronics technician, remembers:

> "I was qualified to work on 23 types of aircraft in the Special Operations Wing. One of our favorites was the A-1, but we did not call them Spads. We referred to them as 'self-lubricating airplanes.' It was covered in oil. There was this stream that ran the length of the aircraft and drained out the port in the tail. The airplane was dangerous to work on after dark, because dew and condensation made the wings so slippery, even with traction pads."

Mark Eyestone shares his vivid recollections as a Spad crew chief:

> "I was a Staff Sergeant and an aircraft general mechanic capable of working on multi-engine prop-driven or jet engine planes. It was March 1971, and I'd been in the Air Force for three years and eight months. I had only four months to go, but I volunteered for any assignment in Thailand to get out of SAC and North Carolina. Now I

was working for the 1st Special Operations Squadron. What was our special operation? We were prepared to help anyone in Vietnam, Laos, and Cambodia. We suspect that A-1s had seen South China from 10,000 feet also.

From this mechanic's viewpoint, the A-1 Skyraider was the only plane I ever crewed that came back for days in a row with no pilot write-ups except a very flattering 'OK flight' notation in the aircraft log book. The only tool any A-1 mechanic carried with him was his big, long screwdriver. Post-flights, of course, required a full toolbox for the fix phase. But for launches, pre-flights, and through flights, the screwdriver could open all panels and service caps. Carried through the belt like a sword, it was also used to check the exhaust stacks, and it was the only tool needed to remove all the engine cowling, except the hot section wrap.

Maintenance was divided into two 12-hour night/day shifts, which we switched every month. There were three rows of revetments named 'Able,' 'Baker,' and 'Charlie.' Hobo 1 Flight handled the planes on Charlie row, while Hobo 2 Flight handled the planes on Baker row. Able row was for those down for long-term maintenance or back-ordered parts, which came all the way from NAS Quonset point, Rhode Island. Night shift pulled basic post-flight inspections, starting as soon as munitions people had unloaded all weapon stores, and the minigun and 20mm cannons had been unloaded. The post-flight inspection consisted of a walk around (looking for bullet holes), a peek in the engine's accessory section for leaks, a fuel strainer inspection, and then a look at the power section for broken studs on exhaust mounts, loose stacks, and the ever-present oil leaks.

The Curtis-Wright R-3350 three-section, twin row, 14-cylinder, 28-sparkplug air-cooled engine (which some called a Curtis-Wright oil pump) produced 2,800 horsepower on high blower. All that power pushed around 39 gallons of 50-weight oil and made for a lot of oil leaks. Let's see; 14 cylinders, each with 2 pushrod tubes, each of which had 2 couplings with 2 oil seals—that's 56 oil seals alone that might, or would, leak. In flight, the engine could use, burn, or leak 5 gallons of oil per hour and still be within limits for oil consumption. Five gallons of oil per hour for an 8-hour flight could run the engine dry and still be within oil consumption specs.

The engine leaked through the stacks, through those 56 oil seals, around accessory drive mounts, and from places that no one ever found. The oil streamed onto the windshield, caked on the side of the fuselage, was tracked into the cockpit, and dripped from the tail. A conscientious crew chief tried to work oil leaks in a different quadrant of the engine every night. This helped to keep the airplane a lot cleaner, but mechanic's opinions varied. There were those who swore that all that oil on the airplane reduced friction and made it slide through the air. Others said that if the pilot didn't get oily climbing in, he'd be more likely to buy the crew chief a beer when he got back—if he got back. Some crew chiefs felt a pilot wouldn't trust a plane that wasn't oily. I preferred the clean policy. I knew this was my last shot on a historical plane, so I tried to have the best-maintained one. Besides, scrubbing dried, caked oil off of a fuselage was hard work under a tropical sun and in high humidity.

Fuel leaks were slightly more important than oil leaks. A fuel leak would get you faster than an oil leak, and usually with more visible and dramatic results. I don't recall any problems with fuel leaks, other than the short little coupling hose between the aircraft and the external drop tank.

The carbs on those Wrights were incredible! For all the backfires and surges and extremes in temps, they were just about perfection. Can you imagine a backfire strong enough to blow off a short stack, but not blow out diaphragms in the carb itself?

Most every night of the monsoon it rained, so the crew chief worked in his rubber poncho. In the heat and humidity, it was a toss-up whether or not to bother wearing the poncho, since it would soak you with your own sweat as fast as any monsoon. That same poncho made an excellent grease apron, though. And for pulling off hot cowlings, it was like a pair of hot mitts.

Even with floodlights, the mechanic usually worked at night with a flashlight in his third hand—his mouth. You crawled under the plane to get into the 'hell holes,' those two access panels that got you under the cockpit. It was 120 degrees in there, with lingering avgas, hot oil, and electronics fumes. It was dark, claustrophobic, and just when you think you are clear of the plane, you stand up and put an antenna in your back. Scraped knuckles,

**The A-1H "Blood, Sweat & Tears" of the 1st SOS escorts an AC-119K "Stinger" gunship over Laos in November 1969. (USAF)**

broken fingernails, and filthy fatigues. Ever change a 'jug' on the bottom of a radial engine, looking up into the oil dripping off the bottom? It took hours getting all the baffles off the jug, just to get at the stud nuts at its base.

During the launching of an A-1, the pilot eventually let the crew chief know he was ready to have ground power pulled. If the chief had a helper he was on the right side of the plane. The pilot was usually doing his mag grounding check when he gave the signal. If all went well, the mechanic could get in there when the engine was at idle, pull the heavy power cord out of the external power socket, and screw down the access panel without getting an eyeful, earful, and nose full of ramp oil, water, and engine exhaust. You were barely four feet from that big spinning prop, but right at the business end of the exhaust stacks. We never wore safety glasses or goggles. Never had them. Never thought of them. The only rule was never to walk towards the prop. Always walk to the rear of the plane. There is only one thing that can get through a prop without getting hurt—a butterfly. Saw it many times.

There never seemed to be enough mechanics for all the planes. Of the 29 aircraft assigned, four to six might be down-country in Bangkok for spar cap mods. Two to four might be on temporary duty at Ubon, Bien Hoa, or Da Nang. One plane would usually be in for the 100-hour phased maintenance inspection. Even with so many aircraft gone, there never was a shortage of work. If all the airplanes got turned and pre-flighted before 4 AM, the 'super sarges' would have us out washing airplanes under a monsoon moon or picking up FOD (Foreign Object Damage—debris) with a flashlight.

Mechanics never cared for their supervisors, but were always willing to go off with the pilots on a mission to prove the sincerity of their efforts. The ultimate pilot's test was whether or not a crew chief was willing to fly in his own plane. When crew chiefs answered 'yes' when asked by their regular pilot if the plane had been inspected, the trusting pilot often didn't bother with his own inspection. Not only was I always willing, I was aching to see how my plane played out its role in the great farce war. I flew only once on a test flight of an A-1. These local hops were called 'flying around the flagpole,' using the call sign 'Carboy.'

We were always losing planes to the VC and to flying accidents, although not too many, considering how many pilots were cross-trained jet jockeys. And late in the war in 1972 we were turning planes directly over to the VNAF.

The last A-1 brought to the war was assigned to NKP for the 1st SOS in 1972. It was an A-1J transferred from Hill AFB, Utah, and taken by ship to the deep-water port at Sattahip, Thailand, on the Gulf of Siam. A couple of our guys went down to U-tapao to receive it. The A-1 was towed down Friendship Highway, wings folded, to the nearby bomber base at U-tapao. There the protective plastic cocoon was removed, the aircraft cleaned mechanically, serviced, and flown north to NKP with its wing stations removed. When that clean-wing '072' arrived, all the mechanics were fighting to be the first one to sign up as its crew chief. We thought it would be a super sleek fast flyer, with easy maintenance. It wasn't two weeks before the nickname 'Greaseball' was hung on it.

Failed to return' aircraft losses were the hardest deaths for a mechanic to take. I launched a Hobo 21 mission one time that never came back. I remember we were carefree and happy because of super weather and a good plane. I took the pilots' hats and wallets with IDs. Officially now they were civilians, since they would be fighting in Laos instead of Vietnam. About 5 PM I was worried. They were long overdue. They just never came back. I stayed in the club until.... The whole squadron, every able plane, even 'Greaseball' and 'Turtle,' took off next morning at 4 AM to look for those two pilots. They were found from the air, and ground troops later confirmed that they had apparently tried to eject, but their plane flipped. Suddenly, the war game became very serious, and it was no longer a one-sided affair.

One of our planes landed with its parking brakes on and went off the runway on a rainy night. One of the pilots was trapped in the burning cockpit. He couldn't be saved because all his ammo was cooking off. 'Twenty-Mike-Mike' and minigun ammo fired all night. The other pilot managed to escape by himself and was able to fly again, but I doubt he'll ever forget that one landing at NKP.

One time we all went to a pilot's party at their 'Hobo Hilton Hootch,' and it was just like those World War I movies of 'Dawn Patrol' with Errol Flynn, where everyone stands around toasting the dead. I gained a lot more respect for the pilots. We were involved. They were committed. With less than one month to go in the Air Force, it seemed that I was doing more and more work with less and less planes. No one was qualified to do any of the work, like towing, parking, and running up, since new guys hadn't yet been trained. New supervisors and senior ser-

**Lt. Col. Vargo, commander of the 1st SOS, makes a final preflight before his "champagne flight" in December 1969. His bomb load was colorfully painted in celebration of the event. (Richard Michaud)**

geants were arriving every day, but they weren't doing any physical work. No one seemed to know that more qualified mechanics was the answer. Fortunately for me the monsoon season came back, and targets were weathered in and the planes couldn't fly. The 1st SOS was no longer a prestigious squadron, but a hard dying relic of a previous war.

During those 12 months I worked hard for myself, my aircraft, and the pilots who flew it. The actual philosophy of the war never entered into things until someone failed to return from a mission. I kept my plane in pretty good condition. The work was hard, heavy, and greasy. The supervisors would rather criticize than reward. No one really seemed to appreciate the crew chief; no one except the pilot who made it back on the crew chief's promise, and who wrote an 'OK Flight' in the crew chief's greasy maintenance forms."

Consolidated Aircraft Maintenance Squadrons (CAMS) were the main suppliers of specialized maintenance personnel to units flying in the war. After starting an aggressive program of rebuilding severely damaged aircraft, the 633rd CAMS at Pleiku had rebuilt three A-1s by mid-1967. After mating the front half of an A-1E with the rear of an A-1G, pilots found the hybrid Spad faster than others. The 633rd during 1966 was reported to have created an even more unusual hybrid by combining the front half of an A-1E and the rear fuselage of an A-1H. Douglas reps gave the go-ahead, and the one-of-a-kind Spad was successfully flown. The primer-painted Spad supposedly wore the tail number 633-66-1. Skyraider overhauls were accomplished by Thai Airways at Bangkok.

Beginning in October 1969 the 6th SOS was dismantled, and its personnel assigned to the 1st, 22nd, and 602nd SOS, all of which had been grouped at NKP. Some of the 6th's assets were used to form the 56th SOW's Operating Location Alpha Alpha at Da Nang. It was then decided that the three squadrons at NKP, which had been specialized, would perform all Spad roles. During the peak years of 1969 and 1970 more than 100 Skyraiders equipped the four squadrons.

**Spad pilot Richard Michaud receives the traditional hosing down in celebration of his champagne flight in November 1970. (Michaud collection)**

Due to the Spad's age, combat attrition, and the Vietnamization program, the 22nd and 602nd squadrons were deactivated during late 1970. It then fell upon the 1st SOS to shoulder the load of close air support in Laos and South Vietnam, escort of special operations helicopters, and "Sandy" search and rescue. The last USAF A-1 sorties were flown from Da Nang in aircraft that had been given to the VNAF. Six A-1s were loaned back from the VNAF to cover the alert commitment for the Christmas "Linebacker" bombing campaign over Hanoi. In January 1973 these A-1s were flown back to bases in South Vietnam.

# 7

# Sandy

Search and rescue was, unquestionably, the Skyraider's crowning achievement. It became dramatically apparent early in the war that lone helicopters were too vulnerable to conduct combat search and rescue (CSAR). Therefore, a SAR task force in 1965 decided that rescue helicopters would work in pairs, and that Skyraiders would provide rescue escort.

Initially the task was performed by Navy A-1s, but by mid-August 1965 the 1st ACS sent a flight of A-1Es to Udorn RTAFB, Thailand, to cover F-105 strikes into high-threat areas. The move signaled the beginning of Air Force combat search and rescue, which evolved into a sophisticated, engrossing program. After several groups of A-1s rotated through Udorn during late 1965, an A-1 replacement flight led by Capt. J.W. "Doc" George inadvertently founded the popular "Sandy" call sign. It was George's Bien Hoa departure call sign. After the flight landed at Udorn, he was asked what call sign he would like to use while there. George replied, "Sandy." It was retained by George's replacement and became the call sign of any A-1 assigned the SAR mission.

Glenn Mackey, an A-1 pilot with the 1st ACS at the time, recounts the early days of the Sandy operation:

"The flight from the 1st ACS remained at Udorn for two weeks and was then replaced by a flight from the 602nd, commanded by Maj. Lou Gang. After their two-week tour they were to be replaced by 'A' Flight from the 1st, which I would lead. When we found out we were next, we quite anxiously debriefed our predecessors on what to expect. Since SA-2 missile sites were already quite active, we found the prospects for the upcoming mission to be rather challenging. We had no special equipment, such as radar warning or munitions, and had not had any training in search and rescue operations. Indeed, there was no operational SAR concept available to us. Apparently, we were just to go to Udorn and do our thing, whatever that was, for a month.

'A' flight departed Bien Hoa on 19 September with our six pilots. Capt. Mel Elliott was out of country on R &

**To replace the Kaman H-43 rescue helicopter in the ever-widening war, the CH-3C arrived in July 1965. The Skyraider's slow speed, and maneuverability at low altitudes allowed it to share the H-3's environment. (USAF)**

R, so his position was covered by Maj. Bernie Fisher. We were greeted at Udorn by Lou Gang, who was still steaming over being recalled by headquarters from an unsuccessful attempt to rescue Lt. Col. Robbie Risner a couple days earlier.

Since we had no training in this operation, I asked Lou to go along in the right seat on an 'orientation flight,' should his group be launched on its last day. Sure enough, on 20 September Lou was notified that an F-105 was down about 20 miles west of Vinh, North Vietnam. We arrived on scene in the afternoon, in good weather, guided to the site by the three remaining F-105s, who were circling at about 12,000 feet. The Air Force rescue helicopter capability at that time consisted mostly of HH-43 'Huskies' positioned at NKP. We were advised that two were on the way. We picked up the survival radio beeper almost immediately and circled over the area, which was hilly and completely covered with trees. The HH-43s arrived shortly thereafter.

We circled again, homing on the survival radio. I was in the right seat with nothing to do but take pictures and observe. The survivor noted the helicopter and popped red smoke; the HH-43 went into a hover and started to lower the sling. I remember thinking, 'This is really a smooth operation.' Suddenly, the rescue helicopter was shot down, crashing almost on top of the survivor. We had seen no ground fire until then. It happened so fast that I didn't actually see the crash. We called in Huskie number two, who started taking fire immediately on arrival in the area. He shortly called an abort, stating he had a crew member hit and was leaking fuel in the cabin.

So much for a rescue. We called in all the fighters in the area and began putting in air strikes around the crash site to cover any escape attempt by the downed crews. We soon had a dozen or more aircraft working the area, and we joined in with our load of rockets and 20mm. At one point I remember looking out and seeing smoke trailing from a rocket pod that had been hit. I called Lou to jettison, and he pulled the handle and dropped all the remaining pods. We stayed in the area for about two hours until dark, trying to give the survivors a best shot at evading. One of the helicopter crew almost made it to the Thai border before being captured. When we got back to Udorn we counted about a dozen holes in the aircraft. Score for the day: one F-105 and one HH-43 down; one HH-43 and two A-1Es damaged; and no rescues. Some orientation ride. I thought, 'This is going to be a very interesting month.'

The 'A' Flight took over the next day. Our operation was the pinnacle of simplicity. We had six pilots, 14 airmen, six A-1Es, and two tents at the end of the runway at Udorn's run-up area. Our supply tent had a few spare tires, radios, tool kits, some extra rocket pods, and a few other odds and ends. Our ops tent had some cots and a table. Midway through our tour we had a field telephone installed so we could be scrambled; before that, the scramble signal was a red flare from the tower. We were billeted in a hotel in town and rode bikes out to the base. We quickly set up a routine, paired off, and established a schedule: each pair on standby for two days, and one day off. On duty days, we got up about 3:30 AM and pedaled out to the command post, where we reviewed the daily frag order and negotiated our flying schedule on the spot.

It was a very informal arrangement which worked well. On days when strikes were going into high threat areas we would position a pair of Sandys at an alert point in Laos, usually near Lima Site 85. The other pair would pull ground alert, and would fly in the afternoon if necessary. If the strikes were in comparatively low threat areas we pulled ground alert. The airplanes were configured with two external fuel tanks and twelve seven-tube 2.75-inch rocket pods. Before leaving Bien Hoa I dug up a few boxes of WP smoke warheads for the rockets, which we installed soon after arriving.

Our month had its highs and lows. Bernie Fisher and Capt. Jack Stover covered one successful pickup, an F-105 pilot down near Dien Bien Phu. The Huskies had been forward deployed to locations like Lima Site 85 since they were very limited in range, load, and speed. We had two very frustrating and unsuccessful missions: an F-105 and an F-4C. Capt. Doyle Ruff took major damage from a large gun he ran across near Route 6 west of Hanoi while we were looking for the F-105 pilot in poor weather. With over 150 holes in the airplane—one in the right wing big enough to jump through—he was fortunate to be able to get the ship back to Udorn. But we all survived."

As the war dragged on and SAR operations became more complex, USAF Spads became a key element of SAR operations conducted by the Aerospace Rescue and Recovery Service (ARRS). SAR missions could be smooth and quick, or they could develop into operations that lasted for days and involved hundreds of aircraft sorties. Besides Sandys, the Search and Rescue Task Force comprised FACs, rescue helicopters, gunships, and fighters for flak suppression (ResCAP) and protection from MiGs (MiGCAP).

**The pure rescue version of the CH-3C was the air-refuelable HH-3E, dubbed the "Jolly Green Giant," seen here being escorted by a pair of 6th SOS A-1Hs in 1969. (USAF)**

Lockheed HC-130Hs "Crown" and HC-130Ps "King" served as airborne command posts; the latter having the capability to air-refuel HH-3E and HH-53 rescue helicopters. The Joint Search and Rescue Center at Saigon, call sign "Joker," coordinated rescue efforts with the NKP rescue center, nicknamed "Jack." They, along with the 3rd Aerospace Rescue and Recovery Group, determined the forces necessary to effect a rescue, which included every conceivable air, sea, and land resource from all services.

Although SAR strategies changed to keep pace with technology, lessons learned, and the tactical environment, a basic procedural plan remained in place throughout the war. The Sandy's mission was to locate the downed aircrew and to escort and provide suppressive fire for the rescue helicopters. Normally, a SAR team consisted of four A-1s, two HH-3 "Jolly Green" helicopters, and an HC-130 control aircraft. The Sandys operated in two flights of two aircraft each. Sandy One and Two were the "low" element, and Sandy Three and Four the "high" element. When concentrated firepower was required all four A-1s could work as a single flight.

The low element leader directed the on-scene effort, and had the awesome responsibility of deciding whether or not a pickup would be attempted. Direct voice contact with the survivor on the ground was especially helpful, since he could provide very useful information about his physical condition and hostile forces, and he could direct air strikes. Normally the low element lead made at least one high speed pass at low altitude to "troll for fire." His wing man carefully watched him from about 4,000 feet, ready to roll in and return fire. During the pickup phase, when one of the helicopters went in for the survivor, all four A-1s flew a "daisy chain" protectively around the helicopter, keeping the area under continuous threat.

Such missions were extremely dangerous, and Spad pilots did their best to maintain their perspective, putting great faith in their fellow pilots. Ed Leonard offers this example:

> "My first combat sortie was on the wing of the 602nd's operations officer in May 1967. During a briefing for the mission into Northern Laos he said, 'If I go down, Leonard will 'cap' me till the Sandys arrive and then will lead the rescue effort.' One of the other pilots said, 'But Leonard isn't qualified.' The ops officer replied, 'If he's alive when the Sandys finally get there, he'll be as qualified as anyone.' I did not find that reassuring."

**A pair of 1st SOS Spads escorts an HH-53C, which eventually replaced the HH-3E. (Leroy Lowe)**

Early in the war, after Spad pilots gained strike experience, they first became the high element wing man, then the low element wing man. They then moved on to high element lead, and when fully qualified, became "Sandy One."

After the consolidation of the 1st, 22nd, and 602nd SOSs under the 56th SOW at NKP, the wing issued a directive to A-1 Sandy alert pilots outlining A-1 SAR procedures and techniques. Included was a schedule that called for each squadron to provide two pilots—one element lead and his wing man—each day. A three-day alert cycle meant that a squadron provided Sandy Five and Six on one day, Sandy Three and Four the next day, and Sandy One and Two on the third day.

During a SAR scramble, Sandys One through Four were launched in sequence, while Five and Six reported to the Tactical Unit Operations Center (TUOC) to become current on intelligence, weather, and geographical information. If additional pairs of A-1s were needed they would assume consecutive Sandy call signs as they were launched. During Barrel Roll and Steel Tiger bombing campaigns, Sandys flew orbits which lasted up to five hours. If a SAR occurred during an orbit the Sandy roles reversed, since the orbiting A-1s were on-scene quickly. Sandys One and Two were then launched to escort the helicopters. The Spad's speed range was compatible with that of the Jolly Green's, enabling it to provide close cover throughout the mission. Besides NKP, Sandys also stood alert at Da Nang and Bien Hoa Air Bases in South Vietnam, and at Ubon RTAFB in Thailand.

Since nearly all strike activity during 1971 took place in Laos, the alert commitment at Bien Hoa was discontinued during early December. When the reduction in numbers of A-1s had reached the point during spring 1972 that additional Spads were needed at NKP for pilot training, the Sandy alert at Da Nang was discontinued.

By 1968 four basic Sandy ordnance configurations had been developed. Special ordnance for SAR operations was often loaded aboard Sandys that stood ground alert. This usually consisted of all smoke bombs to create smoke screens, or area denial ordnance, such as cluster bombs, "gravel," or riot control agents. Spads loaded with special ordnance had their own call signs, which changed daily. Typically, an A-1E/G flying a SAR mission used up its 150-gallon fuel tank on the right wing and dropped it, especially if the lead aircraft was an A-1H/J.

On 9 June 1968 Spad pilot Capt. Michael "Bat" Masterson described in a letter to fellow pilot Herb Meyr the daily SAR operations in Southeast Asia:

> "What really prompted this note was that Carl Light got shot down north of the DMZ Saturday afternoon. A 'Misty' FAC and some Spads from Da Nang went into the area and tried to set up a rescue effort, but the area was bad news, and they were getting hosed by 37s and ZPUs from everywhere. So the Misty worked some 'fast movers' (jet aircraft) on the area, but couldn't even begin to get the area quieted down by nightfall. They briefed us at 5:15 Sunday morning and had the pilot's name for us. When I heard it was Carl I was hoping to get in on it, as I figured

at worst I could pick up his spirits without coming over the air with any touchy information—like tell him he picked a lousy place to bail out, and that we'd figure a way to get him out. But it will cost him a round of drinks at the Cantina. I was Sandy 2 (1and 2 pull alert at Udorn), and Sandy 5 and 6 (two of our alert birds at NKP) went out on the Sunday morning effort after Mistys had worked another load of movers in the area.

It was like a hornet's nest, though. They started in and got driven back three times. After 5 and 6 had been on station four hours, they scrambled Sandy 9 and 10 out of NKP to take over when 5 and 6 got to 'bingo' fuel (enough only to get back to base). They got about halfway out there when a Navy bird went down and they got diverted to SAR that one. That put us as the next to launch. They scrambled and unscrambled us twice, and then decided too late to attempt a pickup—which proves once again the need to implement my suggestion of hanging a J-79 on the centerline and fitting the blue room with JP-4.

King was about to call the effort off and set up for a first light effort today, while continuing to pound the area with fast movers till dark, or later. Lt. Col. Carlson, 'The Mad Bomber,' was Sandy 5, and he said, 'Hell, we've got 40 minutes of fuel left, and I think we can get this guy if the Jollys are game to go in low and stay below the 37's line of sight.' King and Jolly said, 'Press on,' and after some further planning and strikes by the movers they went in on the deck, picked him up, and hauled ass for Da Nang. The Mad Bomber took a ZPU round right through the windscreen and got sprayed with glass, but he says they missed him by a good foot. He's something else. He recovered at Da Nang with only 200 pounds of fuel.

Carl had a few bruises, but other than that he was a damn happy guy. An F-4 was downed in the process, but he made it to the Gulf before punching out, and the other Jolly had both the F-4's front seater and the GIB (guy in back) in the chopper within 15 minutes. Everybody recovered at Da Nang and got together for a bull session about the whole effort. According to the troops when they got back last night, Carl really kept his cool during the whole effort and played a big role in the success of his own pickup.

**The A-1E no. 132444, named "The Abandoned 4's," stands Sandy alert at Da Nang in 1967. (Tom Hansen)**

Meanwhile, the effort on the Navy pilot was still going on about 35 miles from Da Nang. So the Mad Bomber had them rearm his aircraft and he leapt off again—shattered windscreen and all—to back up that effort. He recovered back at Udorn about 7:30 that night.

We had another wild SAR about a week and a half ago that ended up as the biggest SAR effort of the war. It went on for two and a half days and involved 189 strike sorties. It was a pickup of a Navy A-4 jock who was shot down on the second pass of his first combat sortie. Bill Palanc was the first Sandy on the scene, arriving about 4:30 in the afternoon. He got the guy's location pinpointed, then started checking the area and promptly got shot to hell. He pulled out of the area streaming oil with one cylinder shot out and a huge area gone from the mid portion of his left wing. He made it all the way to NKP, although he had an engine fire and zero oil pressure when he hit final approach. Ed Leonard took over as Sandy low and was shot down on his first pass into the area. He bailed out in the middle of the hornet's nest and, although he came up on the radio twice in the next 30 minutes, that was the last contact we ever had with him, and he is now officially MIA.

The effort was finally called for darkness and set up for a real firepower demonstration at first light, with eight Sandys set to launch from NKP in pairs, all day long if necessary, with the whole Alpha Force at their disposal. Palanc went back as the first Sandy low since he had the best knowledge of the area. Weather bogged things down initially, with the valley covered by 3,000-foot overcast. They made contact with the Navy jock and told him to stay hidden until the weather permitted working the area over with fast mover strikes. Everybody orbited outside the immediate area waiting for a weather break.

A couple of hours later the Navy jock came up on the air calling for help. He said *they* were coming through the trees and he was going to have to reveal his position and make a run for it. So Bill said, 'Hang on buddy, I'm coming in.' He hung his balls out one side and his ass out the other and let down through the overcast into the middle of the valley. He picked up the guy's position and hosed down the area around him with rockets and strafe. He lasted about ten minutes before he'd taken enough hits that his engine started coming unglued. He was losing control. He held it long enough to get about three miles outside the valley, then punched out. The Jollys followed his chute down and had him in the chopper within five minutes. He banged both knees on the canopy rail and picked up a chipped tooth and a black eye—other than that he was in good shape. He apparently did good work, as the Navy jock said he didn't hear anybody coming through the trees anymore. The weather broke around noon, and they put in nearly six hours of solid air strikes, then tried for a sundown pickup. But they got driven out again by ZPUs and 37s.

The weather was good on the third day, so a Nail FAC worked six more hours of strike on the area. Finally they decided to make a big move. We put six Sandys in: two escorting the choppers and four strafing, firing rockets, and generally making a lot of noise—and it worked. When they got him in the chopper they found that he'd taken shrapnel in both cheeks of his ass from a CBU dropped earlier in the day. At last report he was smiling and resting (on his stomach) at the NKP hospital. A couple of the troops who have since pulled alert at NKP talked to him at the hospital, and he was a mighty happy and appreciative troop. He said his wife was due to have a baby within four weeks, and that regardless of whether it was a boy or girl its first name is going to be 'Sandy.'"

This was the last Meyr heard from his friend who, less than four months later, himself became the subject of a SAR operation when he bailed out of his Spad on a night strike mission over Laos. He remains on the rolls of the Missing In Action.

As a postscript to the three-day mission Masterson described, on 31 May Navy pilot Ken Fields ("Streetcar 304") was shot down in his A-7 near Tchepone, Laos. Six aircraft were lost, Ed Leonard was captured after he bailed out, and Tom Campbell received the Air Force Cross for leading the rescue of Fields on the third day.

Among the "Old Heads" in the Spad community was Lt. Col. Ralph Hoggatt, whose wealth of experience was gained from flying B-24 bombers during World War II and having served as a C-124 and C-130 instructor. Hoggatt was working as a research psychologist when he was called for combat duty in 1967. He was assigned to the 602nd FS(C) and flew more than 200 combat missions, half of them over North Vietnam.

On 11 November 1967 Hoggatt, along with his wing man, Major William Griffith, led a rescue force for an F-4C crew down near Mu Gia Pass in Laos. While Hoggatt went low to contact a survivor and strafe the area, Griffith circled protectively above. Shortly after Griffith's Spad was badly hit and he ejected. After returning enemy fire Hoggatt called in a Jolly Green to get his wing man, but the chopper was driven off by heavy fire. During the second attempt, with Hoggatt's supporting fire, the helicopter was able to hover and lower a pararescueman (PJ) to Griffith, and both men were pulled into the helicopter.

Although Hoggatt's Spad was badly damaged, he returned to continue the search for the F-4 survivor. He remained to show inbound A-1s the general location of the survivor and enemy guns, and stayed with them until he was *bingo* fuel. With his Spad badly damaged and leaking fluids, and extremely low on fuel, Hoggatt headed for Udorn. When he could not lower his landing gear he had to wait for the runway to be foamed for his crash-landing. Surprisingly, his gear lowered as he prepared to touch down. For his extraordinary courage in the face of overwhelming odds Col. Hoggatt was awarded the Air Force Cross.

No two SAR missions were alike, with each presenting its own special circumstances. Noteworthy is what came to be known as the "Oyster SAR," during which rescue forces had to incapacitate an enemy MiG base in order to pull off the rescue. Spad pilot Dave Preston provides some insight:

"The SAR was for Roger Locher, who was 'Oyster 01B,' an F-4 back-seater whose aircraft went down on 10 May 1972 (the "A" suffix of a call sign denoted the pilot). Oyster 01 was lost on a mission in the 'Bullseye' (Hanoi) area, and no radio contact was obtained with either crewman. Three weeks later, Oyster 01B came up on the emergency *guard* radio channel to contact an F-4 flight transiting the area. Locher reported that he was now in position for a pickup after evading for 21 days. The general area was northwest of Hanoi, and his position was determined to be near the Yen Bai MiG base. After a search by fast movers, his position was determined more precisely to be in some high karst overlooking the base.

A first light mission was planned for the next day, which would surely tax the logistical capabilities of the rescue forces due to the survivor's location so far north. The mission would have to rely upon adequate MiGCAP cover, it would require several refuelings of the Jolly Greens inbound and outbound, and it would require refueling tanker support for the fast mover aircraft, to say nothing of the requirement for 'oversize kahunas' by all the participants flying down low—including the A-1s.

The first day's effort was aborted due mostly to 7th AF failure to ensure that MiGCAP aircraft and adequate tanker support was present. The rescue forces were 'sitting ducks' in a very hostile location and couldn't prosecute beneath the traffic pattern of a MiG base without some pretty dependable fast mover support. The mission was rescheduled for the following day, which gave Locher an opportunity to reposition himself to a location more conducive to a successful pickup.

**A pair of 1st SOS A-1Hs on a Sandy mission in their element over Southeast Asia. (USAF)**

On the second day, for the first time in the war, permission was given to bomb the MiG base at a time coincidental to the time of the rescue attempt. The *rules of engagement* were being bent just this one time to allow this purposeful destruction of the enemy's air base. This would serve as both a diversion and a deterrent to any MiG aircraft trying to take off and interfere with the rescue forces. Despite some further lapses in required support activities, and a lot of tense moments, the pickup was successful. The SAR forces then had to accomplish a very hairy egress and recovery to more friendly confines, which were nearly 300 nautical miles away."

Ron Smith, who flew both days of the Oyster SAR, offers his recollection:

"The fast movers who first made contact with Oyster 01B, and authenticated him successfully, mis-plotted him by about three miles. They thought he was right in the middle of the Red River Valley. In searching for him, I was close enough to Yen Bai to have put the gear down and turned final. Luckily Locher was not that close, but it was obvious we would have to put Yen Bai out of commission for an hour or so in order to make the pickup. I heard that the request to do that went to the president for approval. He had just visited China, and had told them he would begin bombing locations where the Chinese had advisors. This was inside that window, and I give him credit for deciding to go ahead rather than deny permission. The strike on the airfield was runway busting only. The F-4s did a great job cratering the runway in at least two places and not hitting anything else.

Since I had already been to the site I was selected to lead the mission. The squadron commander, Lt. Col. Jim Harding, assumed the Sandy Three position and picked Lt. Col. Don Latham as his wing man. My wing man, Capt. Buck Buchanan, came to the TUOC to look at the intel maps of the area while I was studying them. Had he not done that I might have picked someone else, but I am sure picking Buck was the best decision I made that day. In 24 years in the Air Force, I can honestly say I was never in a flying organization with a better group of people to pick as wing men.

We took off at first light on 2 June with four A-1s and two Jollys from NKP. The rest of the mission package came from other locations, mostly Udorn and Ubon. The plan was to have Sandys Three and Four stay with the Jollys in the mountains south of the valley while Buck and I searched for the survivor. Yen Bai was to be hit as we crossed the river, and the flight designated to take out the guns was to hold until we got them to shoot at us, since these guns had not been plotted before.

I was in radio contact with Roger and authenticated him again with a question that was not on his list (lists of personal information made out by combat aircrew were kept on file so rescue forces could differentiate them from enemy troops with captured radios they used to bait rescue forces). As the guns opened up on us I asked the F-4s if they needed us to mark the targets. They were watching the show and, luckily, could easily see where they were located, so we did not have to turn back to fire marking rockets. Roger also helped, calling that he could hear us and saw them shooting at us.

The only way to get him with helicopters was to go up the Red River, around Yen Bai, and approach him from the northwest. It was mostly mountainous terrain, but it would take much longer and leave little time for mistakes, or we would be out of gas. We had planned for this possibility, so we knew exactly where to cross the river. I had instructed Roger to be ready for us. I also told him that he would not see or hear us until we were on top of him, since we would approach from the other side of the mountain, and he should have his flares ready, and to hit the first A-1 he saw with his signal mirror.

The F-4s had done a great job on the guns. They were still smoking. When Roger flashed Buck with his mirror, Buck directed the lead Jolly toward him. The only ordnance we expended in the area was smoke CBU to block the visibility from the gun sites on a dam a couple of miles away. It took only a couple of minutes to pick up Roger, and we headed out nearly the same way we came in. Although we scared some people off the roads as we departed, it was fairly quiet until we got to the Red River crossing. As we crested the hills north of the river we found ourselves flying over a freight train. Buck and I were past it before we could react, but we warned the Jollys behind us. We took some fire from the train, and Sandys Three and Four, who were last in the flight, attacked it and destroyed the engine.

When they caught up with us we received a MiG warning very close to us. I then found out our MiGCAP fast movers had gone to the tanker. It was hard to be upset with them after the job their buddies had done on the guns, but the plan called for continuous coverage. I sent Sandys Three and Four ahead of the Jollys flying low and straight toward the HC-130 waiting to refuel them about 100 miles away. Meanwhile, Buck and I climbed up and away from the rest of the flight to divert any MiGs that might have been there. The fast movers returned a few minutes later. The rest of the flight was uneventful, except when King ordered us to return to NKP while the Jollys took Roger to Udorn. Since there was no way we were not going to meet the guy I had been talking to for two days, I told them the Jollys needed escort all the way to Udorn."

Besides the Air Force Cross Smith earned that day over North Vietnam, a total of nine Silver Stars were awarded to airmen involved in Oyster 01B's rescue.

Ken Lengfield provides this story, which not only underscores the confusion so prevalent in the heat of battle, but the belief that lives were spared thanks to a much higher authority than 7th Air Force. Lengfield adds, "It describes the events of a night in September 1964 when I almost killed my pal, Bill May, by mistake:"

"The bombing in North Vietnam and Laos, and the truck hunting on the Ho Chi Minh Trail, had not yet started. The most activity was in the IV Corps area south of Saigon. The further south you went, the deeper into enemy territory you were. There were a few small forts down there, and they were the only friendly pockets in the rice paddy country south of the Mekong River. At night the whole area belonged to 'Charlie.' The enemy was pretty much in charge of deciding just when and where any fighting would take place.

We maintained at least two aircraft on alert status at all times. One night in September 1964 my friends Bill May and George Flynn were on alert with two VNAF junior pilots, as required, to support our cover training story. Bill and George got a scramble order to provide air support for a fort that was under heavy attack deep in IV Corps.

There was a full moon that night. I cannot remember ever seeing a brighter night anywhere, and it was not the ideal condition for night combat. Even with lights out the aircraft made good targets.

About 1 AM I was awakened by the command post in Saigon and told that Flynn, the wing man, had been shot down. The C-47 flareship was reporting heavy ground fire in the area. I immediately woke several pilots and called the flightline to set up all available aircraft to support a rescue operation. By the time I got to the flightline the command post called to tell me the lead aircraft was also down. We were going to have an interesting night.

The squadron commander, Lt. Col. John Porter, led the first element of two aircraft, and I led the second. When we arrived in the battle area we could see both aircraft on the ground burning, about two miles apart. The flareship advised us that both pilots of the first aircraft shot down had bailed out. There were no chutes from the lead aircraft. There was a lot of ground fire in the area, and it was especially heavy in the vicinity of the burning A-1s.

Col. Porter initiated the first attack in the area where the ground fire appeared to be coming from. I rolled in behind him to attack the same area. His ordnance was right on target, so I pulled off dry. I knew we would need all the firepower we had to neutralize the area, and I didn't want to waste any on overkill. The ground fire appeared to start up again, and then some young lieutenant with better sense than us veteran fighter pilots yelled on the radio, 'That's not ground fire, that's a survival wink light!' He was absolutely right. We had been trying to kill one of the survivors.

We called in an Army helicopter supporting the rescue effort and they picked up Bill May. Bill said that as the chopper approached him, a huge crew member reached out and grabbed him, pulling him on board and said, 'God bless you. Sir.' I believe that God did indeed bless Bill that night, because the rest of us were trying to kill him.

The helicopter was also able to rescue the VNAF pilot from the other aircraft. He had seen George taken prisoner, put into a sampan, and taken away. A few days later we were told that George had tried to escape and was shot. The VNAF pilot from May's aircraft was also taken prisoner, and was released several years later in very poor condition.

The story doesn't end there; the helicopter that picked up the survivors went down after leaving the battle area. A second chopper picked everyone up and took them to Bien Hoa. When the survivors arrived at the base, the wing commander was so happy to see them he ran out and gave Bill a big bear hug. That cracked one of Bill's ribs, and it was the only injury he received that night."

Often a SAR effort for downed aircrew was compounded when aircraft involved in the rescue were downed. Such was the case when an F-4D, "Stormy 02," was shot down near Tchepone, Laos, on 17 January 1969. The pilot did not get out, but the back-seater was able to eject. Early in the SAR operation Lt. Col. Lurie J. Morris of the 602[nd] SOS was shot down. The next day Stormy 02B was rescued, but Morris' rescue proved more challenging. During the effort to rescue him another 602[nd] Sandy, Capt. Robert F. Coady, was shot down and killed on impact. The SAR force was able to get Morris out, but the Jolly Green helicopter was hit by ground fire and crashed. Another Jolly Green picked up the six survivors, some of whom were badly wounded, including Morris.

Search and rescue operations were often conducted for customers other than downed flyers. For example: on 14 September 1970, 1Lt. Thomas Stump and his wingman, 1Lt. Chris Tateishi, of the 602[nd] SOS were scrambled on a first light rescue attempt for a U.S. Army long-range reconnaissance team trapped deep within an enemy lair. As part of "Operation Tailwind," the team had been under heavy fire for two days. In extremely poor weather, Stump and Tateishi dove to tree-top level to trade blows with enemy gunners, and to clear an escape path for the besieged team. Rather than climb above the overcast and lose sight of the team the Spads hugged the terrain to avoid heavy ground fire.

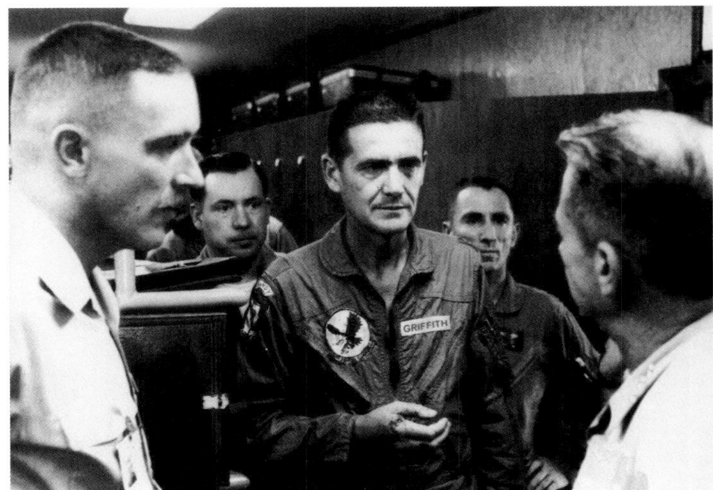


**They wear the war on their faces. Maj. Griffith holds a broken thumb during a briefing shortly after he was rescued during a search and rescue mission on 11 November 1967. Griffith was shot down while searching for an F-4C downed in Laos. His wing man's A-1, flown by Lt. Col. Ralph Hoggatt, was badly damaged. (USAF)**

When the team was a mere 50 meters from the LZ the enemy launched a desperate attack to overrun them. Again the Spads attacked as the enemy fired rocket-propelled grenades at them at point blank range. Stump and Tateishi made 20 passes each, strafing and dropping ordnance within ten meters of the team until the enemy had been beaten. Their courage and skill enabled the recon team to get to the LZ, where they were rescued, climaxing three days of bitter fighting. Stump offers this perspective:

> "When I talked on the radio to the team leader, Gene McCarley, he said, 'We're gettin' the shit kicked out of us!' He was very cool and professional throughout, directing our strikes while he coordinated his people on the ground. The fast movers were unable to help because of the close proximity of the enemy and poor visibility. However, the A-1 was the perfect aircraft for those conditions. We rearmed at Da Nang and returned to knock out several 37mm and 57mm sites along a major interdiction point close by that posed a major threat to the Cobra and HH-53 helicopters making the extraction. We lost the HH-53 McCarley was on to ground fire, but they made it out of the area and another HH-53 was brought in to rescue them. The bad guys were very determined to capture or kill the team because of all the valuable maps and plans the team had captured."

The combat SAR mission during which the largest number of persons was rescued occurred on 6 October 1969. Two CH-53 helicopters ("Knife 61" and "62") of the 21st SOS, with a total of 60 people—8 aircrew and 52 indigenous troops—were down in Laos. They were under continuous attack for about six hours. Repeated low level and close-in strafing and bombing, plus the use of tear gas by six A-1s of the 602nd SOS, enabled two HH-53s to rescue 52 survivors.

As proof of the extent to which Americans would go to accomplish a rescue was the "Boxer 22" SAR during early December 1969. The three-day operation was the largest air rescue effort of the conflict. A total of 430 aircraft took part in a 51-hour operation that was plagued by bad weather, rough terrain, and fierce anti-aircraft defenses. About 100 enemy anti-aircraft guns were attacked by air. A dozen A-1s and as many Jolly Green helicopters were badly damaged during 16 rescue attempts, and a pararescueman was killed—all as testimony to the value Americans placed on a single human life.

Boxer 22 was an F-4 shot down near the Mu Gia Pass in Laos, killing the pilot. The back-seater, Lt. Woodrow Bergeron, Jr., survived. During his three-day ordeal Bergeron was actually lifted off the ground by A-1 strikes and 20mm rounds fired within a meter of him from covering Spads. The enemy used Bergeron as bait to fire on the A-1s and Jolly Greens when they came in close. A total of 11 Sandy lead sessions were conducted by pilots from the three A-1 squadrons at NKP. On the third day, after six hours of bombing and strafing, Maj. Tom Dayton of the 22nd SOS brought in a Jolly, and on its second try snatched Bergeron from the enemy. The number of awards for the operation was a USAF record for a single action.

The last SAR mission in which A-1s participated occurred on 7 November 1972. The day before a U.S. Army Huey helicopter with seven people aboard became trapped in a valley by a typhoon. With little fuel left, and among mountains in heavy clouds, the Huey pilot slowly spiraled downward from 8,000 feet until he landed on a sandbar. Knowing they were in enemy territory and beyond radio range, the crew got away from the aircraft. That night the NVA searched for them as they transmitted emergency beeper signals. By morning the brook where the Huey had landed had become a raging river that washed their helicopter away.

**An A-1J of the 1st SOS flies low during a Sandy mission. (USAF)**

As they moved inland, the crew's spirits were lifted when they heard a Skyraider, whose pilot kept in radio contact with them. Shortly thereafter, Army helicopters appeared and fired on a nearby tree line, where movement had been detected. Then a pair of Jolly Greens came into view to complete the rescue.

The Huey crew later discovered that they were being tracked by two elements of an NVA regiment, and they were close to being captured. That made it easier to explain to their group commander they had no idea where their Huey was.

Nearly 30 years after the incident the Huey copilot, Capt. Bertrand Schreibstein, contacted the A-1 pilot, Don Screws. Screws explained that in 1972 all the A-1s were being retired and replaced by A-7s. That week, 12 A-7s were scheduled for SAR training missions. The last seven A-1s of the 1st SOS were being transferred to the VNAF, so he had to sign a hand receipt for his A-1. Since the Spads flown by Screws and his wing man had plenty of fuel left after the SAR mission, they were directed to fly to Bien Hoa to turn the A-1s over to the VNAF, instead of returning to Da Nang.

Skyraider pilots felt a kinship with helicopter pilots since they operated in the same low and slow environment, sharing danger. Combat chopper pilots knew that only another A-1 could replace an A-1. But only the 1st SOS was left with Spads, and their days were numbered. After three A-1s were downed by SA-7 "Strela" missiles in May-June 1972, a modified flare pod to divert the missiles was added to the Sandy load. In addition, a change in tactics had the wing man above 7,000 feet to watch for missile launches. After feasibility tests conducted during 1971, the 7th Air Force decided the A-7 could perform the rescue role. All A-1s were to be turned over to the VNAF by the end of 1972, and the 1st SOS transferred to Kadena AB, Okinawa. All Stateside USAF A-1s, other than a few retained for training, also went to the VNAF.

The A-7 equipped 354th TFW assumed the Sandy role, prudently employing experienced A-1 and FAC pilots during a crash training course. The A-7s flew their first SAR mission on 16 November for an F-105G shot down over North Vietnam. The effort lasted three days, during which the A-7s, because of their speed, had difficulty staying with the helicopters, often lost sight of key elements, and burned fuel rapidly, necessitating regular trips to the tanker. Nevertheless, A-7D pilot Capt. Colin A. Clarke, in true Sandy tradition, battled bad weather, faulty communications, and heavy ground fire to bring in Jolly Greens.

The Aerospace Rescue and Recovery Service is credited with saving 3,883 lives during the war in Southeast Asia. Had it not been for the Spad and the determination of its pilots, that number would be significantly smaller.

# 8

# Above and Beyond

Of 13 Medals of Honor awarded U.S. Air Force airmen who served in the Southeast Asian conflict, two were earned by Skyraider pilots. The first of those pale blue ribbons was hung by the President around the neck of Major Bernard F. Fisher on 19 January 1967. Bernie Fisher's photograph hung over the bar in the officer's club at Pleiku, an unlikely homage in view of the unassuming Spad pilot's commitment to the strait-laced Mormon religion. But having become the first U.S. Air Force aviator in Southeast Asia to be awarded the nation's highest military award, the photo, hung there by his fellow Air Commando pilots, was fitting tribute.

Fisher earned his fame in the A Shau, a narrow, forbidding valley in South Vietnam's I Corps Tactical Zone, known by airmen and grunts alike as a lethal gauntlet lined with anti-aircraft positions, and home to North Vietnamese Army units. U.S. Special Forces found it an ideal site for observing and impeding Viet Cong and North Vietnamese troops who infiltrated from Laos into South Vietnam. During early March 1966 the Special Forces camp at A Shau, which had a 2,500-foot PSP airstrip, was defended by 17 Green Berets and nearly 400 indigenous troops. The camp was beyond artillery range and depended on air strikes for support. Since the area was of strategic importance to both sides a major battle was inevitable. Knowing that American airpower could decimate their ranks, the enemy wisely waited for the worst seasonal weather to set in to launch their attack. During the early hours of 9 March, with thick clouds blanketing the valley making air support nearly impossible, the attack came.

The determined crew of an AC-47 gunship, "Spooky Two-One," initially managed to find its way down through the clouds, but was shot down before it could set up for a strafing pass. Three of its crew were killed, three were rescued by two Da Nang-based HH-43 helicopters, and the seventh is MIA. The first A-1s into the bitterly contested area were from the VNAF 516[th] Fighter Squadron, flown by Captain Thai Van De, followed by his wingman, USAF advisor Major Lester R. Hewitt. De led Hewitt down through the clouds and a CV-2 Caribou followed. Both A-1s expended their ordnance, and the Caribou dropped its cargo by parachute. De's Spad was pummeled by ground fire, knocking out its hydraulics, so he and Hewitt went back up through the hole. That afternoon Fisher, who was assigned to the 1[st] ACS at Pleiku, was being briefed for a classified mission when it was suddenly changed to A Shau, a place he had never been. When Fisher arrived on scene he found a number of aircraft above the 6,000-foot thick cloud deck, looking for a way down through the soup into the embattled valley.

Fisher found a hole, hugged the valley floor between the peaks, and began strafing the fort's perimeter. In a superb display of airmanship, Fisher went back up through the hole and down again three times, never alone, but escorting a medevac helicopter—which rescued some of the badly wounded—two more flights of A-1Es to lay ordnance around the fort, two C-123 *Providers* for supply drops

**Bernie Fisher and "Jump" Meyers shortly after the daring rescue. Fisher's helmet still carried the silhouette of a jet, reflecting his prior assignment to an F-104 squadron. (Author's collection)**

of medical supplies and ammunition, and a pair of B-57s with napalm and rockets. Before darkness sealed the valley, several helicopters were able to get in to evacuate the seriously wounded. One Marine UH-34 was downed inside the camp. Fisher's copilot that day, Captain Robert Blood, marveled, "He was the bird dog all afternoon. Everybody was just milling around on top until he went in and took charge." The next morning Fisher was told he would get the Silver Star, but the recommendation was lost to the events about to unfold.

That morning, as "Hobo Five-One," he took off on a routine bomb-and-strafe mission, with Captain Francisco "Paco" Vazquez, "Hobo Five-Two," flying another A-1E on his wing. They had been airborne only ten minutes when they were diverted to A Shau. Fisher knew the weather would be the same as the day before. Reaching the cloud-covered area, Fisher found other Skyraiders looking for a hole and, once again, it was he who found it. Two Spads followed Fisher and Vazquez down to the battlefield in trail formation. Two others, Hoboes Two-Seven and Two-Eight, penetrated the overcast soon after and held at a position over an abandoned airfield. Fisher and his wing man roared down the narrow valley, six miles to the besieged camp. Every pilot who came into A Shau that day had to dive 6,000 feet through the clouds, level off above the trees, and then run the gauntlet to the camp. There was little room to maneuver until they reached the camp, where the valley widened. Knowing that, the enemy had set up about 20 anti-aircraft weapons along the valley's ridgelines and prepared to carve meat.

Fisher hugged the ground at about 50 feet altitude and raised the camp's defenders on his FM radio. He said, "I'm the A-1E that just passed over. Where do you want the ordnance?" They answered calmly, "Hit the south wall. They're coming over the south wall." Fisher radioed Vazquez, who was on his tail, to set up for strafe. Behind Vazquez was Major Dafford "Jump" Myers, "Surf Four-One," being followed by his wingman, Captain Hubert King, "Surf Four-Two." All felt ground fire hitting their aircraft. King was almost through the gauntlet when a burst of automatic weapon fire shattered his windshield, missing him by inches. Unable to see through the glass, he pulled up through the clouds and out of the valley.

Myers had just pulled off his second strafing pass when he felt his Spad lurch. Myers said:

> "It was a good solid hit that shook the whole plane and rattled my teeth. I've been hit before by the fifty calibers, and this was something a lot bigger, maybe the Chinese 37mm cannon.
>
> The engine sputtered, and then it conked out for good. The cockpit filled with smoke. I got on the radio and gave my call sign, 'Surf Four-One,' and said, 'I've been hit and hit hard.' Bernie came right back and said, 'Rog, you're on fire and burning clear back to your tail.' I was way too low and said, 'I'll have to put her down on the strip.' I had kept the same angle of bank around the ridgeline after I got hit, and I knew I was coming around toward the north end of the strip. I never saw the runway because of the smoke blowing in my face, but I got a rough fix on my position by looking over my left shoulder and the canopy. From that point on, Bernie talked me down.
>
> He was very cool about it, and that helped. I held my breath for as long as I could, but then I started eating a lot of smoke. Bernie called, 'You look pretty good four-one, take her to the left a little, get your gear down and jettison your ordnance.' I was still carrying 12 frag bombs and two white phosphorous that might go off on impact. I dumped them just short of the runway. Bernie said, 'That looks good, that looks good,' but about five seconds later he said, 'You're too hot, you're too hot, get your gear up—you'll have to belly her in.'"

As Myers touched down the wheels were still coming up and crumpled beneath the Spad. When he dumped his ordnance his centerline fuel tank had not released. Vazquez adds:

> "As Myers approached touchdown I was flying toward him on a reciprocal heading. I was about 500 feet high and 500 feet east of the runway and parallel to it. I saw his belly tank split open and fuel spilled out and ignited. The airplane slid for about one thousand feet, leaving behind a line of burning fuel down the center of the runway. As Surf Four-One slowed to a stop the right wing dragged on the runway and the airplane swerved to the right, finally coming to rest just off the west side of the runway. The remaining belly tank fuel fed an intense fire that immediately swallowed the airplane."

For nearly a minute Fisher saw no sign of life from below.

Right after he impacted the strip Myers opened the left canopy panel, only to be greeted by roaring flames, so he slammed it shut. Deciding that the only way out was by breaking through the right canopy panel, he frantically shed his harness and parachute. "My biggest fear," he said, "was when I pushed that lever to open the right window." But fortune smiled on Jump Myers—the canopy popped open and a stiff breeze opened a path through the flames that, to Myers, seemed like the path through the Red Sea. He ran along the wing, jumped off, and squatted down in a patch of weeds.

"I still thought I was a dead man, because I knew the strip was under enemy control. They don't take prisoners in the middle of a battle." Sustained fire from camp defenders in the bunker nearest Myers kept the enemy from reaching him. A Special Forces sergeant drew heavy fire each time he tried to go over the wall to go to Myers. In a spate of hopelessness, Myers began mulling over his family and the dashed opportunity to take leave in Bangkok and his forthcoming promotion to lieutenant colonel.

Then Fisher roared past not more than 25 feet off the strip. Myers jumped up and waved:

> "I was trying to signal him I was okay and to get the hell out of there. It was like a shooting gallery. The enemy around the fort let loose with what sounded like a thousand automatic weapons, all of then aimed at Bernie."
>
> "When Jump headed into the strip," said Fisher:
>
> "I got on the radio to Control and told them we had a pilot down, and to get a chopper in there real fast. When he hit the runway and burned I waited for almost a minute,

and then I radioed Control, 'Plane on fire, pilot did not get out.' I was sure he was dead. And then I saw him scrambling off the wing with smoke pouring out of his flight suit. I was sure he was burned real bad."

Seeing the enemy closing in on Myers, Fisher dropped bombs while his wingman, Vazquez, strafed, feeling ground fire hit his Spad. Vazquez picks up the story:

"Fisher descended to about 100 feet and circled the burning crash site looking for the pilot. While he searched, I held north, worked on my radio difficulties, and considered our situation. We had lost two airplanes in a matter of minutes, and still did not know the location of the AAA guns. We had expended half our ordnance and I doubted anyone else would be able to penetrate the weather and give us some help before we ran low on gas. As Fisher continued to orbit, AAA tracers came raining down near him. I radioed a warning to Fisher, and told him I'd try to take the gun out.

The gun was about 600 feet from the runway, high on the eastern hills. It had been strategically placed at the same height as the flat deck cloud ceiling, making an attack from above impossible. A level strafing attack seemed best. I climbed to cloud level, centered the target in the windshield, and opened fire. A cluster of at least three guns fired back, suggesting a multiple-gun mount, perhaps a quad. I fired off-and-on for about 10 to 12 seconds to no effect. In retrospect, I believe we were both shooting high, perhaps because of the unfamiliar close-range, level attack.

In short order, I was in a jam. The ridge ahead was an unbroken barrier rising from the valley floor through the solid 700-foot ceiling. To break off the attack and turn away would invite a clear shot at my underside from very close range. The terrain below was rising fast, and climbing would immediately put me in the clouds and out of the fight. I reset the bomb release control to single releases. As the target drew closer I eased the stick back, entered the clouds, and—in a shallow climb—hurriedly punched off my remaining eight bombs, 'walking' the bursts through the target. After all bombs released I banked into a steep, hard left turn and held four Gs. Seconds later the plane dropped through the bottom of the clouds and I was back in the valley. Fisher was about one mile ahead. I tried to radio him but my UHF radio was now dead."

Fisher again asked control about the helicopter and again was told, "15 to 20 minutes." Certain that the North Vietnamese would get to Myers before the rescue chopper arrived, and that it had little chance of getting in and out through the barrage of gunfire, Fisher made his decision. He told Control he was going in and radioed the pair of A-1Es holding near the fort that he was going in and to cover him.

The two Spads, flown by Captain Jon Lucas, "Hobo Two-Seven," and his wingman, Captain Dennis Hague, "Hobo Two-Eight," roared in, with Vazquez falling in behind in a racetrack pattern, and saturated the east side of the runway. Days later a Special Forces Captain told how that ordnance destroyed at least a company of North Vietnamese massed to cross the airstrip, probably kill Jump Myers, and assault the east side of the camp. The captain added, "It took all the pressure off the east wall, and it had a lot to do with us getting out alive."

Lucas, Hague, and Vazquez stayed in a tight left bank so that they were hitting targets every 15 seconds. Certain that the enemy would look for him first at the burning airplane, and concerned that it might explode, Myers crawled to get away from it. He encountered a minefield so he crawled back:

"I said to myself, 'Myers, you have really had it now.' The last thought on my mind was rescue. I knew a chopper would never survive the ground fire, and it simply never occurred to me that somebody would be crazy enough to put an A-1E down on that strip. The steel planking was all buckled up into spikes by mortar rounds, and it was littered with rocket pods, 55-gallon fuel drums, and the debris from my plane. When I heard Bernie's last string of bombs hit and I saw him circle around and then head into the north end of the runway, all I thought was, 'Well, now there are two of us down here.'"

Fisher said:

"I dropped that last string west of the runway to keep their heads down, and also because I wanted to come into that short strip as light as possible. I had it firmly in my mind that the other guys flying cover would give me all the protection I needed. I've flown with these guys, and they are real cool characters, and they hit what they're shooting at."

On his final approach Fisher became enveloped in smoke from the camp, and when he was through it realized he was too fast, so he settled onto the strip for just a couple hundred feet. He saw Myers wave, then gave it power and took off again. Vazquez notes:

"Radio problems had kept me in the dark about Fisher's discussions with the airborne command post that culminated with his decision not to wait for a rescue helicopter. Fisher appeared to be on a left base leg with gear and flaps extended. I assumed he had been hit and was trying to reach the runway. To my surprise his airplane touched down on the runway, rolled for a while, and became airborne again. That's when I realized he planned to pick up the downed pilot."

Fisher bent it around tight in a teardrop turn and came in from the opposite direction, holding it at 95 knots. He just cleared the trees, raised the flaps, and leaned on the brakes even before the tail came down. Riding the brakes, he steered around jagged holes, hitting rocket pods the A-1E's stout gear simply kicked aside. Fisher said:

"Then I saw the end of the runway coming up way too fast. I knew that if I hit the brakes any harder I might burn them up or tip the bird over on her nose. That was the first time all day I was scared. I had to make a decision."

He chose the runway overrun over slamming on the brakes. He swung the Spad around in the mud and grass, applied power, and taxied back down the runway looking for Myers. Myers waved from the weeds, but when Fisher braked he did not see him running. Thinking Myers was badly hurt, Fisher set the parking brakes, unstrapped, and began to exit the aircraft to go and get him. Bullets were smashing into his airplane, one narrowly missing his head.

Meanwhile, the other A-1Es were flying strafing runs 50 feet above the ground. Lucas was still leading the loose string, but he had been hit and was on fire, his cockpit full of smoke. His wingman, Hague, radioed, "You're burning, better get the hell out." "Rog," Lucas answered, "Can't leave Bernie yet. We'll make one more pass." When they both acknowledged they were *Winchester*—out of ammunition—Lucas said, "But they (the enemy) don't know that." Vazquez adds:

> "I went Winchester on the first pass led by Lucas. Though badly damaged by ground fire, Lucas continued to lead through three more passes, giving Fisher time to effect a successful rescue of Surf Four-One. Having expended all ammo, we made a last 'dry' pass while Fisher rolled."

Myers, seeing the Spad on the airstrip, assumed another had been shot down. When he realized it was there for him, he said, "Why, that crazy S.O.B. has come in here to get me out." Amid a hail of gunfire, he ran for the Spad. The run seemed an eternity, both to Myers and to the pilots overhead. He dashed down the middle of the runway in full view of every enemy soldier in the area. Not all the rounds were meant for him, for a bunker on the north wall kept up a heavy volume of fire to cover the rescue. The gunfire was deafening, the bullets whining all around. For the third time that day, Myers was certain he was a dead man.

Fisher was about to jump out the right side when he glimpsed movement in his rearview mirror. It was Myers scrambling up the wing on his hands and knees. He dove into the cockpit, his legs flailing around Fisher and the instrument panel. Fisher grabbed him by the back of his flight suit and set him right side up. Lucas was just coming around for his last pass, his Spad billowing smoke. Fisher whipped the tail around, slammed the throttle forward and, again, did his runway dance around obstacles, adding power and using the last foot of the strip to get airborne. An eye witness in the camp said the soldiers holding the fort cheered as Fisher's Spad roared down the strip and finally lifted off the ground. Vazquez rejoined him, and they hugged the valley floor until clear of the gauntlet, climbed up through the clouds, and leveled off on top of them.

Fisher knew his Spad had taken numerous hits, but he and Vazquez headed for home base at Pleiku. He said:

> "Jump couldn't talk to me because he didn't have a radio headset. He signaled me for a cigarette, and I shook my head, because I don't smoke. He gave me a couple of hugs and held up a finger, meaning 'number one.' He was a mess. He got mud all over everything he touched, and the smoke from his flight suit stunk up the whole cabin. But we couldn't help turning to each other and laughing all the way home."

As soon as Lucas got above the clouds he worked a lever that bypassed the hydraulic system and the fire in his cockpit began to subside. He suspected that's what the problem was, but he wanted his hydraulics working in the middle of a fight. He and his wingman, Hague, flew to Da Nang, the closest airfield. On the ground, crewmen counted 23 holes in Vazquez's Spad, 19 in Fisher's, nine in Lucas', and not a single one in Hague's. That day two more flights of Skyraiders worked the area around the A Shau camp.

Later that day the surviving Special Forces troops were ordered to evacuate the camp. All 13 were wounded. During the bloody two-day battle 213 air strikes were flown by USAF, U.S. Marine Corps, U.S. Navy, and VNAF aircraft. Besides the Skyraiders, three Marine F-4 Phantoms and two A-4 Skyhawks were severely damaged. An estimated 800 of 2,000 North Vietnamese troops were killed, 500 by air strikes. When Marine helicopters were finally able to get into the camp two more UH-34s were shot down. Only 172 defenders of the A Shau camp were brought out by helicopter.

Later, when asked about the less than ten percent chance of getting Myers out, Fisher replied:

> "We had some good wingmen, and that made the odds a lot better. I felt really strong that I could do this. It was something I had to do. We're family."

He also shared the credit with great Americans. He added that another element of the team play began hours before the flight that day—the maintenance crew. The crew chief for '649 was Sergeant Souso, who had done an excellent job of getting it ready to fly. His A-1E had new tires, and the instrument panel was "All bright and shiny." When he accepted the Spad for the day's mission, Fisher said he noted on its maintenance record and flight log, "This is the cleanest airplane I've ever flown." He added, "And I just beat the tar out of it. But if it hadn't been in such good shape I wouldn't have made it." Robert Blood notes:

> "I was the 1st ACS awards and decorations guy when my flight commander, Major Bernie Fisher, did his thing at A Shau. I then got the honor of doing the first draft on what was the write-up for the Medal of Honor. We were in the process of working on a Silver Star for his previous day's work in the valley, and I was told to write his pickup of Jump Myers for the Air Force Cross. The award was rightfully upgraded to Medal of Honor. Bernie did receive the Silver Star for that previous day's work at A Shau. I was in his right seat on what was supposed to have been a trail check-out ride."

For their gallantry, Lucas was awarded the Silver Star, and Hague and Vazquez the Distinguished Flying Cross. Myers asked:

> "What can you do with a guy like Bernie? I would like to furnish him with a year's supply of whiskey. But he doesn't even drink coffee. So I bought him a Nikon camera and had it engraved, *A Shau, March 10, 1966.* It's great to be alive."

Fisher's A-1E, serial number 52-132649, was once again repaired and spruced up, and was placed on display at the U.S. Air Force Museum, where it rests today.

The second Skyraider pilot to distinguish himself by an exceptional selfless act toward his fellow man was Lt. Col. William A. Jones III of the 602[nd] SOS.

On the morning of 1 September 1968 Jones, whose call sign was "Sandy One," led a flight of A-1s comprising his wingman, Captain Paul Meeks, "Sandy Two," along with Sandys Three and Four and two Jolly Green helicopters, on a SAR mission from NKP. Their objective was the two crewmen of an F-4 Phantom, "Carter 02," which had been shot down and crashed 22 miles northwest of Dong Hoi, North Vietnam. Two additional A-1s, Sandys Five and Six, would later join the fray as replacements.

Shortly after he led his flight into the area, Jones established contact with a single F-4, call sign "Liner," who was able to locate and communicate with "Carter 02 Alpha" on his survival radio. "Misty 11," an F-100 FAC, arrived and assumed SAR command, since Jones was having radio trouble. Eventually, Jones learned from the injured pilot on the ground that his back-seater had already been taken prisoner by the North Vietnamese. The pilot tried to guide Jones to his position, but dense foliage and low clouds prevented them from seeing each other.

**Suffering from burns, Jones managed a smile on the afternoon of his Medal of Honor mission. (Tommy Wardlow)**

Jones and his wingman flew down through the clouds towards the survivor's radio beacon, only to be met by antiaircraft weapons and mountains, whose tops disappeared into the overcast. For an agonizing hour the aircraft searched for the pilot when it was discovered the downed pilot's wingman had been leading the search a few miles from the actual location. Misty 11 reestablished contact with the downed pilot and got everyone back on the right track. The *Hun* pilot added that the survivor was well within range of numerous antiaircraft weapons.

On one of his low search passes Jones felt an explosion beneath his airplane and smoke seeped into his cockpit. Disregarding that his aircraft might be burning, he continued looking for the downed pilot. Finally, the survivor's position was pinpointed when he radioed that a Skyraider had just passed overhead. Jones spotted the pilot, but he also saw an antiaircraft weapon firing at him from the top of a karst formation. He was not in position to fire at the gun emplacement, which was too close to the survivor to risk calling in jet fighters, so he maneuvered, making two strafe and rocket passes. On his second pass his low-flying Spad was hit by automatic weapons fire from the ridges. One round slammed into the Yankee Extraction System rocket immediately behind his headrest. The rocket ignited, and the other pilots saw the center fuselage section burst into flames, with flame engulfing the cockpit area.

Jones pulled the ejection handle, which came off in his hands. He pulled the secondary handle, which immediately jettisoned the canopy. However, the sudden rush of air made the fire burn with greater intensity for a few moments. Since the rocket motor had already burned, the extraction system did not work. He disconnected his harness from the Yankee system so he could manually bail out, but discovered the heat had fused his nylon parachute straps to the extraction lanyards, preventing him from leaving the airplane. He then jettisoned his stores and external fuel tank. Despite intense pain from severe burns on his hands, arms, neck, shoulders, and face, Jones pulled his Spad into a climb and tried to transmit the location of the downed pilot and the enemy gun position to the other aircraft. His calls, however, were blocked by others urging him to bail out. Jones then lost his radios and could receive transmissions on only one channel.

The fire subsided, and Jones quickly evaluated the situation. So far he was the only flier to have pinpointed the downed pilot's position. If he tried to bail out, the other aircraft would face the same barrage of antiaircraft fire he had endured. Plus, his going over the side would only compound the difficult search and rescue task already faced by his colleagues. It was discovered later that had he left the airplane, he would not have had a parachute.

Suffering from burns made more excruciating by windblast, Jones chose to fly his crippled Spad 90 miles back to NKP to report his vital information. His wingman, Meeks, led Jones back to base. The 40-minute flight back was extremely difficult for Jones because of his injuries and the damage to his aircraft. His Spad ran rough, and half of his instruments were unreadable due to the fire. The right windshield panel was completely burned away, and the remaining center and left panels were blackened. Jones maintained a slight skid so the remaining panel provided some protection from the windblast. During a taped debriefing, Jones stated that while flying back he took stock of himself. His hands were burned and shredded. His oxygen mask was burned, as was his helmet visor. He was able to get the gear down and the radio was working, so he could hear Meeks leading him in. His eyes were swelling shut and his body was racked with pain.

NKP was shrouded in overcast, but Jones was able to maintain tight formation with Meeks down to the runway, where he made a straight-in, shallow, no-flaps landing.

Waiting for Jones to bring his badly damaged Skyraider to a stop, crash-rescue personnel and ground crewmen stared in disbelief at its blackened, torn fuselage, with nearly all the canopy gone. As he was pulled from the cockpit in extreme pain, he refused medical treatment until he was assured the positions of the downed F-4 pilot and the enemy gun emplacements were known by the pilots still at the scene. He continued passing information to a debriefing officer while on the operating table. Thanks to his tenacity in delivering the information the F-4 pilot was rescued later that day, but not before the gun emplacement was attacked from two different directions by Major Wardlow and Colonel Carlson, both of whom claimed credit for the kill.

His Medal of Honor citation says it best:

> "Col. Jones' profound concern for his fellow man at the risk of his life, above and beyond the call of duty, are in keeping with the highest traditions of the U.S. Air Force and reflect great credit upon himself and the armed forces of this country."

Jones, who had survived more than two decades of flying military aircraft and almost 100 combat missions, was killed in a private plane crash in Virginia on 15 November 1969. President Nixon presented the Medal of Honor to his widow and three daughters on 6 June 1970. Although Jones did not live to see his reward, it is a safe bet that knowing the F-4 pilot was saved as a result of his actions was, for him, sufficient reward.

**One of several Spads named "The Proud American," the A-1H no. 139738 had a distinguished career. It not only served as Jones' mount on his Medal of Honor mission, it was a wing commander's aircraft, and it helped Capt. Ron Smith earn the Air Force Cross on 2 June 1972. Nearly four months later it was shot down during a strike mission in Laos, becoming the last U.S. Skyraider lost in combat. (Tom Novak)**

There is a footnote to Jones' valiant deed. The Skyraider in which he flew the mission, serial number 52-139738, had also distinguished itself. One of a handful named *The Proud American,* the A-1H had previously been assigned to the 1st SOS. It was repaired after Jones' mission and later served as the 56th Special Operations Wing commander's aircraft from 1970 to '72, and then was flown by Captain Ron Smith when he earned the Air Force Cross over North Vietnam on 2 June 1972. It was also the last American Spad lost in combat, having been shot down during a strike mission over Laos on 28 September 1972. The pilot, 1Lt. Lance Smith, was rescued.

# 9

# Tropic Moon

An unconventional application of the A-1 that has seldom, if ever, received its due attention in aviation history annals gives rise to the Skyraider's claim as the first aircraft to successfully employ a self-contained night attack system in combat. The unique concept was born of necessity to address the vexing movement at night of enemy troops and supplies into South Vietnam through Laos. Despite the efforts of a multi-service task force named "Tiger Hound," which began interdiction in southeastern Laos during early 1965, the need for enhanced 'round-the-clock interdiction became obvious.

As of March 1966, the means to destroy the enemy at night became a top priority among the Air Force Research and Development staff. In fact, a special division became engrossed in ten research projects, grouped under "Operation Shed Light," to tackle the problem. Theirs was an overwhelming task, since emphasis during the previous two decades had been on nuclear war and space exploration, not research for air power in limited conflicts. The team worked simultaneously on two approaches: a self-contained attack system using an aircraft carrying every device needed to navigate, locate, and destroy the enemy at night without ground or airborne assistance; and a Hunter/Killer team concept pitting attack aircraft against targets acquired by a single unarmed aircraft.

Air Force planners had set their sights on the new General Dynamics F-111 to fill the role of the self-contained attack system. However, rapid production of the sophisticated F-111 proved difficult and spurred the Air Force, now pressed for time, to focus on interim aircraft for night attack.

Three projects aimed at modifying aircraft for night interdiction were begun during 1966. They were: "Project Lonesome Tiger," using a Douglas B-26K equipped with forward-looking infrared radar; "Operation Black Spot," in which two Fairchild C-123Ks were highly modified with electronic gear and CBU dispensers; and an A-1E, dubbed "Project Tropic Moon I," modified with Low-Light-Level Television (LLLTV). Evaluation of the three aircraft types was conducted at Eglin AFB. The Tropic Moon I program showed promise and was expanded to include the development of four A-1Es for deployment to Southeast Asia. Their serial numbers were 135177, 135187, 135195, and 135211.

Concurrent with the Skyraider project, a new project had come to life in March 1967 when the Air Force decided to modify three Martin B-57Bs with an improved version of the LLLTV installed in the A-1E. This complied with the original Air Force specification that a new night attack system be incorporated into a jet aircraft. Under Tropic Moon II, the three B-57Bs were ferried from Southeast Asia to the Westinghouse Defense and Space Center at Baltimore, Maryland, for modification. The original Tropic Moon I Skyraider (s/n 132643), in the meantime, underwent extensive testing at Eglin's Hurlburt Field. Planning for the project and installation of the special equipment was overseen by Major Zack Hanes of the 1st Combat Applications Group of the Special Air Warfare Center at Eglin.

**The Tropic Moon test aircraft at Hurlburt Field in June 1967. (Vic Kindurys)**

Three crews were formed early in the program and consisted of A-1 instructor pilots who were paired with navigators/systems operators drawn from various commands. According to then-Captain Vic Kindurys:

> "Very few know that seven USAF navigators flew a USAF A-1 combat tour. To this day, one could win many a bar bet in the USAF circles betting whether navs flew combat tours in A-1s."

By June 1967 a total of six crews were assigned to the project. Among the core test crews Kindurys was the tactician, since he had served two tours in Southeast Asia. He and Major Bob Patterson served as check pilots for the other four as the group transitioned into night tactics the pair had developed.

The original A-1E modified under Tropic Moon I was an SAWC asset that operated from Eglin's King Hangar, and was used to test system capabilities, evolve system configuration, and develop tactics and training. The Tropic Moon I package was the first attempt to use low-light-level television as a search and attack system. The Dalmo-Victor Corporation developed the system, the major component of which was a Secondary-Emission-Control-Video-Influenced-Contrast (SECVIDICON) tube, which allowed the crews to see at night with low light levels. Then-Major Bob Christiansen, who was one of the pilots, emphasized, "With a quarter moon or better it was just like watching Green Bay play Dallas at 7,000 feet."

Kindurys explains how the bugs were worked out of the original system:

> "The initial configuration had the system console and operator in the rear compartment, called the 'blue room.' We crews found this to be operationally unacceptable. Consequently, the initial cadre of three crews was allowed to come up with a workable configuration that we would be willing to take into combat. The configuration arrived at was side-by-side seating with an 'attack' monitor in front of the pilot and two vertically-positioned monitors for the right seat nav/operator. We also identified a need for instruments showing the narrow-view search camera's azimuth and elevation readily visible to the pilot. Since the regular gun sights were removed to install the pilot's monitor we obtained CA-202 sights, mounting them to the right of the monitor. To accommodate the new configuration the right seat flight controls were removed. The new configuration was a major departure from the original concept, requiring substantial rework of the instrument panel and causing more than a six-month slip in the mid-1967 Southeast Asia deployment schedule."

During this time the decision was made to install Yankee Extraction Systems for both seats, which added to the delay.

The four A-1Es, destined for a one-year evaluation period in Southeast Asia, were modified by Hayes Aircraft at Birmingham, Alabama, during 1966 and 1967. They were not delivered until November 1967, limiting crew training in them to only six weeks before deployment. At the heart of the system were cameras that served as the pilots' eyes. Telescopic wide and narrow-view low-light cameras were incorporated into a bulbous glass-nosed pod on the left inboard wing stub. The wide-view attack camera, which was mounted on the pod's right side, was gimbaled in elevation only, providing a 30 to 40-degree field of view. It was bore-sighted, and its reticle served as the primary gun sight. The narrow-view, six-power telescopic search camera was housed within the pod. Gimbals allowed azimuth and elevation settings within a seven by seven degree field of view. The navigator/systems operator in the right seat used a joy stick slaved to the narrow-view camera to search for targets.

All three monitors in the cockpit could display the wide (attack) or narrow (search) views. The two facing the nav/operator allowed him to view both camera images simultaneously. The primary flight instruments were grouped under the pilot's single monitor. Using a switch on the throttle, the pilot could alternate between cameras, which was usually done to ensure accuracy during an attack run. By setting a depression angle in the wide-view camera he could make a standard day attack. At night he could position his base leg using the narrow-view camera to look off to the side then, using his monitor, roll in and release ordnance at a predetermined altitude and airspeed, since the monitor was only two-dimensional, having no depth perception. Kindurys adds:

> "The system needed a quarter moon or better to be operationally viable (to see roads). A light source, however, stood out under any conditions. The system was designed to auto-track a locked-on target and to enable level auto-release bombing. However, the auto-track mode was usually unreliable, and the auto-release function could hit the planet, but not a target. Most of the pilots gave up on these features during the early stage of stateside flights."

Pilot Bob Christiansen reminisced:

> "We had some fun and the shit scared out of us learning to use the system while training at Eglin's Auxiliary Field 9. Vic Kindurys flew right seat on my check ride, with Randy Strickland and John Collins on cameras in

**Low-light cameras in a bulbous glass-nosed pod on the A-1E's left wing were the heart of the Tropic Moon system. A wide-view attack camera was attached to the pod's right side. (Vic Kindurys)**

643's blue room. On my final simulated strafing pass against a jeep, driven by Bob Patterson in the Black River region of Eglin's reservation, I started my roll-in late and never could catch the line-of-sight box on my attack screen. I wound it up tighter and tighter, glanced at the altimeter, and said, 'Whoops,' rolled out and pulled up. Vic later said he didn't bother trying to pull up on his right seat stick because I already had us near 'over-G.' We pulled pine tree branches out of a wheel well after we landed."

During training at Eglin the Tropic Moon I Skyraiders were supported by the 4410th CCTS. By late 1967 the six crews were combat ready, having night-qualified with the LLLTV system for dive, skip, and strafe attack using day qualification criteria. Following the year-long test and tactics development phase the project deployed as a unit, including aircrew, system maintenance personnel, tech reps, and the project officer, to Southeast Asia during late December 1967. The four A-1Es were ferried to the West Coast for shipment to Cam Ranh Bay, South Vietnam.

Meanwhile, the B-57Bs of Tropic Moon II had arrived at Phan Rang AB, South Vietnam, during mid-December 1967. Their operations in South Vietnam, however, were short-lived, as they were returned to the U.S. in the wake of disastrous "short-round" incidents. Even before they deployed, the Research and Development staff had begun planning Tropic Moon III, which also used B-57s, but equipped with more sophisticated electronics and weapons. Sixteen improved versions were built, designated B-57Gs, 11 of which went to Ubon RTAFB, Thailand, in September 1970.

Project Tropic Moon I set up shop at NKP, Thailand, during January 1968 as Detachment 2 of the 602nd SOS, which was based at Udorn RTAFB. Flight operations were conducted from the T-28 building, and crews were billeted with those of the 1st SOS. With few exceptions the same pilots and navigator/systems operators flew together throughout the program. Gerry Schwankl reflects:

> "We had ex-WSOs (Weapon System Operators) who operated the LLLTV. My WSO, Buzz Flynn, was a senior major who had been a radar guy on B-52s. It was a new—and not especially happy—experience for him to be able to look out a canopy and see the ground, as well as tracers coming up fast."

The SAWC project officer flew with the unit both stateside and in Southeast Asia.

To conceal the unit's existence, pilots used the "Zorro" call sign used by the T-28s of the 606th ACS, with whom they shared facilities. Kindurys notes:

> "Impact on the bad guys is unknown, but for the first couple of weeks Zorro A-1s totally screwed up the ABCCC controllers' minds. Eventually they caught on as to what we were and, for a time, called us 'Big Zorros.'"

The A-1Es wore standard camouflage for the period, with their undersides painted flat black. The 150-gallon fuel tank carried on the right stub and the LLLTV pod were also flat black. Flash hiders were added to the guns, and the rotating beacon was shielded, making it visible only from above. Standard markings, including the 602nd tail code, were applied in black on the tail fins. From a distance, they appeared to be "normal" A-1s.

With the exception of rockets, which damaged the LLLTV system tubes, any weapon carried by other A-1s could be used. For night tactical reasons and to reduce stress on the TV system tubes, tracer rounds were excluded from 20mm loads. Ordnance usually comprised funny bombs, all variants of CBUs, iron bombs, and finned and unfinned napalm. When Tropic Moon I Skyraiders worked the southern regions of South Vietnam on moonless nights, flares were carried to assist with search and attack. According to Bob Patterson:

> "We were fragged onto the Trail in southern Laos to locate and attack vehicles moving supplies to the south. The primary area of operations was Route 9 to Khe Sanh, to Tchepone and the Ze Bang Yang River crossing, then north and south over the Trail. Defenses in those areas were mainly 37mm and ZPUs. We were limited to times when the moon was about 10 to 20 degrees high, and better than a quarter moon, and we could see individual unlighted targets within about 10,000 feet slant range. We killed about 10 percent of what we found."

Kindurys added:

> "Three missions per night was the norm. We developed moon tables and worked the frag to put the first sortie in the target area when the moon was high enough for the system to see. Two sorties then followed to allow each to take advantage of the moonlight. Missions were scheduled each day, with sorties averaging three hours. Being FAC-qualified, we were cleared to control our own strikes and to operate as FACs for others. However, for credibility's sake, whenever possible, we had 'Candle' or 'Nail' FACs assess our strikes and provide the BDA. Kills were also confirmed by slow-moving FACs the next day."

Patterson continues:

**Extensive redesign of the instrument panel delayed deployment of the system to Southeast Asia by nearly six months. The navigator's monitor is at far right. In the Stateside aircraft, the pilot and nav shared one monitor. (Vic Kindurys)**

"We flew blacked out. Typical convoy attacks were to stop the lead, then the last vehicle, then continue the attack on the vehicles bottled up in between. The latter part of the evening, from midnight to 1 AM until dawn, was very quiet, with most traffic running prior to midnight. Some missions resulted in no kills, and the most we had confirmed in one mission was 26 destroyed."

Vic Kindurys provides the mission details that are not available in official documentation:

"Taking off from NKP, after crossing the Mekong River we checked in with the ABCCC 'Alley Cat.' If he had activity, we gravitated to where the Candle or Nail FACs had 'movers' in hopes of 'instant targets.' Otherwise we motored to our fragged road sector and started searching. Under right conditions we could see blacked out vehicles and 'living was easy.' In less than optimal light, as long as the road could be made out we still had a chance of nailing them. They usually traveled using their blackout lights, which were visible to the Tropic Moon system, but only from their front. Those were the times we really worked.

The tactic was to follow the road in a left-hand spiral search pattern, which allowed for continuous camera coverage of the road and targets while keeping us at the optimal distance for a quick 30 to 35-degree roll-in. We stalked the vehicles, setting up attacks to have the vehicle and the ordnance arrive at the same place at the same time. We attacked down the road, usually head-on.

On the Trail, depending on visibility, I usually flew at 5,000 to 6,000 feet AGL, maintaining a slant range to allow roll-in. This permitted the nav to maintain continuous target tracking. Azimuth and elevation indicators were cross-checked to assist in holding the desired parameters. When we acquired a target I would set up the attack using a normal roll-in to have, on roll-out, the narrow-view tracking box slightly high and centered above the wide-view reticle. 'Going down the chute,' I made quick corrections to center the tracking box, checked airspeed and dive angle, quickly switched to narrow-view for target close-up, back to wide-view, final correction, pickle and pull up with a 1,500 to 2,000-foot left-hand pull-off, maneuver to avoid AAA or go into a left circling climb to reacquire the target and assess its damage.

**The large monitor at left was the pilot's attack/search screen. The optical gunsight is at center. (Vic Kindurys)**

**Tropic Moon pilot and navigator teams pose with the A-1E no. 132643 at Hurlburt in November 1967, just prior to deployment. Test camouflage flight suits were evaluated for six months, but were not worn in combat since new fire retardant nomex flight suits were issued upon the crew's arrival in Southeast Asia. The A-1E wears jeep and tank kill markings from trials at Eglin's ranges. A placard on the mid fuselage says, "Little John." (Bob Christiansen collection)**

On nights when the visibility was good I had nape or CBU. If movers were running and conditions favorable, I would roll in about 4,000 feet using a 15 to 20-degree dive, pickle around 900 feet and go low out of the area. This improved the score and was pretty much my tactic in III and IV Corps. On the Trail, my greatest concern was having a mid-air or becoming an 'innocent bystander' victim to a barrage of 37mm or ZPU 23mm meant for some other guy. Often our search altitudes coincided with the 37mm and ZPU self-destruct slant ranges that were firing at depressed angle at others a few clicks away. It looked like a CBU strike at our altitude."

Strafing and bombing heavily-defended targets at night while relying solely on rudimentary electronics equipment required a special brand of pilot. Testifying to the skill of Tropic Moon I pilots is the following from Bob Christiansen, who was awarded the DFC for a mission flying A-1E 135195 at the 914 Crossing near Tchepone, Laos, on 25 April 1968:

"On that night we succeeded in locating a convoy of four vehicles attempting to ford a river. Making three passes in the face of over 200 rounds of intense 37mm antiaircraft fire, we destroyed all four vehicles and caused six secondary fires and two secondary explosions. With our remaining ordnance we then attacked and silenced one of the gun positions. The citation does not mention our stained flight suits."

One of Christiansen's most memorable missions took place one week later when he and his nav went up against, who he believes, was a Russian pilot. He picks up the story:

"Intelligence always warned that there were probably radar-guided 57mm guns in the vicinity of Mu Gia Pass at the northern entrance to the Ho Chi Minh Trail, but to the south the triple A was limited to manually-operated 37mm guns and ZPUs. I personally chose never to search in the Mu Gia Pass area, as did other crews, discretion being the better part of valor. For my second mission on the night of 2 May I was paired up with Captain Lauren Wood. 'Woody' and his regular pilot, Fred Bosse, had developed strafing tactics that combined the search camera with the pilot's optical gunsight, requiring close verbal communication on the intercom. We did very little strafing in Laos because it was not effective from high altitude, and was flat out dangerous at lower altitudes in karst terrain.

We headed 095 degrees for the southern end of the Trail near Tchepone in eastern Laos, about a 45-minute trip. We started looking at choke points, found nothing, and continued south. After a while Woody said, 'Hey Chris, look at this!' I checked my monitor. Woody had found a convoy of 20 vehicles. He had a reputation of always knowing exactly where he was terrain-wise and said we were looking at Route 9, heading east. He added that we had about five miles of relatively straight road before it began twisting and turning as it climbed into the mountains toward Khe Sanh in South Vietnam.

I positioned us east of the convoy and set up a left-hand orbit, maneuvering to establish a 30-degree dive angle attack on the lead vehicle from east to west. We had learned that gunners listened for changes in engine noises and would fire at the sound, so we held off advancing prop pitch until pulling out from the attack, advancing prop and throttle together. When finally in position I started my roll-in. I had not completed roll-out when a 37mm opened up on us, its tracers coming right under the nose. I aborted the pass, advanced power to climb, and he was on us again with another burst. After some dialogue with Woody I decided to go from west to east. The same thing happened, but this time I cruised back to altitude. I tried three more passes from different compass points, but always met with the tracers, requiring evasive action. Woody, who could perform magic with that search camera, said, 'I've got the gun spotted. He's firing from a position about three-quarters of the way up a piece of karst on the south side of the road. See that black spot on the karst wall? That's him.'

Very frustrated by this time and with a full ordnance load still aboard I decided to go after the gun, since he was definitely cramping our style and the convoy was moving away toward the hills. I flew us 10 miles north of the target area in the river valley, let down to 500 feet AGL, and advanced to military power. Woody raised the search camera to zero elevation and we bored in. I had already armed all ordnance nose and tail, but had not selected anything to drop. This time I selected and primed all four wing guns.

Woody soon picked up the karst at the south end of the valley and the black spot on the screen that was the gun position. Since I couldn't see much through the optical sight I had to rely on the monitor, something I had not done since strafe training at Hurlburt. Woody kept right on the target, and we both watched altitude. About a mile out I centered the spot in the cross hairs on the monitor and put my finger on the trigger. I started a countdown for

**The Tropic Moon A-1E no. 135211. Besides dark camouflage to hide it from enemy gunners at night, the Spad's tail fin light is shrouded in a makeshift cone so it could be viewed only from above. (John Santana)**

Woody . . . 5, 4, 3, 2 . . . Wham! He was right on us with a perfectly-aimed burst. Tracers went just above and below us. I squeezed the trigger while pulling up, sending 20mm skyward. A second later I pulled the right ordnance jettison handle, dropping everything on the wings. I had to get us out of there.

We climbed over the karst and headed south. I slowly climbed to 10,000 feet and warily circled the area. My ordnance was burning harmlessly about a quarter mile north of the road. Woody put the camera on the tail end of the convoy as it snaked into the mountains, safely out of harm's way. I saluted the piece of karst and said, 'You win, you son-of-a-bitch.'

We headed back to NKP. Woody softly asked, 'How did he know, Chris? He always knew what you were going to do next.' More to salve my wounded pride than for any other reason, we agreed that, since *intel* said there were no radar-guided guns this far south, the gun battery must have had a Russian pilot as an advisor—someone who could think like a pilot because he was one. During debriefing I told the lieutenant they may want to update the info on radar-guided guns being on Route 9, but he answered, 'I'll note it, but there have never been any other reports.' For 'effects of my ordnance' I noted 'NVR' for 'No Visible results.' I have often thought of that night and would very much like to meet and shake the hand of the man who accomplished his mission by denying me mine."

Since the A-1's TVs needed clear weather the group moved with the monsoon season. Cloud cover over the Ho Chi Minh Trail in Laos resulted in the unit relocating in June 1968 to Bien Hoa AB, where they were attached to the F-100 "Ramrods." Missions were flown in III and IV Corps, mainly against water traffic in "free-fire zones." At the start of the dry season in November the Big Zorros returned to NKP and were attached to the newly-formed 22nd SOS. Since the combat evaluation period was near completion, Tropic Moon I pilots were assigned to the 22nd SOS and began checking out pilots in night tactics using "clean" A-1E, H, and J model Skyraiders. During the transition period the Tropic Moon I A-1s used call signs "Zorro 51" through "54" so controllers could distinguish them from other Zorro aircraft.

Bob Christiansen flew the last Tropic Moon I mission on 30 November 1968 in A-1E 135211 and the last mission for its pilots in an A-1H on 6 December. The four A-1Es, along with Eglin-based 132643, were returned to their original configuration and assigned to other units. Three were eventually shot down, joining the long list of A-1 combat losses.

Tropic Moon I crews and their special Skyraiders survived hundreds of sorties over Laos and North and South Vietnam. Battle damage was limited to small arms fire, the first of which occurred on 2 September when 135187, flown by Bob Christiansen, took a round in the fuel tank. Although the unit operated single-ship, that was the only mission flown by all four aircraft. Flying blacked out,

**A-1E no. 135211's scoreboard in July 1968 reflected the crew's skill at killing trucks with the Tropic Moon system. Besides 42 truck markings, four sampans are displayed, the one reversed indicating the first destroyed. (Bob Christiansen)**

working strike zones separated by rivers, and maintaining altitude separation, the four attacked a battalion-size Viet Cong unit moving by water in South Vietnam's IV Corps.

Although the original USAF plan called for the installation of the Tropic Moon I package in jet aircraft, the Skyraider, by virtue of its loiter time and experienced pilots, was found to be a more effective anti-truck platform. Bob Patterson summarized the effectiveness of the Tropic Moon I project:

> "The test proved that the concept worked, but was very limited. We needed a quarter moon about 10 to 20 degrees above the horizon to see satisfactorily, and we needed a free strike zone so that anything moving could be attacked, because the system could not differentiate between friendly and enemy. After all, it was stone age equipment compared to current developments."

**Tropic Moon Crews**

| Crew No. | Pilot | Navigator/Systems Operator |
|---|---|---|
| 1. | Lt. Col. Frank Drew | Lt. Col. Randy Strickland |
| 2. | Maj. Robert Patterson | Capt. Herbert Steege |
| 3. | Capt. Victor Kindurys | Capt. Felix Huertas/later Capt. Paul Cummings |
| 4. | Maj. Gerry Schwankl | Maj. Buzz Flynn |
| 5. | Capt. Robert Christiansen | Maj. John Collins |
| 6. | Capt. Fred Bosse | Capt. Lauren Wood |

# 10

## The Son Tay Raid

Adding to the Skyraider's long list of accomplishments was its participation in the Son Tay Prison raid in North Vietnam. Although the Spad's role in the special mission deviated little from its proven combat abilities, the raid itself was, in many ways, unique.

When three American POWs were released by Hanoi in 1969, U.S. leaders heard firsthand how American prisoners were beaten, tortured, and starved by the North Vietnamese. Those brutal accounts confirmed the suspicions of U.S. military leaders, who had long considered the possibility of a POW rescue operation. Although extremely risky, such an operation would not only provide Americans with a positive aspect of the unpopular war, it would force Hanoi to improve POW treatment while demonstrating American resolve.

An ongoing program of aerial reconnaissance kept a special group of analysts within the Pentagon informed about all POW installations. Having tired of the empty rhetoric dispensed by North Vietnamese officials, who hinted only at offering up POWs as bartering power for U.S. withdrawal from Southeast Asia, the Joint Chiefs of Staff (JCS) in the spring of 1970 was at a crossroads.

At that time about 500 Americans were held captive, eighty percent of whom occupied prisons in North Vietnam. More than half of them had been imprisoned for over six years. Many of the MIA were presumed captured. The JCS directed the Special Assistant for Counterinsurgency and Special Activities, Army Brigadier General Donald Blackburn, to study the feasibility of a POW rescue operation. POW rescue attempts in South Vietnam had been largely unsuccessful, and even with the military resources available in Southeast Asia, a rescue of POWs from North Vietnam would be extremely difficult. Nevertheless, a Joint Contingency Task Group was formed in May.

One of the prisons under aerial surveillance by *Buffalo Hunter* drones and high-altitude SR-71 *Blackbirds* was Son Tay, on the Song Con River about 25 miles west of Hanoi. It was believed that more than 50 captives were held at the isolated compound. Despite three North Vietnamese Army installations, an estimated 12,000 enemy troops, and air defense missile batteries, all within a few miles of the compound, planners became certain that a raid could be pulled off before the enemy could react. General Blackburn, working with the CIA, DIA, and NSA, formulated a plan, code-named *Polar Circle*, to rescue POWs with a carefully selected and specially trained force of Army and Air Force combat veterans. After much deliberation the plan was approved by the Joint Chiefs in July 1970.

On 6 August the commander of the USAF Special Operations Force, headquartered at Eglin AFB, Brigadier General LeRoy Manor, was summoned to Washington. Two days later the Chairman of the Joint Chiefs of Staff, Admiral Thomas Moorer, asked General Manor and Army Colonel Arthur "Bill" Simons if they were prepared to explore and carry out the rescue of POWs in North Vietnam. Without hesitation both agreed, and they were offered whatever resources they required.

A team of 26 planners, representing the four services, went immediately to work assembling the all-volunteer force comprising Army Special Forces troops and USAF aircrews. It was determined the primary air element would consist of five HH-53 helicopters and one HH-3, two MC-130 *Combat Talons* (modified with IR navigation gear), and five A-1E Skyraiders. Crewmembers of the 13 aircraft—whose selection was based on their skills and experience—when briefed on the project accepted the monumental task.

Colonel James Yealy was the commander of the 4407th CCTS at Hurlburt, and it became his responsibility to round up the Skyraider pilots for the raid. In his search for the best "stick and rudder" men he could find, he sent to the 56th Special Operations Wing at NKP a message stating, "Send the following pilots stateside for special operation…." The prospective losing end at NKP responded, "This loss would seriously compromise air search and rescue capabilities." Yealy replied, "Send the aforementioned pilots ASAP!" which was answered with, "Loss of concerned pilots would seriously compromise our search and rescue capabilities for the entire Southeast Asian theater." From the still patient Yealy came, "Understand circumstances, but their participation is critical. Send the pilots!" More resistance from NKP; "We really can't spare the number and quality of SAR qualified pilots you are requesting. We respectfully request that you reconsider." Yealy ended the exchange with, " This is bigger than both of us. Now shut up and deal the pilots!"

In the interest of security, Eglin AFB was chosen as the training site with the hope that the presence of 100 *Green Berets* and flight training would blend into the many activities at the sprawling facility. Under tight security, training began on 20 August, mainly at Duke Field—also known as Eglin Auxiliary Number 3—the same site used by the Doolittle Raiders in 1942. Simon's raiders and the helicopter crews trained nearby at a detailed, full scale replica of the Son Tay compound. The mission plan called for a pair of HC-130Ps to refuel the choppers over Laos while an MC-130E guided them to the target area. Another MC-130E would lead the Skyraiders. The ground raiders were to be landed outside Son Tay's compound by three of the HH-53Cs. The remaining two would assume a nearby orbit while the HH-3E landed shock troops inside the compound. The *Hercules* assigned to the helicopters would also drop firefight simulators, while the A-1's pathfinder MC-130E carried a large napalm load. The five A-1s were prudently selected to provide close-in support. Ten F-4Ds from Udorn would fly MIGCAP and work in conjunction with five Korat-based F-105G *Wild Weasels*, which would provide SAM suppression. Mission aircraft were culled from bases throughout Southeast Asia, and additional aircraft were readied as backups. Aircraft comprising the primary element were given code names of fruit—which did not please the aircrew—while the Phantoms used "Falcon" and the Thuds "Firebird." The Navy, in the meantime, would launch nearly 60 aircraft from three carriers of Task Force-77 to draw the attention of Hanoi's air defenses away from the inbound rescue force. Since the bombing halt was still in effect, the Navy aircraft were loaded with flares to be dropped in the port of Haiphong area. They were, however, given permission to attack any radar controlled SAM sites that posed a threat.

Five A-1Es with the best maintenance records were drawn from the three Spad squadrons that had consolidated at NKP—they were the 1st, 22nd, and 602nd Special Operations Squadrons. Some aircraft had black undersides, and all flew without national insignia; however, all retained their codes and serial numbers on their tails. Their external stores consisted of three 150-gal. fuel tanks, plus several 100-pound white phosphorous bombs, rockets, and specially contrived napalm canisters to form flaming pools as reference markers, in case those dropped by the MC-130Es failed. They were also equipped with CBU-58 *Rockeye* cluster bombs to deal with any vehicles that might approach the compound. Since the A-1s were not qualified to carry the Rockeye, which was familiar to Navy jet aircraft, tests were conducted on the Eglin range to establish dive angle, release altitude, and sight settings. Two of the five Spads that participated in the raid are known to be serial numbers 52-133878 and 52-135206. The five pilots were assigned to the 1st Special Operations Wing and would pick up their *right-seaters* when they arrived in Thailand.

When all the players had gathered at Eglin training began in earnest. Practice became the byword, as techniques were perfected and drills were repeated until movements came almost instinctively. Of extreme importance was getting the variety of aircraft to function as a cohesive unit. This was accomplished by first flying the dissimilar types in formation at night. Then came low level flight, which progressed to night aerial refueling and specific tactics, such as helicopter insertions and extractions, and air drops by the MC-130Es of flares, firefight simulators, and napalm. The only training done outside of the Eglin range was two full mission profiles flown just prior to deployment, night flights to perfect map reading with no navigational aids, and runs out over the gulf to test electronic gear.

Flying the mix of aircraft types in formation, at night and blacked out, proved especially challenging. The C-130s would have to fly at near stalling speed, while the heavily loaded HH-53s did their best to keep up. The lone HH-3 rode the crest of the lead C-130's propwash. The Skyraiders, on the other hand, although fully loaded, had to make S-turns and fly near stalling speed to avoid outrunning the C-130s. After the helicopters were refueled enroute to the target area, the MC-130Es were to lead them and the Skyraiders at low level, between mountains, from the refueling point to Son Tay. Aircrews flew more than 1,000 training hours in 268 sorties without an accident, reflecting their exemplary skill.

On 28 September the aerial force and Army raiders joined to practice the complete operation, whose code name was changed to *Ivory Coast*. A final live-fire rehearsal took place on 6 October, after which Generals Manor and Blackburn, along with Colonel Simons, flew to Washington to inform National Security Advisor Henry Kissinger that the assault force was mission ready. They impressed upon Kissinger the importance of launching when the weather and "moonlight window" of 21 October were optimal. However, for political reasons, final approval from President Nixon could not be obtained. The date was disappointingly changed to 21 November, the next best weather and moonlight window.

Meanwhile, air reconnaissance detected signs that activity at the camp had declined, particularly weeds that had grown where prisoners would normally have walked. Film from SR-71s showed no signs of occupants, but planners believed POWs were being kept inside. Since timely and accurate intelligence was a key factor in the mission's success it was closely monitored. Subsequent Blackbird film showed an increase in camp activity.

By 17 November the entire assault force had arrived at Takhli RTAFB, and the mission's code name was changed to *Kingpin*. President Nixon then gave his approval to execute with the coded message *Red Rocket*. Since Typhoon Patsy was bearing down on North Vietnam, General Manor changed the launch date to 20 November. Still, only a small number of the 148-man force knew where the mission would take place. It was not until the afternoon of the raid that they were finally told that at least 70 POWs should be at that night's destination—Son Tay Prison. Photos from a Blackbird flight that afternoon showed signs of habitation, heightening the raiders' anticipation of success.

That night the assault force boarded C-130s which flew them to Udorn RTAFB, where the helicopters and special C-130s waited. One landed at NKP to drop off the A-1E pilots. One of the pilots, John Waresh, recalls:

> "The NKP flightline was blacked out and the tower was empty. The only people out and about were the crew chiefs and us. Of course, the wing commander followed me around like a puppy dog, asking question after question, none of which I could answer. He got rather pissed. Picking up our flight gear we went straight to the birds, cranked up, and taxied out. No taxi, runway, or aircraft lights were used."

Waresh's teammate, Jerry Rhein, added:

> "We took off in radio silence. The wing commander was up in the tower and was told that A-1s would take off at a certain time, and to ignore them."

After takeoff, the A-1Es were to rendezvous with an MC-130E over the base, but it did not appear. They flew two orbits, waiting, which put them ten minutes behind schedule. With no Talon in sight they moved on, flying a prearranged course to Vientiane, Laos, to attempt an alternate rendezvous with the Talon. Again no C-130, so they pressed on for Hanoi. According to Waresh:

> "After Vientiane passed behind there were no lights anywhere—ink black. And then our worst nightmare loomed up—a cloud-bank. Being lead I wasn't worried about being hit, but the rest of the flight exploded like a covey of quail, everyone in God only knows what direction. Pushing it up I climbed straight ahead and soon popped out on top. Not an A-1 in sight, and no hope of joining up again without lights or radio. We were all on our own.
>
> After a short time we noticed a speck of light far ahead. A star? After watching it a while we were sure it was below the horizon, and no Lao in his right mind would have a light on. It had to be something else. Heading straight for it, it took some time to catch. A fully loaded A-1 is no speed demon. Sure enough, there was our Talon with a teeny white light on top of the fuselage and a dim bluish glow coming from the open ramp in the rear. Couldn't see the bluish glow until you were only a few meters from it. There were already two A-1s there, one on each wing. We moved up and the left one moved out, and we took our place on the left wing tip. A few minutes later the other two A-1s slowly pulled up. Once we were all in place the little white light went out, the bluish glow went out, and the Talon descended into the black. From there on it was hold on tight as it bobbed and weaved through the hills and valleys.
>
> The Talon driver was top notch. His power applications during climbs and descents, and gentle banking, allowed our heavy A-1 to hang right in there. The three-day moon window we had for this operation provided good night visibility, with one exception; several valleys we drove through were so deep that mountains, karst, trees, or whatever eclipsed the moon. When that happened it was like diving into an inkwell. You could make out only a few feet of wing tip, and that was because of our own exhaust flame."

A force of 116 aircraft was airborne under complete radio silence. The Wild Weasels got in first to keep the SAM sites at bay, while the Phantoms took up positions to watch for MiGs. The raiding force entered the target area below 500 feet. Almost four miles from the prison, the C-130 leading the helicopters pulled up to 1,500 feet, followed by two HH-53s. Both dropped flares, and the Hercules dropped a firefight simulator over a nearby sapper school. It also released a pallet of napalm before it joined the pair of HH-53s in preplanned orbits. The C-130 leading the Skyraiders was only a minute behind the first. After passing the Initial Point (IP), it disappeared into the night and *Peach Five* peeled off to take up an orbit in case anyone was shot down. Then two more Skyraiders broke away to take up positions near the prison. As the Spads formed a daisy chain to cover the compound, the HH-3E intentionally crash-landed into the camp, and an HH-53's miniguns obliterated the guard towers and guard barracks.

As flares, firefight simulators, and napalm were being dropped by C-130s, the radios came alive when the HH-53 carrying Col. Simons and his assault section landed by mistake at a secondary building, where a fierce firefight took place. Having the benefit of surprise, Simons' team killed more than 100 well-armed Chinese or Russian soldiers. Skyraider pilot Bob Senko remembers:

> "Ed Gochnauer and I were in *Peach Two*, on Major Rhein's wing. We had an automatic frequency change when we entered the target area. Only one aircraft forgot, and that was me. But we were able to keep up with what was going on visually. Both Goch and I knew right away that one of the helos had gone to the wrong area, but we were pretty helpless to do much other than support the troops as best we could. Because they were out of position, we got called to pay close attention to the road from the south, to make sure no one took advantage of our situation. When we got the order to shut down the footbridge between the Citadel and Son Tay, lead and Goch got lined up headed east to take the bridge out with a couple of *Willie-Pete* bombs. I hollered at Goch that he was too shallow, but he let the WPs go anyway and they were pretty short. Fortunately, his run-in line was across what seemed to be a chemical factory and he greased it. There was a beautiful display of different color flames, with the bright green ones going above our altitude. Rhein's bombs were pretty good, and the combination allowed us to get the job done. The reason Goch was so low on his run-in was that the SAMs had already started. They seemed to be random at first, but we noticed they were aimed in the general direction of Son Tay and were being fired on a very low trajectory. So we stayed as low as we could. I don't think any were tar-

geted specifically at us, but they got our attention and we stayed well in the weeds. It wasn't hard, since we had about 15 to 20 percent moonlight to work with and the target area was well marked by small arms fire.

We were circling the camp at about 100 to 200 feet, and when we were on the north side, we'd drop down to water level over the river. Since some of the ground troops were not in position to blow the bridge on the north side of the camp we got called to take it out. Since we couldn't get enough altitude to drop any heavy stuff, we strafed it."

Waresh added:

"There was an infantry camp a few klicks south of the camp and a road directly from it to Son Tay, running right in front of the camp. There was the possibility that they could get their act together quick enough to respond and we didn't want that. Also, the local cops had some jeep things that could respond to the commotion—didn't want that either. As it turned out nothing came towards the camp. Some trucks were running up and down the road paralleling the Red River, but as long as they kept heading into and out of Hanoi we didn't bother them.

The holding point for the choppers while the ground troops did their thing was an island in a nearby lake. They landed there but kept the motor running. Everyone flew blacked out, of course, but the choppers had to use lights to make a touchdown. A truck pulled up to the shore opposite them and pointed their headlights at the choppers, but turned them off after a while. They sat there the whole time, watching, but that's all. We were ready to pounce on them if necessary. It wasn't."

The coded message "Negative items" was repeated on the radio as raiders searched the entire camp. Disappointingly, no American prisoners were found. The HH-3 was ordered destroyed, and the helicopters were called in to pick up the raiding party; they had been on the ground less than 30 minutes and only two of them had been slightly wounded.

The SAM missile sites came to life and were engaged by the Wild Weasels, one of which was hit and severely damaged. Waresh remembers:

"We were at our briefed 3,000 feet until the SAMs started coming our way. Intel told us we wouldn't have any trouble with SAMs at that altitude. A lot some pencil pushing puke knows. We all hit the deck and kept an eye on the launch site closest to us and sure enough, someone decided to try for the guys to the west—us. The site launched one that never got to the horizon. I watched it rise and almost immediately it leveled off. Then the thing stopped moving on my windscreen. I knew what that meant—collision course. We dove into the Red River and turned. Jerry was flying, and I was turned around keeping an eye on the damn thing as it charged over my right shoulder. I kept bumping the stick forward saying, 'Lower, lower,' Jerry kept bumping it back saying, 'We're going to hit the water.' When the rocket plume on the thing seemed as big as the A-1, I yelled, 'Break left!' We went up and over the river bank, about 50 feet, and leveled off at telephone pole height. We never saw the thing again."

Nearly 20 SAMs had been fired at the assault aircraft.

As the helicopters came in for the pickup, the Skyraiders were told to take out a large, heavily constructed bridge northeast of the camp. Since the Spads carried no hard bombs they used their Rockeye munitions on the bridge and strafed until the choppers had all the troops aboard and were leaving the area. MiG warning calls kept anxiety levels high.

**The A-1E no. 135206 of the 602nd SOS at Udorn following the Son Tay Prison raid. It wears no national insignia and has black undersides. (David A. Hansen)**

The relief felt by the outbound aircrews as they checked in at the IP was short-lived. The tension returned when a radio call was heard from one of the helicopters still at the holding point. The pilot was told in no uncertain terms to head for the IP as fast as his machine would take him. The A-1s, which were trailing the helicopters, were near the IP. But, knowing a lone helicopter was an easy target for a MiG, Waresh and Rhein turned around. Waresh continues:

> "We climbed to a nice MiG altitude and 'went Christmas tree.' Every light we had was turned on as we drove slowly back to Hanoi. With MiG calls coming in every few minutes, I was sweating profusely. It seemed an eternity, but as the prison camp and the west side of Hanoi were slipping under our nose we heard the helicopter's IP call. Lights out and split-S. We beat feet west for the IP on the deck."

Eager to get a piece of the remnants of the assault force, a MiG had locked on to the HH-53 and fired a heat-seeking missile. The chopper made a steep diving turn and was able to dodge the missile. Hugging the ground to break the MiG's lock, the HH-53 successfully evaded.

The five Spads were spread out but still in radio contact. As they crossed into Laos they picked up the beeper signal of the F-105 crew that had been downed by a SAM. They contacted four Sandys that had been launched from NKP to cover two HH-53s from the assault force that went in to rescue the pair. The Son Tay raiders then landed at Udorn RTAFB, where they were debriefed and sat on the ramp—silent and disappointed. Although it was difficult for them to imagine at the moment, the raid had a positive affect on POWs. Fearing a repeat performance, North Vietnam consolidated all POWs into the two main prisons in Hanoi. One POW, Colonel Robinson Risner, later stated:

> "The raid may have failed in its primary objectives, but it boosted our morale sky-high! It also put all the POWs captured in North Vietnam together for the first time. This would have a major impact on us."

**Son Tay Raid A-1E Pilot Assignments**

*Peach One*—Maj. Edwin J. Rhein, Jr. and Maj. John C. Waresh

*Peach Two*—Maj. James R. Gochnauer and Capt. Robert M. Senko

*Peach Three*—Maj. Richard S. Skeels and Lt. James C. Paine

*Peach Four*—Maj. Eustace M. Bunn and Capt. Robert H. Skelton

*Peach Five*—Maj. John C. Squires and Capt. William R. Sutton

# 11

## Punch Out

The integration of the *Yankee Extraction System* with the Spads of Southeast Asia was so highly innovative that its development and operational use merit a closer look.

Ejection systems have always been thought of in terms of high speed jet aircraft. However, widespread use in Southeast Asia of prop-driven aircraft—that flew very low and slow and were vulnerable to ground fire—prompted a search for a system that could maximize an aviator's hope for survival in escaping a doomed aircraft. Having recognized the importance of such a system, Robert Stanley of the Stanley Aviation Corporation at Denver, Colorado, had already begun work on a special ejection unit for piston-powered aircraft. Stanley was no stranger to developing unique aircraft crew escape systems, having provided supersonic B-58 *Hustler* bomber crews with ejection escape capsules beginning in 1962.

The U.S. Navy became interested in Stanley's proposal in 1963 and agreed to evaluate the Yankee system. The Naval Air Systems Command (NASC) worked closely with Robert Stanley, who nearly went bankrupt as a result of its development. The Navy, on the other hand, was never as optimistic. Since the operating principle of Stanley's "pull"—or tractor—system was a radical departure from conventional "push" ejection systems, the NASC cited a number of deficiencies it helped Stanley overcome.

Beginning in 1965, testing was done at the Naval Aerospace Recovery Facility (NARF) at NAF El Centro, California. Prior to 1964 the NARF was designated Joint Parachute Facility, comprising the Naval Parachute Unit and the USAF's 6511th Test group (Parachute). A high point in the testing occurred on 17 February 1966 when Harry W. Schmoll, Vice President of Parasystems, Inc, became the first person to be extracted from an aircraft in flight by the Yankee system.

Stanley remained optimistic, but the Navy did not find the system successful, so fleet installations were not approved. Meanwhile, Navy A-1s were being turned over to the Air Force, who expressed an interest in acquiring the Yankee system because its Skyraiders spent a great deal of time at low levels. Since the Navy had originally procured the Stanley equipment, it was directed by the Department of Defense to manage the system's installation in USAF-bound Skyraiders. Despite additional tests by Stanley, which included sled testing, static seat tests, evaluations of parachutes, ex-

**Harry W. Schmoll, Vice President of Parasystems, Inc., is pulled from the cockpit of a T-6 on 17 February 1966 to become the first person extracted from an aircraft in flight by the Yankee system. (Stanley Aviation Corp.)**

traction rockets, and canopy removal systems, plus subsequent human ejections, the Navy Bureau of Weapons vehemently objected to accepting the unproven Yankee system. But it complied with the DoD directive, and the Air Force continued to work the bugs out of the system.

A problem with all ejection seats at low altitudes and air speeds is their inherent instability resulting from propulsion means, which push rather than pull. Unless centers of gravity can be maintained precisely the seat tends to tumble at low speed, causing problems with parachute deployment, low trajectory height, and entanglement. The Yankee escape system used a tractor rocket which pulled the pilot from the aircraft, providing stability at low speed and low altitude where conventional ejection seats proved unstable.

The Navy viewed the Yankee system as having a limited flight envelope requiring straight and level flight for ejection. Navy officials maintained that an ejection could be made only within a given speed range and within only a 45-degree bank without risk to the pilot. To find out if violent maneuvers did, in fact, place limitations on the Yankee system, Stanley installed the unit in a T-6 trainer. Twenty-one flights were made, with the Yankee operated during violent maneuvers including steep dives, rolls, cartwheels, snap rolls, and prolonged spins. The system functioned successfully during all acrobatics and was considered reliable to extract aircrew during the worst possible maneuvering of a stricken aircraft. Stanley also asserted that a pilot could be extracted inverted at 500 feet altitude and be uprighted by the system.

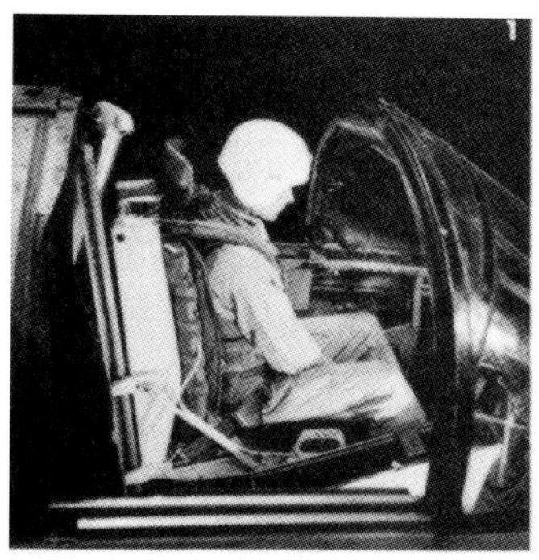

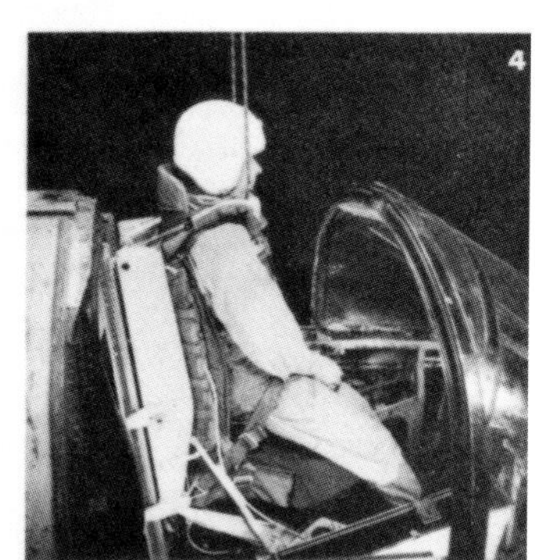


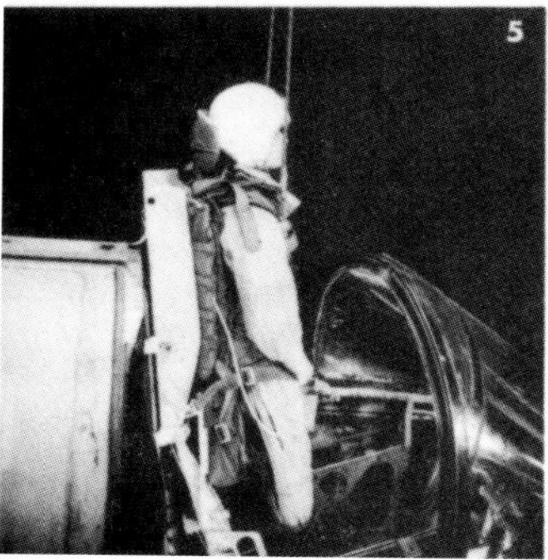


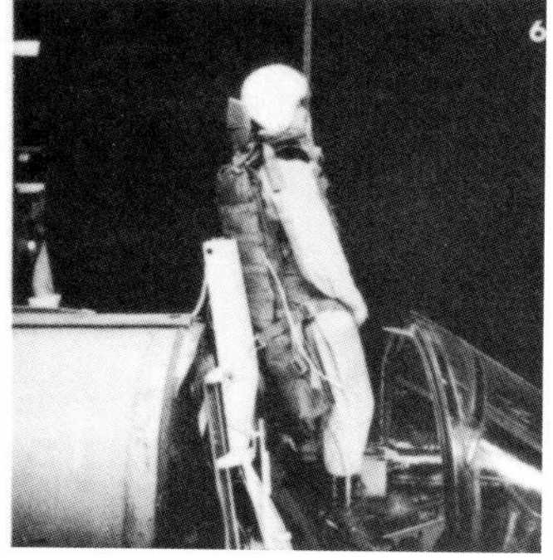


**The extraction sequence of the Yankee system. (Stanley Aviation Corp.)**

USAF Captain Randy Jayne, while assigned to the 4407th CCTS at Hurlburt Field in December 1970, endured a harrowing "out of the envelope" extraction from his A-1H, which proved the system's abilities. Jayne continues:

> "It was during takeoff at approximately 120 knots—the numbers were 50 to 75 feet altitude, 55 degrees left bank, and a high rate of roll. Other than the broken back and multiple joint injuries I can still feel on a rainy day, it was a great experience compared to the alternative of staying with the Spad, which landed on top of and destroyed two A-37s parked on the flight line. After that experience, my subsequent two Southeast Asia combat tours were anticlimactic."

The heart of the Yankee system was the extraction rocket, which had two nozzles on the top to pull the pilot from the cockpit. The rocket launched at 115 feet per second and burned for just over half a second. Connecting the pilot to the rocket were two 12-foot nylon lanyards attached to the pilot's two parachute risers. The rocket nozzles were deflected outward 30 degrees and skewed to make the rocket rotate. Rotation created a conical umbrella beneath which the pilot was suspended, safe from the rocket's intense heat. When 90 percent of the rocket fuel was consumed, the lines detached and the parachute automatically deployed below 15,000 feet.

Thanks to the Yankee's unique capabilities the role of the seat was secondary. The seat's bottom folded downward, allowing the pilot to be pulled in a standing position through an opening much smaller than that required for a pilot seated in a conventional ejection seat. The Yankee's seat remained in the aircraft, however, during the firing sequence it moved up rails far enough to guide the pilot safely through the opening.

The firing sequence was initiated by the pilot pulling a round handle at the front of his seat, which locked the pilot's harness and disconnected the seat actuator. One half second later the canopy was cut free by linear-shaped charges at the metal frame and mild detonating cord around the clear acrylic edges. After another half-second the rocket ignited, pulling the pilot upward by his parachute harness which momentarily attached to the seat sliding up the rails. Once in the opening he was disconnected from the seat and yanked clear. When the rocket and pendant lines disconnected, a parachute drogue deployed 1.3 seconds after he left the airplane.

The Parasystems parachute used with the Yankee system utilized a torso harness with its own lap belt and parachute connections, which absorbed and distributed the extraction rocket's thrust. Users of the system noted that the extraction was surprisingly gentle. In the absence of an ejection seat to support a pilot's spine, the backpack parachute (or a back frame used with a seat parachute)

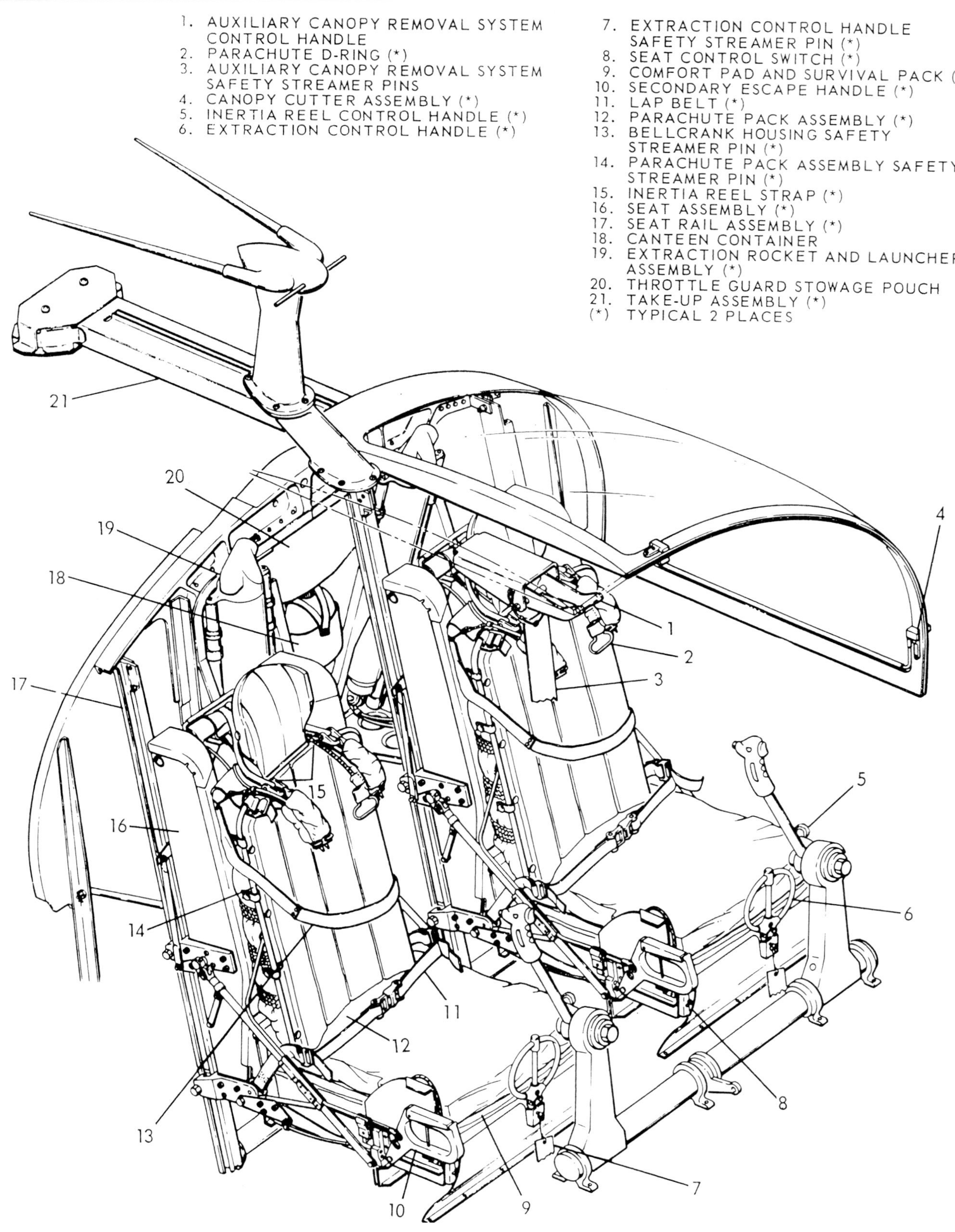


Figure 1-18. E Aircrew Escape System

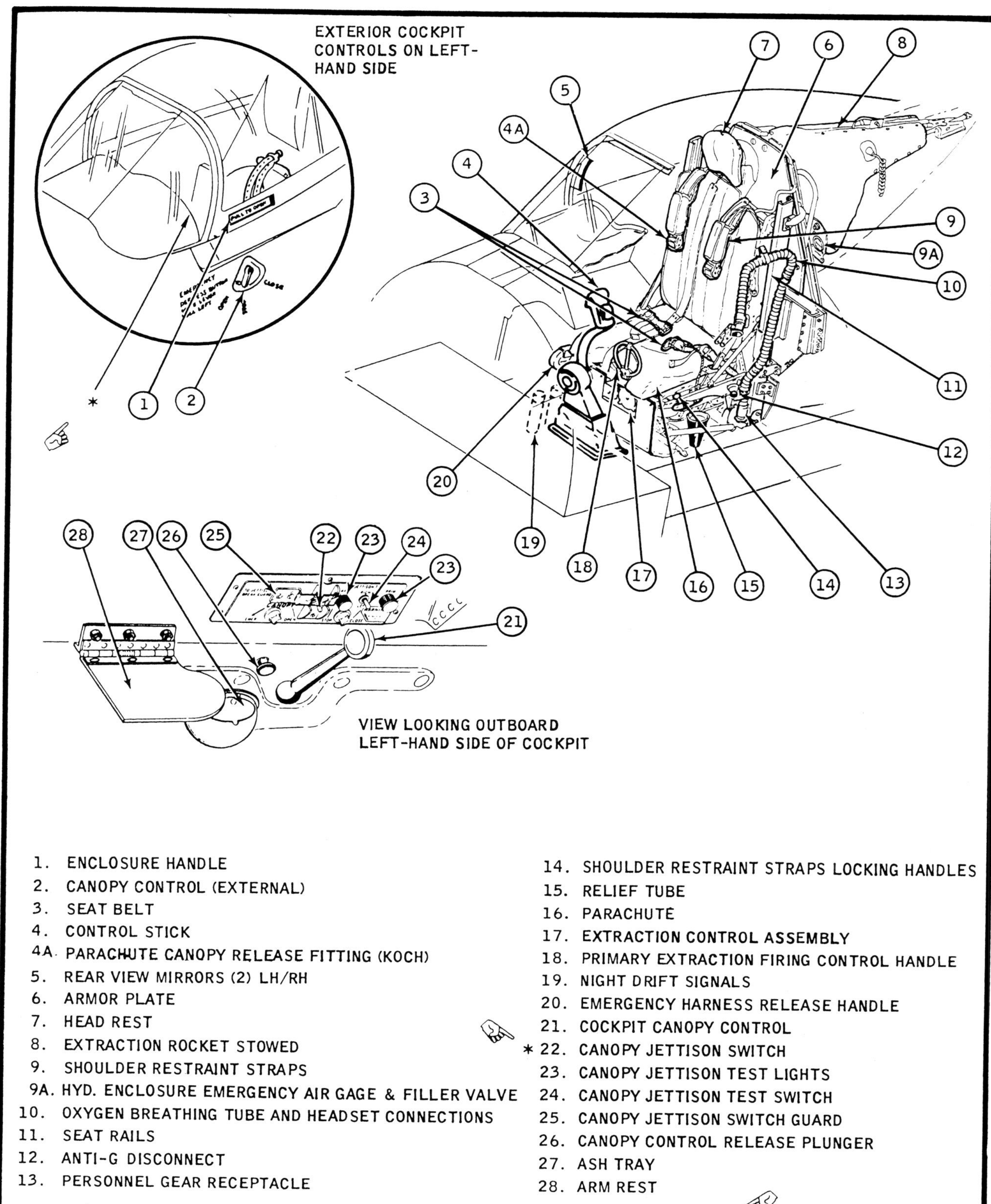


Figure 1-18A. [H] Aircrew Escape System

incorporated a head rest to provide support in wind blast or during shipboard catapults. For extractions over water, the pilot pulled a handle that released a survival container, complete with a self-inflating life raft. During normal flight the container served as a seat cushion, which was attached to the pilot's harness.

Especially noteworthy was the Yankee's zero-zero capability, which meant it could be used at zero altitude and zero airspeed. Testimony to this unusual ability was provided by U.S. Air Force Captain George Porter of the 22nd SOS. Shortly after a night takeoff from NKP on 27 January 1970 Porter's engine started running rough, so he managed a go-around at very low altitude and lined up with the runway. By the time he realized he had not re-lowered his landing gear, his prop was smashing into the runway and he was landing on a full load of fuel and ordnance. He ejected just as the Spad exploded, and he landed close enough to the fireball engulfing his A-1 that his parachute was burned completely. He broke a leg and was put on desk duty until it healed. Porter became the first pilot to rely twice on the Yankee system, having ejected over Laos ten weeks earlier when his engine quit. He would share the title nearly three months later with Captain Friestad of the 602nd SOS, who ejected twice over Laos.

The Yankee system also allowed pilots to leave their airplane by "going over the side"—hurtling toward the wing to avoid hitting the tail—by ditching, or ground egress. A secondary escape handle, located at the seat's lower right side, severed the torso harness, disarmed the firing mechanism, and disconnected the rocket pendants. A Navy pilot's experience illustrates the difficulty and risk involved with a conventional bailout from the A-1: when VA-152's Cdr. G.H. Smith was hit by 37mm fire on 28 August 1966, his Spad was burning so fiercely on both sides that he was forced to eject himself over the vertical stabilizer. Placing one foot on the seat and the other on the stick, and kicking as hard as he could, he still hit the stabilizer, but managed to get his parachute opened before he hit the water. Fortunately, he was rescued.

**This rocket sled was fabricated from an A-1E for high-speed tests of the Yankee system in aircraft with side-by-side seating. (Stanley Aircraft Corp.)**

The A-1E was the first aircraft type to have the Yankee system installed. Although it was a large airplane, the cockpit was far from roomy. A conventional ejection seat installation would have meant costly and time-consuming modifications. To ease installation of the Yankee, attachment points were made interchangeable with the original seat, and the same electric seat actuator was used. Component fasteners were made to conform to standard Navy and Air Force parachute harnesses. Cockpit changes were limited to relocation of a few circuit breakers and spacers to move the armor plate slightly. Total installation time of the Yankee system, which weighed only about 75 pounds, was less than 100 hours, including field installation of the canopy removal system.

In the A-1E/G, fore and aft room permitted the use of a backpack parachute. Original plans called for a Yankee system in the rear cabin, however, the idea was dropped since Air Force mission requirements included only a pilot and copilot. Each rocket was angled slightly away from centerline, eliminating the need for sequenced extractions. Since the rocket was not built into the seat, its placement and firing angle varied slightly. During the Yankee's development, the Navy noted the rocket's dangerous proximity to the pilot, and that it was an explosive hazard if hit by enemy fire. At the Navy's request, Thiokol redesigned the rocket motor with a heavier casing. Even that change, however, could not prevent the serious burns suffered by Lt. Col. William Jones of the 602nd SOS when the rocket of his Yankee system was hit by ground fire during a SAR mission in 1968.

The cockpit of the A-1H/J was even more cramped, necessitating a seat parachute rather than backpack type. The versatility of the Yankee system permitted installation of the rocket behind the pilot, beneath the bubble canopy. When the pilot pulled the handle to eject, the rocket elevated from its somewhat upright stowed position to 45 degrees if the aircraft's speed was more than 300 knots, and 63 degrees if speed was less than that.

The first operational use of the Yankee system occurred on 21 May 1967 when Major C.B. Holler of the 1st ACS ejected from his battle-damaged A-1E over South Vietnam. Less than three weeks later on 11 June, Majors Robert Russell and James Rausch of the 602nd ACS flew an A-1E as part of a two-ship strike mission in North Vietnam. Russell picks up the story:

> "I went along on the late afternoon mission to fulfill a paperwork requirement for a semi-annual proficiency check ride. Jim was the pilot and flight lead; I was the evaluator in the right seat. Over the target, Jim and the other Spad began to expend their ordnance. Our target was the usual suspected truck park in a deep valley, and our recovery left us little clearance between the mountains. After bombing, both aircraft set up for rocket and strafe attacks. On our second rocket pass the engine was not responding to full throttle. The airspeed bled off as Jim tried to gain altitude. We both scanned the cockpit for any indication to explain our predicament. Nothing was working. We decided to get out.
>
> I pulled the handle and was extracted. Jim followed close behind. We knew this new system had seen its first

**The Yankee extraction system in an A-1E. (Tom Hansen)**

operational use the month before and it worked. When we punched out our wings were level, nose about on the horizon, about 1,500 feet altitude and about 180 knots. The canopy went as advertised, but during extraction the canopy frame caught my knees because, after years of drills in other seats, I put my heels tight against the seat.

It was all very fast. The opening of my chute was welcome and, maybe because my adrenalin masked it, I didn't think the shock was remarkable. I had only about 15 seconds from chute opening to landing in trees. Fate picked just the right tree for my chute to hang up. My toes were within a foot of the ground, so I stepped out of my harness and looked for places to hide. With only a .38 caliber revolver I wasn't looking for anyone to argue with, and we had violated one of the cardinal rules of combat—'don't bail out over the area you just bombed.'

Jim's extraction was hairier than mine. He had a 'streamer,' recognized it, shook his chute open and immediately landed on a bamboo platform well above the ground. That was fortunate, since the enemy went first to his location and beat the ground beneath his hiding spot. Our wingman saw our chutes and summoned the rescue force, stayed high and talked with us on our survival radios. Since the A-1 could loiter forever, we knew our wingman would stay as long as necessary. An hour and a half later the Sandys and Jolly Greens arrived and, while taking small arms fire, hauled us up through the trees. Jim and I were back at Udorn sometime after midnight for a party with the rescue guys and the rest of our squadron that didn't have to fly the sunup mission."

Captain Paul Kimminau of the 602[nd] ejected from his A-1H on 12 February 1968. He remembers:

"It was a two-ship escort mission, which involved meeting a helicopter and escorting it to a site in Laos where it would drop off a road watch team, which hid in the jungle and called in air strikes on road traffic. I hadn't flown the A-1H in combat, and when I flew a couple check rides in September 1967, the 602[nd] A-1Hs had yet to have the Yankee system installed; they were retrofit shortly thereafter.

The helo mission was scrubbed due to bad weather, so the controller mentioned he had a target for us. The other aircraft was an A-1E with the operations officer and a new pilot he wanted checked out. Turning the new guy's 'nickel ride' into a checkout flight required that ordnance be delivered. I spotted the target, which was a road being built and what appeared to be a truck, but turned out to be a load of logs. As I pulled off my second rocket pass I felt a 'thump' in the aircraft. I checked the gauges and everything appeared normal. As I was passing through 8,000 feet, back in the clouds, I saw what was probably a puff of smoke go by the canopy. My eyes returned to the instruments and the oil pressure gauge going to zero. The A-1 would fly with major battle damage and get you home, but it would not fly long without oil. After pulling back the power, leveling off, and verifying my position on the radio, the aircraft shuddered, the sump light came on, and the torque meter spun. The engine was deceivingly smooth again, but started a very high RPM scream. I pulled back the throttle and it got very quiet. I got a sinking feeling. I radioed my wingman, 'Firefly 16,' that the engine quit and I was ejecting.

I reached down and pulled the handle. The canopy left immediately. I remember sitting in the seat looking out, realizing the canopy was gone and thinking I should be going pretty soon.

Out I went. Firefly 16 was right behind me and saw me come out of the aircraft. I was tumbling and upside

down when I saw the chute stream out of the seat pack and open. It snapped me upright. When I saw that I had a good chute I let go of the ejection handle. To this day I can clearly see that thing floating away and thinking, 'I wanted to keep that for a souvenir.' I got rid of my oxygen mask, looked around, and waved to Firefly 16 that I was okay.

Although I pulled the risers for all I was worth to land on a high hill, I was directly over a village. I admit, now I was scared. No matter what I did I was headed for the center of the village, where I saw kids running around pointing at me, and a dog running around barking. As soon as I stopped trying to slip the chute I drifted away from the village. I was headed for a tree, and I remember thinking it was a cottonwood tree just like I had seen in Kansas when I was growing up. The tree caught my chute perfectly and I landed standing. I took off running up the hill away from the village, looked up, and saw a helicopter. It wasn't a Jolly Green, so I assumed it was an Air America helicopter. I didn't care what kind it was or whose it was—I was just glad it was there. He was only a couple miles away when he heard my call so he saw my aircraft crash, saw me in the chute, and waited until I landed.

**The system, complete with warning decal, in a single-seat Spad. (Ed Barthelmes)**

**The Yankee system rocket was mounted to the right of the canopy actuator in the A-1H/J model Skyraiders. (Ed Barthelmes)**

Meanwhile I fired my .38 in the direction of two men I spotted running from the village. Firefly 16 said he would strafe anyone who got close. As I chugged to the top of the hill there was the helo in a hover with the 'horse collar' hanging on a cable, and a guy in the doorway waving me over. Once in the helo I lay on the floor gasping for breath. The crewman asked if I wanted to see my aircraft burning and I said, 'No, just take me home.'

A Jolly Green returned me to Udorn where the squadron greeted me with champagne. The mission report showed that I spent five minutes on the ground. It was the most memorable flight—or half flight—I have ever had. Even a VC attack at a base three months later wasn't enough to get my heart beating like it did that day."

Those successes not only boosted the morale of Spad pilots, they encouraged additional installations of the Yankee system. Since the Spad was earmarked for extinction in the Navy, the Yankee was installed in single-seat A-1s earmarked for transfer to the Air Force even before they completed Vietnam cruises. A-1s of both VA-25 and VA-152 are known to have had Yankee systems installed. VA-25 had the Yankee system during the last Navy A-1 deployment aboard *USS Coral Sea* during 1967 and '68. Two Spads were lost during the deployment. In October 1967 Lt.Cdr. Peter Gates crashed into the sea during a VFR approach to the carrier. He was not seen ejecting and did not survive. And there was no indication that Lt j.g. Joseph Dunn used the Yankee system when his A-1H was downed by Chinese MiGs on 14 February 1968. The A-1H, BuNo. 135300, which flew the last Navy A-1H/J combat flight on that deployment, had the Yankee system, which was removed for use in an Air Force A-1 when 135300 was put on display at NAS Pensacola.

Mark Eyestone, who was stationed with the Hobos at NKP, offers the flight line mechanic's perspective:

"When an A-1 pilot got strapped in by the crew chief or a flightline mechanic, his ejection seat was disarmed and safe. There were pins with *Remove Before Flight* streamers that rendered the ejection seat safe. Once the pilot was buckled up and strapped in he signaled the mechanic, who pulled the pins and gave them to the pilot. The pilot stuffed them between the windshield and the dashboard. When the VNAF were training at Hurlburt they would unbuckle and try to get out without waiting for the pins to be inserted. By sign language, I tried to tell them they would go up into the sky if we didn't put in those pins before they unbuckled. I don't know if they got the message."

Among the initial users of the Yankee system in Southeast Asia was Major James Gassman of the 1st ACS, when his A-1G was hit by ground fire on 5 September 1967. During his fourth strafing pass during an armed reconnaissance mission in Laos, Gassman's Spad was hit in the left wing. He continues:

"I had white hot flames coming out of the hole in the wing and the ammo in the gun cans was exploding. I had about three large explosions. I knew I wasn't going to be able to stay with the machine much longer because I held full right rudder and full right aileron. I had to hold it with both hands to keep the wings level. After another explosion I lost control of the airplane. She went into a severe left roll. When I was on my back I said, 'I've got to get out.' I grabbed the handle, waited till the wings got level, and pulled.

I was in a 40-degree dive screaming toward the ground. Altitude was about 2,000 to 2,500 feet. When I pulled the handle the canopy blew immediately. It seemed like an eternity between the time my canopy blew and I got the big charge out of the back. The thing took hold and jerked me out of the seat. The G forces were not severe. My shoulder hit the canopy support bar, and the next thing I remember was looking up. I didn't have an opening shock, but there was the canopy above me. It looked pretty good, but it got awful quiet. Then I heard an explosion, and there was a big fireball directly below me. I was glad I was out of that machine. There was no way I could've climbed over the side, because as soon as I would have unstrapped the old lap belt system, I would have lost control of the airplane and gone in immediately. I wouldn't have been able to open the canopy and dive out. The Yankee system saved me."

Upon landing Gassman raised his teammates on his survival radio and was rescued by helicopter in less than an hour. He concluded:

"Things worked out pretty good for me, just about the way they're supposed to; the ideal situation. I couldn't ask for anything better."

The first seven ejections with the system in Southeast Asia during 1967 were successful, however, the eighth failed to save the pilot. Major Gerald L. Wollington was assigned to the 6th ACS, which had been attached to the 4407th CCTS at Hurlburt for A-1 training in 1967. On 15 November the engine of Wollington's A-1 malfunctioned on takeoff and he ejected. The Yankee got him out of the aircraft, but the chute failed to open and there was not enough altitude to manually bail out. Nor did Majors John Williams and Donald Fincher survive their combat tours when the Yankee system in their A-1Hs failed during 1970. Ken Lengfield remembers:

"I was on the wing of Don Fincher when he went in right after takeoff on 14 March. I saw him struggling to get out of the harness when the canopy went but the seat failed. I almost went in with him because I had joined his wing to see if I could help. It was quite hazy, and before I knew it I was heading straight down with him. I pulled up through his fireball. He never jettisoned his ordnance so he went down like a rock. Fortunately his hard bombs didn't explode, or it would have probably taken my plane as well. John Williams always swore he would never trust

**The system's rocket and the canopy actuator were in the zippered canvas enclosure behind the seat and armor plate. This A-1H has a replacement canopy. Its ordnance load is noted within the armament decal. (Richard S. Drury)**

the seat, but all the missions out of Da Nang were low-level, so we didn't have much choice."

More than one former Spad pilot recalls that, in view of Jones' injuries, a representative from the Stanley Corporation was flown in to inspect the Yankee systems and determine if shielding could be added to prevent rockets from being ignited by hostile fire. Emphasizing the need for inspections was the plight of several Pleiku-based pilots who did not eject at low level after radioing that they were getting out. Reportedly, the rep discovered that the Yankee systems were improperly installed, although they were installed in accordance with the installation manual. The theory held that the manual was written in haste for a system that had not been sufficiently tested. Other failures occurred on 6 April 1970 when Lt. James Matthews of the 602nd SOS went over the side after the seat failed, and on 28 July 1970 when Major Otis Morgan of the 602nd was killed after trying to eject. Of 73 reported extractions from 63 aircraft, 65 were successful. Of the eight failures, five were determined to be system failures and three were of undetermined causes.

Clearly, the Yankee Extraction System was immersed in controversy, and the recollections of its use bittersweet. Despite failures, the fact remains that more pilots would have died had their Spads not been equipped with the Yankee extraction system. In the end, the pilots are left with the final verdict, which is based either on having watched their wingman auger in, or their own survival thanks to the Yankee system. The Yankee was also considered for use in the A-3B, T-28, A-37, B-26K, O-2, and even in the HH-43 helicopter aircraft. None, however, would compare with the unique system's involvement with the Skyraider.

**The angle brace at the bottom of this A-1E Yankee seat is a seat pan support strut. The yellow handle is a secondary escape handle. (Ted A. Morris)**

# 12

## Passing the Torch

The line dividing North and South Vietnam had been drawn shortly after World War II, when communist leader Ho Chi Minh gained control over what would become North Vietnam. France, in its effort to stem the communist tide and reestablish colonial rule over Indo-China, deployed air elements throughout the country. In March 1949, the Vietnamese Army requested from the French permission to form an aviation unit. Citing limited assets, the French denied the request. Shortly after China fell in October 1949, its leaders and those of the Soviet Union backed Ho's Viet Minh, forcing the French to request American assistance. President Truman, firm in his belief that the spread of communism was a direct threat to U.S. interests, authorized military aid to the French.

After harsh criticism from the U.S. that the Vietnamese were doing little to oppose the Viet Minh, the French conceded their domination over the struggle and supported an independent Vietnamese military. After much deliberation, an aviation battalion was formed during July 1951, followed by the Vietnamese Military Aviation School at Nha Trang, which officially opened on 8 May 1952. It was not until 1 July 1955 that aircraft were transferred to Vietnamese control. That date is officially recognized as the birth of the Vietnamese Air Force (VNAF). On 1 June 1956, the 1st Fighter Squadron (FS) was activated at Bien Hoa with Grumman F8F Bearcats, becoming the first VNAF combat squadron.

The U.S. commitment to stop communism in Southeast Asia began in earnest in 1956, when the Air Force Advisory Group began assisting the VNAF with combat operations, logistics, maintenance, and personnel management. Each member of the Group had a Vietnamese counterpart. Eventually, more than 500 officers and airmen worked in advisory positions to the VNAF: 170 at Group Headquarters in Saigon, with the remainder assigned to Air Force Advisory Teams at key bases. In 1957, the U.S. Air Force became involved with the training of VNAF personnel, although on a limited basis. When the number of communist guerilla attacks in South Vietnam rose sharply during 1959, the VNAF response comprised little more than one squadron of weary Bearcats. South Vietnam's President Diem grounded the obsolete F8Fs and requested American jet aircraft as replacements. Six Lockheed T-33s were initially promised, but never arrived since the Geneva Accords prohibited the delivery of jet aircraft, which it termed "sophisticated weaponry." After conferring with his military advisors, President Eisenhower decided to supply South Vietnam with Skyraiders.

The American Military Advisory Group first planned to send U.S. Navy AD-4s. Since parts replacement and overhaul of the obsolete AD-4s were sure to prove troublesome, it was decided in April 1960 to supply the VNAF with AD-6s, which were still operational with the U.S. Navy. On 23 September 1960, six AD-6s were offloaded from the carrier *USS Core* at the Saigon dock.

**The French left behind more than 20 Grumman F8F-1B Bearcats, giving the VNAF its first high performance strike aircraft. They formed the 1st Fighter Squadron at Bien Hoa in 1956, which became the 514th FS when equipped with A-1s. Oversize national insignias were common on early VNAF aircraft. (Lt. Col S. Johnson/Norm Taylor collection)**

**The unique camouflage of this A-1H at Da Nang in 1966 indicates its assignment to the equally unique 522nd FS of the 83rd Special Operations Group. (Terry Love)**

Spare engines, spare parts, and ground support equipment had previously been shipped to Bien Hoa. An additional 19 AD-6s arrived in May 1961. The Skyraiders, which VNAF personnel nicknamed "Trau Dien," for "crazy water buffalo," replaced aging Bearcats of the 1st Fighter Squadron.

To provide the VNAF with training and support, a seven-man U.S. Navy advisory team accompanied the first-arriving Skyraiders. Under the Military Assistance Program, six pilots from the VNAF's 1st Fighter Squadron were sent in 1959 to the Navy's Aviation Training Unit 301 (ATU-301) at NAS Corpus Christi, Texas, where the Navy conducted Skyraider training.

Ralph Poore offers his recollections as a Navy Skyraider instructor with ATU-301:

> "We began to receive VNAF students in late 1959, in groups of four. The first 12, or so, were quite experienced in that they had several hundred flying hours, mostly in the old F8F. These initial students were multilingual and very easy to manage. They took to the Skyraider with ease. They were given a shortened version of the advanced training syllabus we taught, since there was no need to teach them to land on an aircraft carrier. The shortened syllabus was about 100 hours, divided into Instrument Navigation, Weapons Delivery, and Formation Flying.

As time passed the quality of the students, in terms of flying experience and linguistic skills, was much less. However, what they lacked in experience was surpassed by their enthusiasm. In all fairness, and to the best of my knowledge, they never damaged an aircraft, although they did have us growing more gray hair from time to time.

I recall one such event, wherein a "Fam" (familiarization) flight of three VNAF students, with two airborne flight instructors, managed to cause quite a stir. This was to be their very first flight in the AD, and they were briefed extensively concerning how this fam mission was to be conducted. It was our practice to have a lead instructor and a chase instructor on these fam flights, with the students sandwiched between, flying very loose formation. Well, once airborne, none of these students arrived at the rendezvous point, and the chase instructor could only wring his hands as each, in turn, flew off in a separate direction. Within moments they had all disappeared. Radio contact was attempted repeatedly, to no avail. So, the instructors joined up and returned to base, very leery of what might occur.

Some four hours later, at about the end of fuel endurance, each of these fledglings appeared overhead, requesting landing instructions. They each landed, taxied in, deplaned, and walked to the hangar. Naturally, they were interrogated at length as to their behavior. Each explained that they were just sightseeing, and wanted to see more of Texas! So flight discipline was proven to be a problem.

There were other shenanigans, but there was no realistic means of controlling this kind of behavior. There was also no way to measure their individual political bias, since

**During the early 1960s, the VNAF 514th FS used this colorful fuselage band to identify some of its Spads. (Author's collection)**

**Wearing a seat-pack parachute, a VNAF pilot of the 516th FS prepares for a mission in his napalm laden A-1 in 1966. (Tom Hansen)**

**Partially loaded with 500-pound fire bombs, and wearing the checked band of the 23rd Tactical Wing, a VNAF A-1H taxis at Bien Hoa AB in 1967. Gray cowl rings and flaps were common on VNAF Spads. (Richard Oliver)**

the 1963 bombing of the palace in Saigon was accomplished by an early set of these students."

The pilots then went to Attack Squadron 122 (VA-122) at NAS Lemoore, California, for tactical training.

As the VNAF expanded, the U.S. Air Force established a VNAF training program at U.S. bases. First, aviation cadets attended basic military training at Nha Trang Air Training Center, or at some other training camp in Vietnam. Before flight training could begin, candidates underwent an English language course in Vietnam, followed by 15 weeks of language study at Lackland AFB, Texas. That was followed by a 42-week basic flight course at Randolph AFB, Texas, which was moved to Keesler AFB, Mississippi, during late 1966. Students then moved on to Eglin's Hurlburt Field for an 18-week stint, which offered nearly 90 hours of flying time in the A-1E. After graduation, cadets with 24 months of service were granted the rank of 2nd Lieutenant, while those with less than 24 months of service were titled "Aspirants," which was equivalent to a U.S. Warrant Officer. One of those students, Ngoc Van Tran, shares his feelings about the stateside training:

> "Lack of communication was the common problem among VNAF cadets. We could listen and understand about 70 percent of what the instructors said, but we could only say about 30 percent of what we needed to say."

Tran was channeled into rotary-wing training, which was conducted at U.S. Army bases:

> "There," he says, "things got worse. There was a lot of pressure, a lot of misunderstanding, a lot of yelling for nothing, and a lot of humiliating language was used. We endured this pain just for the honor of our country, and mostly for the glory of having wings on our chests."

By the end of 1964, 117 A-1 pilots and 32 maintenance personnel of the VNAF had been trained in the U.S. While in-country familiarization by USAF A-1 pilots and maintenance personnel continued, the scope of training within the VNAF increased to reduce the dependency on U.S. training. One of the 602nd instructors remembers:

**Nguyen Cao Ky, wearing a yellow flight suit and purple scarf, at a ceremony on 7 May 1966 when he accepted control of Binh Thuy Air Base. (Herbert C. Meyr, Jr.)**

**An A-1H of the 520th FS about to be recovered after it came to rest alongside Binh Thuy's runway in 1966. (Herbert C, Meyr, Jr.)**

**Surrounded in a VNAF hangar by F-5 jet fighters, a Spad undergoes overhaul in March 1971. (Neal Schneider)**

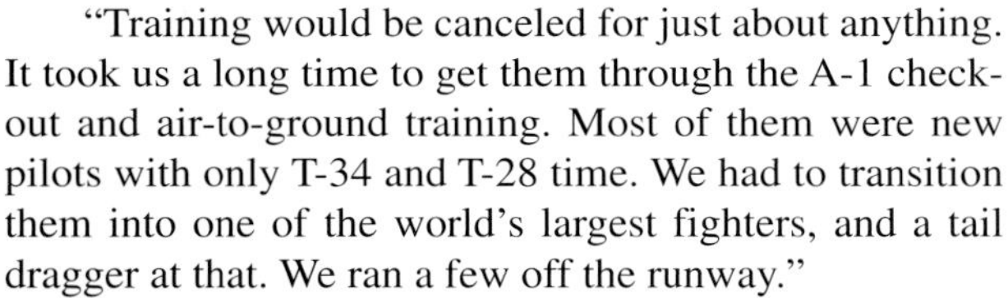

"Training would be canceled for just about anything. It took us a long time to get them through the A-1 check-out and air-to-ground training. Most of them were new pilots with only T-34 and T-28 time. We had to transition them into one of the world's largest fighters, and a tail dragger at that. We ran a few off the runway."

Many Vietnamese pilots found the transition to the Skyraider difficult. Those with T-28 experience found it hard to break the habit of landing the A-1 with the tail high. The Spad's size and power taxed the smaller Vietnamese, who had difficulties with rudder control to counter the A-1's tremendous torque. As a result, a number of VNAF Spads ended up on their backs or nosed into the ground. To ease handling, VNAF Skyraiders seldom flew with full ordnance loads.

Although "Vietnamization" meant different things to different groups of people, its overwhelming goal was to make the Vietnamese self-sufficient. The lack of self-sufficiency in the VNAF made its need more pronounced. Some U.S. leaders were convinced that need could be fulfilled best through training. Accordingly, the importance the USAF Air Training Command placed upon training the VNAF is evidenced by the following statistic: of a total of 1,443 foreign pilots who completed the T-28 primary-basic pilot program, which ran from 1958 to 1973, approximately 900 were Vietnamese.

Prior to shipment to Saigon, the AD-6s were overhauled at NAS Quonset Point's rework facility. Their refurbishment included fresh U.S. Navy paint jobs, although with VNAF national insignia and 1st FS insignia on the cowls. During familiarization at Bien Hoa, under the stewardship of U.S. Navy Lt. Kenneth Moranville, the AD-6s flew alongside the few remaining Bearcats. Live ordnance was frequently carried during the transitional period, and combat missions were flown if the need arose. Moranville's advisory team finished their job by the end of 1960. After the "Jungle Jim" squadron arrived at Bien Hoa during late 1961, VNAF AD-6 pilots worked closely with USAF pilots during combat training, and by year's end the 1st FS had logged 251 combat missions. The initial training

**An A-1G of the 23rd Tactical Wing lands at Bien Hoa AB in 1971. (Neal Schneider)**

**The pilot of this Spad was killed when he crash-landed with battle damage at Bien Hoa during late 1964. (Martin P. Jester)**

**This A-1H of the 518th FS was badly damaged in June 1968. (Author's collection)**

conducted by USAF advisors was handed over to the 34th Tactical Group, which was augmented by 18 U.S. Navy instructor pilots and maintenance personnel of VA-152's "Detachment Zulu." Although some USAF pilots felt that VNAF pilots had enough time in the A-1 to train their fellow pilots, the two-month program was ordered by USAF staff officers. Both VNAF and American pilots flew pre-strike, escort, and bombing missions, often accompanied by VNAF T-28s.

Dat Nguyen, a pilot with the 516th Fighter Squadron, has these observations about the training:

> "Starting in early 1963, most VNAF pilots had their basic flight training in T-28s at Randolph AFB. After graduation they went back to Bien Hoa, where they went through three training phases: right seat as an observer in 1st ACS or 602nd ACS A-1Es, for familiarization and to get a feel for combat missions. This lasted two to three weeks. Phase Two was checkout in the A-1H, and gunnery school with VA-152. U.S. Navy instructors told students to forget what they learned from the USAF, because only the Navy knew how to fly the A-1. Phase Three students went back to the 1st ACS to fly combat missions. They then flew left seat with an instructor.
>
> There were no solos. We were constantly reminded that only the USAF knew how to land the aircraft correctly, and that what we learned from the Navy should be disregarded."

While the Skyraiders gave the VNAF the firepower necessary for close air support, they were not the answer to many of the VNAF's inherent problems. Poor maintenance, which plagued the air arm throughout much of its existence, and political infighting prevented the VNAF from exploiting the Skyraider's proven potential. Fearing a coup attempt, President Diem did not allow VNAF Skyraiders to operate from bases other than Bien Hoa. Despite his efforts to concentrate the A-1s where their activities could be closely monitored, a pair of disgruntled VNAF pilots managed to break away from a flight on 26 February 1962 to bomb and strafe the presidential palace in Saigon. One AD-6 was downed by ground fire, and the other escaped to Cambodia. Although the incident was

**A VNAF crew chief surveys the remains of his A-1, no. 139757, following a rocket attack at Bien Hoa AB on 12 May 1967. (Embry via Ernest L. Connors)**

**This A-1G of the 518th FS suffered extensive damage to its vertical fin. (Author's collection)**

**This VNAF flightline includes A-1s of the 522nd FS in 1966. Eventually "hard" revetments replaced sand bag barriers to protect aircraft during ground attacks. (Tom Hansen)**

deemed not to be a coup attempt, Diem restricted Skyraiders in the Saigon area to 20mm ordnance loads.

As the VNAF grew in size and proficiency new Skyraider squadrons were formed. Newly arriving aircraft replaced AT-28B/Cs of the 2nd FS at Nha Trang, significantly increasing the VNAF's tactical support coverage in other regions. As part of a major reorganization on 1 January 1963, the VNAF redesignated its 1st FS the 514th FS, and the 2nd FS became the 516th FS. In the VNAF three-digit unit numbering system the first number identified the unit mission, while the remaining two identified the squadron. The 500 series identified fighter squadrons.

A major defeat for the South Vietnamese at Ap Bac in January 1963, and heavy T-28 losses at the hands of enemy gunners, prompted the decision to improve VNAF performance by retiring all T-28s and standardizing VNAF fighter squadrons with A-1s. As more Skyraiders arrived at Bien Hoa during 1964, the 518th FS traded in its T-28s for A-1s. The 520th FS was activated at Bien Hoa during June 1964, and the Special Mission 522nd FS went into business at Tan Son Nhut in 1965. An influx of A-1s resulted in the establishment of the 524th FS at Nha Trang in September 1965. The seventh and final VNAF Spad squadron, the 530th FS, was organized at Pleiku during December 1970. Squadrons typically had 24 Skyraiders assigned, the majority of which were single-seat A-1s.

By early 1963 U.S. support for President Diem had diminished to the extent that a coup was carried out, in which four VNAF Skyraiders and two T-28s attacked the presidential compound.

Diem's ousting and subsequent murder resulted in new leadership for the VNAF under Colonel Nguyen Cao Ky, who supported the coup. Ky had gained notoriety by volunteering for most of the early clandestine forays into North Vietnam. Known for his swaggering manner and leadership abilities, Ky organized and led the elite 83rd Special Operations Group, which used a variety of aircraft to conduct clandestine missions into enemy strongholds. To give the special unit strike capability, the 522nd Fighter Squadron was formed with A-1H Skyraiders on 1 April 1965. Their primary mission was to provide cover for patrol boats picking up agents who had parachuted into North Vietnam. Beginning in 1966, USAF and VNAF A-1s dropped camouflaged supply containers to CIA and Department of Defense sponsored agent teams infiltrated into North Vietnam. Although other low-flying, prop-driven aircraft could accurately drop the containers, they were slower and more vulnerable than the A-1 in the North's air defense environment. Other missions included strikes against enemy sanctuaries in neighboring countries and support of cross-border operations. When Thieu was elected President and Ky his Vice President in 1967, discord between them prompted Theiu in January 1968 to disband the 83rd SOG, for fear that it would be used in a coup against him.

**Since VNAF personnel seldom worked weekends, this ground-looped A-1 blocked one of Bien Hoa's runways from a Friday until Monday in July 1972, during which time the base was limited to one runway. (Dwayne Meyer)**

**Wearing fresh paint and colorful markings, an A-1H of the 516th FS is readied for a flight from Da Nang AB in November 1966. (Tom Hansen)**

**Skyraiders of the 524th FS on the flightline at Nha Trang in 1966. (Terry Love)**

**This battle damaged Spad of the 514th FS crash-landed at Bien Hoa on 17 September 1964. It was repaired and flew until March 1973, when it was lost. (Martin P. Jester)**

As the VNAF continued to expand, its air assets were reorganized, so that by 1965 each Corps area had an A-1 squadron for support. At the beginning of 1965 the VNAF possessed 89 A-1s, which increased to 146 when six squadrons had become operational by year's end.

Unfortunately, the expansion generated additional problems that reduced the A-1s' availability rate by one-third. Major losses, such as that which occurred on 16 May 1965, did not help matters. That day a B-57 on Bien Hoa's ramp exploded during engine start. The resulting chain reaction of explosions destroyed 11 VNAF A-1s, 10 B-57s, and a Navy F-8, as well as killing 20 USAF and 8 VNAF personnel, and injuring 105.

Bien Hoa-based A-1s were periodically sent north to Da Nang for larger operations against defended targets. Foremost among such missions was a strike on 8 February 1965 involving 24 Skyraiders culled from other VNAF squadrons. Hand picked and led by Ky himself, the pilots flew from Da Nang to attack supply and troop concentrations in North Vietnam. Although heavy anti-aircraft fire scored hits on all aircraft and downed one Skyraider, 90 percent of the military establishment at Vinh Linh was destroyed. The strike raised VNAF morale and boosted Ky's political standing, but the introduction of Soviet radar-guided air defense weapons during 1965 brought an end to such raids. Ky's use of the VNAF to rise to power in June 1965 garnered additional U.S. support, which coincided with the infusion of American air units.

The primary mission of VNAF Skyraiders was the support of ground forces, although air strikes were regularly flown in South Vietnam. Some VNAF A-1 pilots became proficient at supporting covert operations. Qui Nguyen, who flew A-1s with the 516th FS, says:

> "We used the call sign 'Batman' when we flew special missions out of Pleiku to support MACV SOG teams. These carried out reconnaissance missions along the Ho Chi Minh Trail, penetrating deep into Laos and Cambodia. They also rescued pilots and attempted POW rescue.

**Indicative of the clandestine operations prevalent during the conflict, a VNAF A-1E, which has had its markings removed, taxis past a C-123, also void of markings in 1966. (Terry Love)**

**The A-1G no. 133922 of the 524th FS was lost on 5 May 1967. (Terry Love)**

**Some of the approximately 40 VNAF A-1s seen here on Bien Hoa's flightline in 1964 have full ordnance racks, an unusual occurrence during the VNAF's existence. (Gene Traczyk)**

At Pleiku AB during 1969 and 1970 there was one A-1 detachment deployed from Bien Hoa AB to fly these special missions. Pilots and aircraft from the 514th and 518th rotated to Pleiku every two weeks. We worked with 'King Bee' H-34s of the VNAF 219th Helicopter Squadron and 'Pretzel,' 'Covey,' and 'Nail' FACs to support the SOG teams from insertion through extraction. Around the end of 1970 we handed the mission over to the 530th 'Jupiter' Squadron after it was established at Pleiku."

The 514th Squadron also flew combat air support, air cover, and escort missions. Dat Nguyen describes his most harrowing experience from his days as an A-1 pilot:

"I was with the 516th Squadron, based at Da Nang. In late 1966 it was the only VNAF squadron to continue the air war against North Vietnam. Four VNAF pilots were shot down in that campaign, and I was the only one who survived. I was detained at the infamous Hoa Lo prison camp, also called the 'Hanoi Hilton' by the American POWs.

I was shot down on 14 May 1966 while flying along the Ho Chi Minh Trail looking for targets. It was my 26th mission over North Vietnam. I was hit by AAA fire, and I could see a large hole in my left wing. I still had some 400 rounds of 20mm ammunition, and it started to explode like firecrackers on the 4th of July. A hydraulic line was severed, which intensified the fire. One explosion was so strong that it almost turned my airplane upside down.

Since I tried to gain as much speed as possible to reach the DMZ I was too low to bail out. I saw a small rice paddy and decided to crash-land on it. Before touching the ground, I glanced at the airspeed indicator and it showed 230 knots. 'Too high,' I said to myself, but I had no other choice. It was my first crash-landing, but it was a perfect one! I thought I was going to die. It's hard to believe that the A-

**A small number of fat face Spads were passed to the VNAF, some of which were A-1Gs. This example, seen in March 1967 at Da Nang AB, belonged to the 516th FS. (Neal Schneider)**

**VNAF A-1s participate in a flyby at the military academy at Dalat in November 1965. (Pham Quang Khiem)**

**This A-1G of the 524th FS received a direct hit during a mortar attack at Pleiku in June 1966. The attack was launched after sunset from Pleiku's bomb dump, making a counterattack difficult. (Robert E. Blood)**

1 was so strong and so well built. I got out of the airplane without a scratch.

I took off my black flying suit and tried to make people in the area believe I was a North Vietnamese peasant. But when I realized I was wearing American 'Jockey' underwear, I said to myself, 'This is not a good idea.' I was also worried that the choppers from Da Nang would not be able to recognize me when they came for my rescue. I was on the ground for almost an hour and was finally captured. I was the flight leader, and my two wing men, who had just come from flight school, were shocked and disoriented when I was shot down, which caused the delay in getting a rescue team to the area.

'Max' was the code name I used during my seven years of imprisonment. I was released with the rest of the camp in 1973 during 'Operation Homecoming.'"

Little did military leaders realize that the ever-increasing role of Americans in the air war would have an adverse effect on the lesser-equipped and less motivated VNAF. Some felt the solution lay in modernizing the VNAF aircraft inventory. The VNAF's first jets were Northrop F-5s, which replaced A-1s of the 522nd FS in June 1967. Three other A-1 squadrons (the 516th, 520th, and 524th) converted to A-37s in 1969. As the U.S. enlarged the VNAF with nearly 300 aircraft during 1970, an A-1 squadron, the 530th, was formed at Pleiku. Edd Barnes recalls his tenure as a VNAF advisor at Pleiku:

"When I arrived in September 1970 there were no VNAF aircraft at Pleiku. The VNAF wing commander was in place, as were the squadron commander and a few A-1 and UH-1 Huey helicopter pilots. Aircraft maintenance personnel began arriving in September, and the flow continued throughout my tour.

Some A-1s were flown to Pleiku by pilots of the losing unit, however, I accompanied the 530th squadron commander and five VNAF pilots to NKP, where we returned from the 56th SOW with six A-1s on 9 December 1970. The 530th pilots were generally older and more experienced than the helicopter pilots. All squadron commanders, however, were extremely well qualified to perform their assigned duties. The Hueys and Skyraiders were in pristine condition when accepted by the VNAF.

Lam Son 719 was in progress from early February through early March 1971. The 530th and the 235th (Huey) Squadrons participated in this operation as the first taste of combat for each unit. We had almost daily contact with NVA units in the Dak To and Tan Canh areas. There was enemy activity in the area at all times while our training was in progress. Candidly, it was of little consequence.

A most disruptive aspect of the training program was family separation amongst the Vietnamese officers and airmen. Most officers had their families in Saigon. Some families were at Nha Trang, and some located elsewhere. Few were at Pleiku, as it was not considered to be a choice assignment. Weekends were preceded by an exodus of personnel. We seldom flew on weekends. I had no emotional problem with that concept, however, I did have a problem of logic. I was leaving after a year, and we, the Americans, were leaving soon thereafter, and permanently.

Those aircrews who attained combat ready status were as ready to fight as anyone. There were some significant discrepancies in other areas. Aircraft maintenance was a bright spot. For the most part, Vietnamese mechanics were eager to learn and did a commendable job. When the necessary parts could be procured, they could fix it. Unfortunately, as in every unit I've been assigned, parts were not always available."

From 1960 to 1972 a total of 329 A-1s are recorded as having been delivered to the VNAF, all of them under provisions of the MAP program. Evidence shows that more than 350 A-1s were actually operated by the VNAF, nearly one-third of which were A-1Es and A-1Gs. This increase is the result of aircraft transfers that occurred late in the war between the USAF and VNAF to fulfill needs as they arose. Of the total officially documented 240 were in

**This VNAF A-1E, believed to be no. 132627, was destroyed by an engine fire at Bien Hoa in 1967. (Embry via Ernest L. Connors)**

a Navy configuration, with the balance having come from Air Force bases in the U.S., especially Hurlburt Field, and those in the Pacific theater. Adding to the confusion in determining the exact number and type of VNAF A-1s are the designations A-1E and A-1G, which were used interchangeably by all three services to identify VNAF dual-seat Spads.

The VNAF suffered heavy Skyraider losses, and by the end of 1973, after the U.S. had ceased A-1 operations, only 70 A-1s remained in the VNAF inventory. To replenish losses and supply additional aircraft before an impending 1972 cease-fire restricted deliveries of war materiel, "Project Enhance," a large-scale movement of hundreds of aircraft, including 23 A-1H/Js, quickly got under way. A follow-on program, called "Project Enhance Plus," which was designed to fully modernize the VNAF, accounted for 21 A-1E/G Skyraiders.

The massive infusion of aircraft created the predictable maintenance and logistics nightmares. These problems, when coupled with the lack of mechanical experience of VNAF personnel, and their passive disposition, contributed to the demise of the gargantuan air arm.

Although the January 1973 Paris Peace Treaty ended U.S. involvement in the war, the fighting continued, with the VNAF facing battles on new fronts. By the time the feeble cease-fire had been signed, the U.S. had engorged the VNAF with more than 2,000 aircraft equipping 65 squadrons, making it the fourth largest air force in the world. Aware that the VNAF could not operate the massive air force, U.S. leaders honored continuous VNAF requests for additional aircraft as a means to persuade President Thieu to agree to a cease-fire. It was imprudently hoped that, over time, the VNAF would somehow develop the ability to handle the large force. Those hopes were dashed in 1974 when the VNAF placed more than 200 aircraft in storage, including the remaining 61 Skyraiders.

Enemy air defenses challenged South Vietnamese air superiority, and the introduction of the portable SA-7 heat-seeking missile all but halted A-1 operations. Budget cuts within the Vietnamese government, a dry pipeline from the U.S., and an ever-aggressive enemy signaled the VNAF's impending fate, and that of the nation itself. As bitter battles were fought during the early months of 1975, in which the North Vietnamese gained territory, air support for the ARVN seldom was adequate. After the NVA overwhelmed the ARVN defenders during the major battle at Xuan Loc, which guarded the approaches to Saigon and Bien Hoa, the fate of the South was sealed.

On 30 April, the day after President Ford ordered the evacuation of Saigon, a handful of VNAF airmen, in utter defiance, flew their AC-119K gunship against the North Vietnamese divisions surrounding the capitol. The gunship was joined by a pair of VNAF Skyraiders. An SA-7 missile found its mark on the gunship, and the two Spads, along with another pair over southwest Saigon—one of which was shot down—became the last VNAF aircraft to oppose the enemy in Southeast Asia. The Skyraider had fought the war from beginning to end.

The communist takeover produced an exodus among VNAF pilots. During South Vietnam's final days, VNAF pilots flew aircraft to safe haven in Thailand, or took refuge aboard U.S. carriers. Often, their families were crammed into the aircraft, making the flight more perilous.

One pilot somehow managed to escape with his wife and two children in the cockpit of an A-1H, while another fit his tall wife into an H model's cockpit for the flight. Another VNAF pilot tells of taking off in an A-1E with his crew chief in the right seat and 20 people, some of them infants, in the "blue room." A few miles out after takeoff he jettisoned the Spad's ordnance, which allowed him to gain altitude.

Among 165 VNAF aircraft flown to U-tapao RTAFB, 11 were Skyraiders—five A-1Es, five A-1Hs, and an A-1G. There, they crowded the airfield along with nearly 100 Cambodian aircraft that had arrived when Phnom Penh fell on 12 April. U.S. personnel at U-tapao were kept busy, not only painting over VNAF markings and stripping aircraft of ordnance, but handling the flood of refugees.

Of approximately 1,000 VNAF aircraft captured intact in Vietnam more than 40 were Skyraiders. At Saigon's Tan Son Nhut alone, 26 A-1s fell into enemy hands.

Throughout its troubled life the Vietnamese Air Force suffered setbacks that prevented its function as a well-organized and motivated air arm under sound leadership. As a result, it came under harsh scrutiny and enduring criticism. No single issue can be pinpointed as the heart of the matter. Rather, like the U.S. Air Force, after which it was patterned, the VNAF had strengths and weaknesses, and varying degrees of problems throughout its organizational structure.

The VNAF's rapid growth may have actually worked against its gaining independence. The glutting of aircraft into an air arm beset with problems, and one which fought an enemy who was motivated, well equipped, well trained, and who always possessed the initiative, proved a poor substitute for the experience, aggressiveness, and motivation necessary for victory.

Although VNAF fixed-wing pilots, all of whom were volunteers, emerged from the upper crust of Vietnam's social order, they remained overshadowed by U.S. intervention. On an individual basis some Vietnamese were anxious to go it alone, while others were content to have the Americans shoulder the load. The latter percep-

**This A-1H, no. 139622, of the 518th FS crashed at Bien Hoa in 1964 after being damaged by antiaircraft fire. The pilot had the canopy open only a few inches and drowned in mud before he could be dug out. The Spad was repaired. (Martin P. Jester)**

tion was shared by many U.S. pilots, who were accustomed to getting the job done, and found it easier simply to do so.

Political infighting and instability within the South Vietnamese government had a detrimental effect on military leadership, and resulted in corruption and low morale. Wavering U.S. support and political indecision meant that targets were poorly selected, and that VNAF A-1s stood alert duty unloaded. Maintenance standards seldom rose above marginal, contributing to low availability rates. Nor did the VNAF have the capability to perform aircraft recovery, field maintenance, and many other tasks critical to the successful operation of a massive air arm.

The Vietnamese were quick to point out that war had been a part of their lives since childhood, and they expected that to continue. It was their reason for flying less missions than the Americans, especially at night, during bad weather, and on weekends. Such attitudes served only to widen the vast cultural gap between the Americans and Vietnamese. Even more difficult to understand was the psychology of the VNAF pilot, which held that if he experienced problems with the aircraft, the Buddhist philosophy was to be passive and not aggressively handle the situation. As one VNAF pilot stated, "So it was not always a matter of the airplane simply being too much to handle because of our physical stature."

Lost on many was the fact that Vietnamese pilots had no rest and recuperation leave, nor an end to their tour of duty. Consequently, some logged thousands of combat flying hours. Some flew until they were wounded, some until they died.

Quan Trung Tran, a former VNAF Spad pilot and survivor, provides this perspective:

> "The ones left behind after the war were sent to re-education camps. Some never made it out alive.
>
> Their families were told of their deaths years after the fact. Their remains were never sent home, and no one can really tell where they are buried. My cousin is one of those. The ones that got to go home were always treated as the lowest class. I still remember that every single holiday we had to report for civic duties, including cleaning the streets, the riverbanks, the market, the city drainage system, etc., and we could not go home at the end of the day. We had to carry our own food, and we did not get a dime for our labor. We were then sent to the public schools to spend the night under guard because we were considered 'dangerous' to society. We had no citizenship, we could not vote, and we had to keep a book recording our daily activities, which the local police would check once a week. Those who made it to the U.S., either at the end of the war or during the later war years, were fortunate. But even we had to start from scratch. Many members of the VNAF now in the U.S. succeeded in new careers. A few continued their flying career as U.S. airline pilots. One of my classmates made it to the rank of Lt. Commander in the U.S. Navy."

**A VNAF Spad makes a bomb run on an enemy position. (David A. Hansen collection)**

**A USAF advisor oversees an engine change on a VNAF A-1 at Bien Hoa AB in 1965. (USAF)**

# 13

## Colors and Markings

Throughout the course of the war in Southeast Asia, the three services that operated Skyraiders underwent sweeping changes that affected the appearance of their Spads. As the war gained momentum, color and marking directives necessarily kept pace with changes in tactics and technology. The color code system was titled Federal Standard (FS) 595a, and used five-digit numbers for color identification. The first digit of the guide established sheen: 1 for gloss; 2 for semi-gloss; and 3 for flat, sometimes called non-specular. While the majority of Skyraider color schemes and markings complied with U.S. Navy, U.S. Air Force, and Vietnamese Air Force command directives and unit policies, personal markings, usually in the form of names applied to cowls, were apparent. Since World War II, Navy attack aircraft had been painted overall glossy Sea Blue. It was not until February 1955 that a new painting policy was issued, which called for non-specular Light Gull Gray (FS 36440) upper surfaces over glossy Insignia White (FS 17875). Both sides of the ailerons, elevators, and rudders also became white, along with wheel wells and the inside surfaces of landing gear doors. A high visibility training scheme was also introduced that used a blend of glossy Insignia White and International Orange (FS 12197).

A directive issued during February 1959 introduced semi-gloss Fluorescent Red Orange (FS 28913) to replace International Orange. The directive also called for the edges of landing gear doors to be painted gloss Insignia Red (FS 11136). The light colored livery served as a backdrop for an overabundance of colorful and flashy markings for two decades. Among the few exceptions were land-based aircraft, and those which had their markings toned down for deployment to the war zone.

A September 1958 directive specified two-letter tail codes for Carrier Air Groups. Navy and Marine Corps aircraft assigned to the

**Up until July 1960, Advanced Training Unit 301 was the Navy's Skyraider training unit, which used this high visibility white and International Orange "split" scheme. (Tom Hansen)**

**Fluorescent red-orange panels were standard on Spads of VA-122, the Navy's A-1 training unit. (Ivan B. Shinski)**

True to Navy tradition, this A-1H, which served as the mount for the commander of Attack Carrier Air Wing 19, wears colorful markings in 1967. The name beneath the canopy is "Cdr. Billy Phillips." This Spad served all three air arms in Southeast Asia, and was lost in combat during late 1972. Unusual are the black bomb racks. (Neal Schneider)

Blue-painted practice ordnance and a Navy Unit Commendation ribbon on the vertical fin indicate this VA-145 A-1J's non-combat status in September 1966. It would see combat in three Navy squadrons, two USAF squadrons and a VNAF squadron. (Robert Burgess)

Atlantic Fleet used codes with the first letter taken from the first half of the alphabet (A through M), while codes of units assigned to the Pacific Fleet began with letters N through Z. The second letter could be any letter of the alphabet. The code was displayed in black on both sides of the vertical stabilizer, and on upper starboard wing surfaces.

Navy A-1s on WestPac cruises also followed the time honored Navy policy of having three-digit side numbers, which were applied in black to the Spad's cowl, and its upper starboard wing surfaces. The number, or part of it, was usually repeated, although in smaller size, on the flaps, vertical tail, and on landing gear strut covers. Side numbers were used as call sign suffixes and aided in ground and deck handling, as well as in air traffic control. Skyraiders bearing a side number ending in 00, called "double nuts," denoted a carrier air wing commander's aircraft, while those numbers ending in 01 were assigned to squadron commanders. The side number's first digit was based on the numerical order in which squadrons were assigned to carrier air wings. Groups from 100 through 600 were used, with 700 typically assigned to early warning and "Electric Spad" detachments. Trim colors, which were usually applied to tail fin tips and were incorporated into squadron emblems, corresponded to the assignment order.

As part of the Navy's commitment to training South Vietnamese A-1 pilots, an August amendment to a directive issued during April 1960 included specifications for South Vietnamese national insignia. The amendment ordered that A-1s earmarked for delivery to the VNAF be painted with the South Vietnamese national insignia on both sides of the fuselage and wings, and a rectangular fin flash of the national colors on the tail fin.

Besides red "zaps" and footprints the width of the aircraft maliciously applied to VA-115's A-1H BuNo. 137612, white-painted flaps were also unusual. (Tom Hansen)

This striking bumblebee design was applied to VA-176 Spads for the squadron's 1966 combat tour. This A-1H, call sign "Papoose 12," wears 29 combat mission symbols. (Tom Doll collection)

**This new arrival to the Air Force inventory wears an armament placard below the "blue room," and the crew chief's name, "SSGT J. Walker," below the canopy. Noteworthy is a statement painted in white on the Spad's tire cautioning against FOD (Foreign Object Damage). (Jack M. Friell)**

A major deviation from the standard Navy gull gray and white scheme was an experiment with camouflage begun in 1965. Naval Aviation officials, interested in determining the importance of camouflaging its aircraft to blend with Vietnam's predominantly green terrain, deployed in early 1966 camouflaged aircraft assigned to CVW-11, aboard *Kitty Hawk,* and CVW-15, aboard *Constellation.* Among the aircraft evaluated were A-1s of VA-115. The color scheme consisted of Dark Green (FS 34079) and Olive Green (FS 34102) over the existent white undersides. Jim Salter, who was a Spad pilot with VA-115, shares his recollections of the "new camo décor":

> "The thinking at the time was that it would aid in hiding us from the ground and from the air as we zigzagged through the mountains on our way to targets. In reality, I don't think it accomplished either task, and I believe most of our pilots thought it had just the opposite effect. While flying support in South Vietnam we went in high to stay clear of random ground fire and commercial traffic around Saigon. This negated any benefit from ground cover. In the North, we never worried about being seen by enemy aircraft as our Phantoms ruled the skies, keeping North Vietnamese planes well to the north of Hanoi.
>
> Upkeep was a real pain. The camouflage was painted over the peacetime gray and durability was poor. Washing, although infrequently at sea, was harsh by nature, and it didn't take long for the gray to start showing through the camo. Touch-up painting could only be accomplished when a bird was 'hard down' or when we put into port for a little R and R. Thus, our birds had that 'rode hard and put away wet' appearance most of the time."

Due to the reasons noted by Salter, plus the fact that camouflage impeded visibility for deck hands during night carrier operations, the scheme was discontinued in mid-1966.

As Skyraiders passed through Navy rework facilities, prior to being transferred to the Air Force they were painted overall Gray (FS 36473), which was commonly called "COIN Gray." A few A-1Es and A-1Gs entered the USAF inventory in the standard Navy livery of Gull Gray and Insignia White.

For the first two years of operations in Southeast Asia, the only markings applied to USAF A-1s were national insignia (first South Vietnamese, then U.S.), the serial number on the tail in black, and large black numbers (1 through 4), or the letters A or B on the cowls. The letters initially differentiated 602nd ACS A-1s from those of the 1st ACS. The digits also helped in organizing the large number of Spads at one base, and they facilitated identification for maintenance and ramp parking. Unique to the overall gray scheme were various patterns of black-painted areas on the fuselage to mask the engine exhaust for which the Skyraider was notorious.

**USAF Spads carried on the tradition of decorating ordnance during holidays, or for special occasions. This 1st ACS A-1E at Bien Hoa is loaded for a mission on Easter Sunday 1964. The aircraft was lost in a mid-air collision 14 months later. (Gene Traczyk)**

**Although pilots' names were often worn on aircraft, pilots frequently were assigned other aircraft, depending on availability and mission line-up. The wings of this A-1H reflect the busyness of Spad squadrons. (Tom Hansen)**

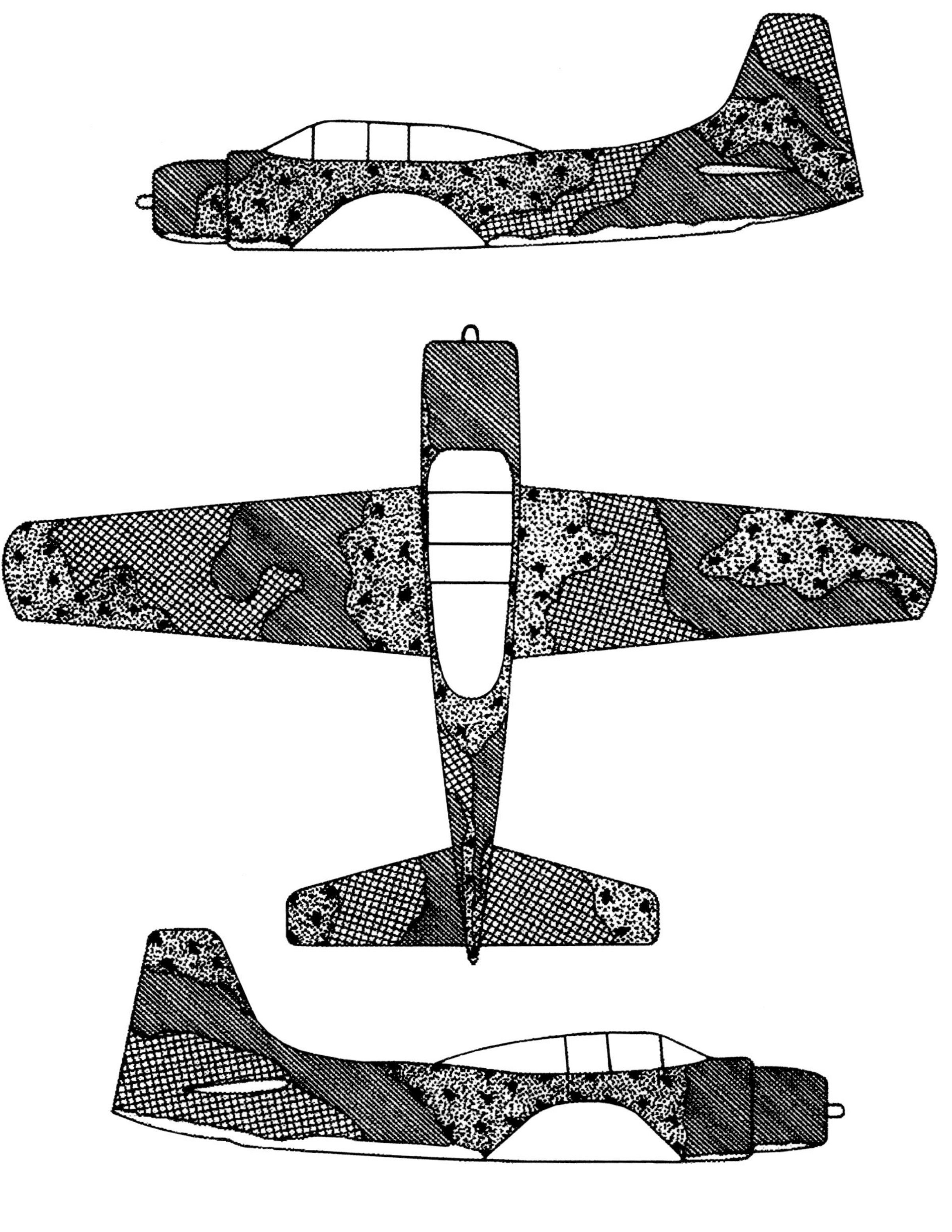
TAN
No. 30219
GRAY
No. 36622
GREEN
No. 34079
GREEN
No. 34102

**The colorful fuel tanks of VA-152's Spads were not used in the combat zone. (Gary L. Gottschalk)**

As camouflage was introduced during late 1965 for USAF aircraft in Southeast Asia, the COIN Gray familiar to Air Commando aircraft gave way to a "Tactical" scheme consisting of Dark Green (FS 34079), Medium Green (FS 34102), and Dark Tan (FS 30219) over Camouflage Gray (FS 36622). In some cases, the original COIN Gray was retained as the underside color. Although the Air Force issued a standard guide for camouflaging aircraft, called "T.O. 1-1-4," patterns, and sometimes colors, applied to A-1s varied. Beginning in 1969, Spads regularly flown on night missions had their undersides painted black. With camouflage came reduced-size national insignia, which eventually were left off of the aircraft.

As Spads were camouflaged, two-digit tail codes, which were introduced for USAF aircraft in 1966, were painted on the vertical stabilizers, usually in white. Spads with black undersides had black tail codes. Below the tail codes were partial serial number blocks in black or white, or combinations thereof. A common Air Force practice had the last three digits of the serial number repeated on both landing gear strut fairings.

When the 4407th CCTS was activated at Hurlburt Field on 1 December 1967 it was assigned the tail code AD. The squadron color was red, which appeared on the aircraft as a band on the vertical stabilizer. When A-1s came under control of both the 4407th CCTS and the 317th SOS in 1972 they were given the tail code AH, and green became the squadron color, which was also worn as a tail band. Stateside Spads often wore the TAC emblem on the vertical tail and the 1st SOW emblem on the cowl.

Air Force Spads flown by commanding officers of units in Southeast Asia were identified by tan stripes applied diagonally around the aft fuselage. A wing commander's Spad wore five stripes, a squadron commander's wore four, and a base commander's had three.

**VA-115 advertised their unit name and call sign "Arabs" with a camel silhouette on the tail fin tips of their Spads. (Tom Hansen)**

**Details of VA-52's battle mace on the A-1's fuselage. (Tom Hansen)**

**Pilots and airplanes of VA-152 proudly displayed the squadron color, pale yellow. It was used for the pilots' helmets, unit patch, and chevrons worn on the Spads' tails and external fuel tanks. Even the pilot's headrest bore the color onto which a black spade was applied. (Gottschalk collection)**

**In keeping with VAW-13's name "Zappers," a lightning bolt emblem was carried on the outer wing store of this EA-1F. The motif also appears on the tail band. Navy Spads seldom were seen with black-painted exhaust areas. (Nick Williams collection)**

Miscellaneous markings that appeared on USAF Spad fuselages included an ordnance data panel, ejection seat warnings, and a panel indicating the pilot's and crew chief's names, all of which were changed from high visibility colors to black on the camouflage scheme.

Since few official documents exist that record the color and marking system used by the Vietnamese Air Force, photographs, and the recollections of former VNAF members, are the primary sources from which those important details can be gleaned. The VNAF's first Skyraiders, acquired in 1960, retained their standard U.S. Navy scheme. Skyraiders later supplied by the U.S. Air Force were finished in overall COIN Gray. Some of the first aircraft camouflaged in Southeast Asia were A-1s of the VNAF's 83rd SOG, 522nd Fighter Squadron. Although their patterns and colors varied, the predominant colors on the special Spads were brown and green upper surfaces over gray. Particularly interesting was a purple-brown shade used with dark green. Adding to the uniqueness of 83rd SOG A-1s was a colorful emblem worn on the fuselage and Vietnamese/Chinese characters on the cowls.

When the U.S. Air Force introduced camouflage, VNAF A-1s also began wearing the three-tone Tactical scheme in 1966. Skyraiders were at the forefront of the VNAF's efforts to make their aircraft some of the most colorful in existence. VNAF units made liberal use of trim colors and unit markings. Striking fuselage bands, which were used to differentiate units, became the most recognizable feature of VNAF Spads. Four band designs were first used to identify the flights that comprised the 514th FS at Bien Hoa during 1962 and 1963. Shortly thereafter similar distinctive bands were used to identify tactical groups, which later became tactical wings. Squadron emblems normally appeared on the cowls of VNAF Spads.

**Test camouflage applied to VA-115 Spads in 1965 was anything but durable. The last digit of this A-1H's side number was repeated on the flaps, tail fin and upper right wing. (NMNA)**

**Clearly visible on this A-1H is the Navy's practice of painting flight control surfaces white. The side number and tail code are repeated on the right wing. (Tom Hansen)**

**This view shows to good effect the complete markings worn by VA-145 Spads during the squadron's 1967 combat cruise. (Tom Hansen)**

**On a training flight over Eglin AFB, Florida, this A-1E displays an early style exhaust mask. (USAF)**

South Vietnam's national insignia was a modification of the U.S. design, and incorporated the national colors of orange and red. The insignia was adopted when the U.S. took over Vietnam's Military Assistance Program. Its similarity to the U.S. insignia eased their constant exchange which, it was hoped, averted attention to U.S. combat involvement early in the war. Rectangular fin flashes of the national colors were worn on the rudders of A-1s.

Like their USAF counterparts, VNAF A-1s wore tail codes, not only for identification, but to facilitate mission scheduling and maintenance. Large, black single-digit tail codes were worn by A-1s of the 514th FS during the early to mid-1960s. The only other single-digit tail codes observed were smaller, white letters worn on A-1s of the 23rd Tactical Wing later in the war. As additional squadrons were formed a two-digit tail code was created, which had a small letter denoting the unit, behind which a larger letter was placed to identify the aircraft. The VNAF rapidly expanded to the extent that a third letter, which identified the aircraft, was added to the tail code; the first two then became squadron identifiers.

Apparently, the number of aircraft pumped into the Vietnamese Air Force eventually overwhelmed efforts to adhere to the color and marking guidelines established early in the conflict. Although some VNAF A-1s were necessarily devoid of markings for clandestine operations, many simply did not have the colorful markings, or even national insignia, applied.

**Even camouflage could not diminish the impressive lines of the Skyraider. The upper surface of centerline fuel tanks was frequently painted. The red landing gear door edges of this A-1J were a carryover from the Navy's color standards. Number 142043 is seen here at Sheppard AFB, Texas during March 1970. (Merle Olmsted)**

The A-1H no. 135243 in the final stages of rework at NAS Quonset Point prior to being turned over to the Air Force. A 150-gallon Mk 8 fuel tank, undoubtedly from Navy stock, is attached to the centerline station. (Tom Hansen)

In this view of A-1E BuNo. 132655 at Webb AFB, Texas in 1967, it's obvious how the cargo compartment behind the cockpit came to be called the "blue room." (Ron Picciani)

A red tail band identified Spads assigned to the 4407th CCTS, 1st SOW at Hurlburt in 1972. That year the squadron's "AD" tail code was replaced by "AH." (Ron Picciani)

The A-1G no. 132577 of the 1st SOS is masked for repainting at the Phase Facility at Don Muang Airport, Thailand in 1970. (Roger Youngblood)

A-1E no. 132410 was one of the first of its type in the USAF inventory, and one of the first to be camouflaged. It is seen here at Pleiku in December 1965. The oxidizing effect of the Spad's exhaust served to create its own camouflage pattern. A large black "A" on the cowl indicates its assignment to the 602nd FS(C). (Raymond A. Young III)

**"Miss Carolyn" of the 602nd SOS had black undersides and served as a commander's aircraft during 1970, as indicated by five diagonal tan stripes. The 56th SOW emblem was worn on the tail fin. (Richard Michaud)**

**The cartoon character "Snoopy," atop his flying doghouse in his relentless pursuit of the Red Baron, became an endearing symbol of combat aviators in Southeast Asia. The landing gear knees of Skyraiders also were adorned with various colors and the names of crew chiefs. (Tom Hansen)**

**Barely visible on the fuel tank of A-1G no. 135043 is the title "Commando One." The Playboy bunny on the prop was an early 1st ACS marking. (Tom Hansen)**

**The A-1E no. 135141 wore a white kangaroo silhouette on its cowl during late 1967. The ubiquitous Snoopy zap was applied to the Australian symbol and the inboard bomb rack. The Mk 8 centerline fuel tank was painted Sea Blue, indicating its original Navy ownership. (Robert C. Mikesh)**

**"Miss Eileen," A-1H no. 135263, flown by the commander of the 56th SOW, Col. Richard White in 1969, wore emblems of units to which he previously had been assigned. (Scott Roe/Richard White collection)**

In long standing tradition, "The Ragin' Cajun," A-1H no. 134494 of the 1st SOS, has ordnance decorated to recognize Easter 1970. External 300-gallon fuel tanks often were painted COIN Gray, which was darker than the Spad's underside color. (Richard S. Drury)

As part of their night strike mission, Spads of the 22nd SOS at NKP had their undersides painted black. (Neal Schneider)

The only markings worn by this camouflaged A-1H of the 1st SOS in 1971 were those on the tail fin. (USAF)

This A-1E wears the tail code of the 1st SOS, 14th SOW at Pleiku. A green shamrock appears on the fuselage. Portions of the cowl ring and cowl flaps are black. The Glossy Sea Blue centerline fuel tank came from the Navy inventory. (Marty Isham collection)

The A-1H flown by the commander of the 514th FS in 1962 and 1963 displayed a fuselage band that incorporated all four bands worn by the flights within the squadron. (Elof S. Lundh)

Few VNAF A-1s were seen with this stylized form of tail code or tail markings, which matched the fuselage band. This A-1J belonged to the 516th FS during 1966. (Tom Hansen)

Skyraiders of the 83rd SOG's 522nd FS wore distinctive emblems that matched the unit's unique mission. The legend "Than Phong" on the squadron's fuselage emblem translated means "God of Wind." (Richard Oliver)

This A-1H of the 83rd SOG, 522nd FS is painted a unique purple-brown and dark green camouflage. The scheme was complemented by distinctive markings, which included the unit emblem and ethnic characters on the cowl. (Tom Hansen)

Seen in October 1962, this pair of A-1Hs wears the markings worn by the 514th FS. The fuselage bands were used only during late 1962 and 1963. (Author's collection)

Although the tiger pattern fuselage band on this A-1H was no longer used after 1963, the original 514th FS markings remained when this photo was taken in 1967. The cowl band is black. (Neal Schneider)

VNAF Spads typically wore their squadron emblems on their cowls. The title "Thien Loi" within the 524th Fighter Squadron's emblem translates to "God of Thunder." (Richard Oliver)

A common practice among VNAF A-1 units was the addition of ground crewmens' names below the squadron emblem. "Co-Truong" means "mechanic," which was followed by his name. This cowl belonged to the 514th FS at Bien Hoa AB in 1963. (Elof S. Lundh)

A-1H no. 139622 of the 518th FS in February 1966 after it was rebuilt following a fatal crash in 1964. The large national insignias were later reduced in size, but tail markings remained the same. (Author's collection)

It was standard practice for the VNAF to leave the rudders of A-1s COIN Gray. On this A-1H, no. 139796 of the 516th FS at Da Nang in 1966, the rudder serves as a backdrop for the national insignia. (Tom Hansen)

A pair of A-1Hs of the VNAF 516th FS during 1966 when the transition to camouflage was made. The Gray Spad, no. 135352, was lost during February 1967. (Tom Hansen)

# 14

## Survivors

Although the majority of Skyraiders, especially those that served in Southeast Asia, were lost through attrition or at the hands of enemy gunners, a small number survive thanks to the diligence and perseverance of those who recognize the Spad's role in the development of American airpower. Foremost among them is General Heinie Aderholt.

Among the more than 160 VNAF aircraft that escaped to Thailand during the communist takeover in April 1975 were 11 Skyraiders. The A-1H number 139606 was the last Spad out of Vietnam, flown by a VNAF pilot with his family jammed into the aircraft's "hell hole."

As a dispute between the U.S., Thailand, and Hanoi over rightful ownership of the aircraft ensued, Aderholt, then in command of the U.S. Military Assistance and Advisory Group in Thailand, knew he had to act. He had former Spad pilots Capt. Roger Youngblood and Maj. Jack Drummond fly four A-1s to Takhli AB. Youngblood adds, "On 5 May the A-1 number 139606 was the last A-1 ever to fly under the U.S. flag." At Takhli they were hidden in a hangar until 1979.

Fearful that North Vietnam might enter Thailand to collect their spoils, and determined to preserve the Spads, Aderholt rented tractors to pull the A-1s to the Chao Prya River, where they were loaded onto barges. When the barges became stuck in the shallows Aderholt bribed the overseer of the Chainat Dam to open the floodgates. The barges were freed, allowing them to float to the Bangkok port, where they were loaded aboard ship—destination United States.

Other survivors were relegated to storage in the Arizona desert as residents of the Military Aircraft Storage and Disposition Cen-

**The A-1H BuNo. 135332 served the U.S. Navy, U.S. Air Force, and South Vietnamese Air Force, and was one of only four A-1s brought out of Southeast Asia at the war's end. It is seen here awaiting rework and transfer to the USAF inventory. (Author's collection)**

**This AD-4, BuNo. 123827, served as a gate guard at Dekalb Peachtree Airport, Georgia from 1959 to 1966. It was then acquired by David Forrest who restored it to flying condition by 1978. (Author's collection)**

Missing major tail components, A-1E no. 132428 occupies a Bien Hoa revetment with the hulk of an A-37 during the early 1990s. The A-1 had been repainted and given Peoples Vietnamese Air Force markings. (Roger Youngblood)

Roger Youngblood, who, with Jack Drummond, rescued four A-1s from Vietnam at war's end, poses with A-1H no. 135344 at Bien Hoa during the early 1990s. The Spad was captured during the 1975 North Vietnamese takeover. (Roger Youngblood collection)

ter, which became the Aircraft Maintenance and Regeneration Center. A handful were resurrected to serve as impressive gate guards, while others have been painstakingly and lovingly restored to airworthy condition. The Spad's appeal as a warbird is based upon its rarity, power, beauty, and classic distinction. Tracking and documenting their status and ownership since retirement from military service proves challenging, mainly because they frequently change hands.

During the 1970s a number of AD-4NAs operated by the French Armee de l'Air in African regions became surplus, and several were brought to the U.S. by collector Jack Spanich. Walt Darran, who says his main claim to fame is having flown combat missions in Spads with both the U.S. Navy and U.S. Air Force, plus a civilian trans-Atlantic delivery, provides the details of his involvement with the French Ads:

"My love affair with the Spad started at Corpus Christi, with the Navy's Advanced Training Command in 1963. I arrived at Yankee Station with VA-165, and embarked *USS Coral Sea* (CVA-43) in January 1964. My first combat flight was a ResCAP for A-4 driver Ed Dickson on 8 February. After flying for Air America towing gliders, corporate flying, Alaska bush flying, flying transports on Kwajalien, and finally flying fire bombers, in April 1977, ten years to the day after my discharge from the Navy, I ferried one of the first two civilian AD-4Ns back to the U.S.

In the fall of 1976 I saw a sale ad for AD-4 Skyraiders, 'From $40,000.' I was on the phone immediately with Jack Spanich of Michigan, who said he had purchased nine AD-4Ns from the French Armee de l' Air. Jack had a total of

A once proud Spad rests forlornly on flat tires and in disrepair in a Bien Hoa revetment during 1990. (Roger Youngblood)

A-1G no. 132589 was rotated back to the U.S. following service with the 602nd SOS and South Vietnamese Air Force. It is displayed at Hurlburt Memorial Park among a host of Air Commando aircraft. (Author's collection)

Following French service, this AD-4NA, BuNo. 127888, named "Super Spad," was operated by Kal-Aero under contract to the U.S. Army as a target tug during the 1970 and 1980s. It is now owned by the Kalamazoo Aviation History museum in Michigan. Its cowl, wing tips and rudder are dark blue. (Stephen Miller)

Bernie Fisher's A-1E after it was put on display at the USAF Museum at Wright-Patterson AFB, Ohio, where it remains today. (Leo Kohn)

about 200 hours, and the biggest airplane he had flown was a Cherokee 6, so he contracted Scott Nielsen from St. Louis to ferry them to Michigan from Chateaudun, France. I called Scott, who said he had a stable of pilots who could fly anything with a reasonable facsimile of wings.

A couple months later Scott called to ask if I was interested in ferrying one of two Spads sitting on the ramp in Dublin, and could I find someone to fly the other. It seemed his warriors only made it to Dublin before their nerves and shaky right legs got the better of them. They locked up the birds and went home. I couldn't find any buddies with a passport, reasonable experience, available time, and an inclination to tour iceberg country in a 30-year old single-engine single-seater. Our only nav aid was a portable fixed-card ADF mounted on its side between the rudder pedals, and a portable VHF for communication. No life vests or rafts—if we went in that time of year, why prolong the agony. So Hank Parker, Scott's partner, was elected to fly the second bird to St. John, Newfoundland, where Scott would relieve him.

Hank and I arrived in Dublin, appropriately, on April Fool's Day. A preflight and a run-up confirmed the birds were in great shape, so the local tower controllers, who had been guarding the aircraft, took us in tow for a tour of their fantastic city. The details of Dublin after that are a bit hazy, but my log says we left three days later—you can fill in the blanks.

Hank was a transport type with no formation experience, so I gave him a briefing on how to fly lead, visual signals, how to open the canopy and start the engine—probably an hour, if that, and off we went. Hank was in BuNo. 124156/N91935, and I was in BuNo. 126882/N91945. I think Hank cheated and read NATOPS. The five and a half-hour leg to Reykjavik, Iceland, went without a hitch.

Two legs were planned for the next day, with refueling at the Danish weather station at Narssag, Greenland, then on to St. John. Forecast over the icecap was clear and visibility unlimited. Not so. We were in and out of the clag most of the first half, then on top of a solid overcast. Some-

Warbird collector Jack Spanich used the colorful markings of VA-176 to turn this AD-4NA into a facsimile of Lt. j.g. Patton's MiG killer. (Author's collection)

BuNo. 139606 underwent a number of paint scheme changes as it passed through the hands of different collectors. (Flying Images)

how we didn't pick up any ice, which was good, because my situation was complicated by two other factors. First, Hank's lead was a bit spastic, and I had the worst vertigo I'd ever encountered. Then over half way there, my sump light came on. I did the only thing I could think of; I unscrewed the bulb. Fixed. I concentrated on sphincter control. Just prior to total panic, a few breaks appeared in the overcast. Then, right on schedule, the ADF needle swung hard right as we crossed some peaks. After nearly four hours, we were about ten miles off course. Hank was more than forgiven. We shot the published approach just to be sure, and Hank did his second Spad landing into 50 knots of wind coming off the glacier. Swinging the tail around into the wind to taxi crosswind was the fun part.

My sump light was only ring fuzz, so after a great Danish buffet and refueling, we headed for St. John. The only thing I remember about that five-hour leg was shooting a night IFR (instruments) approach, trying to keep the blue side up while figuring out where the hell I was with a fixed card ADF set sideways between my feet. Luckily, the ceiling wasn't too low.

Scott replaced Hank for the remaining legs to Fredricton, New Brunswick, Canada, and Detroit and Yipsilanti, Michigan. At Fredricton the Turkey (TBM Avenger) drivers of Forest Protection Ltd. were drooling over our Spads. At Detroit, some snotty little customs broad jumped on me for 'hitting the head' before she'd cleared us. She searched my bags thoroughly for excess booze,

This AD-4NA was resurrected from the African desert by a collector who sold it to Pacific Fighters at Chino, California. It was then resold to Dr. Michael Schloss. (Author)

The variety of serial numbers that have appeared on this A-1H during different time frames suggest it was a hybrid comprised of A-1s that suffered battle damage. Former Thailand-based A-1 pilots agree. It was displayed at NKP and was later given by General Aderholt to the Thai Air Force Museum at Don Muang. In this 1979 view, its cockpit armor has been removed, revealing the original external canopy control and pilot step. (Ivan B. Shinski)

The same Spad in November 1979. A number of USAF Spad pilots are certain this A-1H wears a bogus serial number, and was instead a hybrid based on serial number 134472 of the 1st SOS. (Neal Schneider)

The A-1H no. 139674 was captured during the communist takeover and placed on display at the War Remnants Museum at Ho Chi Minh City, Vietnam. Not only is its paint scheme inaccurate, the once proud aircraft was originally displayed with a centerline rocket launcher that would have fired into the propeller. (Istvan Toperczer)

> but didn't question the four 20mm cannons still mounted in each aircraft. If she'd asked, I was going to tell her they were pegs to hang helmets on. Then it was a short hop to Yipsilanti, a nice carrier break over the numbers, and I headed home with 23.1 more Spad hours in my log.
>
> Jack didn't get all nine Spads back to the U.S.A., as the French reneged and sent a few back to Chad. Jack was killed, along with his wife, when he put a hole in the side of a mountain with a Spad while scud running."

The four Spads brought out of Thailand in 1979 were acquired by warbird collector David Tallichet of Military Aircraft Restoration Corporation, who stored them at Orange County Airport at Los Angeles, California, until the mid-1980s. All were refurbished, and today they preserve the Spad's dignity in the warbird and air show circuit.

The likelihood of enlarging the Skyraider warbird fleet with aircraft still in Vietnam and, possibly, the Khmer Republic, remains uncertain. Vietnam's government continues to resist efforts by collectors to purchase A-1s that languish at its air bases. At least 30 Skyraider airframes, although in various stages of dismantlement, are known to occupy revetments at Bien Hoa and DaNang air bases. Especially perturbing are sizeable, salvageable portions of A-1s periodically spotted in scrap heaps throughout the country.

In contrast, a single Spad remains in Thailand, displayed at the Royal Thai Air Force Museum at Bangkok. The aircraft is reported to have been assigned to the 1st SOS at NKP in 1969. After suffering combat damage, it was deemed unrepairable and placed on display at the base entrance. It wore the name "The Proud American" on its cowl, which may have been carried over from its operational duty, or to memorialize another A-1. General Harry Aderholt later presented the aircraft to the museum. After it fell into a state of disrepair the Spad was renovated and again wears a bogus serial number, plus the word "American" on the cowl.

Nearly 20 Skyraiders are displayed at museums and military facilities across the United States, some of which are veterans of the war in Southeast Asia. The A-1E 52-132598, for example, dis-

Although painted in the popular markings of U.S. Navy Attack Squadron 176, the dorsal air intake and fuselage door reveal this Skyraider's true identity as an AD-4NA. (Robert S. DeGroat)

A beautifully restored EA-1E in 1998. (Robert S. DeGroat)

This AD-4NA, Buno. 126970, crashed in 1984 at a warbird show, killing owner Jack Spanich and his wife. (WI ANG)

played in the proud company of other Air Commando aircraft at Hurlburt Field Memorial Air Park, served the 602nd SOS and the South Vietnamese Air Force.

The A-1E in which Bernie Fisher earned his Medal of Honor is preserved at the U.S. Air Force Museum. Especially noteworthy is an unidentified A-1H stored at the museum which could potentially be displayed to honor the Air Force's second Medal of Honor recipient, William Jones.

The National Museum of Naval Aviation at NAS Pensacola, Florida, is home to the A-1H, BuNo. 135300, which flew the last Navy single-seat Skyraider combat mission in 1968 while assigned to VA-25. Another A-1H, BuNo. 137602, is displayed at NAS Lemoore, California, in the markings of 135300, commemorating the final flight.

Compared to the large number of Skyraiders produced, many of which saw combat, less than 50 remain worldwide to pay tribute to the Spad's long list of accomplishments.

This AD-4NA, BuNo. 126882, was among several recovered from Chad and made available for sale to warbird collectors. It is seen here in April 1977. (Baldur Sveinsson)

One of two former French AD-4NAs owned by Richard Bertea and Donald Hanna. This is BuNo. 126959, while its mate is BuNo. 126935. Both aircraft wear the same color and marking scheme. (Eugene "Mule" Holmberg)

# Skyraider Warriors

Lt. j.g. Gary L. Gottschalk at NAS Alameda in March 1966. Lt. E.D. "Bud" Edson is in the cockpit. (Gary Gottschalk collection)

Maj. Peter B. Lee (left) and Maj. John C. Waresh pose with a Spad named "The Judge" in July 1970 after Waresh led a difficult mission to rescue Lee. Lee's Spad had been cut in half by 37mm fire while attacking trucks at night in Laos. (John Waresh collection)

"B" Flight of the 1st Air Commando Squadron at Pleiku in February 1966. Back row includes (left to right) – Capt. Frank Urbanic, Capt. Ken Shatzer, Capt. Ken Rhuman, Capt. Robert Blood. Front row – Capt. "Paco" Vazquez, Maj. Bernie Fisher, Capt. Jon Lucas, Capt. Bruce Wallace, Lt. Col. William Gutches. (Robert Blood collection)

Cdr. Gordon H. Smith, Executive Officer VA-152 aboard CVA-34 in 1965. The "2" on his helmet denotes his position in the squadron. (Gary L. Gottschalk)

VNAF advisor Capt. Joe Reynes at Da Nang AB in July 1964 with a 516th Fighter Squadron Spad. (Joe Reynes collection)

1Lt. Jim George of the 602nd SOS at NKP in 1969. (James George collection)

Personnel of the 1st SOS at NKP in 1970. (USAF)

VNAF Lt. Thien in June 1964. Thien was killed later that year. (Joe Reynes)

**Capt. Jerry Bracken, one of six USAF pilots who replaced Capt. Joe Reynes at Da Nang in 1964, poses with a VNAF 516th FS A-1H. His Swedish K sub-machine gun was acquired from Special Forces troops. (Joe Reynes)**

**Chief Petty Officer G.E. Searles of VA-152. (Gary L. Gottschalk)**

**Roger Youngblood and his crew chief, SSGT Smith, of the 1st SOS during a post-SAR mission briefing. (Roger Youngblood collection)**

**Framed by the cannons of his A-1E, no. 135215, named "LA Woman," James Easterly and his crew chief of the 1st SOS prior to takeoff at Da Nang in 1971. (Author's collection)**

Capt. Robert E. Blood preflights his A-1E at Pleiku in May 1966. (Robert Blood collection)

Capt. William Prescott of the 602nd SOS in 1966. (USAF)

Lt. Jack S. Smith of VA-152 aboard *Oriskany* in 1965. (Gary L. Gottschalk)

Lt. Thien of the 516th FS at Da Nang in 1964. (Joe Reynes)

Richard S. Drury with the A-1H "Firebird" at NKP in 1969. (Richard S. Drury collection)

Spad crew chief SSGT. James Wadman washes his A-1G, no. 132514, at NKP in 1970. (Ernest L. Connors)

Spad pilot Bob Gochenour of the 6th SOS celebrates the last mission in 1968 of his second tour in Southeast Asia. Looking on is Don Dineen (left), along with Richard Ives and the squadron's ground liaison, an Army sergeant. (USAF)

Lt. E.D. "Bud" Edson of VA-152 in 1965. (Gary L. Gottschalk)

Capt. Larry Haight of the 1st ACS and friends Janis Paige and Anita Bryant during the 1964 Bob Hope Christmas Show at Bien Hoa. Haight wears the 34th Tactical Group patch—as if anyone noticed. (USAF)

Lt. Col. Richard Michaud, commander of the 602nd SOS, with his Sandy Spad in November 1970. (Richard Michaud collection)

VNAF advisor Herb Meyr with a VNAF A-1, formerly of the 1st ACS as indicated by the Playboy bunny on the prop. (Herb Meyr collection)

Maj. Alfred of the 1st SOS still managed a smile after he left large pieces of his Spad in enemy territory. (Richard S. Drury)

1Lt. James Matthews of the 602nd SOS prepares to climb into the cockpit of his A-1J, no. 142021, at NKP. His crew chief, SGT. Ernest L. Connors, assists. (Ernest L. Connors collection)

"Hobo" pilot Capt. R. Crowder and a black-bellied A-1H at NKP in 1969. Crowder carries a .38 cal. revolver in his flight suit pocket. (Richard S. Drury)

Lt. Gordon C. Wileen at NAS Alameda in March 1966. In the background, VA-152's A-1H BuNo. 137502 displays its impressive tally of combat missions. (Gary L. Gottschalk)

Capt. Zack Pryse of the 602nd SOS at Udorn in 1966. (USAF)

Jim George (center) helps Jim Costiri (left) and Stu Bischoff of the 602nd SOS celebrate their "fini flight" on 1 April 1970. (James George collection)

Personnel of the 6th SOS pose with an A-1E loaded with LAU-3/A rocket launchers and 750-pound fire bombs decorated for Easter 1966. (Win DePoorter)

Pilots of the 520th Fighter Squadron and USAF advisor at Binh Thuy in 1966. (Author's collection)

Spad drivers and friend of VA-215 aboard *Hancock* in 1965. (USN)

Spad pilots of VA-152 pose for a change-of-command ceremony at NAS Alameda in early 1965. Cdr. Gusenert (center, back row) was replaced by Cdr. Knutson (to his left). Lt. j.g. Scott Mailhes (second from left, front row), who designed the squadron patch and the aircraft marking scheme, was killed in action. Lt. j.g. Ed Davis (fourth from left, front row) became a prisoner of war. (USN)

USAF advisors to the VNAF 520th FS at Binh Thuy in 1966. From left are Maj. James Bales, Capt. Zeke Zalinsky, 1Lt. Herb Meyr, and Col. T. Johnson. (Herb Meyr collection)

Pilots and officers of the 6th SOS at Pleiku in March 1968. (USAF)

VNAF Capt. On Van Tai of the 518th FS at Da Nang in 1964. (Joe Reynes)

Capt. Robert A. Marron of the 602nd SOS in 1967. (USAF)

1st SOS Spad mechanic/crew chief Mark Eyestone at NKP in 1971. (Mark Eyestone collection)

Maj. Albro L. Lundy, Jr. confers with Sergeants Hinely and Stanton of the 1st SOS prior to takeoff during October 1970. Two months later, Maj. Lundy was declared missing in action. (Ernest L. Connors)

Personnel and A-1E of Project "Tropic Moon" at NKP during November 1968, on the eve of the system's teardown. (Vic Kindurys)

The MiG killers four in VA-25's ready room aboard *Midway* shortly after deplaning on 20 June 1965. From left are Lynn, Greathouse, Johnson, and Hartman. Each wears different flight clothing. (USN)

An A-1E and crew chiefs of the 1st Air Commando Wing at Eglin AFB in 1963. (USAF)

1st SOS Spad pilots, from left, Moffatt, Nordhaus, Drury, and Hair, celebrate their last combat flight. (USAF)

A VNAF 516th Fighter Squadron pilot poses with an A-1 of the 514th Squadron in May 1964. (Joe Reynes)

**Lt. Richard White, Jr. (center) visited his father, Col. Richard White, at NKP in 1969. Both Spad pilots, the younger White flew a sortie with his father as lead, and he and Maj Walt Davis (right) as wing men. "Miss Eileen," A-1H no. 135263, was named after Col. White's wife. (Scott Roe/Richard White collection)**

**Skyraider men at an A-1 reunion. Medal of Honor recipient Bernie Fisher is at center. (Roger Youngblood collection)**

**Of these 30 VNAF Skyraider pilots of the 514th FS posing at Bien Hoa AB in 1967, 9 were killed in combat. All were 1st or 2nd lieutenants, except for the squadron commander, Capt. Thanh Nha Hoang, to the left of the USAF major, who was the squadron advisor. (USAF)**

# Spad Emblems

True to military tradition, there was an abundance of emblems in the Skyraider community during the war in Southeast Asia. Nearly every unit of the three services that flew Spads had an official emblem, whose design had to fall within set guidelines and was subject to approval. Many units, however, devised unofficial emblems, which usually outnumbered official versions, and sometimes were considered unsavory. Nevertheless, these colorful emblems bolstered the morale, camaraderie, and pride necessary for the effective operation of a combat Skyraider unit. Most of these interesting emblems appeared in the form of patches and some were applied to the Skyraider's massive fuselage. "Party suits," which were black or blue-dyed flight suits adorned with patches, served as fraternal billboards advertising Spad drivers' unit assignments and skills, much like the time-honored flight jacket.

Variations of a particular emblem usually indicated a change within the unit, or simply the location it was made. Often, that was a small tailor shop just outside an air base, where locals toiled to produce these interesting and colorful emblems, which have become an important part of the Skyraider's rich history.

**U.S. Navy carrier air groups that served Vietnam cruises became known as the Tonkin Gulf Yacht Club, whose members, both pilots and aircraft, wore these emblems.**

**This patch was designed for the Spad pilots of VA-152 by one of the squadron's pilots, Lt. j.g. Lawrance S. "Scotty" Mailhes, who was KIA in 1965.**

Carrier Airborne Early Warning Squadron Eleven (VAW-11).

Airborne Early Warning Squadron 33.

So many coups against the South Vietnamese occurred early in the war that USAF Spad pilots came up with this emblem.

U.S. pilots used this patch to exploit North Vietnam's accusation that American flyers were "Yankee Air Pirates."

↑
Pacific Air Forces personnel.

This emblem was embroidered fully across the back of some Spad pilots' party suits.

Even the enemies' introduction of the dreaded SA-7 Strela missile prompted a special patch.

22nd Special Operations Squadron

1st Air Commando Squadron.

1st Special Operations Squadron.

**U.S., Laos, Cambodia, Thailand, and South Vietnam flag grouping worn on the arm of a party suit.**

**This design was submitted as the official patch for the 1st Air Commando Squadron at Bien Hoa AB in 1965, but it was disapproved because it was not in the form of a shield or circle.**

**Above: 34th Tactical Group - 1963. This patch did not conform to USAF guidelines, which prohibited the illustration of equipment or locations. Above Right: The replacement emblem introduced in 1964.**

**Pacific Air Forces Standardization/Evaluation Group at Kadena AB, Okinawa.**

**A-1 Flight Examiner Pacific Air Forces Standardization/Evaluation Group at Kadena AB, Okinawa.**

**1st Special Operations Wing.**

**4409th Combat Crew Training Squadron.**

**Patch worn by the pilots who flew the first A-1Es to arrive at Bien Hoa AB.**

**6th Special Operations Squadron.**

**6th Air Commando Squadron.**

6th Special Operations Squadron.

22nd Special Operations Squadron.

22nd Special Operations Squadron.

1st Special Operations Squadron.

The cartoon flying Snoopy character was probably the most popular form of nose art applied to aircraft in Southeast Asia, and was easily identified with Spad pilots.

The call sign "Sandy" became synonymous with rescue in Southeast Asia, and to attain the position of "Sandy One" indicated a wealth of experience in combat search and rescue.

South Vietnamese Air Force.

The emblem of the VNAF 83rd Special Operations Group as it was applied to the Skyraider's fuselage.

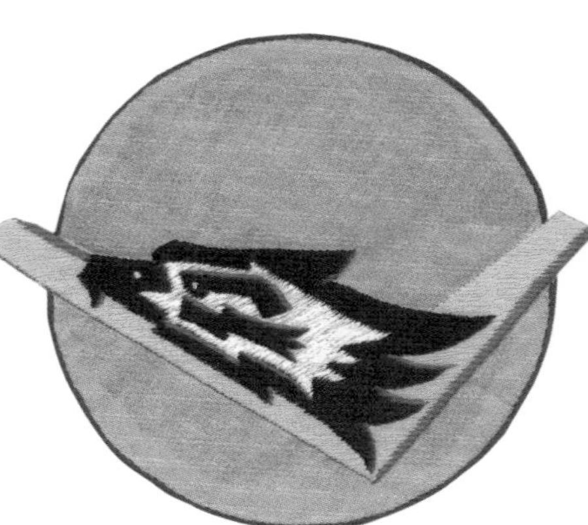

VNAF 514th Fighter Squadron.

VNAF 516th Fighter Squadron.

South Vietnamese Air Force.

4410th Combat Crew Training Squadron "Tropic Moon."

This "Tropic Moon I" patch is seen in its original colors of black and white.

Topic Moon I

# Appendix A: U.S. Air Force Skyraider Squadrons in Southeast Asia

1st SOS – ex-1st Air Commando Squadron; activated June 1963; operated from Bien Hoa AB, Pleiku, Qui Nhon, Nha Trang, and Nakhon Phanom RTAFB; call signs "Hobo" and "Sandy;" tail code "TC;" deactivated December 1972

6th SOS – ex-6th Fighter Squadron (Commando); activated November 1967; operated from Pleiku and OLAA (Da Nang); call signs "Spad" and "Super Spad;" tail code "ET;" deactivated November 1969

22nd SOS – activated October 1968; operated from Nakhon Phanom RTAFB; call signs "Zorro" and "Sandy;" tail code "TS;" deactivated September 1970

602nd SOS – ex-602nd Fighter Squadron (Commando) and 602nd Air Commando Squadron; activated April 1963; operated from Bien Hoa AB, Pleiku, Udorn RTAFB and Nakhon Phanom RTAFB; call signs "Firefly" and "Sandy;" tail code "TT;" deactivated December 1970

Note: Tail code "EC" was used to identify A-1s of composite 1st and 6th SOS while at Pleiku under 14th SOW. Tail code "6T" identified 6th SOS A-1s under 14th SOW.

# Appendix B: U.S. Navy A-1 Squadron WestPac Combat Cruises

| Squadron | Air Wing/Group | Carrier | Tail Code | Side No. | Dates on Station |
|---|---|---|---|---|---|
| VA-25 | CVW-2 | *Midway* | NE | 570-581 | 3-22-65/11-14-65 |
| | CVW-2 | *Coral Sea* | NE | 571-582 | 8-11-66/2-16-67 |
| | CVW-15 | *Coral Sea* | NL | 401-414 | 8-10-67/3-29-68 |
| VA-52 | CVW-5 | *Ticonderoga* | NF | 300-311 | 4-13-64/12-6-64 |
| | CVW-5 | *Ticonderoga* | NF | 300-311 | 10-25-65/5-7-66 |
| | CVW-19 | *Ticonderoga* | NM | 300-311 | 10-15-66/2-29-67 |
| VA-95 | CVW-9 | *Ranger* | NG | 500-511 | 8-17-64/4-25-65 |
| VA-115 | CVW-11 | *Kitty Hawk* | NH | 501-513 | 10-17-63/7-20-64 |
| | CVW-11 | *Kitty Hawk* | NH | 500-513 | 11-15-65/6-6-66 |
| | CVW-5 | *Hancock* | NF | 500-513 | Jan 1967/July 1967 |
| VA-145 | CVW-14 | *Constellation* | NK | 500-511 | 6-11-64/1-24-65 |
| | CVW-14 | *Ranger* | NK | 501-514 | 1-3-66/8-18-66 |
| | CVW-10 | *Intrepid* | AK | 500-511 | 6-9-67/12-9-67 |
| VA-152 | CVW-16 | *Oriskany* | AH | 581-592 | 4-5-65/12-6-65 |
| | CVW-16 | *Oriskany* | AH | 500-511 | 6-11-66/11-8-66 |
| | CVW-16 | *Oriskany* | AH | 500-512 | 6-26-67/1-23-68 |
| VA-165 | CVW-16 | *Oriskany* | AH | 581-592 | 8-1-63/3-10-64 |
| | CVW-15 | *Coral Sea* | NL | 200-212 | 1-23-64/10-23-65 |
| | CVW-10 | *Intrepid* | AK | 200-211 | 5-1-66/10-30-66 |
| VA-176 | CVW-10 | *Intrepid* | AK | 400-412 | 5-1-66/10-30-66 |
| VA-196 | CVW-19 | *Bon Homme Richard* | NM | 600-612 | 2-24-64/11-16-64 |
| | CVW-19 | *Bon Homme Richard* | NM | 601-612 | 5-12-65/1-4-66 |
| VA-215 | CVW-21 | *Hancock* | NP | 560-571 | 11-16-64/5-11-65 |
| | CVW-21 | *Hancock* | NP | 560-571 | 12-6-65/7-21-66 |
| | CVW-21 | *Bon Homme Richard* | NP | 560-571 | 2-10-67/8-17-67 |

### VAW-11

| | | | | | |
|---|---|---|---|---|---|
| Det Q | CVSG-59 | *Bennington* | RR | 71-73 | Feb 1964/Aug 1964 |
| Det R | CVSG-53 | *Kearsarge* | RR | 700-703 | July 1964/Dec 1964 |
| Det T | CVSG-55 | *Yorktown* | RR | 710-715 | Nov 1964/May 1965 |
| Det R | CVSG-53 | *Kearsarge* | RR | | June 1966/Dec 1966 |

### VAW-13

| | | | | | |
|---|---|---|---|---|---|
| Det L | CVW-21 | *Hancock* | VR | | April 1962/Dec 1963 |
| Det | CVW-15 | *Coral Sea* | VR | | 1-23-64/10-23-65 |
| Det A | CVW-2 | *Midway* | VR | 701-703 | 3-22-65/11-14-65 |
| Det E | CVW-19 | *Bon Homme Richard* | VR | 701-703 | 5-12-65/1-4-66 |
| Det | CVW-16 | *Oriskany* | VR | | 4-5-65/12-6-65 |
| Det 1 | CVW-7 | *Independence* | VR | 771-774 | May 1965/Dec 1965 |
| Det | CVW-15 | *Constellation* | VR | 772-780 | May 1966/Dec 1966 |
| Det A | CVW-19 | *Coral Sea* | VR | 721-723 | 8-11-66/2-16-67 |
| Det M | CVW-9 | *Enterprise* | VR | 771-773 | Nov 1966/July 1967 |
| Det | CVW-15 | *Coral Sea* | VR | | 8-10-67/3-29-68 |
| Det 31 | CVA-31 | *Bon Homme Richard* | VR | 771-773 | 1-26-67/8-25-67 |
| Det 42 | CVW-1 | *Roosevelt* | VR | | June 1966/Feb 1967 |
| Det 43 | CVW-15 | *Coral Sea* | VR | 771-773 | 7-26-67/4-6-68 |
| Det 64 | CVW-14 | *Constellation* | VR | 771-773 | May 1967/Dec 1967 |
| Det | CVW-16 | *Oriskany* | VR | | 6-26-67/1-23-68 |
| Det 63 | CVW-11 | *Kitty Hawk* | VR | 011-013 | 11-18-67/6-28-68 |

### VAW/VAQ-33

| | | | | | |
|---|---|---|---|---|---|
| Det 11 | CVSG-56 | *Intrepid* | AK | | 1963/1964 |
| Det 11 | CVW-10 | *Intrepid* | AK | 601-603 | May 1967/Jan 1968 |
| Det 14 | CVW-19 | *Ticonderoga* | NM | 704-706 | Jan 1968/Aug 1968 |
| Det 11 | CVW-10 | *Intrepid* | AK | 801-803 | 6-4-68/2-8-69 |

### Carrier Designations

| **Attack** | **ASW Support** |
|---|---|
| *USS Ticonderoga*CVA-14 | *USS Yorktown*CVS-10 |
| *USS Hancock*CVA-19 | *USS Intrepid*CVS-11 |
| *USS Bon Homme Richard*CVA-31 | *USS Bennington CVS-20* |
| *USS Oriskany*CVA-34 | *USS Kearsarge CVS-33* |
| *USS Midway*CVA-41 | |
| *USS Franklin D. Roosevelt*CVA-42 | |
| *USS Forrestal*CVA-59 | |
| *USS Ranger*CVA-61 | |
| *USS Independence*CVA-62 | |
| *USS Kitty Hawk*CVA-63 | |
| *USS Constellation*CVA-64 | |
| *USS Enterprise*CVAN-65 | |

| **Squadron** | **Name** | **Call Sign** |
|---|---|---|
| VA-25 | *Fist of the Fleet* | *Canasta* |
| VA-52 | *Knightriders* | *Viceroy* |
| VA-95 | *Skyknights* | *Green Lizard/Fortress* |
| VA-115 | *Arabs* | *Arab* |
| VA-145 | *Swordsmen* | *Electron* |
| VA-152 | *Wild Aces* | *Locket* |
| VA-165 | *Boomers* | *Firewood* |
| VA-176 | *Thunderbolts* | *Papoose* |
| VA-196 | *Main Battery* | *Milestone* |
| VA-215 | *Barn Owls* | *Barn Owl* |
| VAW-11 | *Early Eleven* | *Overpass* |
| VAW-13 | *Zappers* | *Robbie* |
| VAW/VAQ-33 | *Knighthawks* | *Snowshoe* |

# Appendix C: Vietnamese Air Force Skyraider Units

514th FS – redesignated from 1st FS on 1 January 1963; operated from Bien Hoa AB; call sign "Phoenix;" tail code "L" ("W" on A-1E/G)

516th FS – activated 1 January 1963; operated from Da Nang AB and Nha Trang; det. at Pleiku called "ABAT 5;" call sign "Tiger;" tail code "L" ("P" on A-1E/G); converted to A-37 July 1969

518th FS – activated 18 October 1963; operated from Bien Hoa AB; call sign "Dragon;" tail code "K" ("kW" on A-1E/G)

520th FS – activated 16 June 1964; operated from Bien Hoa AB; relocated to Binh Thuy August 1965; call sign "Divine Bear;" tail code "V" ("vW" on A-1E/G); converted to A-37

522nd FS – activated 1 April 1965; attached to 83rd SOG, which became 83rd Tac. Gp. On 1 January 1966; operated from Tan Son Nhut AB; call sign "Divine Wind;" tail code "U;" converted to F-5 June 1967

524th FS – activated 15 September 1965; operated from Nha Trang AB; detachments at Pleiku (call sign "Jupiter"), Binh Thuy, and Tan Son Nhut AB (call signs "Dragon" and "Phoenix"); tail code "P;" converted to A-37 April 1969

530th FS – activated 1 December 1970; operated from Pleiku AB; call sign "Jupiter"

**Tactical Wings**

23rd TW – Bien Hoa AB; 514th, 518th, and 520th FS
33rd TW – Tan Son Nhut AB; 522nd FS
41st TW – Da Nang AB; 516th FS
62nd TW – Nha Trang AB; 524th FS
72nd TW – Pleiku AB; 530th FS

# Appendix D: U.S. Air Force Skyraiders

| Type | Serial Number | Units, Cowling Designations, Remarks |
|---|---|---|
| A-1H | 52-129668 | 6th SOS; crashed on fire at Dak To after damaged by AAA on 4-25-70, Maj. D.E. DeTar "Spad 03" ejected and was rescued |
| A-1H | 52-132260 | |
| A-1H | 52-132340 | |
| A-1H | 52-132352 | |
| A-1E | 52-132392 | 602nd ACS/A; shot down North Vietnam during SAR for F-4C "Phantom 12" on 11-11-66, Capt. R.P. Rosecrans "Sandy 05" ejected and was rescued |
| A-1E | 52-132398 | 4407th CCTS, 1st SOW |
| A-1E | 52-132400 | 602nd ACS; shot down Laos on 6-9-66, Maj. J.L. Caskey "Firefly 17" ejected and was rescued |
| A-1E | 52-132401 | 1st ACS; crash-landed after damaged by AAA in Laos on 2-10-65, Capt. William Y. Duggan rescued, VNAF student MIA |
| A-1E | 52-132403 | 1st ACS/1, tail code EC |
| A-1E | 52-132408 | 602nd ACS; shot down North Vietnam on 6-11-67, Maj. James F. Rausch and Maj. Robert Russell ejected and were rescued |
| A-1E | 52-132409 | 602nd ACS/A |
| A-1E | 52-132410 | 602nd ACS/A; shot down Laos on 10-20-66, Capt. David R. Wagner "Sandy 08" KIA |
| A-1E | 52-132411 | 1st ACS; shot down South Vietnam during close support mission on 10-26-64, 1Lt. Glen C. Dyer and VNAF 2Lt. KIA |
| A-1E | 52-132412 | 1st ACS; shot down South Vietnam on 1-28-66, Maj. Fred L. McPherson "Spad 45" KIA |
| A-1E | 52-132414 | 1st ACS; 602nd ACS/1; crash-landed at Chu Lai after damaged by AAA on 7-22-65, Capt. Oliver C. Chase, Jr. KIA |
| A-1E | 52-132415 | 4407th CCTS, 4410th CCTW; later VNAF |
| A-1E | 52-132416 | |
| A-1E | 52-132417 | one of two AD-5s evaluated at SAWC August 1962 through January 1963; 602nd ACS/A, shot down Laos 5-16-66, Capt. H. Lewis Smith "Dragonfly 23" ejected and was rescued |
| A-1E | 52-132418 | |
| A-1E | 52-132419 | 602nd ACS; lost in mid-air over Laos on 1-26-67, pilot rescued |
| A-1E | 52-132421 | 1st ACS/1; shot down North Vietnam 7-31-66, Capt. D.W. Lester, Jr. "Dragonfly 21" ejected and was rescued |
| A-1E | 52-132423 | 602nd ACS; shot down Laos on 7-6-66, Capt. J.R. Crane "Sandy 21" rescued |
| A-1E | 52-132425 | VNAF; 602nd ACS/A and 1; shot down Laos on 4-19-66, Capt. Richard J. Robbins "Sandy 31" KIA |
| A-1E | 52-132428 | 4407th CCTS, 1st SOW; VNAF; captured during takeover, currently at Bien Hoa |
| A-1E | 52-132433 | 4407th CCTS, 1st SOW; VNAF |
| A-1E | 52-132436 | 4407th CCTS, 1st SOW |
| A-1E | 52-132439 | One of two AD-5s evaluated at SAWC August 1962 through January 1963; 602nd ACS/4; shot down North Vietnam during SAR for F-105 "Oak 01" on 11-6-65, Capt. George G. McKnight "Sandy 14" POW |
| A-1E | 52-132441 | 1st ACS; shot down South Vietnam supporting outpost under attack on 9-23-64, 1Lt. George E. Flynn III bailed out, was captured and killed in captivity, VNAF student POW (wing man Capt. May, in 132656, also hit and crashed-landed nearby) |

| | | |
|---|---|---|
| A-1E | 52-132442 | 602nd ACS; crash-landed near battle after damaged by AAA during support of Plei Me, South Vietnam on 10-22-65, Capt. Myron W. Burr rescued |
| A-1E | 52-132443 | display at Texas Air Museum |
| A-1E | 52-132444 | 602nd ACS "The Abandoned 4's"; Lt.Col. Ralph Hoggatt Air Force Cross during SAR for F-4C "Awol 01" on 11-11-67; VNAF |
| A-1E | 52-132445 | 602nd ACS/1; shot down Laos while dive bombing target on 3-10-70, Capt. Donald R. Combs "Firefly 23" and Capt. George E. Luck rescued, Luck wounded |
| A-1E | 52-132447 | 602nd ACS; shot down Laos during SAR for F-105D "Nash 02" on 5-26-66, Capt. Robert I. Bush "Sandy 12" ejected and was rescued |
| A-1E | 52-132448 | 1st ACS; VNAF |
| A-1E | 52-132449 | 1st ACS; crash-landed Cambodia after damaged by AAA during close support mission on 6-7-66, Capt. Robert L. Sander "Elbow 65" KIA |
| A-1E | 52-132450 | 1st ACS; shot down during close support mission South Vietnam on 9-26-64, Maj. W.G. Harris and VNAF pilot rescued |
| A-1E | 52-132453 | 1st SOS |
| A-1E | 52-132454 | 602nd ACS; shot down Laos on 11-15-66, Capt. G.E. Fowler "Firefly 12" rescued |
| A-1E | 52-132455 | VNAF; 1st SOS; 602nd SOS; crashed following engine failure Laos on 11-1-69, Maj. Peter Williams "Fire fly 27" ejected and was rescued, Maj. Richard W. Lytle's ejection seat failed and he was killed |
| A-1E | 52-132456 | 602nd SOS; operational loss on 1-11-69 |
| A-1E | 52-132459 | 1st SOS |
| A-1E | 52-132460 | 4407th CCTS, 1st SOW |
| A-1E | 52-132464 | 1st ACS; shot down Laos on 1-31-66, Capt. J.R. Gearhart "Hobo 20" rescued |
| A-1E | 52-132465 | 1st ACS; on training mission, crashed short of runway in South Vietnam after possible damage from ground fire on 8-29-64, Capt. Richard D. Goss and VNAF student pilot killed |
| A-1E | 52-132468 | 1st ACS; written off after landing accident at Pleiku on 1-12-66; display at McClellan AFB |
| A-1E | 52-132469 | 602nd ACS/4; shot down North Vietnam during SAR for F-105 "Oak 01" on 11-6-65, Capt. Richard E. Bolstad "Sandy 12" POW |
| A-1E | 52-132471 | 1st ACS; crashed during training flight 15 miles from Bien Hoa AB on 2-24-65, Capt. Kurt W. Gareiss and Capt. Thomas C. McEwen, Jr. killed |
| A-1E | 52-132472 | 4407th CCTS, 1st SOW; 1st SOS |
| A-1E | 52-132474 | 4407th CCTS, 1st SOS; VNAF |
| A-1E | 52-132476 | 1st ACS/3; crashed due to equipment failure 5 miles from Bien Hoa AB on 10-29-64, Capt. John C. Knaggs and Capt. Edward Blake killed |
| A-1G | 52-132481 | VNAF |
| A-1G | 52-132482 | VNAF |
| A-1G | 52-132484 | |
| A-1G | 52-132485 | VNAF |
| A-1G | 52-132487 | VNAF |
| A-1G | 52-132494 | VNAF |
| A-1G | 52-132496 | 602nd ACS |
| A-1G | 52-132497 | VNAF |
| A-1G | 52-132498 | VNAF; 1st SOS/2 |
| A-1G | 52-132503 | VNAF; |
| A-1G | 52-132508 | VNAF |
| A-1G | 52-132514 | 602nd ACS; 1st SOS "Hot Wad Wagon;" VNAF, scrapped South Vietnam |
| A-1G | 52-132524 | VNAF |
| A-1G | 52-132528 | 606th SOS; 6th SOS "War Monger;" 1st SOS; VNAF |
| A-1G | 52-132535 | 4407th CCTS, 4410th CCTW; crashed following mid-air with 132644 while dogfighting on 6-24-65, Capt. James J. Jines, Jr. and Maj. Robert W. Robinson killed |
| A-1G | 52-132542 | VNAF; tail code EC, 602nd SOS; crashed near Ban Ban, Laos, pilot experienced vertigo during night mission when gyro went out on 10-13-68, Capt. Michael J. Masterson "Firefly 26" bailed out and remains MIA |
| A-1G | 52-132546 | 1st SOS; 602nd SOS; crashed Thailand returning from mission on 2-12-69, 1Lt. Richard D. Chorlins "Firefly 31" rescued |
| A-1G | 52-132548 | 1st ACS; shot down Laos on 6-21-67, Capt. Darrell J. Spinler "Hobo 21" KIA |
| A-1H | 52-132550 | |
| A-1G | 52-132551 | VNAF |
| A-1G | 52-132559 | VNAF |

| | | |
|---|---|---|
| A-1G | 52-132562 | VNAF 1131st Special Squadron; crashed during demonstration strafing pass near Bien Hoa AB on 9-5-65, Capt. Richard C. Marshall and U.S. Army Warrant Officer 2 William J. LaGrand killed |
| A-1G | 52-132569 | 602nd ACS; 1st ACS; shot down Laos during SAR for F-4C "Awol 01" on 11-11-67, Maj. William C. Griffith ejected and was rescued |
| A-1G | 52-132577 | 1st ACS; 602nd SOS |
| A-1G | 52-132579 | 1st ACS' shot down Laos on 9-5-67, Maj. J.O. Gassman "Hobo 34" ejected and was rescued |
| A-1G | 52-132582 | VNAF; 1st ACS; tail code EC; shot down Laos on 4-26-68, Lt. Col. John A. Saffell "Hobo 65" ejected and was rescued |
| A-1G | 52-132585 | |
| A-1G | 52-132587 | VNAF; 602nd ACS/4; shot down Laos on 3-13-68, Maj. Donald E. Westbrook "Sandy 01" MIA, later KIA |
| A-1G | 52-132588 | 602nd ACS; lost in mid-air Laos on 9-8-66, pilot rescued |
| A-1G | 52-132593 | 1st ACS/3; lost in mid-air with A-1E 133880 South Vietnam during direct support mission on 10-2-65. Capt. Donald C. Patch KIA |
| A-1G | 52-132596 | 4407th CCTS, 1st SOW |
| A-1G | 52-132598 | 602nd SOS; VNAF; display at Hurlburt Field |
| A-1G | 52-132600 | 1st ACS; shot down on administrative flight from Nha Trang to Udorn RTAFB on 11-16-66, Lt. Col. C.A. Smith "Commando 01," Col. G.F. Bradburn, and SSgt. Souza rescued, A1C Allan D. Pittman MIA |
| A-1G | 52-132601 | 1st ACS; after releasing bomb on target in South Vietnam, followed bomb into ground, probably as a result of ground fire on 4-18-65, Capt. James A. Wheeler KIA |
| A-1G | 52-132605 | VNAF; 1st ACS; shot down South Vietnam on 12-30-66, Capt. E.R. Maxson "Hobo 26" rescued |
| A-1G | 52-132607 | 1st ACS/4; crashed on close support mission South Vietnam 8-3-65, possibly operational loss |
| A-1G | 52-132612 | VNAF; 6th SOS "Jan;" 602nd SOS; shot down during combat air support mission on 1-9-70, Capt. J.L. Hudson "Firefly 43" ejected and was rescued |
| A-1G | 52-132614 | VNAF; 602nd SOS; back to VNAF |
| A-1G | 52-132615 | |
| A-1G | 52-132616 | VNAF |
| A-1G | 52-132619 | 602nd ACS/B and 4 "Carolyn's Folly;" VNAF |
| A-1G | 52-132620 | VNAF |
| A-1G | 52-132622 | 4407th CCTS, 1st SOS |
| A-1G | 52-132624 | VNAF; 602nd ACS/A "Cheerie;" crashed Thailand during SAR for F-104 "Fresno 01" on 9-1-66, Capt. Alvie Lee Minnick "Sandy 32" ejected and was rescued |
| A-1G | 52-132625 | 1st ACS, 1131st Special Squadron; shot down Laos on 2-25-67, Lt. Col. Joseph L. Hart "Hobo 36" KIA |
| A-1G | 52-132627 | VNAF |
| A-1G | 52-132628 | 6th SOS; VNAF |
| A-1G | 52-132629 | VNAF |
| A-1G | 52-132630 | VNAF |
| A-1G | 52-132633 | 602nd ACS/3; 1st ACS; shot down Laos on 11-10-66, Capt. John L. O'Brien "Hobo 29" KIA |
| A-1G | 52-132634 | 1st ACS/3; one of two A-1s destroyed during ground attack at Nha Trang on 4-22-66 |
| A-1G | 52-132635 | VNAF |
| A-1G | 52-132636 | VNAF |
| A-1E | 52-132637 | 1st ACS/3; operational loss at Bien Hoa AB on 12-26-65. Maj. Lewis R. Raleigh killed |
| A-1E | 52-132638 | VNAF; 602nd ACS/4 "Corn Fed;" 1st ACS; shot down Laos on 5-4-67, Maj. Charles E. Rogers "Hobo 21" KIA |
| A-1E | 52-132640 | 1st ACS; shot down South Vietnam during training mission on 12-1-64, 1Lt. K.P. Roedeman rescued, VNAF Warrant Officer D.S. Tam KIA |
| A-1E | 52-132641 | 4407th CCTS; 1st SOW; crashed near Hurlburt Field on 6-17-70, Lt. Col. James J. Mihalick and Maj. O'Dell L. Riley killed |
| A-1E | 52-132643 | *Tropic Moon* aircraft; 1st SOS "Minnesota Fats," "Winona," "Iron Butterfly;" VNAF |
| A-1E | 52-132644 | 4407th CCTS, 4410th CCTW; crashed following mid-air with 132535 while dogfighting with F-100s 12 miles from Masayhead, Florida on 6-24-65, instructors Capt. Edward L. Doyle and Maj. Donald L. Lumadue killed |
| A-1E | 52-132646 | 1st SOS; shot down Laos on 10-21-68, Maj. William L. Bagwell "Hobo 32" ejected and was rescued |
| A-1E | 52-132648 | 602nd ACS; shot down South Vietnam during SAR for F-104 "Fresno 01" on 9-1-66, Maj. Hubert C. Nichols, Jr. "Sandy 31" MIA, later KIA |
| A-1E | 52-132649 | 1st ACS; crash-landed Can Tho, South Vietnam after damaged by AAA on 3-21-65, Capt. William H. Campbell and Capt. Jerry P. Hawkins KIA, aircraft recovered; 1st SOS; Maj. Bernard Fisher Medal of Honor aircraft, display U.S. Air Force Museum |
| A-1E | 52-132653 | 4407th CCTS, 4410th CCTW; 1st SOS; VNAF |

| | | |
|---|---|---|
| A-1E | 52-132654 | 1st ACS; shot down and crashed into water North Vietnam during strike mission on 10-2-64, Capt. Kenneth E. Walker and VNAF 2Lt. KIA |
| A-1E | 52-132655 | 4407th CCTS, 4410th CCTW; VNAF |
| A-1E | 52-132656 | 1st ACS; shot down supporting outpost under attack South Vietnam on 9-22-64, Capt W. H. May rescued, wing man Lt. Flynn forced to bail out, both of their VNAF students reportedly captured |
| A-1E | 52-132657 | VNAF |
| A-1E | 52-132659 | 1st ACS; shot down South Vietnam on 9-13-66, Lt. Col. E. Deatrick "Hobo 26" rescued |
| A-1E | 52-132661 | TAC; wing separated and crashed on training flight near Hurlburt on 10-22-68, Capt. John J. Stark and Maj. James C. Phillips killed |
| A-1E | 52-132663 | VNAF; 1st ACS/1 and 2; shot down Laos on 10-6-67, Maj. Frank A. Armstrong "Hobo 34" KIA |
| A-1E | 52-132665 | VNAF; 1st ACS/4; shot down Laos on 2-14-66, Maj. John R. Hills "Sandy 02" KIA |
| A-1E | 52-132666 | VNAF; 1st ACS; crashed during landing at Bien Hoa AB on 1-27-65, Maj. George F. Vlisides and VNAF observer killed |
| A-1E | 52-132667 | VNAF; 1st ACS; shot down and collided with 133925 South Vietnam during mine-laying mission on 6-6-68, Maj. David J. Gunster "Hobo 17" KIA, Capt. Edward E. Kirkpatrick rescued |
| A-1E | 52-132668 | VNAF; 602nd ACS/4; 1st ACS; shot down attacking bunkers North Vietnam on 7-21-68, Maj. Billy M. Mobley "Zorro 67" ejected and was rescued |
| A-1E | 52-132669 | VNAF; 1st ACS; shot down North Vietnam and crashed into sea during SAR for A-4E "Silver Fox 500" on 9-10-65, Capt. Paul V. Graybill "Sandy 12" bailed out and was rescued, Capt. Graybill Silver Star |
| A-1E | 52-132670 | VNAF; 1st ACS; crash-landed and burned at Qui Nhon, South Vietnam on 7-29-65, Maj. Lou Gang uninjured |
| A-1E | 52-132673 | 4407th CCTS, 1st SOW; VNAF |
| A-1E | 52-132674 | 1st SOS; 602nd ACS; crashed shortly after takeoff at NKP on 1-27-70, Capt. George H. Porter "Zorro 21" ejected and was rescued |
| A-1E | 52-132675 | VNAF; 1st ACS/3; shot down North Vietnam on 9-10-66, Maj. Lawrence B. Tatum "Hobo 27" ejected, MIA |
| A-1E | 52-132678 | 602nd ACS/1; shot down North Vietnam on 8-9-67, Capt. Allen S. Cherry KIA |
| A-1E | 52-132680 | 602nd ACS; shot down by MiGs North Vietnam during SAR on 4-29-66, Capt. Leo S. Boston "Sandy 22" MIA, later KIA |
| A-1E | 52-132681 | 1st ACS; shot down Laos on 6-4-67, Lt. Col. Lewis M. Robinson "Hobo 34" KIA |
| A-1E | 52-132682 | |
| A-1E | 52-132683 | 4407th CCTS, 1st SOW; VNAF; civil U.S. reg. warbird |
| A-1E | 52-132686 | 4407th CCTS, 1st SOW; VNAF |
| A-1G | 52-132691 | 602nd ACS |
| A-1G | 52-132698 | display at Carson City, Nevada |
| A-1E | 52-133855 | 1st ACS/3; shot down South Vietnam on 5-21-67, Maj. C.B. Holler "Hobo 01" rescued |
| A-1E | 52-133856 | TAC; crashed near Hurlburt Field during training flight on 11-8-66, VNAF 2Lt. Ha Xuong killed |
| A-1E | 52-133857 | 602nd SOS "Supper Mex;" 22nd SOS "Midnight Special;" 1st SOS shot down during strike mission Laos on 6-17-72, Maj. Esequiel M. Encinas "Hobo 42" KIA, last USAF A-1 pilot KIA |
| A-1E | 52-133858 | 4407th CCTS, 1st SOW; 1st SOS; VNAF |
| A-1E | 52-133860 | 4407th CCTS, 1st SOW; VNAF (test flown with wings folded by USN in 1951) |
| A-1E | 52-133861 | 4407th CCTS, 4410th CCTW; VNAF |
| A-1E | 52-133862 | 4407th CCTS; 4410th CCTW; VNAF |
| A-1E | 52-133864 | 1st ACS; shot down South Vietnam 3-12-66, Maj. M.E. Blaylock rescued |
| A-1E | 52-133865 | 602nd SOS; 1st SOS; shot down by SA-7 South Vietnam during SAR for 0-2A "Bilk 34" on 5-2-72, Maj. James Harding "Hobo 20" rescued |
| A-1E | 52-133866 | VNAF |
| A-1E | 52-133867 | 602nd ACS; shot down South Vietnam 3-10-66; Maj. Dafford W. Myers rescued by Maj. Bernard Fisher |
| A-1E | 52-133868 | 4407th CCTS, 4410th CCTW |
| A-1E | 52-133869 | 602nd ACS/3; 1st ACS; crashed North Vietnam after mid-air with A-1E 133899 during SAR for F-105D "Buick 01" on 6-9-66, Maj. Theodore J. Shorack, Jr. "Sandy 31" KIA |
| A-1E | 52-133871 | 602nd ACS "Dottie;" shot down Laos on 5-1-66, Capt. J.M. Ingalls "Firefly 19" bailed out and was rescued |
| A-1E | 52-133872 | VNAF;1st ACS/3; 602nd ACS; shot down Laos on 8-4-66, Capt. John R. Burns "Firefly 19" KIA |
| A-1E | 52-133873 | 4407th CCTS, 4410th CCTW; 1st ACS; crashed 3-13-66, aircraft recovered, shot down Laos 3-19-67, Capt. Michael J. Dugan "Hobo 33" bailed out and was rescued |
| A-1E | 52-133876 | 1st ACS/2; VNAF; 602nd SOS; written off following battle damage 12-6-67 |
| A-1E | 52-133878 | 1st SOS; Son Tay raid aircraft; VNAF |
| A-1E | 52-133879 | VNAF |

A-1E 52-133880 602nd ACS/2; lost in mid-air with A-1G 132593 during direct support mission South Vietnam on 10-2-65, Capt. Donald R. Hood KIA

A-1E 52-133882 1st ACS/4; shot down South Vietnam on 4-8-66, Capt. S. Knickerbocker "Hobo 41" rescued; VNAF

A-1E 52-133883 1st SOS; tail code EC; 6th SOS; shot down during close support mission South Vietnam on 7-23-69, Maj. Franklin W. Picking "Spad 33" and Maj. Thomas H. McCarty KIA

A-1E 52-133884 4407th CCTS, 1st SOW; 1st SOS

A-1E 52-133885 VNAF; 602nd ACS; shot down Laos on 2-15-66, Maj. Oscar Mauterer "Sandy 22" MIA

A-1E 52-133886 1st ACS; crash-landed South Vietnam after damaged by ground fire on 4-17-65, Capt. Lawrence D. Haight rescued, following day aircraft destroyed with explosives

A-1E 52-133888 1st ACS; shot down Laos on 3-13-68, Lt. Col. Joseph H. Byrne "Hobo 11" and Lt. Col. Guy F. Collins KIA

A-1E 52-133889 1st ACS/3; lost in mid-air with A-1E 135040 during strike mission near Pleiku, South Vietnam on 6-16-65, Capt. Robert D. Gallup KIA

A-1E 52-133890 602nd ACS; shot down North Vietnam during SAR for "Lightning 01" on 7-1-66, Maj. Robert C. Williams "Sandy 42" MIA, later KIA

A-1E 52-133891 4407th CCTS, 1st SOW; VNAF

A-1E 52-133892 4407th CCTS, 1st SOW; VNAF

A-1E 52-133893 1st ACS/3; tail code EC

A-1E 52-133896 4407th CCTS, 1st SOW; VNAF

A-1E 52-133897 VNAF; 1st ACS; shot down during support mission of Plei Me Special Forces camp South Vietnam on 10-22-65, Capt. Melvin Elliott bailed out and was rescued the following day

A-1E 52-133898 VNAF; 1st ACS; shot down South Vietnam during close support mission on 11-14-65, Capt. Paul T. McClellan, Jr. "Hobo 09" KIA

A-1E 52-133899 VNAF; 602nd ACS/1; flew 400th A-1 combat mission on 11-6-65, mid-air North Vietnam with A-1E 133869 during SAR for F-105D "Buick 01" on 6-9-66, Capt. Robert I. Bush "Sandy 41" KIA

A-1E 52-133900 TAC; crashed at Hurlburt Field on 11-9-64, Capt. William J. Walsh and 2Lt. William A. Shagner killed

A-1E 52-133901 1st ACS; destroyed during ground attack at Bien Hoa AB on 5-14-65

A-1E 52-133904 4407th CCTS, 1st SOW

A-1E 52-133905 602nd ACS; downed by MiG-17 North Vietnam during SAR for F-105 "Kingfish 02" on 4-19-67, Maj. John S. Hamilton KIA, Hamilton Air Force Cross

A-1E 52-133906 4407th CCTS, 1st SOW; VNAF

A-1E 52-133907 3rd TFW; operational loss South Vietnam on 1-28-66, pilot rescued

A-1E 52-133908 1st ACS; shot down Laos during SAR mission on 2-24-66, Capt. Raymond H. Hetrick KIA

A-1E 52-133909 602nd ACS; shot down Ban Naka Tew, Laos on 5-19-67, Maj. Roy A. Knight, Jr. "Firefly 11" KIA, Knight Air Force Cross

A-1E 52-133910 1st ACS; shot down and crashed into sea South Vietnam on 10-12-65, Capt. D.W. Rice rescued

A-1E 52-133911

A-1E 52-133913 1st ACS; shot down Laos on 7-13-67, Maj. Frank A. Armstrong "Hobo 36" ejected and was rescued

A-1E 52-133914 VNAF; 1st ACS/4; tail code EC; 602nd SOS; shot down Laos on 3-4-70, Capt. D.E. Friestad "Firefly 32" ejected and was rescued

A-1E 52-133915 VNAF; 1st ACS/1; 602nd ACS; shot down during strafing run South Vietnam on 10-4-65, Capt. Charles F. Allen KIA

A-1E 52-133918 602nd ACS; shot down Laos on 6-29-66, Capt. N.J. Baker "Dragonfly 25" ejected and was rescued

A-1E 52-133919 4407th CCTS, 1st SOW; VNAF

A-1E 52-133920 USAF; VNAF

A-1E 52-133921 Used by Stanley Aviation Corp. for Yankee seat tests; tail code EC, crash-landed 1968 and scrapped at Tan Son Nhut AB

A-1E 52-133922 VNAF

A-1E 52-133923 TAC; crashed during training flight near Hurlburt Field on 9-26-67, Lt. Col. Albert C. Hamby and Maj. William N. Kuykendall killed

A-1E 52-133925 602nd ACS' 1st ACS; shot down and collided with 132667 South Vietnam on 6-6-68, Maj. Rudolph L. Nunn, Jr. "Hobo 16" KIA

A-1E 52-133926 602nd ACS; shot down Laos on 11-29-66, Capt John M. Roper "Firefly 14" KIA

A-1E 52-133927 1st SOS; shot down Laos on 6-28-69, Lt. Col. William D. Neal, Jr. "Hobo 22" bailed out when ejection seat failed, Maj. William L. Bagwell ejected, both rescued

A-1E 52-133928 602nd ACS; shot down North Vietnam on 9-12-66, Maj. Stanley G. Sprague "Firefly 14" KIA

A-1E 52-133976

A-1E 52-133989 1st ACS; lost in mid-air with C-123 during night strike South Vietnam on 1-13-66, Capt. Robert M. Middlebrooks KIA

| | | |
|---|---|---|
| A-1H | 52-134257 | 1st SOS "Hell Bender" |
| A-1H | 52-134471 | 602nd SOS; crashed shortly after takeoff from NKP on 3-14-70, Maj. Donald B. Fincher "Firefly 22" tried to eject but system failed and he was killed |
| A-1H | 52-134472 | VNAF; 1st SOS; RTAF museum at Don Muang, Thailand |
| A-1H | 52-134484 | VNAF |
| A-1H | 52-134488 | VNAF |
| A-1H | 52-134494 | 1st SOS "The Ragin Cajun;" VNAF |
| A-1H | 52-134500 | VNAF |
| A-1H | 52-134502 | 6th SOS; tail code 6T |
| A-1H | 52-134507 | VNAF |
| A-1H | 52-134508 | 602nd SOS; shot down attacking troops Laos on 12-10-68, Capt. Jerry J. Jenkinson "Firefly 22" ejected and was rescued |
| A-1H | 52-134515 | 22nd SOS; shot down during strike mission Laos on 3-26-69, 1Lt. Michael J. Faas rescued |
| A-1H | 52-134518 | 602nd ACS; shot down during SAR for two F-4s North Vietnam on 1-17-68, Lt. Col. Robert F. Wilke "Sandy 05" KIA, Air Force Cross |
| A-1H | 52-134520 | Maj. David E. Hinsen Silver Star for saving Ben Het Special Forces camp on 2-25-69; VNAF |
| A-1H | 52-134526 | 1st SOS "Little Prince;" Capt. Edward R. Jayne II Silver Star for "Ashcan 01/A" SAR on 12-11-71; 1Lt. Glen C. Priebe "Sandy 05" Silver Star for "Bat 21" SAR from 4-3 to 6-72; Capt. Edward R. Jayne II Silver Star for "Nail 31A/B" SAR on 3-18-72 |
| A-1H | 52-134535 | 4407th CCTS, 4410th CCTW; crashed on takeoff from Hurlburt Field on 12-17-70, Capt. Randy Jayne ejected and survived, aircraft repaired and transferred to VNAF |
| A-1H | 52-134540 | VNAF |
| A-1H | 52-134550 | VNAF |
| A-1H | 52-134551 | 1st SOS "Cool Fool," "Jello Liver;" shot down by SA-7 during SAR and crashed into sea on 5-1-72, 1Lt. William Seitz "Sandy 08" rescued |
| A-1H | 52-134555 | 602nd ACS; 22nd SOS; 1st SOS "The Proud American;" VNAF |
| A-1H | 52-134557 | VNAF |
| A-1H | 52-134562 | 602nd SOS "Fight'n Polish Eagle" "Gomer Getter," crashed on takeoff at NKP on 3-15-69, Capt. Wayne A. Warner "Sandy 04" rescued |
| A-1H | 52-134565 | 1st SOS; VNAF |
| A-1H | 52-134568 | 6th ACS; written off after crashing during landing at Pleiku on 6-23-68, Capt. Richard L. Russell "Spad 31" KIA |
| A-1H | 52-134569 | 22nd SOS; VNAF |
| A-1H | 52-134570 | VNAF; Commander's aircraft 633rd SOW; 6th SOS "Honey;" 602nd SOS; shot down attacking trucks Laos on 1-11-70, 1Lt. Richard D. Chorlins "Firefly 31" KIA |
| A-1H | 52-134575 | VNAF |
| A-1H | 52-134577 | 602nd SOS |
| A-1H | 52-134585 | VNAF |
| A-1H | 52-134588 | 602nd SOS; shot down during SAR for F-4D "Stormy 02" on 1-18-69, Capt. Robert F. Coady "Sandy 01" KIA |
| A-1H | 52-134589 | VNAF; operational loss on 9-12-71, 602nd pilot was rescued |
| A-1H | 52-134600 | VNAF |
| A-1H | 52-134602 | VNAF |
| A-1H | 52-134605 | VNAF |
| A-1H | 52-134606 | |
| A-1H | 52-134607 | VNAF |
| A-1H | 52-134609 | 6th SOS; 1st SOS; VNAF |
| A-1H | 52-134614 | 602nd SOS "Ol Half-Fast," shot down attacking trucks Laos on 6-13-69, 1Lt. Neal C. Ward "Firefly 20" MIA, later KIA |
| A-1H | 52-134622 | 1st SOS "Balls A Fire;" Capt. Fred C. Boli made emergency landing at LS-20A Long Thien, Laos on 9-16-71, destroyed during recovery next day when high winds caused Army CH-54 to release aircraft at end of strip |
| A-1H | 52-134625 | disappeared during test flight from Da Nang AB on 8-2-65, Capt. William W. Hail MIA |
| A-1H | 52-134626 | 1st SOS |
| A-1H | 52-134631 | VNAF |
| A-1H | 52-134632 | VNAF; 602nd SOS; shot down during SAR for F-4D "Stormy 02" Laos on 1-17-69, Lt. Col. Lurie J. Morris "Sandy 02" ejected and was rescued next day |
| A-1H | 52-134634 | VNAF |

| | | |
|---|---|---|
| A-1H | 52-134636 | VNAF |
| A-1H | 52-134638 | |
| A-1H | 52-134665 | |
| A-1G | 52-134976 | VNAF |
| A-1G | 52-134987 | VNAF; 1st ACS/3; 3rd TFW; operational loss Thailand on 12-8-65, Capt. Ronald M. Canter killed |
| A-1G | 52-134988 | |
| A-1G | 52-134990 | 1st ACS; 22nd SOS; shot down during strike mission Laos on 4-10-69, Maj. R.A. Shumok "Zorro 80" rescued |
| A-1G | 52-134997 | 1st ACS; shot down South Vietnam on 11-22-66, Capt. R.H. Armstrong rescued, aircraft recovered, but scrapped at Pleiku |
| A-1G | 52-135005 | 1st ACS; crashed during training mission South Vietnam on 3-6-65 |
| A-1G | 52-135007 | 1st ACS/4 "Miss Pussy Galore;" shot down Laos on 12-31-67, 1Lt. Glenn A. Belcher "Hobo 19" KIA, aircraft recovered |
| A-1G | 52-135021 | 602nd ACS/3; one of two A-1s destroyed during ground attack at Nha Trang on 4-22-66 |
| A-1G | 52-135034 | transferred from USN to USAF but not converted to USAF standard |
| A-1G | 52-135036 | 4407th CCTS, 1st SOW |
| A-1G | 52-135038 | 4407th CCTS, 4410th CCTW; 602nd ACS "Corn Fed;" tail code EC; VNAF |
| A-1G | 52-135040 | 1st ACS/3; lost in mid-air with A-1E 133889 during strike mission near Pleiku on 6-16-65, Capt. John Rumph bailed out and was rescued |
| A-1G | 52-135042 | 4407th CCTS, 1st SOW; VNAF |
| A-1G | 52-135043 | 1st ACS; shot down attacking tanks near Khe Sanh on 2-8-68, Maj. Robert G. Lapham "Hobo 01" KIA, Maj. Lapham Silver Star |
| A-1G | 52-135047 | 1st ACS; VNAF |
| A-1E-5 | 52-135139 | 1st SOS; 6th SOS; destroyed during ground attack at emergency strip in Laos on 8-8-68 |
| A-1E-5 | 52-135141 | 22nd SOS "Up Tight;" 1st SOS, squadron commander's aircraft; tail code EC, shot down by SA-7 during SAR for 0-2A "Bilk 34" South Vietnam on 5-2-72, Capt. Donald Screws "Hobo 21" rescued |
| A-1E-5 | 52-135154 | 602nd SOS; shot down during SAR for F-4D "Wolf 06" Laos on 3-20-70, 1Lt. D.H. Townsend "Strike 63" ejected and was rescued |
| A-1E-5 | 52-135165 | 1st ACS; aircraft lost power at low altitude and crashed Thailand on 3-11-68, Maj. Lee D. McIntosh "Hobo 21" rescued |
| A-1E-5 | 52-135177 | *Tropic Moon* aircraft |
| A-1E-5 | 52-135185 | VNAF |
| A-1E-5 | 52-135187 | *Tropic Moon* aircraft; 602nd SOS; 1st SOS; shot down attacking enemy troops Laos on 9-30-71, 1Lt. George W. Kamenicky "Hobo 42" and Capt. Halton R. Vincent KIA |
| A-1E-5 | 52-135195 | *Tropic Moon* aircraft, Maj. Robert B. Christiansen Distinguished Flying Cross for destroying 4 trucks Laos on 4-25-68; 22nd SOS; shot down Laos on 2-11-70, Col. William L. Kieffer, Jr. "Hobo 53" KIA |
| A-1E-5 | 52-135201 | 6th SOS; 22nd SOS; shot down Laos on 3-25-69, Capt. K.E. Gilmore "Hobo 34" ejected and was rescued |
| A-1E-5 | 52-135202 | tail code EC; crashed due to power loss Laos on 5-23-68, Maj. Robert E. Raynor "Hobo 66" ejected and was rescued |
| A-1E-5 | 52-135206 | 602nd SOS "Georgia Ann;" 1st SOS; Son Tay raid aircraft; Capt. Robert F. Burke Distinguished Flying Cross for medevac support on 1-11-72 |
| A-1E-5 | 52-135211 | 602nd ACS; *Tropic Moon* aircraft; 22nd SOS; shot down during strike Laos on 11-11-69, Capt. George H. Porter "Zorro 65" ejected and was rescued |
| A-1E-5 | 52-135215 | 1st SOS "LA Woman," "Orient express" |
| A-1H | 52-135223 | VNAF; crashed South Vietnam during armed recon mission on 12-23-65, Capt. James C. Wise, Jr. KIA |
| A-1H | 52-135228 | VNAF |
| A-1H | 52-135236 | 6th SOS; shot down supporting Special Forces team Laos on 8-9-68, Maj. Wayne B. Wolfkeil "Spad 36" KIA |
| A-1H | 52-135242 | 602nd SOS; 6th SOS "Pappy Yokum's Country Store"; tail code 6T; Crashed due to engine failure on takeoff at Da Nang AB on 8-14-70, Maj. Van Buren "Spad 01" rescued |
| A-1H | 52-135243 | 4407th CCTS, 4410th CCTW; VNAF |
| A-1H | 52-135245 | VNAF |
| A-1H | 52-135251 | 602nd ACS; shot down attacking bunkers Laos on 7-10-68, Maj. Howard R. Jennings "Firefly 12" ejected and was rescued |
| A-1H | 52-135257 | 602nd SOS; 1st SOS "Sopwith Camel," "Midnight Cowboy;" VNAF |
| A-1H | 52-135258 | 1st SOS "Marty D;" "Peregrine" VNAF |
| A-1H | 52-135260 | VNAF |

| | | |
|---|---|---|
| A-1H | 52-135263 | 1st SOS "Miss Eileen," wing commander's aircraft; 602nd SOS "Miss Kate;" shot down Laos on 7-28-70, Maj. P.B. Lee "Hobo 20" rescued |
| A-1H | 52-135272 | 1st ACS; shot down while dropping ordnance in support of Kham Duc evacuation on 5-12-68, Lt. Col. James N. Swain "Hobo 01" ejected and was rescued, Lt. Col. Swain Silver Star |
| A-1H | 52-135273 | 6th SOS; crashed on approach to Da Nang AB on 12-17-69, Capt. G. Manning "Spad 03" KIA |
| A-1H | 52-135275 | 1st SOS; 602nd SOS; returning from mission to NKP lost power and crashed in Laos on 3-19-70, Maj. L. Evenson "Firefly 26" ejected and was rescued |
| A-1H | 52-135279 | VNAF |
| A-1H | 52-135281 | VNAF |
| A-1H | 52-135282 | 602nd ACS; shot down during SAR for A-7A "Streetcar 304" Laos on 5-31-68, Capt. Edward W. Leonard, Jr. "Sandy 07" bailed out and taken POW |
| A-1H | 52-135286 | 1st SOS; 602nd SOS "Funny Honey"; VNAF |
| A-1H | 52-135289 | VNAF |
| A-1H | 52-135291 | 6th ACS; shot down attacking trucks Laos on 6-28-68, Maj. Paul F. Johns "Spad 37" MIA |
| A-1H | 52-135292 | 602nd SOS "Proud Mary;" VNAF |
| A-1H | 52-135293 | VNAF |
| A-1H | 52-135295 | VNAF |
| A-1H | 52-135298 | VNAF |
| A-1H | 52-135305 | 6th SOS; shot down supporting Special Forces team Laos on 9-29-68, Capt. Wayne E. Newberry "Spad 04" KIA |
| A-1H | 52-135308 | VNAF |
| A-1H | 52-135310 | VNAF |
| A-1H | 52-135314 | 602nd SOS; 1st SOS; shot down supporting medevac Laos on 6-18-71, Capt. Roger E. Witte "Hobo 30" KIA |
| A-1H | 52-135322 | 4407th CCTS, 4410th CCTW; VNAF |
| A-1H | 52-135324 | 602nd SOS; engine quit during strafe attack Laos on 2-12-68, Capt. Paul F. Kimminau "Firefly 15" ejected and was rescued |
| A-1H | 52-135325 | VNAF |
| A-1H | 52-135332 | 4407th CCTS, 1st SOW; VNAF; civil U.S. reg. warbird |
| A-1H | 52-135336 | 22nd SOS; shot down during SAR for USMC OV-10A "Hostageman" Laos on 4-21-70, Capt. J.M. Dyer "Sandy 01" ejected and was rescued |
| A-1H | 52-135338 | |
| A-1H | 52-135339 | VNAF |
| A-1H | 52-135340 | VNAF |
| A-1H | 52-135343 | VNAF |
| A-1H | 52-135344 | VNAF; captured during takeover, currently at Bien Hoa |
| A-1H | 52-135355 | VNAF |
| A-1H | 52-135356 | 22nd SOS; crashed on takeoff from NKP when engine failed on 6-8-69; 1Lt. Lloyd M. Scott "Zorro 61" killed |
| A-1H | 52-135370 | |
| A-1H | 52-135371 | 4407th CCTS, 1st SOW |
| A-1H | 52-135376 | VNAF |
| A-1H | 52-135387 | VNAF |
| A-1H | 52-135392 | VNAF |
| A-1H | 52-135399 | VNAF |
| A-1H | 52-135406 | VNAF |
| A-1H | 52-135472 | 1st SOS "The Love Machine;" 602nd SOS |
| A-1H | 52-135596 | |
| A-1H | 52-135599 | VNAF |
| A-1H | 52-135608 | 1st SOS |
| A-1H | 52-137493 | VNAF |
| A-1H | 52-137496 | 6th SOS; shot down providing air cover for ground troops South Vietnam on 1-10-69, Maj. James B. Wheeler "Spad 03" ejected and was rescued |
| A-1H | 52-137499 | VNAF |
| A-1H | 52-137502 | 6th SOS; VNAF |
| A-1H | 52-137505 | VNAF |
| A-1H | 52-137506 | VNAF |
| A-1H | 52-137511 | 1st SOS "Stump Jumper;" squadron commander's aircraft |
| A-1H | 52-137512 | 602nd SOS; shot down Laos on 7-4-69, Col. Patrick M. Fallon "Firefly 26" ejected and taken POW |

| | | |
|---|---|---|
| A-1H | 52-137514 | VNAF |
| A-1H | 52-137517 | 602nd SOS; VNAF |
| A-1H | 52-137520 | 6th SOS "Boisterous Ben;" destroyed on takeoff at Da Nang AB on 7-19-69, 1Lt. L.C. Jensen "Spad 12" rescued |
| A-1H | 52-137522 | VNAF |
| A-1H | 52-137524 | 6th SOS "Annie's Fanny," "Little Annie Fanny;" 22nd SOS "Nancy Lou;" VNAF |
| A-1H | 52-137526 | VNAF |
| A-1H | 52-137532 | VNAF |
| A-1H | 52-137535 | VNAF |
| A-1H | 52-137537 | VNAF |
| A-1H | 52-137539 | 602nd SOS; shot down Laos on 10-27-69, 1Lt. James W. Herrick, Jr. "Firefly 33" MIA |
| A-1H | 52-137543 | 602nd SOS; 1st SOS; shot down during strafing pass Laos on 7-2-69, Capt. John L. Flynn "Hobo 30" KIA |
| A-1H | 52-137546 | 22nd SOS; shot down attacking trucks Laos on 12-18-68, Maj. Gregory I. Barras "Zorro 50" MIA, later KIA |
| A-1H | 52-137551 | VNAF |
| A-1H | 52-137552 | 6th SOS "Spad Dad," tail code 6T, crashed near NKP after damaged from AAA on strike mission on 12-29-69, 1Lt. N. Frisbie "Firefly 13" rescued |
| A-1H | 52-137558 | VNAF |
| A-1H | 52-137559 | 6th SOS; shot down during SAR mission Laos on 1-10-69, Maj. Arthur R. Sprott, Jr. "Spad 12" KIA |
| A-1H | 52-137560 | VNAF |
| A-1H | 52-137564 | VNAF |
| A-1H | 52-137569 | VNAF |
| A-1H | 52-137570 | VNAF |
| A-1H | 52-137579 | 6th SOS |
| A-1H | 52-137586 | 6th SOS "Chitty Chitty Bang Bang;" VNAF |
| A-1H | 52-137593 | 602nd SOS; "The Mighty Red Baron" VNAF |
| A-1H | 52-137597 | 1st SOS "Miss Judy;" VNAF |
| A-1H | 52-137599 | VNAF |
| A-1H | 52-137601 | 6th SOS, shot down during SAR for F-105D "Scotch 03" South Vietnam on 7-2-68, Maj. Henry A. Tipping "Spad 11" ejected, KIA |
| A-1H | 52-137609 | 6th SOS; tail code 6T "Bad News;" VNAF |
| A-1H | 52-137612 | VNAF; 6th ACS; shot down South Vietnam on 5-5-68, Capt. Lyn D. Oberdier "Spad 32" KIA |
| A-1H | 52-137616 | 1st SOS |
| A-1H | 52-137618 | |
| A-1H | 52-137620 | 6th ACS; crashed during strafing pass Laos on 5-24-68, Lt. Col. Wallace Ford "Spad 28" KIA, Ford was squadron's first CO, suspected wing gun explosion |
| A-1H | 52-137622 | VNAF; lost due to engine failure Thailand on 3-23-72, 602nd pilot rescued |
| A-1H | 52-137624 | VNAF |
| A-1H | 52-137628 | 1st SOS "Balls A Fire;" shot down supporting Special Forces team Laos on 4-9-71, Capt. Carroll B. Lilly "Sandy 10" MIA |
| A-1H | 52-137664 | VNAF |
| A-1H | 52-137746 | VNAF |
| A-1E-5 | 52-139575 | 602nd ACS; shot down Laos on 7-9-68, Lt. Col. William R. Bruce "Firefly 16" ejected and was rescued |
| A-1E-5 | 52-139577 | 602nd ACS; 1st SOS; VNAF |
| A-1E-5 | 52-139579 | 22nd SOS; shot down attacking structures Laos on 3-18-69, 1Lt. M.A. Riopelle "Zorro 32" ejected and was rescued; suspected wing gun explosion |
| A-1E-5 | 52-139584 | 602nd ACS; shot down during SAR for Navy A-7A "Streetcar 304" Laos on 6-1-68, Maj. William G. Palanc, "Sandy 01" ejected and was rescued |
| A-1E-5 | 52-139594 | 1st SOS; crashed during landing at NKP on 8-11-68 |
| A-1E-5 | 52-139595 | |
| A-1E-5 | 52-139598 | 1st SOS "Barbie Doll;" crashed during medevac escort Laos on 12-24-70, Maj. Albro L. Lundy, Jr. "Sandy 03" ejected, KIA |
| A-1H | 52-139606 | 6th SOS; VNAF; civil U.S. reg. warbird |
| A-1H | 52-139608 | 1st SOS "Blood, Sweat & Tears;" Capt. Robert F. Burke "Sandy 03" Silver Star for "Bat 21" SAR on 4-6-72; VNAF |
| A-1H | 52-139609 | 1st SOS "The Good Buddha," Capt. Ronald Smith Silver Star for "Nail 31" SAR on 3-19-72, tail code 6T; VNAF |
| A-1H | 52-139612 | VNAF |

| | | |
|---|---|---|
| A-1H | 52-139616 | Capt. Eugene A. Bardal Silver Star for "Bat 21" SAR on 4-3/4-72, Capt. Eugene A. Bardal Distinguished Flying Cross for gunship crew SAR on 3-31-72 |
| A-1H | 52-139618 | 1st SOS "Magnet Ass;" VNAF |
| A-1H | 52-139621 | 602nd SOS "The Peace Maker;" shot down during SAR for F-4D "Laredo 02" Laos on 4-6-70, 1Lt. J.R. Matthews "Sandy 03" bailed out and was rescued |
| A-1H | 52-139622 | VNAF |
| A-1H | 52-139626 | VNAF |
| A-1H | 52-139634 | VNAF; 1st SOS "Devil's Disciple," "Suzy-Q" "D.J. Special" |
| A-1H | 52-139637 | |
| A-1H | 52-139638 | 602nd SOS "Miss Noreen," squadron commander's aircraft; VNAF |
| A-1H | 52-139641 | 602nd SOS "Maggie's Orange Blossom Special," crashed near NKP when engine failed on 3-1-69, Capt. Wayne A. Warner "Sleepy 84" bailed out and was rescued |
| A-1H | 52-139643 | VNAF |
| A-1H | 52-139653 | VNAF |
| A-1H | 52-139656 | VNAF |
| A-1H | 52-139661 | VNAF |
| A-1H | 52-139662 | VNAF |
| A-1H | 52-139663 | VNAF |
| A-1H | 52-139665 | 1st SOS "Pumpkin Pie," "Spad Dad II," "Martha Lynn;" 602nd SOS "Miss Sandra K;" VNAF; civil U.S. reg. warbird |
| A-1H | 52-139668 | 1st SOS; 602nd SOS; shot down near Dak To, South Vietnam on 4-25-70, Maj. D.E. DeTar "Spad 03" rescued |
| A-1H | 52-139674 | VNAF; War Remnants Museum, Ho Chi Minh City, Vietnam |
| A-1H | 52-139678 | 602nd ACS; crash-landed Thailand after damaged by AAA on 3-18-68, Capt. Edward W. Leonard "Firefly 15" rescued |
| A-1H | 52-139680 | |
| A-1H | 52-139689 | VNAF |
| A-1H | 52-139690 | 602nd SOS |
| A-1H | 52-139691 | VNAF |
| A-1H | 52-139702 | 1st SOS; shot down attacking trucks Laos on 7-28-71, Maj. J.D. Patton "Sandy 09" rescued |
| A-1H | 52-139703 | VNAF |
| A-1H | 52-139706 | VNAF |
| A-1H | 52-139707 | VNAF |
| A-1H | 52-139711 | VNAF |
| A-1H | 52-139713 | 602nd SOS |
| A-1H | 52-139714 | VNAF |
| A-1H | 52-139715 | VNAF |
| A-1H | 52-139718 | VNAF |
| A-1H | 52-139723 | VNAF |
| A-1H | 52-139730 | VNAF; 22nd SOS; crashed and was destroyed during landing at NKP on 7-26-71, Lt. Col. R. Kaiser "Sandy 04" rescued |
| A-1H | 52-139734 | 1st SOS; shot down during SAR for U.S. Army UH-1H "Witch Doctor 05" on 3-6-71; 1Lt. C.L. Tipton "Sandy 04" ejected and was rescued |
| A-1H | 52-139735 | 6th SOS; shot down attacking storage area Laos on 10-27-68, Lt. Col. Victor J. Cole "Spad 01" rescued |
| A-1H | 52-139738 | 1st SOS "The Proud American," 602nd SOS; Lt. Col. William A. Jones III Medal of Honor aircraft 9-1-68; wing commander's aircraft 1970-1972; Capt. Ronald E. Smith Air Force Cross aircraft for F-4E "Oyster 01/B" SAR North Vietnam on 6-2-72; shot down during strike mission Laos on 9-28-72, 1Lt. Lance L. Smith "Hobo 42" ejected and was rescued |
| A-1H | 52-139739 | 1st SOS; 602nd SOS; shot down Laos on 9-22-68, Maj. Charles F. Kuhlman "Sandy 03" KIA |
| A-1H | 52-139744 | VNAF |
| A-1H | 52-139746 | VNAF |
| A-1H | 52-139752 | 1st SOS |
| A-1H | 52-139757 | VNAF |
| A-1H | 52-139758 | VNAF |
| A-1H | 52-139762 | VNAF |
| A-1H | 52-139765 | VNAF |
| A-1H | 52-139770 | 1st SOS "Big White Horse;" VNAF |
| A-1H | 52-139771 | VNAF |

| | | |
|---|---|---|
| A-1H | 52-139775 | VNAF |
| A-1H | 52-139776 | 1st SOS; 602nd SOS; experienced runaway prop and loss of oil pressure South Vietnam 7-28-70, Maj. Otis C. Morgan "Spad 02" tried to eject but egress system inoperative and he was killed when aircraft crashed |
| A-1H | 52-139778 | 602nd SOS "Bubbles 'N Bust;" VNAF |
| A-1H | 52-139779 | 602nd SOS "Mafia Madness;" VNAF |
| A-1H | 52-139780 | 1st SOS "Firebird," Capt. Robert F. Burke "Sandy 03" Silver Star for "Bat 21" SAR on 4- 3/6-72 |
| A-1H | 52-139785 | VNAF |
| A-1H | 52-139788 | 4407th CCTS, 1st SOW; VNAF |
| A-1H | 52-139789 | 22nd SOS; 6th SOS; experienced engine failure South Vietnam on 10-7-70, Maj. John V. Williams "Spad 02" tried to eject but egress system inoperative and he was killed in crash trying to land in A Shau Valley |
| A-1H | 52-139791 | 4407th CCTS, 4410th CCTW; 1st SOS "Close To You," Capt. Ronald E. Smith Air Force Cross aircraft for F-4E "Oyster 02/B" SAR North Vietnam on 6-1-72; VNAF |
| A-1H | 52-139797 | VNAF |
| A-1H | 52-139799 | 22nd SOS; shot down 25 miles from NKP Laos on 1-22-70, Capt. E.F. Anderson "Zorro 16" ejected and was rescued |
| A-1H | 52-139802 | VNAF |
| A-1H | 52-139803 | 1st SOS; VNAF |
| A-1H | 52-139808 | VNAF |
| A-1H | 52-139810 | 1st SOS; VNAF |
| A-1H | 52-139811 | 22nd SOS "El Malo," base commander's aircraft 1968-69; Col. Dale W. Brink Distinguished Flying Cross aircraft for O-1 "Raven 48" SAR Laos 6-16-69; crashed near NKP during escort mission on 12-21-69, Maj. R.L. Bohan "Firefly 11" rescued |
| A-1H | 52-139814 | VNAF |
| A-1H | 52-139820 | 1st SOS; 4407th CCTS. 1st SOW |
| A-1H | 52-139821 | 602nd SOS; 6th SOS "Chitty Chitty Bang Bang;" shot down supporting SAR Laos for F-4 "Packard 01" and U.S. Army helo on 11-12-69, Maj. Gerald R. Helmich "Spad 02" MIA, later KIA |
| A-1J | 52-142014 | 602nd SOS "Miss Kate," squadron commander's aircraft; VNAF |
| A-1J | 52-142015 | 602nd SOS; shot down during SAR for USMC OV-10A "Hostageman" Laos on 4-22-70 Capt. Friestad "Spad 01" ejected and was rescued |
| A-1J | 52-142016 | 6th SOS; VNAF |
| A-1J | 52-142021 | 6th SOS; 602nd SOS "Su Nan Sam," Maj. Thomas E. Dayton Air Force Cross for SAR for F-4 Laos on 12-5/7-69; 1st SOS "Devilish Diane," Capt. Edward R. Jayne II Silver Star aircraft for F-105G "Ashcan 01/A" SAR on 12-10-71; VNAF |
| A-1J | 52-142023 | 602nd SOS; shot down during combat air support mission near LS 36, Laos on 3-1-69, 1Lt. Clyde W. Campbell "Firefly 24" KIA |
| A-1J | 52-142028 | 602nd SOS; 1st SOS "Priscilla's Princess," squadron commander's aircraft, Capt. Robert F. Burke Distinguished Flying Cross for combat air patrol mission Cambodia on 11-8-71, and Silver Star for "Bat 21" SAR on 4-4-72, Capt. Fred C. Boli Silver Star for "Bat 21" and "Jolly Green 67" SAR on 4-6-72; VNAF |
| A-1J | 52-142029 | 602nd SOS "Sock It To Em;" shot down attacking mortar position near LS 32 Laos on 4-26-69, Maj. James B. East "Sandy 06" KIA |
| A-1J | 52-142030 | 602nd SOS; crashed after takeoff abort at NKP enroute for SAR for USN A-7 "War Ace 300" on 10-2-69, 1Lt. Donald R. Moore "Sandy 04" KIA |
| A-1J | 52-142033 | 602nd SOS; shot down supporting troops in contact near LS 85 Laos on 12-8-68, Maj. Thomas H. O'Connor "Firefly 34" rescued |
| A-1J | 52-142035 | 602nd SOS; shot down during strafing pass during SAR for A-1J "Firefly 34" on 12-8-68, Capt. Joseph S. Pirruccello, Jr. "Sandy 06" KIA |
| A-1J | 52-142042 | 4407th CCTS, 1st SOW |
| A-1J | 52-142043 | 1st SOS, shot down during ordnance pass during SAR for F-8 "Nickel 102" South Vietnam on 6-20-72, Capt. Lawrence G. Highfill "Sandy 07" ejected and was rescued |
| A-1J | 52-142048 | 6th ACS, shot down attacking target Laos on 4-25-68, Lt. Col Harold D. Shultz "Spad 31" ejected and was rescued |
| A-1J | 52-142053 | 602nd SOS "Anita Michelle;" 1st SOS; shot down during escort mission Laos on 8-2-71, 1Lt. Glen J. Taliaferro "Hobo 42" KIA |
| A-1J | 52-142056 | 602nd SOS "Tiny Tim;" VNAF |

| | | |
|---|---|---|
| A-1J | 52-142058 | 1st SOS; 602nd SOS "Julie," "Rita," wing commander's aircraft, Capt. Fred C. Boli Distinguished Flying Cross aircraft for SAR for "Seafox 01" on 2-11-72, Capt. Robert F. Burke Silver Star aircraft for SAR for OV-10A "Nail 31A/B" Laos on 3-19-72; VNAF |
| A-1J | 52-142059 | 6th SOS; shot down South Vietnam on 5-7-68, Capt. John G. Hayes "Spad 02" ejected and was rescued, suspected wing gun explosion |
| A-1J | 52-142062 | 1st SOS; Capt. Fred C. Boli Distinguished Flying Cross for SAR for F-105G "Ashcan 01/A" on 12-10-72 |
| A-1J | 52-142063 | 602nd SOS "The Hasler," "Squirrel;" 1st SOS; shot down during SAR for OV-10A "Nail 31" Laos on 3-18-72, Capt. Michael J. Faas "Hobo 01" ejected and was rescued |
| A-1J | 52-142065 | 602nd ACS; 6th SOS "The 777 Jackpot;" Maj. David E. Hinsen Silver Star aircraft North Vietnam mission on 10-20-68; 22nd SOS; hit by AAA attacking gun position during SAR for F-4D "Wolf 06" Laos on 3-21-70, Maj. Edward M. Hudgens "Sandy 06" KIA |
| A-1J | 52-142070 | 602nd SOS; shot down during SAR for OV-10A "Hostageman" Laos on 4-22-70, Maj. C.E. Whinery "Sandy 03" ejected and was rescued |
| A-1J | 52-142072 | 602nd SOS; crash-landed at Ubon RTAFB following combat damage on 12-20-68, Maj. Albert J. Roberts, aircraft reportedly stricken |
| A-1J | 52-142076 | 602nd SOS; 1st SOS; written off following combat damage and crash landing March 1972 |
| A-1J | 52-142077 | 602nd SOS; 1st SOS; experienced engine malfunction during medevac escort Laos on 4-6-71, Capt. J.W. Steward "Hobo 30" ejected and was rescued |
| A-1J | 52-142080 | 602nd SOS; shot down during SAR for F-4D "Pintail 01" Laos on 2-15-69, Lt. Col. Richard A. Walsh III "Sandy 01" KIA, Walsh Silver Star for mission |

Note: Some A-1s originally earmarked as MAP deliveries to the VNAF went instead to USAF units, while others assigned to VNAF units were actually flown by USAF pilots. Some A-1s were turned over to the VNAF following USAF service, then borrowed back. A number of those ended up back on the VNAF inventory. To cover losses, some A-1s were later drawn from U.S. Navy stocks. Some A-1 wrecks were scattered outside air base peripheries, where they remained, but were stripped of ordnance and usable parts. Downed aircraft that were considered salvageable, but in remote areas, were recovered by helicopter, or destroyed in place with explosives or air strikes.

Not listed in this appendix since their A-1 serial numbers are unknown, but also killed flying A-1s in Southeast Asia are USAF Col. Thomas Hergert, 1st ACS on 3-8-64: Capt. Walter Draeger on 4-4-65: Maj. William Richardson on 4-2-66: and Lt. Col. Robert Wilke on 1-17-68.

# Appendix E: U.S. Navy Skyraiders on Vietnam Cruises

| Type | Bureau Number | Units, Side Numbers, Remarks |
|---|---|---|
| EA-1F | 132513 | VAW-13 Det. One/708 |
| EA-1F | 132529 | VAW-13 Det. L |
| EA-1F | 132540 | VAW-13; shot down during SAR for A-4E North Vietnam on 6-2-65, Lt. j.g. McMican, Lt. j.g. Gerald M. Romano, AT3 William H. Amspacher and ATN3 Thomas L. Plants KIA |
| EA-1F | 132543 | VAW-13; ditched at sea off North Vietnam on 9-10-66 after generator loss and engine fire, pilot and three crewmen rescued |
| A-1G | 132555 | VAW-13/012 |
| EA-1F | 132575 | VAW-12 Det. One/772 |
| EA-1F | 132576 | VAW-13/728 |
| A-1G | 132581 | VAW-13/779 |
| EA-1F | 132591 | VAW-33/783; VAW-13 Det. L/707 |
| A-1G | 132621 | VAW-33 |
| EA-1E | 133770 | VAW-13/780; operational loss from Cubi Point on 9-25-67, four crewmen rescued |
| A-1H | 134449 | VA-25/404; flying with an EA-1F, became lost on a ferry mission from Cubi Point and attacked by Chinese MiG-17s near Hainan Island on 2-14-68, Lt. j.g. Joseph P. Dunn bailed out and EA-1 crew saw good chute, Dunn MIA, later KIA (last USN A-1 loss) |
| A-1H | 134472 | VA-176/402 |
| A-1H | 134482 | VA-196/607; shot down during strike mission to Qui Vinh bridge on 9-28-65, Lt. Cmdr. Carl J. Woods bailed out over water, but KIA |
| A-1H | 134511 | VA-25/575 |
| A-1H | 134515 | VA-52/304 |
| A-1H | 134517 | VA-25 |
| A-1H | 134518 | VA-152/585 |
| A-1H | 134526 | VA-95; VA-115/502; credited with 1/2 MiG kill |
| A-1H | 134531 | VA-115/505 |
| A-1H | 134534 | VA-165/208; shot down during overwater recon mission on 9-13-66, Lt. j.g. T.J. Dwyer bailed out and was rescued |
| A-1H | 134535 | VA-25 |
| A-1H | 134546 | VA-215 |
| A-1H | 134551 | VA-196 |
| A-1H | 134555 | VA-25/580 |
| A-1H | 134563 | VA-152/584 |
| A-1H | 134567 | VA-152/510 |
| A-1H | 134568 | VA-115/508 |
| A-1H | 134569 | VA-52/300 (Commander Air Wing aircraft) |
| A-1H | 134570 | VA-52/302 |

| | | |
|---|---|---|
| A-1H | 134575 | VA-152/511 "Foo Foo Juice" |
| A-1H | 134577 | VA-52/306; VA-165/209 "Miss Pussy Galore" |
| A-1H | 134586 | VA-145/515; crashed into sea after damaged by AAA during recon mission North Vietnam on 8-3-66, Lt. D. Franz rescued |
| A-1H | 134588 | VA-115/505 |
| A-1H | 134589 | VA-145/504; VA-25/403 |
| A-1H | 134605 | VA-152/203 |
| A-1H | 134609 | VA-25/579 |
| A-1H | 134614 | VA-52/307 |
| A-1H | 134619 | VA-152/586; lead flight of two on SAR mission North Vietnam when shot down on 8-29-65, Lt. Edd D. Taylor KIA |
| A-1H | 134622 | VA-176/410 |
| A-1H | 134625 | VA-115; lost at sea after mid-air with 135225 during SAR mission on 3-17-67, pilot rescued |
| A-1H | 134670 | VA-52/302 |
| EA-1E | 134818 | VAW-11 Det. R; crashed South Vietnam |
| EA-1F | 134974 | VAW-13 Det. One/704 |
| EA-1F | 135010 | VAW-13; crashed into sea during night launch, Lt. John McDonough killed, two crewmen rescued |
| EA-1F | 135028 | VAW-13 |
| A-1G | 135034 | VAW-13/777 "Jackpot" |
| EA-1F | 135040 | VAW-13 |
| A-1G | 135049 | VAW-13/776 |
| EA-1F | 135050 | VAW-13/779; crashed into sea during night catapult launch on 6-20-66, Lt. John R. McDonough killed, Lt. j.g. Robert D. Carlton and Lt. j.g. Jay G. Lagres rescued |
| EA-1F | 135051 | VAW-13 Det. L |
| EA-1F | 135053 | VAW-13 Det. L |
| EA-1F | 135054 | VAW-13 Det. L |
| EA-1E | 135139 | VAW-11/71 |
| EA-1E | 135141 | VAW-11/73 |
| EA-1E | 135207 | VAW-11 Det. T/715 |
| A-1H | 135225 | VA-115/503; lost at sea after mid-air with 134625 during SAR mission on 3-17-67, Lt. j.g. Gene W. Goeden KIA |
| A-1H | 135226 | VA-95/508; shot down during armed recon mission Laos on 4-11-65, Lt. j.g. William E. Swanson KIA |
| A-1H | 135231 | VA-152/586; shot down North Vietnam on 8-28-66, Cmdr. G.H. Smith bailed out at sea and was rescued |
| A-1H | 135236 | VA-215/567; VA-152; crashed into sea following carrier launch on 8-25-66, pilot rescued, aircraft recovered |
| A-1H | 135239 | VA-176/401; shot down during armed recon mission, Lt. Charles A. Knochel bailed out over water, but KIA |
| A-1H | 135243 | VA-52/310 |
| A-1H | 135244 | VA-152/588; shot down and crashed into sea during search mission North Vietnam on 11-17-65, Lt. Cmdr. Jesse J. Taylor KIA |
| A-1H | 135257 | VA-115/507 |
| A-1H | 135272 | VA-165/210 "Shush Boomer;" VA-215/567 |
| A-1H | 135274 | VA-196/611; shot down during ferry mission from Chu Lai to carrier *Bon Homme Richard* on 9-24-65, Lt. Cmdr. J. Gallager bailed out over water and was rescued |
| A-1H | 135275 | VA-25/582; VA-152/512 |
| A-1H | 135286 | VA-25/577 |
| A-1H | 135288 | VA-152/504; shot down attacking barges in the Gulf of Tonkin on 7-15-67, Lt. j.g. Robin B. Cassell KIA |
| A-1H | 135292 | VA-115/510 |
| A-1H | 135297 | VA-25/572 "Paper Tiger II;" VA-115/514; shot down and crashed into sea attacking barges on 3-17-67, Lt. Cmdr. A.H. Henderson rescued |
| A-1H | 135300 | VA-52/305 "Battle Axe;" VA-25/405, flew last USN A-1 attack mission 1968, display Naval Aviation Museum |
| A-1H | 135305 | VA-115/511 |
| A-1H | 135323 | VA-25/572; shot down during recon mission North Vietnam on 10-12-66, Lt. Robert D. Woods bailed out, evaded for two days and was captured |

| | | |
|---|---|---|
| A-1H | 135324 | VA-25/581; VA-215/563 |
| A-1H | 135326 | VA-176/412 |
| A-1H | 135329 | VA-25; crashed while dropping ordnance at Dong Hoi, North Vietnam on 8-7-65, Lt. Cmdr. Harold E. Gray, Jr. KIA |
| A-1H | 135332 | VA-52/301 |
| A-1H | 135336 | VA-52/303 |
| A-1H | 135338 | VA-145/505; VA-165/205 "Glider Rider" |
| A-1H | 135341 | VA-52/309; crash-landed at sea after damaged by AAA attacking barges North Vietnam on 11-27-66, Lt. j.g. William H. Natter rescued |
| A-1H | 135344 | VA-196/609; VA-145/506 |
| A-1H | 135356 | VA-25/571 |
| A-1H | 135366 | VA-215/572; crashed into sea after hit by AAA attacking vessels North Vietnam on 5-25-67, Ens. Richard C. Graves KIA |
| A-1H | 135370 | VA-145/506 |
| A-1H | 135371 | VA-152/501 |
| A-1H | 135375 | VA-95/512; developed engine problem possibly due to AAA enroute to target North Vietnam on 3-15-65, pilot attempted to return to carrier but crashed at sea, Lt. j.g. Charles F. Clydesdale KIA |
| A-1H | 135377 | VA-95/507 |
| A-1H | 135384 | VA-25 |
| A-1H | 135390 | VA-25/412; shot down while attacking vessels North Vietnam on 8-30-67, Lt. j.g. L.E. Gardiner rescued |
| A-1H | 135398 | VA-115/511; lost on night mission over water North Vietnam on 4-17-66, Lt. j.g. William L. Tromp captured and later KIA |
| A-1H | 137496 | VA-176/405 |
| A-1H | 137502 | VA-152/516 and 587 |
| A-1H | 137512 | VA-152/504 "Jimbo," "Little Bit" |
| A-1H | 137516 | VA-215/572; one of three A-1s supporting naval gunfire near Hon Me Island, North Vietnam on 3-21-67, became lost in overcast, Lt. Paul C. Charvet KIA |
| A-1H | 137517 | VA-25/575 |
| A-1H | 137520 | VA-152/581; VA-115/520 (experimental camouflage 1966) |
| A-1H | 137521 | VA-25; flight of eight, shot down on strike mission against Co Dinh power plant, North Vietnam on 6-10-65, Lt. j.g. Carl L. Doughtie KIA |
| A-1H | 137523 | VA-25/573; credited with 1/2 MiG kill, crashed into sea when power was lost on approach to carrier on 6-24-65, Lt. Cmdr. Robin Bacon rescued |
| A-1H | 137534 | VA-165/206; shot down on recon mission near Vinh Son, North Vietnam on 9-2-66, Cdr. William S. Jett III bailed out at sea and was rescued |
| A-1H | 137537 | VA-52/305 |
| A-1H | 137539 | VA-165/202 |
| A-1H | 137543 | VA-176/409; credited with MiG kill |
| A-1H | 137545 | VA-215; hit by ground fire during armed recon mission Mu Gia Pass region on 4-27-65, Lt. j.g. Scotty B. Wilkes nursed the aircraft to Thailand, where he bailed out and was rescued |
| A-1H | 137546 | VA-152/513 "The Swamp Rat" |
| A-1H | 137552 | VA-115/501 |
| A-1H | 137559 | VA-52/309; VA-145/502 |
| A-1H | 137566 | VA-152/590; crash-landed at sea after damaged by AAA on 11-9-65, Lt. Cmdr. Paul G. Merchant rescued |
| A-1H | 137570 | VA-145 |
| A-1H | 137575 | VA-25; lost power and crashed into sea on 8-19-67, Lt. Cmdr. Fred H. Gates II KIA |
| A-1H | 137576 | VA-152/581VA-215/567; shot down during bombing pass Laos on 4-29-66, Lt. Cmdr. William E. Egan KIA |
| A-1H | 137584 | VA-215; crashed while attacking target North Vietnam on 3-31-65, Lt. j.g. Gerald W. McKinley KIA |
| A-1H | 137588 | VA-215/506 |
| A-1H | 137589 | VA-215; shot down North Vietnam on 3-5-66, Cmdr. Robert C. Hessom KIA |
| A-1H | 137590 | VA-52; lost at sea when oil system failed on 11-16-65, pilot rescued |
| A-1H | 137593 | VA-25/572 |
| A-1H | 137601 | VA-115/506 |
| A-1H | 137610 | VA-152/513 and 588; crashed into sea during recon mission at night in bad weather on 10-5-66, Lt. j.g. |

| | | |
|---|---|---|
| | | James A. Beene KIA |
| A-1H | 137612 | VA-115/504 |
| A-1H | 137616 | VA-145/511 |
| A-1H | 137618 | VA-165/203 "Gloppita Gloppita Machine" |
| A-1H | 137621 | VA-52; crashed when engine failed North Vietnam on 12-1-65, pilot rescued |
| A-1H | 137622 | VA-145/510 and 512; VA-52/386; VA-25/406 |
| A-1H | 137627 | VA-145/506; crashed near target during armed recon mission North Vietnam on 2-10-66, Lt. Gary D. Hopps KIA |
| A-1H | 137628 | VA-215/564; VA-152/564 |
| A-1H | 137629 | VA-152/510; shot down during armed recon mission North Vietnam on 10-8-66, Lt. John A. Feldhaus MIA, later KIA |
| A-1H | 137690 | VA-52; lost after experienced oil problem on 11-16-65 |
| EA-1E | 139603 | VAW-11 Det. T; crashed due to engine failure during training flight on 4-15-65, crew of three rescued |
| A-1H | 139612 | VA-215/508 |
| A-1H | 139616 | VA-215/570; crash-landed at sea on 5-9-66, Lt. Cmdr. C.W. Sommers II rescued, aircraft recovered |
| A-1H | 139634 | VA-52/308 |
| A-1H | 139636 | VA-152/589; lost at sea when engine failed on 7-21-65, pilot rescued |
| A-1H | 139641 | VA-95/506; VA-152/514 |
| A-1H | 139645 | VA-52/385 |
| A-1H | 139652 | VA-52/380 |
| A-1H | 139653 | VA-25/577 |
| A-1H | 139662 | VA-145/512 |
| A-1H | 139665 | VA-152/584; civil U.S. reg. warbird |
| A-1H | 139680 | VA-25/581; VA-145; VA-165/210 |
| A-1H | 139691 | VA-145/505; VA-25 |
| A-1H | 139692 | VA-52/381; shot down by SAM enroute to target North Vietnam on 4-13-66, Cmdr. John C. Mape KIA |
| A-1H | 139693 | VA-165/203; while firing rockets at target, exploded and crashed into Gia Hoi River North Vietnam on 9-5-65, Lt. j.g. Edward B. Shaw KIA |
| A-1H | 139695 | VA-152/591 |
| A-1H | 139700 | VA-115/504 |
| A-1H | 139701 | VA-152/501; crashed at sea after hit by AAA while attacking train North Vietnam on 8-7-66, Lt. Charles W. Fryer KIA |
| A-1H | 139702 | VA-145/513; VA-196/601 |
| A-1H | 139708 | VA-152; operational loss Laos on 6-30-65, pilot rescued |
| A-1H | 139713 | VA-25/573 |
| A-1H | 139715 | VA-196/605 |
| A-1H | 139720 | VA-152/592; shot down North Vietnam on 8-26-65, Lt. j.g. Edward A. Davis bailed out and was captured |
| A-1H | 139721 | VA-215; shot down during armed recon mission Laos on 4-2-65, Lt. Cmdr. James J. Evans KIA |
| A-1H | 139726 | VA-115/501 |
| A-1H | 139728 | VA-152/514 |
| A-1H | 139730 | VA-165/201 |
| A-1H | 139731 | VA-115/505; VA-152/511 and 591; crashed attacking target with rockets North Vietnam on 10-14-66, Ens. Darwin J. Thomas KIA |
| A-1H | 139734 | VA-196/610 |
| A-1H | 139735 | VA-152/513 |
| A-1H | 139738 | VA-196/603 |
| A-1H | 139748 | VA-52/306; after combat mission, crashed into sea attempting to land aboard carrier on 1-18-67, Lt. j.g. Marlowe E. Madsen KIA |
| A-1H | 139752 | VA-152/505 |
| A-1H | 139755 | VA-196/612; downed by ground fire attacking bridge North Vietnam on 12-2-65, Lt. Cmdr. Gerald R. Roberts KIA |
| A-1H | 139756 | VA-25/580; crashed into sea when hit by SAMs during post-strike recon mission on 9-14-66, Cmdr. Clarence W. Stoddard, Jr. KIA |
| A-1H | 139760 | VA-145; crashed into sea during low-angle rocket attack on torpedo boat North Vietnam on 8-5-64, Lt. j.g. |

| | | |
|---|---|---|
| | | Richard C. Sather KIA, (first USN A-1 loss in SEA) |
| A-1H | 139768 | VA-25/577; credited with MiG kill; VA-115/504; crash-landed into sea after damaged by AAA attacking barges on 3-17-67, Lt. R.B. Moore rescued |
| A-1H | 139770 | VA-152/507; VA-215/565 |
| A-1H | 139772 | VA-165/206; crashed into sea after hit by AAA during recon mission on 8-13-65, Lt. R.J. Hyland rescued |
| A-1H | 139776 | VA-215/511 |
| A-1H | 139778 | VA-115/206 (experimental camouflage 1966) |
| A-1H | 139779 | VA-25/574; VA-152/506 |
| A-1H | 139789 | VA-115/510 |
| A-1H | 139790 | VA-215; VA-152/563; crash-landed at Da Nang AB after damaged by AAA attacking Ha Tinh radar site North Vietnam on 3-26-65, Lt. j.g. C.E. Gudmunson rescued |
| A-1H | 139792 | VA-176/404 |
| A-1H | 139803 | VA-25/578; VA-152/511 |
| A-1H | 139805 | VA-115/511; crashed into sea following launch from carrier on 2-14-67, Lt. Robert C. Marvin killed |
| A-1H | 139806 | VA-145; crashed into sea following launch from carrier on 6-20-66, Lt. Cmdr. John W. Tunnell killed |
| A-1H | 139808 | VA-25 |
| A-1H | 139810 | VA-152/589 |
| A-1H | 139818 | VA-215; shot down attacking trucks North Vietnam on 4-20-65, Lt. j.g. James P. Shea KIA |
| A-1H | 139820 | VA-145/506 |
| A-1H | 139821 | VA-25/579 |
| A-1H | 139848 | |
| A-1J | 142012 | VA-152/583; operational loss at sea North Vietnam during ResCap on 8-10-65, Lt. j.g. Lawrence S. Mailhes killed |
| A-1J | 142016 | VA-145/507; VA-115/501 (experimental camouflage 1966) |
| A-1J | 142021 | VA-145/504; VA-152/504; VA-25/574 |
| A-1J | 142023 | VA-52/384 "Bucky;" VA-52/311 |
| A-1J | 142028 | VA-176/402; VA-145/504 |
| A-1J | 142029 | VA-25 |
| A-1J | 142031 | VA-145/504; crash-landed Laos after damaged by AAA on 2-1-66, Lt. Dieter Dengler captured, but escaped on 6-29-66 and was rescued 7-20-66 |
| A-1J | 142032 | VA-52/391; shot down Tiger Island, North Vietnam on 4-18-66, Lt. A.D. Wilson rescued |
| A-1J | 142033 | VA-145/501 "Baby" |
| A-1J | 142035 | VA-165/204 |
| A-1J | 142038 | VA-196/601; VA-115/513; shot down attacking AAA position Laos on 2-1-66, Lt. j.g. B.S. Eakin bailed out and was rescued |
| A-1J | 142043 | VA-215/561 |
| A-1J | 142045 | VA-25/570 |
| A-1J | 142047 | VA-215/503; VA-152 |
| A-1J | 142048 | VA-25/570 |
| A-1J | 142050 | VA-215; crashed following loss of controls South Vietnam on 5-14-66, pilot bailed out and was rescued |
| A-1J | 142051 | VA-152/582; VA-115; crashed at sea following engine failure on 5-19-66, pilot rescued |
| A-1J | 142056 | VA-152/501 |
| A-1J | 142057 | VA-196/600; crashed from explosion of own bomb attacking target South Vietnam on 9-14-65, Lt. Cmdr. James T. Kearns KIA |
| A-1J | 142058 | VA-145/502; VA-25 |
| A-1J | 142059 | VA-165/204 "Puff The Magic Dragon" |
| A-1J | 142060 | VA-25 |
| A-1J | 142063 | VA-115/306 |
| A-1J | 142064 | VA-25/571 |
| A-1J | 142065 | VA-145; VA-165/200 |
| A-1J | 142070 | VA-25/414 "North Vietnamese Crop Duster" |
| A-1J | 142071 | VA-115; operational loss Laos on 3-11-66, pilot rescued |
| A-1J | 142076 | VA-25/410 |
| A-1J | 142077 | VA-25/411 |
| A-1J | 142081 | VA-215/501; VA-52/387; shot down attacking troops South Vietnam on 1-3-66, Lt. J.W. Donahue rescued |

# Appendix F: South Vietnamese Air Force Skyraiders

| Type | Bureau Number | Units, Tail codes, Remarks |
|---|---|---|
| A-1E | 132415 | 530th FS; lost on 4-3-72 |
| A-1E | 132425 | |
| A-1E | 132428 | PA |
| A-1E | 132433 | 514th FS |
| A-1E | 132437 | 518th FS/KWC |
| A-1E | 132444 | 518th FS; lost on 3-31-71 |
| A-1E | 132448 | 530th FS; lost on 4-16-71 |
| A-1E | 132455 | |
| A-1E | 132474 | |
| A-1G | 132481 | 522nd FS; lost on 12-25-67 |
| A-1G | 132482 | 514th FS/wA, lost on 4-16-70 |
| A-1G | 132485 | 518th FS; 530th FS/wE. lost on 12-19-71 |
| A-1G | 132487 | 518th FS/KWB, combat loss on 4-9-72 |
| A-1G | 132488 | 518th FS; lost on 1-29-66 |
| A-1G | 132494 | 518th FS/KWE |
| A-1G | 132497 | 518th FS/KWB, lost on 8-16-71 |
| A-1G | 132498 | lost on 1-29-66 |
| A-1G | 132503 | 516th FS/wJ |
| A-1G | 132508 | lost on 3-25-68 |
| A-1G | 132510 | 514th FS; lost on 4-4-66 |
| A-1G | 132514 | 530th FS; written off following crash at Tan Son Nhut AB on 3-2-71 |
| A-1G | 132524 | 516th FS; 514th FS; lost on 4-12-70 |
| A-1G | 132528 | 516th FS/PA; 518th FS; flown to Thailand 1975 |
| A-1G | 132542 | 518th FS/KWc |
| A-1G | 132551 | 518th FS/KWD/wI, lost on 11-16-66 |
| A-1G | 132557 | 520th FS; lost on 9-1-68 |
| A-1G | 132559 | 518th FS/KWD; 524th FS; 530th FS |
| A-1G | 132560 | |
| A-1G | 132562 | 514th FS; crashed at Bien Hoa AB on 9-5-65 |
| A-1G | 132575 | |
| A-1G | 132576 | |
| A-1G | 132582 | |
| A-1G | 132587 | |
| A-1G | 132598 | |
| A-1G | 132602 | 522nd FS; operational loss at Tan Son Nhut AB on 10-1-66 |

| | | |
|---|---|---|
| A-1G | 132605 | 522nd FS |
| A-1G | 132612 | 516th FS/PD; 524th FS |
| A-1G | 132614 | 516th FS/wF; 518th FS; combat loss at Thu Duc on 9-5-69, recovered and scrapped at Bien Hoa AB |
| A-1G | 132616 | 516th FS/PB; disappeared near Nong Son on 10-5-66 |
| A-1G | 132618 | |
| A-1G | 132619 | 516th FS/wG |
| A-1G | 132620 | 516th FS/PG; lost on 1-29-68 |
| A-1G | 132624 | |
| A-1G | 132626 | 530th FS; operational loss at Cu Hanh on 2-8-72 |
| A-1G | 132627 | 518th FS; lost on 3-6-67 |
| A-1G | 132628 | 516th FS/wE; 530th FS/WH, lost on 2-2-72 |
| A-1G | 132629 | 518th FS/KWE; 514th FS, lost on 2-3-69 |
| A-1G | 132630 | 516th FS/wG |
| A-1G | 132635 | 520th FS/vWc, lost on 2-1-68 |
| A-1G | 132636 | 514th FS; 518th FS/KWc, lost on 2-4-70, scrapped at Tan Son Nhut AB |
| A-1G | 132638 | |
| A-1G | 132643 | |
| A-1G | 132647 | |
| A-1G | 132652 | |
| A-1G | 132653 | 518th FS; lost on 3-3-73 |
| A-1G | 132655 | 530th FS; flown to Thailand 1975 |
| A-1G | 132657 | 524th FS |
| A-1G | 132661 | |
| A-1G | 132663 | |
| A-1G | 132665 | |
| A-1G | 132666 | 520th FS |
| A-1G | 132667 | |
| A-1G | 132668 | |
| A-1G | 132669 | 520th FS |
| A-1G | 132670 | |
| A-1G | 132673 | |
| A-1G | 132675 | 520th FS |
| A-1G | 132683 | 514th FS; flown to Thailand 1975; civil U.S. reg. warbird |
| A-1G | 132686 | |
| A-1E | 133858 | lost on 1-11-74 |
| A-1E | 133860 | 514th FS; flown to Thailand 1975 |
| A-1E | 133861 | lost on 4-15-72 |
| A-1E | 133862 | |
| A-1E | 133866 | 530th FS; lost on 5-31-74 |
| A-1E | 133872 | |
| A-1E | 133875 | |
| A-1E | 133876 | |
| A-1E | 133878 | |
| A-1E | 133879 | 514th FS; lost on 5-25-66 |
| A-1E | 133882 | lost on 1-18-73 |
| A-1E | 133885 | |
| A-1E | 133891 | 514th FS; lost on 4-20-73 |
| A-1E | 133892 | 514th FS; lost on 1-18-73 |
| A-1E | 133896 | 514th FS/E |
| A-1E | 133897 | |
| A-1E | 133898 | |
| A-1E | 133899 | lost on 9-1-70 |
| A-1E | 133906 | 514th FS; operational loss on 2-19-73 |
| A-1E | 133914 | |
| A-1E | 133915 | |

| | | |
|---|---|---|
| A-1E | 133919 | 514th FS/FFU; flown to Thailand 1975 |
| A-1E | 133920 | 518th FS; flown to Thailand 1975 |
| A-1E | 133922 | 524th FS; lost in mid-air with 139663 on 5-5-67 |
| A-1E | 133927 | |
| A-1H | 134469 | 514th FS; lost at Soc Trang on 8-25-62 |
| A-1H | 134472 | 518th FS; lost on 1-16-73 |
| A-1H | 134473 | 514th FS/A, lost on 7-17-63 |
| A-1H | 134479 | 514th FS/E, lost on 5-18-64 |
| A-1H | 134482 | 514th FS/O |
| A-1H | 134483 | 518th FS/KS |
| A-1H | 134484 | 514th FS/O, badly damaged twice, combat loss on 11-20-67 |
| A-1H | 134488 | 514th FS/U/A; 518th FS, lost on 10-8-72 |
| A-1H | 134493 | 516th FS |
| A-1H | 134494 | 530th FS, lost at Cu Hanh on 2-15-73 |
| A-1H | 134497 | 514th FS/G |
| A-1H | 134498 | 514th FS/K, lost on 5-15-67 |
| A-1H | 134499 | 520th FS/vH; 518th FS; operational loss at Pleiku on 8-19-70 |
| A-1H | 134500 | 518th FS/KC |
| A-1H | 134505 | 514th FS/B |
| A-1H | 134507 | 516th FS; 518th FS/KB; 514th FS; lost on 9-21-69 |
| A-1H | 134511 | |
| A-1H | 134514 | 514th FS/H, crashed at Bien Hoa AB 1964, scrapped |
| A-1H | 134517 | |
| A-1H | 134519 | 514th FS/J; 518th FS, combat loss on 5-10-66 |
| A-1H | 134520 | 514th FS/R, lost on 1-18-73 |
| A-1H | 134522 | 520th FS/vG |
| A-1H | 134525 | 522nd FS; lost on 9-22-65 |
| A-1H | 134526 | lost on 1-17-73 |
| A-1H | 134528 | 518th FS; lost on 12-21-64 |
| A-1H | 134531 | 514th FS; lost on 6-25-66 |
| A-1H | 134534 | 516th FS |
| A-1H | 134535 | |
| A-1H | 134536 | 520th FS; operational loss at Bien Hoa AB on 4-7-65 |
| A-1H | 134539 | 518th FS; lost on 10-17-65 |
| A-1H | 134540 | 514th FS/M; 516th FS/LII/LN, lost on 5-5-68 |
| A-1H | 134546 | 520th FS; operational loss at Long Binh on 5-5-65 |
| A-1H | 134549 | 514th FS; lost on 1-3-64 |
| A-1H | 134550 | 520th FS; 518th FS/KN/KZ, lost on 11-10-69 |
| A-1H | 134553 | 522nd FS; lost in mid-air with 137610 at Tan Son Nhut AB on 7-16-65 |
| A-1H | 134555 | 514th FS/C; 518th FS; lost on 4-3-72 |
| A-1H | 134557 | 520th FS; 518th FS/vE/KQ, lost on 7-25-72 |
| A-1H | 134561 | 518th FS/KQ |
| A-1H | 134565 | 514th FS/U |
| A-1H | 134569 | 514th FS/O, lost on 10-24-72 |
| A-1H | 134570 | |
| A-1H | 134575 | lost on 6-21-74 |
| A-1H | 134580 | 516th FS; lost on 6-5-65 |
| A-1H | 134585 | 514th FS/Q/J, combat loss on 5-13-72 |
| A-1H | 134589 | 514th FS; operational loss on 9-12-71 |
| A-1H | 134590 | 514th FS/H, scrapped at Bien Hoa AB 1964 |
| A-1H | 134592 | 518th FS; lost on 2-5-65 |
| A-1H | 134595 | 514th FS/J, operational loss on 12-3-62 |
| A-1H | 134598 | 518th FS; 530th FS; lost on 9-12-71 |
| A-1H | 134600 | 514th FS/Q/E; 520th FS/vQ |
| A-1H | 134602 | 514th FS/H, lost in mid-air with 139653 on 8-24-67 |

| Type | Serial | Notes |
|---|---|---|
| A-1H | 134605 | 514th FS/L/J; 518th FS; combat loss on 11-30-71 |
| A-1H | 134607 | 514th FS/KO/LQ/T; 516th FS; lost on 3-29-74 |
| A-1H | 134609 | lost on 11-12-72 |
| A-1H | 134610 | 522nd FS |
| A-1H | 134613 | 516th FS; lost on 1-15-69 |
| A-1H | 134616 | 514th FS; lost at Ca Mau on 11-24-63 |
| A-1H | 134620 | 514th FS/G, lost at Pleiku on 8-15-63 |
| A-1H | 134631 | 518th FS/KC; 520th FS/vU |
| A-1H | 134632 | 524th FS |
| A-1H | 134634 | 516th FS; combat loss on 1-10-69 |
| A-1H | 134636 | 514th FS/I/G |
| A-1G | 134976 | 516th FS; 524th FS, lost on 2-12-68 |
| A-1G | 134981 | 524th FS; crashed 1966 |
| A-1G | 134987 | |
| A-1G | 134997 | |
| A-1G | 135036 | 514th FS; lost on 9-19-72 |
| A-1G | 135037 | 520th FS; lost on 11-24-65 |
| A-1G | 135038 | 520th FS; 530th FS; lost on 4-13-72 |
| A-1G | 135042 | 514th FS; lost on 4-19-74 |
| A-1G | 135043 | |
| A-1G | 135047 | 518th FS/KWF/K/wK, lost on 3-27-74 |
| A-1E | 135177 | 514th FS/wA |
| A-1E | 135185 | 530th FS; lost on 7-27-73 |
| A-1E | 135206 | 530th FS |
| A-1E | 135215 | 530th FS |
| A-1H | 135223 | 522nd FS/UE |
| A-1H | 135224 | 514th FS/A, commander's aircraft, destroyed mortar attack at Bien Hoa AB 11-1-64 |
| A-1H | 135226 | 514th FS/X |
| A-1H | 135228 | 514th FS/X; 518th FS; lost on 12-2-68 |
| A-1H | 135229 | 514th FS/C |
| A-1H | 135237 | 514th FS/YX/Y; 520th FS, combat loss on 6-1-65 |
| A-1H | 135243 | lost on 12-31-72 |
| A-1H | 135245 | 514th FS; lost on 11-5-67 |
| A-1H | 135256 | 514th FS/C, lost on 4-6-65 |
| A-1H | 135257 | |
| A-1H | 135258 | 514th FS; lost on 5-7-72 |
| A-1H | 135260 | 516th FS/LJ/H |
| A-1H | 135276 | 516th FS; crashed on 5-14-64 and scrapped at Bien Hoa AB |
| A-1H | 135278 | 516th FS; lost on 9-20-64 |
| A-1H | 135279 | 514th FS; lost on 4-6-71 |
| A-1H | 135281 | 518th FS/KA |
| A-1H | 135283 | 516th FS; crashed at Da Nang AB on 12-8-65 |
| A-1H | 135286 | 518th FS/KL, lost on 12-27-73 |
| A-1H | 135288 | 514th FS/Z |
| A-1H | 135289 | 514th FS/Z/D, lost on 3-29-73 |
| A-1H | 135292 | 530th FS; lost Laos on 5-7-71 |
| A-1H | 135293 | 514th FS; operational loss on 9-28-68 |
| A-1H | 135295 | 522nd FS; 520th FS; lost on 11-28-65 |
| A-1H | 135298 | 522nd FS/UG; 520th FS; combat loss on 4-14-67 |
| A-1H | 135308 | 514th FS/P, combat loss on 8-21-69 |
| A-1H | 135310 | 514th FS; 518th FS/KL, lost on 5-5-68 |
| A-1H | 135311 | 518th FS; lost on 1-3-65 |
| A-1H | 135322 | 514th FS/M, lost on 5-20-72 |
| A-1H | 135325 | 516th FS |
| A-1H | 135332 | 514th FS/T; civil U.S. reg. warbird |

| | | |
|---|---|---|
| A-1H | 135334 | 522nd FS; lost on 3-5-66 |
| A-1H | 135335 | lost on 10-24-70 |
| A-1H | 135339 | 514th FS/A/D, operational loss on 8-29-67 |
| A-1H | 135340 | 516th FS; 518th FS/KJ; 514th FS/LR, lost on 3-28-73 |
| A-1H | 135343 | 516th FS |
| A-1H | 135352 | 516th FS/LT, lost on 2-4-67 |
| A-1H | 135355 | 514th FS/C; 516th FS; 518th FS; lost on 10-22-70 |
| A-1H | 135367 | 516th FS; lost at Cu Hanh on 12-11-64 |
| A-1H | 135373 | 522nd FS; lost at Tan Son Nhut AB on 9-27-65 |
| A-1H | 135374 | 522nd FS; 520th FS; lost on 5-27-67 |
| A-1H | 135376 | 518th FS/S, operational loss on 3-13-69, scrapped at Tay Ninh |
| A-1H | 135384 | 516th FS; lost at Bien Hoa on 6-29-64 |
| A-1H | 135386 | 518th FS; lost on 10-23-64 |
| A-1H | 135387 | 530th FS/R; combat loss on 1-12-70 |
| A-1H | 135392 | 522nd FS/US; 518th FS; disappeared during flight on 4-6-72 |
| A-1H | 135399 | 520th FS; 518th FS/KE, lost on 9-1-67 |
| A-1H | 135402 | 522nd FS; disappeared during flight on 4-22-65 |
| A-1H | 135406 | 524th FS; lost on 11-21-67 |
| A-1H | 135433 | |
| A-1H | 135527 | lost on 10-8-64 |
| A-1H | 135599 | |
| A-1H | 137493 | 514th FS/Z; 516th FS; 520th FS/vH; 518th FS/LH, combat loss on 5-15-72 |
| A-1H | 137498 | 516th FS; 524th FS; lost on 2-21-66 |
| A-1H | 137499 | 520th FS/vH, lost on 3-14-68 |
| A-1H | 137502 | 518th FS; 514th FS/K, lost on 7-8-72 |
| A-1H | 137505 | 518th FS/KI; 520th FS/vB |
| A-1H | 137506 | 514th FS/F, lost on 8-2-67 |
| A-1H | 137513 | 518th FS/KN |
| A-1H | 137514 | 518th FS |
| A-1H | 137517 | 514th FS/P |
| A-1H | 137519 | 520th FS/vP, lost on 8-22-66 |
| A-1H | 137522 | 518th FS; lost on 2-5-69 |
| A-1H | 137524 | 530th FS; lost on 6-12-71 |
| A-1H | 137526 | 520th FS; lost on 3-10-67 |
| A-1H | 137531 | 524th FS; lost at Nha Trang AB on 11-12-65 |
| A-1H | 137532 | 518th FS/KP, lost on 12-30-67 |
| A-1H | 137535 | 518th FS/ lost on 5-12-73 |
| A-1H | 137537 | 518th FS; lost on 8-17-68 |
| A-1H | 137540 | 514th FS; 516th FS/M |
| A-1H | 137541 | 518th FS; lost on 2-2-68 |
| A-1H | 137551 | 514th FS/B |
| A-1H | 137553 | 522nd FS; lost on 12-3-65 |
| A-1H | 137554 | 520th FS/vI, lost on 4-25-65 |
| A-1H | 137558 | 518th FS/KO; 514th FS; lost on 6-24-68 |
| A-1H | 137560 | 518th FS/KX; 530th FS; lost on 5-26-72 |
| A-1H | 137564 | 514th FS/Y; 518th FS/KH |
| A-1H | 137567 | 524th FS; operational loss on 1-3-66 |
| A-1H | 137569 | 520th FS/vA |
| A-1H | 137570 | 514th FS; lost on 11-3-69 |
| A-1H | 137571 | 522nd FS; 514th FS; disappeared during flight on 10-31-70 |
| A-1H | 137574 | shot down on 7-23-64 |
| A-1H | 137577 | |
| A-1H | 137586 | 530th FS; disappeared during flight on 2-4-71 |
| A-1H | 137587 | 518th FS/KJ |
| A-1H | 137588 | 518th FS; lost on 3-17-66; hulk in Military Museum, Ho Chi Minh City, Vietnam |

| | | |
|---|---|---|
| A-1H | 137593 | 518th FS |
| A-1H | 137595 | 514th FS; lost on 7-3-66 |
| A-1H | 137596 | 524th FS; lost on 12-8-66 |
| A-1H | 137597 | |
| A-1H | 137599 | 518th FS/KE, lost on 1-3-73 |
| A-1H | 137609 | 518th FS/KM |
| A-1H | 137610 | 522nd FS; lost in mid-air with 134553 at Tan Son Nhut AB on 7-16-65 |
| A-1H | 137619 | 516th FS; lost on 6-12-65 |
| A-1H | 137622 | |
| A-1H | 137624 | 518th FS; lost on 8-12-68 |
| A-1H | 137625 | 516th FS; disappeared during flight on 8-2-65 |
| A-1E-5 | 139577 | combat loss 9-11-73 |
| A-1H | 139606 | 518th FS/KB; flown to Thailand 1975; civil U.S. reg. warbird |
| A-1H | 139607 | 514th FS/T, lost on 4-27-64 |
| A-1H | 139608 | |
| A-1H | 139609 | 518th FS/KP; 514th FS, combat loss on 11-12-72 |
| A-1H | 139610 | 518th FS |
| A-1H | 139612 | 518th FS/KN; 514th FS/O, crashed on takeoff at Bien Hoa AB on 1-20-70 |
| A-1H | 139616 | |
| A-1H | 139618 | 518th FS/KS |
| A-1H | 139619 | 516th FS; 518th FS; lost on 3-14-66 |
| A-1H | 139622 | 518th FS/KG; 514th FS; 530th FS; lost on 4-24-72 |
| A-1H | 139624 | 514th FS; lost on 1-11-66 |
| A-1H | 139626 | lost at Cu Hanh on 2-8-72 |
| A-1H | 139629 | 514th FS/E, operational loss on 11-5-62 |
| A-1H | 139634 | 530th FS; lost on 5-15-73 |
| A-1H | 139638 | 530th FS; lost on 4-13-72 |
| A-1H | 139640 | lost 1965 |
| A-1H | 139643 | 514th FS/X; 518th FS; lost on 2-28-70 |
| A-1H | 139649 | 524th FS; combat loss at Cu Hanh on 5-2-66 |
| A-1H | 139653 | 530th FS; 514th FS; lost in mid-air with 134602 on 8-24-67 |
| A-1H | 139656 | 518th FS/KR |
| A-1H | 139661 | 518th FS/G, lost on 5-1-70 |
| A-1H | 139662 | 516th FS; lost on 4-29-68 |
| A-1H | 139663 | 524th FS; lost in mid-air with 133922 on 5-5-67 |
| A-1H | 139664 | 514th FS/LI; 516th FS; 520th FS; combat loss at Binh Thuy on 12-15-67 |
| A-1H | 139665 | 514th FS; flown to Thailand 1975; civil U.S. reg. warbird |
| A-1H | 139667 | |
| A-1H | 139673 | lost on 9-1-67 |
| A-1H | 139674 | 518th FS/KM; 520th FS/vV |
| A-1H | 139676 | 514th FS/A, crashed at Bien Hoa AB on 6-4-62 (first VNAF A-1 loss) |
| A-1H | 139685 | |
| A-1H | 139686 | 516th FS; lost at Qui Nhon on 4-9-65 |
| A-1H | 139689 | 514th FS/L; flown to Thailand 1975 |
| A-1H | 139690 | 522nd FS/UA; 524th FS; combat loss at Vung Ro on 10-3-66 |
| A-1H | 139691 | 524th FS; 514th FS; lost at Dak To on 5-16-67 |
| A-1H | 139703 | 524th FS; 514th FS/N; 530th FS; lost on 6-27-72 |
| A-1H | 139705 | 524th FS; lost on 7-30-66 |
| A-1H | 139706 | 514th FS; lost on 1-10-67 |
| A-1H | 139707 | 516th FS/LM, lost on 2-16-68 |
| A-1H | 139711 | 520th FS/vF, crashed at Binh Thuy on 2-12-67 |
| A-1H | 139714 | 522nd FS; 524th FS; lost on 4-5-68 |
| A-1H | 139715 | 524th FS; lost on 2-2-67 |
| A-1H | 139718 | 524th FS/B; 514th FS; lost on 7-11-74 (last recorded VNAF loss) |

| | | |
|---|---|---|
| A-1H | 139723 | 514th FS/zK; 518th FS/KF |
| A-1H | 139730 | |
| A-1H | 139733 | 522nd FS; crashed at Tan Son Nhut AB on 7-28-65 |
| A-1H | 139737 | 522nd FS/UL |
| A-1H | 139744 | 522nd FS/U/UL; 514th FS |
| A-1H | 139746 | 518th FS/KY; 530th FS |
| A-1H | 139749 | 516th FS |
| A-1H | 139753 | 522nd FS; lost at Muc Hoa on 9-16-65 |
| A-1H | 139757 | 522nd FS/UT, destroyed during rocket attack at Bien Hoa AB on 5-12-67 |
| A-1H | 139758 | 520th FS/vS, lost at Binh Thuy on 12-23-66 |
| A-1H | 139762 | 520th FS; lost on 6-21-68 |
| A-1H | 139764 | 522nd FS; lost on 1-28-66 |
| A-1H | 139765 | 518th FS; lost on 11-27-66 |
| A-1H | 139769 | 516th FS/K, lost on 8-16-66 |
| A-1H | 139770 | 530th FS; lost on 5-9-72 |
| A-1H | 139771 | 516th FS/KT/LP |
| A-1H | 139775 | 516th FS; 514th FS; lost on 5-29-70 |
| A-1H | 139778 | |
| A-1H | 139779 | 530th FS; lost on 5-27-72 |
| A-1H | 139785 | 520th FS; lost in mid-air with 142045 on 8-24-67 |
| A-1H | 139788 | 518th FS; lost on 4-3-72 |
| A-1H | 139791 | |
| A-1H | 139796 | 516th FS; 514th FS; lost on 11-25-68 |
| A-1H | 139797 | 522nd FS/UL; 516th FS' 518th FS; lost on 4-30-70 |
| A-1H | 139798 | 514th FS; lost on 7-23-66 |
| A-1H | 139802 | 522nd FS/UB; 516th FS/LU; 514th FS; lost on 12-7-70 |
| A-1H | 139803 | 514th FS; lost on 11-12-72 |
| A-1H | 139808 | 518th FS; lost on 3-3-67 |
| A-1H | 139810 | |
| A-1H | 139812 | 522nd FS; lost on 9-22-65 |
| A-1H | 139814 | 520th FS; vY |
| A-1J | 142014 | 530th FS; lost on 9-30-71 |
| A-1J | 142016 | 530th FS; lost on 5-23-72 |
| A-1J | 142021 | lost on 12-26-72 |
| A-1J | 142028 | |
| A-1J | 142034 | 516th FS; crashed at Da Nang AB on 5-17-67 |
| A-1J | 142045 | 516th FS/LC; 520th FS; lost in mid-air with 139785 on 8-24-67 |
| A-1J | 142046 | 516th FS/LB; 520th FS; combat loss on 6-13-68 |
| A-1J | 142054 | |
| A-1J | 142056 | 518th FS/X/wA, lost on 12-20-71 |
| A-1J | 142058 | |
| A-1J | 142060 | 516th FS; shot down North Vietnam on 5-14-66, pilot captured |
| A-1J | 142064 | 516th FS/LP, lost on 10-31-67 |
| A-1J | 142079 | 516th FS |

Note: The majority of VNAF A-1 losses occurred in South Vietnam, with a loss of 68 pilots and aircrew. Nearly 60 VNAF Skyraiders listed as "badly damaged" were actually losses since, although they were recovered, they were never made flyable. A total of 24 VNAF A-1s were reported destroyed at Bien Hoa AB on 16 May 1965, when a B-57 starter ignited 500-pound bombs on the flight line. Several VNAF and USAF A-1s, along with many other aircraft, were damaged.

# Appendix G: USAF Hurlburt Field A-1 Training Fatalities

| Date | Name |
|---|---|
| 11-9-64 | Capt. William J. Walsh |
| 11-9-64 | 2Lt. William A. Shagner, III |
| 2-24-65 | Capt. James J. Jines, Jr. |
| 2-24-65 | Maj. Robert W. Robinson |
| 2-24-65 | Capt. Edward L. Doyle |
| 2-24-65 | Maj. Donald L. Lumadue |
| 11-8-66 | VNAF 2Lt. Ha Xuong |
| 9-26-67 | Lt. Col. Albert C. Hamby |
| 9-26-67 | Maj. William N. Kuykendall |
| 11-15-67 | Maj. Gerald L. Wollington |
| 10-22-68 | Capt. John J. Stark |
| 10-22-68 | Maj. James C. Phillips |
| 6-17-70 | Lt. Col. James L. Mihalick |
| 6-17-70 | Maj. O'Dell L. Riley |

# Appendix H:
# VNAF A-1s Flown to Thailand at War's End

A-1G 132528

A-1E 132655

A-1E 132683

A-1E 133860

A-1E 133919

A-1E 133920

A-1H 135332

A-1H 139606

A-1H 139665

A-1H 139689

A-1H 139744

# Bibliography

**Books**

Barthelmes, Ed and Dann, Richard S. *Walk Around A-1 Skyraider*, Squadron Signal Publications, Inc.: Carrollton, TX, 2001.

Birdsall, Steve. *The A-1 Skyraider.* Arco Publishing Co. Inc.: New York, 1970.

Burgess, Richard R., Lt. Cdr., USN (Ret.). *The Naval Aviation Guide.* Naval Institute Press: Annapolis, MD, 1996.

Chinnery, Philip D. *Any Time, Any Place.* Naval Institute Press: Annapolis, MD, 1994

Cutler, Thomas J. *Brown Water, Black Berets: Coastal and Riverine Warfare in Vietnam.* Naval Institute Press: Annapolis, MD, 1988.

Dorr, Robert F. *Douglas A-1 Skyraider.* Osprey: London, 1989.

Drury, Richard S. *My Secret War.* St. Martin's Press: New York, 1979.

Francillon, Rene J. *Tonkin Gulf Yacht Club: U.S. Carrier Operations Off Vietnam.* Naval Institute Press: Annapolis, MD, 1988.

Gann, Harry. *The Douglas Skyraider.* Hills & Lacy Ltd.: London, 1965.

Grossnick, Roy A. *Dictionary of American Naval Aviation Squadrons.* Naval Historical Center, 1995.

Haas, Michael E., Col., USAF (Ret.). *Apollo's Warriors: United States Air Force Special Operations during the Cold War.* Maxwell AFB, AL, 1997.

Jackson, B.R. *Douglas Skyraider.* Aero Publishers, Inc.: Fallbrook, CA, 1969.

Johnsen, Frederick A. *A-1 Skyraider: A Photo Chronicle.* Schiffer Publishing Ltd.: Atglen, PA, 1994.

Jones, William A. *Maxims for Men-At-Arms.* Dorrance & Company: Philadelphia, 1969.

Mikesh, Robert C. *Flying Dragons: The South Vietnamese Air Force.* Osprey: London, 1998.

Mutza, Wayne. *Lockheed P2V Neptune.* Schiffer Publishing Ltd.: Atglen, PA, 1996.

Rahn, Bob. *Tempting Fate: An Experimental Test Pilot's Story.* Specialty Press: North Branch, MN, 1997.

Schlight, John. *The War in South Vietnam: The Years of the Offensive 1965-1968.* Office of Air Force History: Washington, 1988.

Staaveren, Jacob V. *Interdiction in Southern Laos 1960-1968.* Center for Air Force History: Washington, 1993.

Sullivan, Jim. *AD Skyraider In Action.* Squadron/Signal Publications, Inc.: Carrollton, TX, (nd).

Tilford, Earl H. *The United States Air Force: Search and Rescue in Southeast Asia.* Center for Air Force History, 1980.

Trest, Warren A. *Air Commando One.* Smithsonian Institution Press: Washington, 2000.

**Governmental Publications**

Office of Safety, Headquarters, South Vietnamese Air Force. *Listing of Destroyed and Badly Damaged Aircraft.* 1975.

U.S.A.F. 4410th Combat Crew Training Wing. *A-1E Aircrew Training Manual.* 1 October 1967.

U.S.A.F. 4410th Combat Crew Training Wing. *Air Delivered Ordnance: A Resume of Technical Data on Conventional Munitions used in Special Air Warfare Activities.* 22 May 1968.

U.S.A.F. Headquarters, Air Training Command. *History of Foreign Training in ATC 1941-1976.* (n.d.).

U.S.A.F. Department of Field Training Manual. *Aircraft Maintenance (A-1E).* 30 November 1967.

U.S.A.F. News Release. *Skyraider Pilots Tour 4th Division Complex.* March, 1968.

U.S.A.F. Reference Series. *Air Force Combat Wings: Lineage and Honors Histories 1947-1977.* (n.d.).
U.S.A.F. SAWC Technical Documentary Report. *Evaluation of A-1E Skyraider Aircraft.* April 1963.
U.S.A.F. TACM/PACAFM 55-1. *Aircrew Operational Procedures.* September, 1969.
U.S.A.F. Technical Order 1A-1E-1.
U.S.A.F. Technical Order 1A-1H-1.
U.S.A.F. 56 SPOPWGM 55-2. *A-1 SAR Operational Procedures and Techniques.* 15 February 1970.
United States Pacific Fleet. *Analysis Staff Study: Replacement of the A-1 by Jet Aircraft For Sea Dragon Spotting and RESCAP.* August 1967.

**Magazines**

Aero Album. Ehrengardt, C.J. *French ADs.* Winter, 1971.
Aero Digest. *Douglas Skyraider.* November, 1971.
Aerospace Safety. Shacklock, John D. *Hit the Ground Running.* October, 1970.
Air Combat. Bowman, M. and O'Leary, M. *Skyraider.* March/April 1998.
Air Enthusiast. Dorr, Robert F. *Southeast Asian Spad . . . The Skyraider's War.* No. 36.
Air Force Magazine
  Frisbee, John L. *On-Scene Commander.* May, 1995.
  Frisbee, John L. *The Valley of Death.* July, 1998.
  Glines, C.V. *The Son Tay Raid.* November, 1995.
  Zoeller, Laurence W. *To Major Bernard F. Fisher, USAF: The Medal of Honor.* March, 1967.
Air News. Hare, Robert C. *50 m.p.h. Faster – The Douglas BT2D.* April, 1946.
Air Progress. Drury, Richard S. *Douglas Skyraider.* May, 1970.
Air & Space. Wetterhahn, Ralph. *Escape to U Taphao.* December1996/January 1997.
All Hands
  *Piped Ashore: Out on Twenty.* September, 1968.
  *Skyraider.* September, 1957.
  *Skyraider, A-Number One.* January, 1969.
Argosy. Taylor, Ron. *You've Just Been Had by a Spad, Dad.* October, 1967.
Aviation. Heinemann, E.H. *Skyraider's High Performance Stems from Pin-Point Performance.* April, 1946.
Behind The Lines. Chinnery, Philip D. *Spads of the 6th SOS.* January/February, 1994.
FineScale Modeler. Mutza, Wayne. *Vietnam A-1 Skyraider MiG Killers.* January, 1999.
Flight Journal. Hukee, Byron. *Down There Amongst Them.* October, 1998.
Friends Journal. Birdsong, G.P., Col., USAF (Ret.). *Ben Het.* Summer, 1994.
Journal, American Aviation Historical Society. Heinemann, E.H. *AD Douglas Skyraider.* Spring, 1997.
Meccano. Taylor, John. *The Spads of A Shau.* February, 1968.
Naval Aviation News. *Remember When.* June, 1966. *Skyraider.* January, 1972.
RAF Flying Review. *Venerable Able Dog.* Vol. XVIII, No. 3.
The AIRMAN
  Everett, Robert P., Capt., *Rescue at Do Khe.* February, 1968.
  Everett, Robert P., Capt., *Sandys of the Six-Oh-Second.* February, 1968.
  George, James A., SMsgt., *He Had To Help.* December, 1968.
  Sherril, Clay A., A1C, *Routine Strike Mission.* February, 1968.
The Saturday Evening Post
  Armstrong, Richard. *It's Great To Be Alive.*
  Dengler, Dieter, Lt. j.g., *I Ecaped from a Red Prison.*
V.F.W. Kilbourne, Jimmy W., Maj., *One of a Thousand.* September, 1968.
Wings. Marrett, George J. *Sandy to the Rescue.* April, 2000.

**Internet**

Davis (2000) *The Able Dogs.* (On-Line). Available:http//www.abledogs.com/
Hukee, Byron (2000) *The A-1 Skyraider Association.* (On-Line). Avialable:http//skyraider.org/skyassn/index.htm

Manor, Leroy J., Lieut. Gen., USAF (Ret.) (1999) *The Son Tay Raid.* (On-Line). Available:http//home.earthlink.net/~aircommando1/SONTAYRAI.htm
Pike, John (2000) *Dumb Bombs.* (On-Line). Available:http://www.fas.org/man/dod- 101/sys/dumb/

**Newspapers**
Highland Air Times. *6th SOS pilots credited with 33 enemy kills verified, possibly more.* 1968. *Spads fly high sortie- high load aircraft.* November, 1968.
Navy Times. Ennis, John. *Navy's Skyraiders Bound for the AF.* 18 October 1967.
Seventh Air Force News. *Specialists at Pleiku Rebuild Combat-Damaged Skyraiders.* 2 August 1967.
VA-25 Newsletter Johnson, Clinton B., Capt., USNR (Ret.). *Skyraider vs. MiG-17.* December 1997.

**Other Documents**
Air Commando Association Newsletter, excerpts from various issues.
Douglas Aircraft Group, Douglas Report 49784B. *Study Reactivating A-1J Skyraider Production.* 23 April 1965.
Larrison, John, Lt. Col., USAF (Ret.). *How the Sandys got started: The Day the First A-1s Went to Thailand.* Daedalus Flyer, Winter 1999.
Lowe, Leroy W. *A Case Study: Search and Rescue Operations in Southeast Asia.* July, 1972.
Masterson, Michael J., Capt., *Search and Rescue in SEA.* Personal communication to Herb Meyr, 20 June 1968.
McDonnell Douglas News Release. *Study to Reactivate A-1J Skyraider Production.* 2 October 1969.
Pacific Stars & Stripes, excerpts from various issues.
Skyraider Association Newsletters, excerpts from various issues.
Stanley Aviation Corporation Engineering Bulletin No. 1515. *Yankee Escape System.* September 1967.